War Veterans and Fascism in Int

This book explores, from a transnational viewpoint, the historical relationship between war veterans and fascism in interwar Europe. Until now, historians have been roughly divided between those who assume that 'brutalization' (George L. Mosse) led veterans to join fascist movements and those who stress that most ex-soldiers of the Great War became committed pacifists and internationalists. Transcending the debates of the brutalization thesis and drawing upon a wide range of archival and published sources, this work focuses on the interrelated processes of transnationalization and the fascist permeation of veteran politics in interwar Europe to offer a wider perspective on the history of both fascism and veterans' movements. A combination of mythical constructs, transfers, political communication, encounters and networks within a transnational space explain the relationship between veterans and fascism. Thus, this book offers new insights into the essential ties between fascism and war and contributes to the theorization of transnational fascism.

Ángel Alcalde is currently a Humboldt Postdoctoral Fellow at the Ludwig Maximilian University of Munich. He earned his PhD in history and civilization from the European University Institute. He is a specialist on the social and cultural history of war, transnational history and the history of fascism. He has published numerous works on the Spanish Civil War and the Franco dictatorship, including two books, *Los excombatientes franquistas* (2014) and *Lazos de Sangre* (2010).

Studies in the Social and Cultural History of Modern Warfare

General Editor
Jay Winter, *Yale University*

Advisory Editors
David Blight, *Yale University*
Richard Bosworth, *University of Western Australia*
Peter Fritzsche, *University of Illinois, Urbana-Champaign*
Carol Gluck, *Columbia University*
Benedict Kiernan, *Yale University*
Antoine Prost, *Université de Paris-Sorbonne*
Robert Wohl, *University of California, Los Angeles*

In recent years the field of modern history has been enriched by the exploration of two parallel histories. These are the social and cultural history of armed conflict, and the impact of military events on social and cultural history.

Studies in the Social and Cultural History of Modern Warfare presents the fruits of this growing area of research, reflecting both the colonization of military history by cultural historians and the reciprocal interest of military historians in social and cultural history, to the benefit of both. The series offers the latest scholarship in European and non-European events from the 1850s to the present day.

A full list of titles in the series can be found at:
www.cambridge.org/modernwarfare

War Veterans and Fascism in Interwar Europe

Ángel Alcalde

Ludwig Maximilian University of Munich

CAMBRIDGE
UNIVERSITY PRESS

CAMBRIDGE
UNIVERSITY PRESS

University Printing House, Cambridge CB2 8BS, United Kingdom

One Liberty Plaza, 20th Floor, New York, NY 10006, USA

477 Williamstown Road, Port Melbourne, VIC 3207, Australia

314-321, 3rd Floor, Plot 3, Splendor Forum, Jasola District Centre, New Delhi - 110025, India

79 Anson Road, #06-04/06, Singapore 079906

Cambridge University Press is part of the University of Cambridge.

It furthers the University's mission by disseminating knowledge in the pursuit of education, learning and research at the highest international levels of excellence.

www.cambridge.org
Information on this title: www.cambridge.org/9781316648186
DOI: 10.1017/9781108182423

First published 2017
First paperback edition 2019

A catalogue record for this publication is available from the British Library

Library of Congress Cataloging in Publication data
Names: Alcalde, Ángel, author.
Title: War veterans and fascism in interwar Europe / Ángel Alcalde (Ludwig Maximilian University, Munich).
Description: Cambridge, United Kingdom ; New York, NY :
Cambridge University Press, 2017. | Series: Studies in the social and cultural history of modern warfare | Includes bibliographical references.
Identifiers: LCCN 2017003668 | ISBN 9781107198425 (Hardback)
Subjects: LCSH: Fascism–Europe–History–20th century. | Veterans–Political activity–Europe–History–20th century. | Veterans–Europe–Social conditions–20th century. | World War, 1914-1918–Veterans–Europe. | World War, 1914-1918–Influence. | Europe–Politics and government–1918–1945. | Europe–Social conditions–20th century. | BISAC: HISTORY / Europe / General.
Classification: LCC D726.5 .A54 2017 | DDC 320.53/309409042–dc23
LC record available at https://lccn.loc.gov/2017003668

ISBN 978-1-107-19842-5 Hardback
ISBN 978-1-316-64818-6 Paperback

Les Combattants ne sont pas fascistes, mais ...
Il y a un mais.

– Henri Pichot

(*La Revue des Vivants,* February 1927)

Contents

Figures and Tables

Acknowledgements

This book is based on a doctoral dissertation defended at the European University Institute (Florence, Italy) in June 2015. Researching and writing this book have been an extraordinary period of my life, in which I have received the support and help of many people and institutions. I would like to thank the Spanish Ministry of Education for granting me a full scholarship through the 'Salvador de Madariaga' Program to undertake my PhD studies and for providing financial support during the months I spent as a visiting fellow at Konstanz Universität (Germany) and the Università di Roma–La Sapienza (Italy). The Department of History and Civilization at the European University Institute generously sponsored my research missions abroad and provided many other facilities. My work was also enhanced by being a member of the research project 'Discursos e identidades de género en las culturas políticas de la derecha española, 1875–1975', funded by the Spanish Ministry of Economy and Competitiveness. In June 2016, my dissertation was awarded the Ivano Tognarini Prize in Contemporary History by the Istituto Storico della Resistenza in Toscana, a distinction for which I am very thankful. During the last stages of completing the manuscript, I was a post-doctoral fellow at the Leibniz Institute of European History (Mainz, Germany), which also provided many facilities and a stimulating academic environment.

For their insightful comments on my work, I am sincerely grateful to my supervisor, Professor Federico Romero, and to the members of the jury that examined my dissertation, Professors Ángela Cenarro, Sven Reichardt and Lucy Riall. I owe a special debt of gratitude to Professor Ángela Cenarro, who guided me in my first years as a historian and also supervised my doctoral research. In addition, Professor Sven Reichardt gave me crucial advice during the time I spent as a research fellow in Konstanz, for which I am very much indebted. I would also like to express my deepest appreciation to Professor Giovanni Sabbatucci, who with great generosity and hospitality received me in Rome to talk about historical issues he had masterfully investigated four decades ago.

In addition, my work was also improved by the constructive critiques of many other scholars. Professors Heinz-Gerhard Haupt, Laura Lee Downs and Robert Gerwarth read parts of my work and gave me useful feedback. The anonymous reviewers of the manuscript also made valuable remarks to improve it. Dónal Hassett and Stephanie Wright not only commented on my research but also collaborated in carefully proofreading my manuscript. Jessica Bate also contributed to make the final text more readable. Jay Winter and Michael Watson guided me through the final process of editing. Of course, I bear sole responsibility for any errors or inaccuracy that might be found in this book.

I want also to express my gratitude to many other historians with whom I enjoyed discussing different scientific and professional concerns over the last few years: David Alegre, Giulia Albanese, Miguel Alonso, Miguel Ángel del Arco, Aurora Artiaga, Arnd Bauerkämper, Romain Bonnet, Zira Box, David Brydan, Jesús Casquete, Antonio Cazorla, Gustavo Corni, Robert Dale, Lourenzo Fernández Prieto, Miriam Franchina, Ferran Gallego, Bernhard Gissibl, Claudio Hernández, Anke Hoffstadt, Mark Jones, Daniel Knegt, Anna Lena Kocks, Nicola Labanca, Daniel Lanero, José Luis Ledesma, Francisco Leira, Elissa Mailänder, James Matthews, David A. Messenger, Jaremey McMullin, John Paul Newman, Xosé Manoel Núñez Seixas, Stephen R. Ortiz, Rubén Pallol, Mercedes Peñalba-Sotorrío, Alejandro Pérez-Olivares, Pierluigi Pironti, Alejandro Quiroga, Javier Rodrigo, Miguel Ángel Ruiz Carnicer, Pedro Rújula, Alessandro Salvador and Martina Salvante. Many other people, scholars and professionals from the different academic institutions, archives and libraries that I visited during the last few years contributed directly or indirectly to make my work easier to access and more rewarding. A special mention must go to my friends and colleagues Natalia Galán, Cloe Cavero, Miguel Palou and José Miguel Escribano, who helped and supported me at different stages of my research. Last but not the least, I would like to pay a warm tribute to my family and especially to Neha: this book is a very small compensation for all the time I did not spend with them.

Abbreviations

ACS	Archivio Centrale dello Stato
AGA	Archivo General de la Administración
AMAE	Archivio del Ministero degli Affari Esteri
AN	Archives Nationales
ANC	Associazione Nazionale Combattenti
ANMIG	Associazione Nazionale fra Mutilati e Invalidi di Guerra
ANRZO	Associazione Nazionale Reduci Zona Operante
ARAC	Association républicaine des anciens combattants
BArch	Bundesarchiv
BUF	British Union of Fascists
CAUR	Comitati d'Azione per l'Universalità di Roma
CIAMAC	Conférence internationale des associations de mutilés et anciens combattants
CIP	Comitato Internazionale Permanente
CR	Carteggio Riservato
DDI	Documenti Diplomatici Italiani
DNE	Delegación Nacional de Excombatientes
DNSE	Delegación Nacional del Servicio Exterior
DNVP	Deutschnationale Volkspartei
FET-JONS	Falange Española Tradicionalista y de las JONS
FIDAC	Fédération interalliée des anciens combattants
JONS	Juntas de Ofensiva Nacional Sindicalista
LFC	Légion française des combattants
MAE-AD	Ministère des Affaires Étrangères. Archives Diplomatiques
MI	Ministero dell'Interno
MP	Member of Parliament
MVSN	Milizia Volontaria per la Sicurezza Nazionale
NCO	Non-commissioned officer
NSDAP	Nationalsozialistische Deutsche Arbeiterpartei
NSKOV	Nationalsozialistische Kriegsopferversorgung
ONC	Opera Nazionale Combattenti

xii

PNF	Partito Nazionale Fascista
PPI	Partito Popolare Italiano
PS	Pubblica Sicurezza
PSdA	Partito Sardo d'Azione
PSF	Parti Social Français
PSI	Partito Socialista Italiano
RFB	Rote Frontkämpferbund
RSI	Repubblica Sociale Italiana
SA	Sturmabteilung
SDNA	League of Nations Archives
sf.	Sottofascicolo
SPD	Segreteria Particolare del Duce
UF	Union fédérale
UNC	Union nationale des combattants
UNCi	Unione Nazionale Combattenti
UNRG	Unione Nazionale Reduci di Guerra
UNUS	Unione Nazionale Ufficiali e Soldati

Introduction

This book analyzes the transnational relationship between war veterans and fascism in interwar Europe.[1] For decades, historians have strived to explain why the European continent, only twenty years after a cataclysmic war of unprecedented murderous dimensions, became involved in a new, even more horrendous world conflict. Although there were important democratic experiences and remarkable advances in many facets of human life, the interwar period saw the progressive demolition of the peaceful order for which many people had hoped in the wake of the Great War. While at the beginning of 1919 democracies clearly dominated Europe, by June 1940, they were the exception to the rule. This eclipse of democracy, marked by violent conflicts and civil wars, cannot be understood without placing fascism at its centre. Fascism was a product of the First World War experience, and fascism can also be considered to have triggered the Second World War. In this scenario, explaining the links between fascism and war veterans, the men who were also a direct legacy of the Great War, remains crucial.

One can easily find an abundance of superficial evidence to suggest that First World War veterans were closely linked to the origins of fascism. For example, it is a truism to say that Hitler was just one among millions of soldiers demobilized from the defeated German army. Likewise, Mussolini had been a serviceman during the Great War. Historians have mentioned on innumerable occasions that paramilitary groups in the early post-war period, such as the Freikorps and the early Italian fascist movement, were composed of many former combatants. Furthermore, during the 1920s and 1930s, fascist movements in practically every European country rose to prominence with their members staging quasi-military parades, dressed in their uniforms and decked out in the medals they had usually obtained in the trenches. Militarism was a defining characteristic of fascism. And, seemingly, war and fascism walked hand

---

[1] In this book, *fascism* in lower case refers to the transnational phenomenon, and *Fascism* in upper case refers exclusively to the Italian original movement and regime.

1

in hand. Were these facts mere circumstantial coincidences, or do they reveal a substantial, essential connection between the fascist phenomenon and war veterans? A definitive response to this question remains, as yet, elusive.

This book aims to provide a new account of the highly complex relationship between veterans and fascism. By examining processes of transnationalization and the fascist permeation of veteran politics and by analyzing the cultural, sociological and political origins of fascism as well as its European expansion, this work aims to offer an interpretation of this phenomenon and to fill gaps in existing historical knowledge. Although much has been written about interwar veteran movements and the historiography on fascism is vast, only a limited number of works have dealt directly with their historical interconnections. Most of these studies have revolved around the controversial 'brutalization' thesis of historian George L. Mosse. Yet they have not reached any universally accepted interpretation. In the meantime, many facets of the relationship between veterans and fascism have been neglected.

War Veterans

This book is concerned with the interwar veterans or, in other words, with the history of veterans of industrialized warfare. In the modern era, as German military theorist Carl von Clausewitz put it,[2] participation in war became an initiation to politics. Since the French Revolution, military service had been closely connected with notions of citizenship, and participation in the defence of the nation began to be generously rewarded by the state. The adoption of universal military service, linked to the nationalization of the army, was a transnational process. However, an unresolved tension remained: whereas universal military service guaranteed the future political liberty of male citizens, it also implied their submission to a coercive system isolated from the wider society: the army.[3] Furthermore, during the nineteenth century, European armies embraced new roles, which also shaped the social and political functions of their veterans. Armed forces fought to expand and retain colonial empires, to further national unification processes and to resolve internal civil wars. The state authorities often charged the military with the maintenance of public order. In different countries, the state relied on

---

[2] Carl von Clausewitz, *On War* (ed. and trans. Michael Howard and Peter Paret), Princeton, NJ, Princeton University Press, 1984, p. 605.

[3] Thomas Hippler, *Citizens, Soldiers and National Armies. Military Service in France and Germany, 1789–1830*, London, Routledge, 2008.

the armed forces to repress working-class protests and to defend property.[4] Forced conscription became highly unpopular.[5] Thus, the figure of the soldier became associated with the defence of the establishment, with nationalist or imperial aggression and with coercion.[6]

It was in this context that ex-soldiers moved to create associations, as part of the wider emergent civil society. These organizations embodied the memory of national wars and performed functions of mutual assistance; they were also closely linked to the active military. In Italy, for instance, veteran patriotic groups from the wars of independence were influential.[7] And certain patriotic veteran associations, such as the Deutscher Kriegerbund (Kyffhäuserbund) in Wilhelmine Germany, became bulwarks of social conservatism and anti-socialism.[8] And yet, the number of former soldiers in proportion to the overall national population was miniscule, as was the weight of veterans in politics. This would drastically change in the advent of the First World War.

We may reasonably surmise that all veterans from across distinct periods share a set of common traits based on a comparable experience of combat.[9] Much can be learnt about the veterans of the interwar period by looking into the experiences of the soldiers of the Great War. However, if historians have spoken of a 'war generation', composed of young bourgeois men who volunteered and sometimes returned from war believing that they had become different and better individuals,[10] no unitary pattern of political response to the war experience can be identified. The war experience differed sharply according to the social class and background of the actors.[11] Although some historians believe that all

---

[4] John Gooch, *Army, State and Society in Italy, 1870–1915*, Houndmills, Macmillan, 1989; Anja Johansen, 'Violent Repression or Modern Strategies of Crowd Management? Soldiers as riot police in France and Germany, 1890–1914', *French History*, 15 (2001), pp. 400–20.

[5] Rafael Núñez Florencio, *Militarismo y antimilitarismo en España*, Madrid, CSIC, 1990.

[6] See, for example, Gérard de Puymége, *Chauvin, le soldat-laboureur: contribution à l'étude des nationalismes*, Paris, Gallimard, 1993.

[7] Marco Fincardi, 'I reduci risorgimentali veneti e friulani', *Italia contemporanea*, 222 (2001), pp. 79–83.

[8] Alex Hall, 'The War of Words: Anti-Socialist Offensives and Counter-Propaganda in Wilhelmine Germany 1890–1914', *Journal of Contemporary History*, 11, 2–3 (1976), pp. 11–42.

[9] Stéphane Audoin-Rouzeau, *Combattre. Une anthropologie historique de la guerre moderne, XIXe–XXIe siècle*, Paris, Seuil, 2008; David A. Gerber (ed.), *Disabled Veterans in History*, Ann Arbor, University of Michigan Press, 2000.

[10] Robert Wohl, *The Generation of 1914*, Cambridge, MA, Harvard University Press, 1979; Paul Fussell, *The Great War and Modern Memory*, Oxford University Press, 1975; Mario Isnenghi, *Il mito della Grande Guerra*, Bari, Laterza, 1970.

[11] See Richard Bessel, 'The Front Generation and the Politics of Weimar Germany', in Mark Roseman (ed.), *Generations in Conflict. Youth Revolt and Generation Formation in Germany, 1770–1968*, Cambridge University Press, 2005, pp. 121–36.

veterans share a set of characteristics that reflect the nature of their war experience,[12] it would be wrong to maintain that veterans also shared a common *political* instinct.

In addition, the very notion of the 'veteran' could embody significantly different meanings depending not only on the nation-state but also on the language. What was a war veteran? Even before the concept was officially defined by legislation, historical actors had already endowed it with implicit, subjective connotations that varied according to the language employed. It was not exactly the same to say, as in Britain, *ex-servicemen*, as it was to use the more aggressive word *combattenti*, as in Italy. Nor was it neutral to call them *Kriegsopfer* ('war victim') or *Front-kämpfer* ('front fighter'), as the Nazis sometimes did, instead of naming them *ehemalige Kriegsteilnehmer* (literally, 'former participants in war'). The explanations for such a variety of notions and meanings must be sought in the national and regional contexts that conditioned and shaped political struggles over the very definition of the symbol of the veteran, as we will see. In this book, the concept of 'veteran', most common in the United States, was the most unbiased term available to analyze this chapter of European history.

Despite the difficulty of defining veterans as a politically coherent and well-defined historical group, historiography on interwar veterans has often tried to discern their predominant political orientation. During the 1950s and 1960s, scholars often recalled the affinity of veteran associations with right-wing and fascist parties.[13] The paramilitary groups that emerged after the war, many of them composed of ex-combatants, were viewed as the 'vanguard of Nazism'.[14] Later, a developing historiography would revise this perception of veterans as potential fascists. German historians were aware that interwar veterans had created politically diverse associations.[15] In Italy, where the common idea of the veterans as potential fascists had remained alive, historian

---

[12] Eric J. Leed, *No Man's Land: Combat & Identity in World War I*, Cambridge University Press, 1979; Martin Crotty and Mark Edele, 'Total War and Entitlement: Towards a Global History of Veteran Privilege', *Australian Journal of Politics and History*, 59, 1 (2013), pp. 15–32.

[13] René Remond, 'Les anciens combattants et la politique', *Revue française de science politique*, 5ème année, 2 (1955), pp. 267–90; Graham Wootton, *The Politics of Influence. British Ex-Servicemen: Cabinet Decisions and Cultural Change (1917–57)*, London, Routledge & Kegan Paul, 1963; Elliott Pennell Fagerberg, 'The "Anciens Combattants" and French Foreign Policy', unpublished PhD thesis, Université de Genève, 1966.

[14] Robert G. L. Waite, *Vanguard of Nazism: The Free Corps Movement in Postwar Germany 1918–1923*, Cambridge, MA, Harvard University Press, 1952.

[15] Volker R. Berghahn, *Der Stahlhelm. Bund der Frontsoldaten*, Düsseldorf, Droste, 1966; Alois Klotzbücher, 'Der politische Weg des Stahlhelm, Bund der Frontsoldaten in der

Giovanni Sabbatucci told the story of the ambitious, albeit failed, democratic project for a political 'renewal' of Italy (*rinnovamento*) that the veterans pursued during 1919–20.[16] Antoine Prost's exhaustive study of the French veteran movement argued that the French veterans, far from representing a fascist threat, had, in fact, constituted a barrier against the expansion of fascism in France.[17] During the 1970s, a set of studies on interwar veterans showed that no clear political orientation could be ascribed to them; veterans embraced not only rightist but also leftist causes, and different organizations within a single country were often political rivals. In the place of a general tendency to see the veteran groups as predominantly right wing and potentially fascist, these works produced a more nuanced picture.[18]

At the same time, the importance of veteran politics and ideologies in the origin of fascism has not been ignored, as important contributions to the study of Fascism and Nazism demonstrate. Emilio Gentile addressed the origins of fascism as a revolutionary and totalitarian ideology stemming from the First World War experience.[19] According to Gentile, *combattentismo*, a kind of rebellious instinct that characterized the returning veterans, was one of the crucial components of the fascist ideology. George L. Mosse argued that the revolutionary national-socialist ideology and *völkisch* nationalism acquired a mass basis only after the Great War and that veteran organizations (such as the Stahlhelm) had contributed to expanding such an ideology.[20] In his book,

Weimarer Republik. Ein Beitrag zur Geschichte der "Nationalen Opposition" 1918–1933', inaugural dissertation, Friedrich-Alexander-Universität zu Erlangen-Nürnberg, 1964; Karl Rohe, *Das Reichsbanner Schwarz Rot Gold: Ein Beitrag zur Geschichte und Struktur der politischen Kampfverbaende zur Zeit der Weimarer Republik*, Düsseldorf, Droste, 1966; Kurt G. P. Schuster, *Der Rote Frontkämpferbund 1924–1929*, Düsseldorf, Droste, 1975; C. J. Elliot, 'The Kriegervereine and the Weimar Republic', *Journal of Contemporary History*, 10, 1 (1975), pp. 109–29; Ulrich Dunker, *Der Reichsbund jüdischer Frontsoldaten 1919–1938. Geschichte eines jüdischen Abwehrvereins*, Düsseldorf, Droste, 1977.

[16] Giovanni Sabbatucci, *I combattenti nel primo dopoguerra*, Rome-Bari, Laterza, 1974. See also Ferdinando Cordova, *Arditi e legionari Dannunziani*, Padua, Marsilio, 1969.

[17] Antoine Prost, *Les Anciens Combattants et la Societé Française 1914–1939*, 3 vols., Paris, Presses de la Fondation Nationale des Sciences Politiques, 1977; see also Antoine Prost, *In the Wake of War: The 'Anciens Combattants' and French Society*, Oxford, Berg, 1992. Cf. Chris Millington, *From Victory to Vichy: Veterans in Inter-war France*, Manchester University Press, 2012.

[18] Stephen R. Ward (ed.), *The War Generation: Veterans of the First World War*, Port Washington, NY, Kennikat Press, 1975.

[19] Emilio Gentile, *Le origine della ideologia fascista*, Bari, Laterza, 1975; see also Emilio Gentile, *Storia del partito fascista. 1919–1922: Movimento e milizia*, Rome-Bari, Laterza, 1989.

[20] George L. Mosse, *The Crisis of German Ideology: Intellectual Origins of the Third Reich*, New York, Universal Library, 1964, pp. 254–7.

Fallen Soldiers, Mosse defined the interwar persistence of violence as the 'brutalization' of politics.[21] Mosse affirmed that the experience of trench warfare, with its daily confrontation with death, was the origin of a dehumanizing trivialization of violence during the interwar period, which ultimately led to genocide. The political right and, conspicuously, the war veterans appeared as the chief agents of the 'brutalization' of politics.

The ensuing debate around the 'brutalization' thesis continues to the present day. The notion of 'brutalization' has become an analytical tool for some historians to understand the violence of the interwar period. Works on the cultural history of war have argued that the Great War was the matrix of totalitarianism, pointing to the veterans as important conveyors of violence.[22] Other scholars, in contrast, are sceptical regarding the long-term destructive consequences of the Great War experience and even deny that such 'brutalization' ever existed.[23] They underline the fact that the French veterans, as Prost argued, remained committed to pacifism. Richard Bessel, who carefully analyzed the situation of Germany in the aftermath of the Great War, noted that the reintegration of front-line soldiers was effective and peaceful; only a tiny minority of them joined the mercenary Freikorps.[24] Benjamin Ziemann, indeed, has recently highlighted the importance of a republican, democratic culture among German veterans, maintaining that the war experience had, in fact, engendered pacifist sentiments among ex-combatants.[25]

Most recently, the concepts of 'cultural demobilization', 'cultures of victory' and 'cultures of defeat' have permitted historians to explain why the traumatic, violent war experiences, whilst being similar for all

[21] George L. Mosse, *Fallen Soldiers: Reshaping the Memory of the World Wars*, New York, Oxford University Press, 1990.

[22] Omer Bartov, *Mirrors of Destruction: War, Genocide, and Modern Identity*, Oxford University Press, 2000, pp. 16–22; Stéphane Audoin-Rouzeau and Annette Becker, *14–18, retrouver la Guerre*, Paris, Gallimard, 2000, pp. 313–14; Angelo Ventrone, *La seduzione totalitarian: Guerra, modernità, violenza politica (1914–1918)*, Rome, Donzelli, 2003; Enzo Traverso, *A ferro e fuoco : La guerra civile europea, 1914–1945*, Bologna, Il Mulino, 2007; Alexander Mesching, *Der Wille zur Bewegung. Militärischer Traum und totalitäres Programm. Eine Mentalitätsgeschichte vom Ersten Weltkrieg zum Nationalsozialismus*, Bielefeld, Transcript, 2008.

[23] Dirk Schumann, 'Europa, der Erste Weltkrieg und die Nachkriegszeit: eine Kontinuität der Gewalt?', *Journal of Modern European History*, 1, 1 (2003), pp. 24–43; Antoine Prost, 'Les limites de la brutalisation : Tuer sur le front occidental, 1914–1918', *Vingtième Siècle. Revue d'histoire*, 81 (2004), pp. 5–20.

[24] Richard Bessel, *Germany after the First World War*, Oxford, Clarendon Press, 1993.

[25] Benjamin Ziemann, *War Experiences in Rural Germany 1914–1923*, Oxford, Berg, 2007, pp. 211–68; id., *Contested Commemorations, Republican War Veterans and Weimar Political Culture*, Cambridge University Press, 2013.

combatants, had 'brutalizing' effects only in some countries.[26] By focusing on the processes of demobilization, historians have offered insights into the separate paths that the veterans of different countries walked after 1918. In Britain and France, the population in general, and veterans in particular, abandoned war mentalities and attitudes more easily than, for instance, in Germany or Italy.[27] In the latter countries, the circulation of post-war myths, such as the 'stab in the back' (*Dolchstoß*) and the 'mutilated victory', probably thwarted demobilization of the minds.[28] In Germany and Austria, counter-revolutionary paramilitary units included many veterans, particularly ex-officers, alongside younger nationalist students. Yet, rather than the war experience, it was defeat and revolution that catalyzed their violent reaction.[29] Post-war violence was the result of the collapse of state authority and of the political radicalization of many different social groups – not only the war veterans – as a consequence of military mobilization and demobilization.[30]

The case of Italy, victorious in 1918 but suffering from the 'brutalization' of politics, is crucial to understand the context in which Fascism was born. However, there are many gaps in this knowledge.[31] The prevalent interpretation says that the Italian liberal state and the political left failed to demobilize and welcome returning troops; therefore, some veterans turned into fascists or into supporters of D'Annunzio in Fiume, whilst the army officers' neutrality and obedience to the state weakened.[32] In the first part of this book, I will revise this interpretation by looking into

---

[26] John Horne (dir.), 'Démobilisations culturelles après la Grande Guerre', *14–18 Aujourd'hui, Today, Heute*, 5 (2002); Julia Eichenberg and John Paul Newman (eds.), *The Great War and Veterans' Internationalism*, New York, Palgrave, 2013.

[27] Bruno Cabanes, *La Victoire endeuillée : La sortie de guerre des soldats français (1918–1920)*, Paris, Seuil, 2004; Jon Lawrence, 'Forging a Peaceable Kingdom: War, Violence, and Fear of Brutalization in Post-First World War Britain', *Journal of Modern History*, 75, 3 (2003), pp. 557–89; Adam R. Seipp, *The Ordeal of Peace. Demobilization and the Urban Experience in Britain and Germany, 1917–1921*, Farnham, Ashgate, 2009.

[28] Boris Barth, *Dolchstoßlegenden und politische Desintegration. Das Trauma der deutschen Niederlage im Ersten Weltkrieg 1914–1933*, Düsseldorf, Droste, 2003.

[29] Robert Gerwarth, 'The Central European Counter-Revolution: Paramilitary Violence in Germany, Austria and Hungary after the Great War', *Past and Present*, 200 (2008), pp. 175–209.

[30] Robert Gerwarth and John Horne (eds.), *War in Peace: Paramilitary Violence in Europe after the Great War*, Oxford University Press, 2012; Mark Edele and Robert Gerwarth (eds.), Special Issue: 'The Limits of Demobilization', *Journal of Contemporary History*, 50, 1 (2015).

[31] Giulia Albanese, 'Brutalizzazione e violenza alle origini del fascismo', *Studi Storici*, 55, 1 (2014), pp. 3–14.

[32] Marco Mondini, *La politica delle armi: Il ruolo dell'esercito nell'avvento del fascismo*, Rome-Bari, Laterza, 2006; Marco Mondini and Guri Schwarz, *Dalla guerra alla pace: Retoriche e pratiche della smobilitazione nell'Italia del Novecento*, Verona, Cierre edizioni/Istrevi, 2007, pp. 23–113.

8   Introduction

demobilization from a transnational and cultural point of view. Beyond the paradoxes of the 'brutalization' paradigm, transnational perspectives are required to answer the questions of how, and to what extent, war veterans were connected to the new fascist ideas, movements and regimes of the interwar period.

Fascism

As a history of the European fascist movements and regimes, this book has a wider chronological and geographical scope than most works on post-war veteran demobilization. Examining the history of fascism in its relations with the veterans in interwar Europe requires transcending the nation-state frameworks that usually shape existing research on the topic,[33] as well as observing more than two decades of historical developments. By analyzing the many layers of the long-term historical relationship between veterans and fascism in a transnational perspective, this book addresses important gaps in knowledge and contributes to the new understanding of fascism as a transnational phenomenon.

Whereas the existing bibliography on fascism is truly immense, historians have only begun to understand how fascist symbols, myths and discourses about war were translated into social practice and politics. In particular, the relationship between veterans and fascism has not been sufficiently studied. Whereas many works on fascism have focused on assessing the presence of ex-combatants and soldiers within the movements,[34] few studies have taken the notion of the combatant as a cultural construct that was manipulated by the fascist movements and regimes.[35] However, scholars have stressed the seminal importance of the war

---

[33] Ángel Alcalde, *Los excombatientes franquistas. La cultura de guerra del fascismo español y la Delegación Nacional de Excombatientes (1936–1965)*, Zaragoza, Prensas de la Universidad de Zaragoza, 2014; Nils Löffelbein, *Ehrenbürger der Nation. Die Kriegsbeschädigten des Ersten Weltkriegs in Politik und Propaganda des Nationalsozialismus*, Essen, Klartext, 2013; Robert Weldon Whalen, *Bitter Wounds. German Victims of the Great War, 1914–1939*, Ithaca, NY, Cornell University Press, 1984; Deborah Cohen, *The War Come Home: Disabled Veterans in Britain and Germany, 1914–1939*, Berkeley, University of California Press, 2001.

[34] Michael Mann, *Fascists*, Cambridge University Press, 2004; Sven Reichardt, *Faschistische Kampfbünde. Gewalt und Gemeinschaft im italienischen Squadrismus und in der deutschen SA*, Köln, Böhlau, 2002.

[35] Matthias Sprenger, *Landsknechte auf dem Weg ins Dritte Reich? Zu Genese und Wandel des Freikorpsmythos*, Paderborn, Ferdinand Schöning, 2008. See also Benjamin Ziemann, 'Die Konstruktion des Kriegsveteranen und die Symbolik seiner Erinnerung 1918–1933', in Jost Dülffer and Gerd Krumeich (eds.), *Der verlorene Frieden: Politik und Kriegskultur nach 1918*, Essen, Klartex-Verlag, 2002, pp. 101–18.

experience for fascism[36] and, in particular, for German National Socialism.[37] Yet, these works usually place themselves within the 'brutalization' debate[38] and seldom provide transnational and long-term perspectives. Reconstructing the history of fascist veteran discourses and organizations in interwar Europe is a task that remains to be done, and it is from a transnational perspective that we can attain new insights.

But what do I mean when I talk about fascism in this book? Currently, there is an increasing tendency to consider 'fascism' as a rather vague and contradictory category that historical actors used to pursue their objectives within a transnational context.[39] Following this trend, I assume as a premise the existence of a nonspecific *transnational* fascism phenomenon, in which different movements and regimes were involved, starting with Italian Fascism and German National Socialism. I do not intend, therefore, to take fascism as a static object or abstract category whose essential core should be identified. Fascist movements and regimes were never hermetically isolated from other authoritarian, para-fascist and counter-revolutionary political manifestations.[40] 'The category of fascism is the product of the actions, struggles and the self-identification of the political actors themselves,' as Michel Dobry has put it.[41] The best way to fully understand fascism, therefore, is to situate it within its historical context and rendering visible its evolution and diffusion throughout Europe.[42] We will observe fascism in action, as a fast-evolving and expanding process that, after its birth in Italy, took place fundamentally in the

---

[36] Simonetta Falasca-Zamponi, *Fascist Spectacle: The Aesthetics of Power in Mussolini's Italy*, Berkeley, University of California Press, 1997, pp. 162–82; Philip Morgan, *Italian Fascism, 1915–1945* (2nd edn.), New York, Palgrave Macmillan, 2004.

[37] Gerd Krumeich (ed.), *Nationalsozialismus und Erster Weltkrieg*, Essen, Klartext, 2010; Thomas Kühne, *Kameradschaft. Die Soldaten des nationalsozialistischen Krieges und das 20. Jahrhundert*, Göttingen, Vandenhoeck & Ruprecht, 2006.

[38] Arndt Weinrich, *Der Weltkrieg als Erzieher. Jugend zwischen Weimarer Republik und Nationalsozialismus*, Essen, Klartext Verlag, 2013, pp. 21–5; Alessandro Salvador and Anders G. Kjøstvedt (eds.), *New Political Ideas in the Aftermath of the Great War*, Cham, Palgrave Macmillan, 2017, p. xiv.

[39] Kevin Passmore, 'L'historiographie du "fascisme" en France', *French Historical Studies*, 37, 3 (2014), pp. 466–99; Samuel Huston Goodfellow, 'Fascism as a Transnational Movement: The Case of Inter-War Alsace', *Contemporary European History*, 22, 1 (2013), pp. 87–106.

[40] Aristotle A. Kallis, '"Fascism", "Para-fascism" and "Fascistization": On the Similarities of Three Conceptual Categories', *European History Quarterly*, 33, 2 (2003), pp. 219–49.

[41] Michel Dobry, 'Desperately Seeking "Generic Fascism": Some Discordant Thoughts on the Academic Recycling of Indigenous Categories', in António Costa Pinto (ed.), *Rethinking the Nature of Fascism*, pp. 53–84; cf. Roger Griffin, *The Nature of Fascism*, London, Printer Publishers, 1991.

[42] Robert O. Paxton, *The Anatomy of Fascism*, New York, Knopf, 2004; Philip Morgan, *Fascism in Europe, 1919–1945*, London, Routledge, 2003.

transnational context of Europe during the interwar period. In short, this is a book on 'transnational fascism'.

Studying an ideology and a political movement such as fascism from a transnational point of view involves observing the 'multidirectional transfer' and circulation of 'ideas, information, resources'.[43] Transnational history looks 'beyond national boundaries and seek[s] to explore interconnections across borders', 'whether through individuals, non-national identities, and non-state actors, or in terms of objectives shared by people and communities regardless of their nationality'.[44] Works on 'transnational fascism', therefore, have focused on the interconnectedness, the contacts and sometimes the rivalries between Fascist Italy and Nazi Germany, leading to the entanglement of the two powers at the end of the 1930s. They have shown not only the similarities and the differences between both regimes but also their kinship, bonds and mutual influence. Fascist movements and regimes were simultaneously ultranationalist and transnational phenomena. And by focusing on connections and exchanges, historians have demonstrated the wide – even transatlantic – circulation of fascism during the interwar period.[45] It is now clear that during the 1920s, Italian Fascism became the model and the inspiration for different right-wing, nationalist and counterrevolutionary groups abroad.[46] But by 1934, Hitler had overtaken Mussolini as the lodestar of the European extreme right; the first attempts at cooperation and the fight for leadership between fascists and national socialists ended in the consolidation of National Socialism as the new model for European fascists and as the leading force of the Axis.[47] This strong interpenetration reveals the extent of the fascist phenomenon in interwar Europe and provides a glimpse into its complex 'nature'. The transnational perspective promises a redefinition of

---

[43] Martin Durham and Margaret Power (eds.), *New Perspectives on the Transnational Right*, New York, Palgrave Macmillan, 2010, p. 3; see also Sven Reichardt and Armin Nolzen (eds.), *Faschismus in Italien und Deutschland: Studien zu Transfer und Vergleich*, Göttingen, Wallstein, 2005.

[44] Akira Iriye, *Global and Transnational History: The Past, Present and Future*, Basingstoke, Palgrave Macmillan, 2012, pp. 11 and 15.

[45] Federico Finchelstein, *Transatlantic Fascism: Ideology, Violence, and the Sacred in Argentina and Italy, 1919–1945*, Durham, NC, Duke University Press, 2010.

[46] Hans Woller, *Rom, 28. Oktober 1922. Die faschistische Herausforderung*, Munich, DTV, 1999, pp. 20–57; Christian Goeschel, 'Italia Docet? The Relationship between Italian Fascism and Nazism Revisited', *European History Quarterly*, 42 (2012), pp. 480–92.

[47] Arnd Bauerkämper, 'Transnational Fascism: Cross-Border Relations between Regimes and Movements in Europe, 1922–1939', *East Central Europe*, 37 (2010), pp. 214–46; see also Salvatore Garau, 'The Internationalisation of Italian Fascism in the Face of German National Socialism, and Its Impact on the British Union of Fascists', *Politics, Religion & Ideology*, 15, 1 (2014), pp. 45–63.

fascism.[48] This book contributes to the practice of transnational history by observing not only the role of political networks, international institutions and migrants but also the cross-border transmission of myths and stereotypes that synthesized the fascist ideology, as we will see.

If the idea of transnational fascism is a very recent historiographical development, a transnational analysis of the historical relationship between veterans and fascism is a new endeavour. Existing research has suggested the importance of the international contacts of fascist veterans and approached the transnational dimension of veteran politics during the interwar period.[49] A small number of publications have examined the international contacts and mutual influences between fascist, national-socialist and other veteran leaders from different countries.[50] But the wider transnational phenomenon behind these bilateral encounters has remained unexplained. This book traces the web of major connections, encounters, transfers and entanglements that shaped the historical relationship between veterans and fascism in Europe during the interwar period.

Methodologies

Analyzing the transnational relationship between fascism and war veterans during the European interwar period requires us to ask why and how the figure of the war veteran became associated with the emerging fascist ideology and movement. In doing so, this book does not assume an essentialist reading of Mosse's 'brutalization' thesis, nor that war veterans may be seen as coherent, integrated historical actors that could become either internationalist pacifists or belligerent nationalists. Historians have sometimes posed the question of *how many* veterans became 'brutalized' fascists and how many did not in order to draw conclusions based on quantitative analysis. But this perspective often leads to inconclusive and superficial interpretations, and it implies uncritically assuming a given and essentialist notion of 'veteran'. As we will see, the category of 'veteran' was, above all, a cultural construct; its meaning was defined through discursive *and* organizational struggles. To explain

---

[48] Glenda Sluga, 'Fascism and Anti-Fascism', in Akira Iriye and Pierre-Yves Saunier (eds.), *The Palgrave Dictionary of Transnational History*, Basingstoke, Palgrave Macmillan, 2009.

[49] Martina Salvante, 'The Italian Associazione Nazionale Mutilati e Invalidi di Guerra and its International Liaisons in the Post Great War Era', in Eichenberg and Newman (eds.), *The Great War and Veterans' Internationalism*, pp. 162–83.

[50] See, for example, Claire Moreau Trichet, *Henri Pichot et l'Allemagne de 1930 à 1945*, Bern, Lang, 2004.

this process, I will have recourse not to the notion of 'brutalization' but to the concepts of 'symbolic appropriation', 'stereotype' and 'myth'.

'Symbolic appropriation' is a notion usually employed by social and cultural anthropologists. Here it refers to the process by which symbols, cultural materials or objects acquire a specific meaning, becoming associated to a human group or political power. In particular, I start from the position that the 'war veteran' was an existing transnational symbol that acquired new meanings as a result of the First World War experience. In Chapter 1, I will discuss the particularities of the transnational process of symbolic appropriation that took place roughly between 1917 and 1919 in Western Europe, the outcome of which was the widespread consolidation of a set of beliefs about what I call the 'anti-Bolshevik veterans'. In this sense, I will analyze the veteran-related discourses and representations employed at that time in different countries, in particular, in postwar Italy. As a result, a stereotypical notion of the 'fascist veteran' emerged.

The concept of 'stereotype' will allow us to observe the beginning of the European circulation of fascism. 'A stereotype is a set of beliefs about the personal attributes of a social group.'[51] Although stereotypes often are negative, they are also 'aids to explanation ... energy-saving devices, and ... shared group beliefs'; they always contain a kernel of truth.[52] It is striking to see how the theory of stereotyping[53] is applicable to the formation of the conviction that many Italian fascists were war veterans, and vice versa. The stereotype of the fascist veteran circulated, thereafter, throughout Europe by means of communication processes that according to the theory 'may play a major part in the spread and perpetuation of social stereotypes'.[54] In this way, the fascist veteran became one of the most iconic incarnations of fascism. As we will see, this stereotype greatly influenced politics, since not only the fascists were believed to be – for the most part – war veterans but also because on many occasions *veterans* in general were either warily or enthusiastically

---

[51] Tood D. Nelson, *Handbook of Prejudice, Stereotyping, and Discrimination*, New York, Psychology Press, 2009, p. 201.

[52] Craig McGarty, Vincent Y. Yzerbyt and Russell Spears, *Stereotypes as Explanations: The Formation of Meaningful Beliefs about Social Groups*, Cambridge University Press, 2002, p. 2.

[53] Perry R. Hinton, *Stereotypes, Cognition and Culture*, East Sussex, Psychology Press, 2000, pp. 7–8.

[54] Anthony Lyons, Anna Clark, Yoshihisa Kashima and Tim Kurz, 'Cultural Dynamics of Stereotypes: Social Network Processes and the Perpetuation of Stereotypes', in Yoshihisa Kashima, Klaus Fiedler and Peter Freytag (eds.), *Stereotype Dynamics: Language-Based Approaches to the Formation, Maintenance, and Transformation of Stereotypes*, New York, Erlbaum Associates, 2008, pp. 59–92, here p. 83.

seen as fascists or potential fascists. Understanding this phenomenon is extremely important because in reality, as historians know, a negligible proportion of ex-soldiers became fascists, at least at the beginning.

The existence and circulation of the 'fascist veteran' stereotype might have been innocuous had the fascist movement never conquered power, but as the March on Rome succeeded, an important myth crystallized. This widespread belief that the Italian veterans had been the core of a political movement that had swiftly conquered power, destroying the Bolshevik menace and bestowing on the community of ex-combatants the leading role to which they were allegedly entitled, I will call the 'myth of the fascist veterans' a narrative that helped make sense of events, providing them with deep-rooted significance.[55]

This book not only sets out to understand how a pervasive idea of the 'fascist veteran' was constructed, but it also examines how the fascist model of veteran politics circulated throughout Europe over time, particularly during the 1930s. Therefore, it studies historical cross-border processes, such as 'transfers', 'networks', 'circulation' and 'encounters'.[56] These processes took place within a porous geographical space that mainly corresponded to four countries – Italy, Germany, Spain and France – but not only to them. Fascism was born in Italy, and therefore events taking place in this country will be of the utmost importance to the analysis. The German case demands attention not only for the 1930s but also going back to 1919. Also, Spain and France were countries deeply affected by what happened in their environs. In these two countries, new fascist-inspired dictatorships were imposed in 1939–40. Cross-border transfers and contacts between fascists and veterans occurred in several directions, particularly within the region formed by the four countries just named. Yet, relevant events also took place far from this crucial space of communication. What was happening at particular moments in, for example, Russia, Romania, Britain or the United States is for us as important as what occurred in Milan in 1919, Rome in 1922, Berlin in 1933, Paris in 1934 or Madrid in 1939. I hope that an intelligent reader will not take my unconventional narrative leaps from one country to another as a symptom of methodological inconsistency. On the contrary, this particular geographical framework adjusts to the transnational political space of fascism.

---

[55] For an explanation of political myths as basic narratives that respond to a need for significance, see Chiara Bottici, *A Philosophy of Political Myth*, New York, Cambridge University Press, 2007.
[56] On these analytical tools, see Pierre-Yves Saunier, *Transnational History*, New York, Palgrave Macmillan, 2013.

In short, this book argues that the manipulation of a complex of transnational, culturally constructed and mythical ideas of the war veteran(s) marked the historical relationship between veterans and fascism. First, this manipulation allowed Italian Fascism to become a distinct, original and influential political movement. Second, it contributed to its rise, seizure of power and consolidation within Italy. Third, it permitted the transformation of Italian Fascism into a *transnational* phenomenon in Europe: fascism, in the lower case. Fourth, it paved the way for the creation of an international fascist entente between – fundamentally but not only – Italian Fascism and German National Socialism. And fifth, it became a crucial element for fascist military expansion and for the imposition of new fascist and fascist-inspired regimes in Spain and France.

To make these points, this book draws on a strong empirical basis. I have used both archival and contemporary published sources from different countries, especially Italy, Germany, France and Spain. In particular, the veterans' press is the most common primary source employed,[57] along with contemporary books and brochures. State archives, including archives of the Foreign Ministries, have provided an important component of the primary evidence. Other historians have already consulted most of this material. However, I have analyzed these records from new points of view, searching for traces of the often-neglected transnational dimension and the evolution and cross-border circulation of symbols and discourses. By transcending the nation-state perspective, my systematic comparison of periodicals published simultaneously in different countries during the interwar period often reveals a different and more complete picture of historical events. In addition, I have retrieved a set of published sources that had never been systematically used before, for example, the journals of the fascist Associazione Nazionale Combattenti, *L'Italia combattente* and *L'Italia grigio-verde*. For this book, I have also collected information about the deeds and ideas of historical actors who have been largely neglected by historians until now.

The structure of the book is relatively simple. There are three parts, each composed of two chapters. Part I deals with the beginning of the transnational relationship between veterans and fascism: Chapter 1 examines the origins of this link during the Great War and its aftermath; Chapter 2 focuses on Italy to show how Italian Fascism was constructed on that basis and how it had a profound impact abroad. Part II examines the 1920s: Chapter 3 analyzes the fascist impregnation of veteran politics

---

[57] For an overview of the Italian veteran press, see Giovanni Sabbatucci, *La stampa del combattentismo (1918–1925)*, Bologna, Cappelli, 1980.

in Italy, and Chapter 4 shows how the mythical link between veterans and fascism circulated in Europe, contributing to the emergence of other fascist movements. Part III deals with the 1930s: Chapter 5 explains the highly complex process of entanglement of fascist veteran politics in Western Europe, and Chapter 6 discusses the final events of the transnational relationship between veterans and fascism, namely, new wars and the imposition of dictatorships in Spain and France.

Part I

Fascism and Veterans after the Great War

1   Great War Veterans and the Origins of Fascism, 1914–1919

This chapter examines the origins of the historical relationship between veterans and fascism, starting with the history of Italian participation in the Great War. The primary origin of both European 'generic' fascism and Italian Fascism lies in the First World War, which was simultaneously a global and European event and a cluster of disparate national experiences. Italy's participation in the Great War did not differ radically from that of other belligerent countries. However, it is necessary to take into account some particularities of Italy's involvement in the European conflict. Just as the war experience was fundamental for many future fascists, so too Mussolini's trials and tribulations during the First World War determined the process of ideological genesis of the fascist movement. I will address this issue in the first section of this chapter. I will show how, in the critical context of 1917, while the Bolshevik revolution was under way in Russia and Italy suffered a grave military setback at Caporetto, Mussolini began to develop a new ideology in which war veterans would play a crucial role.

The birth of fascism and its early relations with the ex-soldiers of the Great War were not isolated Italian phenomena. The deep post-war crisis that affected the country was part of a wider trend. Italy, like all the European nation-states, was plagued with social unrest, economic distress, and political instability. Paramilitarism and the formation of veteran movements were transnational consequences of the First World War. In the second section, I will offer an overview of the wider framework into which the Italian case must be considered. By focusing on international events in 1919, I will provide a description of the European context in which the birth of Fascism must be understood, including the emergence of veterans' organizations and paramilitary movements. The interconnectedness of all these historical forces is the key to understanding the evolution of the link between veterans and fascism.

The two last sections of this chapter focus on the Italian post-war experience, for I argue that the link between fascism and veterans was originally established in Italy. In Italy, the emergence of veterans' associations had certain distinctive characteristics that reflected the particularity of the Italian Great War experience. These specific characteristics intersected with wider understandings of momentous European events, such as those of the Central European counter-revolution. Transnational factors, therefore, explain the appearance of the original fascist movement in Italy, as well as the fascists' drive to absorb veterans into their ranks. The long process by which Italian veterans were politicized will be analyzed here as a conflictive process of symbolic appropriation that took place above all in the discursive and ideographic realm and that had transnational origins and consequences. The consolidation of a common, albeit unhistorical, perception of the veteran as an anti-Bolshevik, nationalist figure set a crucial precedent for the future symbolic fusion of war veterans and Fascism.

The Italian Experience of the First World War

The social and intellectual ferment that defined European societies before the outbreak of the war was also a feature in Italy. Like other states in Europe, Italy had been locked into the system of international alliances. In Italy, there were representatives of a new form of bellicose nationalism, with links to the French revolutionary rightist ideology typical of the years prior to the war.[1] However, despite its uneasy Triple Alliance with Germany and Austria-Hungary, Italy did not immediately join the conflict in August 1914: the expectations of some Italians, who saw the war as the catalyst for a new and better world, remained temporary unfulfilled. If one wants to understand why Fascism originated in Italy and the role veterans played in its development, the inquiry should start at this period.

The roots of Fascism lie in the Italian interventionist movement. While the young volunteers and soldiers of Germany, France and Britain started to kill each other along the European Western Front, in Italy, writers such as Giuseppe Prezzolini and Giovanni Papini spurred the Italian 'war generation' on in their articles in the review *La Voce*. Authors such as Gabriele D'Annunzio and Filippo Tommaso Marinetti did the same through their poems. Their writings attributed an existential meaning to war.[2] These apostles of intervention, together with young politicians, revolutionaries and republicans advocated joining the war on the

---

[1] Zeev Sternhell, *La droite révolutionnaire 1885–1914: Les origines françaises du fascisme*, Paris, Fayard, 1997.

[2] Walter L. Adamson, *Avant-Garde Florence: From Modernism to Fascism*, Cambridge, MA, Harvard University Press, 1993; Wohl, *The Generation of 1914*, pp. 168–70.

side of France and Britain. Most Italian intellectuals agreed with this aggressive stance, but for a variety of reasons. Some saw the war as a historical opportunity to complete the *Risorgimento* and Italian unity; others as the long-awaited chance to redeem the proletariat and overthrow the old political elites. War – they believed – would be a palingenetic experience for the Italian nation. Diverse groups and organizations from the nationalist far right to the revolutionary left converged in interventionism, a movement that acquired anti-democratic traits. Although all this agitation would be presented as successfully imposing the will of the interventionists against the decadent bourgeois nation during the 'radiant days' (*radiose giornate*) of May 1915, the decision to enter the war on the Entente side had been carefully negotiated; the Italian government had secretly reached an agreement with the British, the French and the Russians in the Pact of London.[3]

A striking characteristic of the Italian Great War experience, largely unparalleled elsewhere, was the social and political division that intervention provoked, especially within the Socialist Party. The fact that Italy would receive the territories of the Tirol and Dalmatia – among others – in case of victory was of no interest to the vast majority of the Italian population, which was, in general, utterly opposed to war. Whereas the interventionists were usually young middle-class educated men, the working class reasonably feared that the war would bring scarcity and worse living conditions. The national truce of the 'Sacred Union' that took place in France and Germany in 1914, involving support of the war effort by the socialists in these countries, did not exist in Italy. In France and Germany, the anti-militarist socialists were marginalized; Jean Jaurès was soon assassinated, and Karl Liebknecht would be expelled from the German Socialist Party. In contrast, anti-militarism and internationalism prevailed in Italian socialism, where it was the interventionists who were in the minority. Thus, if the so-called Spirit of 1914 was a myth in Germany,[4] May 1915 was similarly not marked by enthusiasm and voluntary enlistment across Italian society. However, the political left was not a firm and unanimously pacifist, internationalist and neutralist bloc. Socialists such as Leonida Bissolati and Gaetano Salvemini,

---

[3] The intellectual and social climate previous to Italian intervention can be seen in Mario Isnenghi, *Il mito della grande guerra*, Bologna, Il Mulino, 1989 (1st edn. 1970), pp. 11–178; Angelo Ventrone, *La seduzione totalitaria. Guerra, modernità, violenza politica (1914–1918)*, Rome, Donzelli, 2003, pp. 3–48; Mario De Nicolò (ed.), *Dalla trincea alla piazza: L'irruzione dei giovani nel Novecento*, Rome, Viella, 2011, *passim*.

[4] Jeffrey Verhey, *The Spirit of 1914: Militarism, Myth and Mobilization in Germany*, Cambridge University Press, 2000.

representatives of democratic interventionism, seeking to fight German imperialism, advocated Italy's entry into the war.

At this time, Benito Mussolini's attitude must be understood in the context of interventionism. He had been a revolutionary socialist and editor of the socialist newspaper *Avanti!* in Milan since 1912. His political ideas were often in tension with socialist orthodoxy, but his evolution towards the political right would take place in the context of the interventionist movement and during the war.[5] In line with his particular version of revolutionary ideology and galvanized by his readings of the intellectuals of *La Voce*, Mussolini supported intervention in the autumn of 1914. He founded his own interventionist paper, *Il Popolo d'Italia: Quotidiano socialista*, and severed ties with the Italian Socialist Party (PSI) in November. Subsequently, he participated in the founding meeting of the Fasci d'azione rivoluzionaria, a group that advocated revolutionary intervention. After repeated bitter confrontations with the socialists in the pages of his newspaper, Mussolini welcomed the declaration of war and was called up by the Italian army as a simple conscript. Like Mussolini, many other young men followed similar paths towards the war experience, some volunteering, but the overwhelming majority obliged to serve by conscription.

The Italian army of the First World War recruited almost six million people who had to be persuaded to fight and make sacrifices in the name of the nation. Peasants composed 45 percent of the army, whereas industrial workers were often exempt from front-line service. Extremely hierarchical relationships between soldiers and officers defined military life. Officers and junior officers typically came from a middle-class background and constituted a military elite of around 250,000 men, of which at least 200,000 were not professional military men. Although the figure of the 'peasant soldier' (*contadino soldato*) was cultivated in the propaganda as a model of obedience, devotion and resignation, this myth, developed by middle-class officers, contrasted with the harsh realities of the front.[6] Severe discipline was applied to recruits. During the first years of the war, there was no consensus about the war effort among Italians. The socialists adopted an ambiguous position, expressed in the motto 'neither support, nor sabotage' (*né aderire, né sabotare*). The struggle against the Austro-Hungarian forces seemed pointless for many men,

---

[5] Renzo De Felice, *Mussolini il rivoluzionario, 1883–1920*, Turin, Einaudi, 1965, pp. 221–418; Paul O'Brien, *Mussolini in the First World War: The Journalist, the Soldier, the Fascist*, Oxford, Berg, 2005.

[6] Giovanna Procacci, *Soldati e prigionieri italiani nella Grande Guerra. Con una raccolta di lettere inedite*, Rome, Editori Riuniti, 1993, pp. 90–3.

exasperated by the minimal but exhausting front-line advances and retreats in the region of the Alps, along the Piave River, on Mount Grappa, across the rocky plateau of the Carso, or in the repetitive battles of the Isonzo River.[7] It was on this river that Mussolini experienced his own baptism as a soldier.

How did Mussolini's interest in the combatants as future political actors materialize? His belief in war as a revolutionary event was already clear in 1914, but his faith in soldiers and veterans as political agents would mature over time. In reality, although the war experience conferred an aura of a warrior on Mussolini, his combat record was far from heroic. He spent a long time hospitalized in the rearguard and saw his last action in February 1917 when he was accidentally wounded. Although he could not fulfil his desire to become a junior officer, Mussolini identified himself with the officers, and junior officers became the main readers and contributors to his newspaper.[8] His nationalist commitment to attain Italian territorial demands pushed him to exalt the front soldiers as the spearhead of the war effort. In December 1916, he wrote that in the trenches he was witnessing the birth of a new and better elite that would govern Italy in the future: the 'trenchocracy' (*trincerocrazia*).[9] However great his enthusiasm for trench soldiers may have been, after February 1917, he returned definitively to Milan as a journalist and editor of *Il Popolo d'Italia*. Later, during the critical year of 1917, Mussolini's ideology would undergo a crucial turn.

The revolutionary process in Russia was the first and most consequential factor in Mussolini's evolution towards a new ideology that would celebrate future veterans as champions. When the Russian Revolution of February 1917 took place, the interventionists of *Il Popolo d'Italia* believed that the purported revolutionary nature of the war was giving positive results.[10] But soon they feared that the revolution could bring the withdrawal of Russia from the war.[11] Mussolini was aghast at such a possibility because this 'treason' would be detrimental to Italy and the allied countries and, more importantly, because the outcome of an agreed peace in Russia, as the result of the revolution, would directly contradict his own interpretation of the revolutionary nature of war. *Il Popolo d'Italia* insisted that the war was revolutionary: the Russian

[7] Mark Thompson, *The White War: Life and Death on the Italian Front, 1915–1919*, New York, Basic Books, 2009.
[8] See Mussolini's war diary, published in several chapters in *Il Popolo d'Italia* during the war: Edouardo and Duilio Susmel (eds.), *Opera Omnia di Benito Mussolini*, Vol. XXIV, Florence, La Fenice, 1961, pp. 1–113.
[9] *Il Popolo d'Italia*, 27 December 1916.   [10] *Ibid.*, 19 March 1917; 4 April 1917.
[11] *Ibid.*, 13 April 1917.

front soldiers, especially the young officers, backed the revolution, but Russians had to continue the war until victory.[12] In July 1917, Mussolini was euphoric because Russian soldiers were advancing against the Germans, and he supported the possibility of a Kerensky dictatorship.[13] Mussolini's inclination was clearly towards continuing war at all costs, so he subordinated any social improvement for the population – including the masses of soldiers – to the superior interests of the war effort and the nation. When the last Russian offensive failed due to the soldiers' lack of enthusiasm to fight, he held the Bolshevik agitators responsible. In general, for the interventionist bourgeoisie, the bad turn taken by the Revolution in Russia offered a troubling precedent for what might happen in Italy. This parallel was extremely present in the minds of many like Mussolini when the Italian army, after years of brutal struggle, nearly collapsed in the autumn of 1917. The twelfth battle of the Isonzo, the so-called disaster of Caporetto, was a traumatic defeat that threw the Italian army and society into crisis.[14]

Combined with the ongoing Russian Revolution, Caporetto was the second event that drove Mussolini to designate veterans as the harbingers of a new emergent ideology. It is important to realize that when this massive retreat happened – between October and November 1917 – not only were other belligerent armies such as that of France experiencing problems of mutinies and weariness among the troops,[15] but in Russia a second revolution was taking place. The Bolsheviks had succeeded in winning the allegiance of Russian soldiers who, enthusiastic about peace, were the protagonists of a revolution at the front.[16] Meanwhile, in Italy, the divisions among socialists became more acute, shocked as they were by both the Russian events and the invasion of national territory. The Italian socialists, scrutinized through the lens of the Russian example, were blamed for debilitating the morale of the troops and for having provoked the disaster at Caporetto. Even though General Cadorna used the Italian socialists as a scapegoat, he was replaced by General Armando Diaz as the new Chief of General Staff. This change would not be enough to renew the Italian war effort, nor would it stop

[12] *Ibid.*, 15 April 1917; 5 May 1917.
[13] B. Mussolini, 'Bandiere rosse', *Il Popolo d'Italia*, 5 July 1917; B. Mussolni, 'Il tramonto di Zimmerwald', *Il Popolo d'Italia*, 7 July 1917; B. Mussolini, 'Viva Kerensky!', *Il Popolo d'Italia*, 26 July 1917.
[14] Isnenghi, *Il mito della Grande Guerra*, pp. 261–394.
[15] André Loez and Nicolas Mariot, *Obéir/desobéir: Les mutineries de 1917 en perspective*, Paris, Éditions La Découverte, 2008.
[16] Allan K. Wildman, *The End of the Russian Imperial Army*, Princeton, NJ, Princeton University Press, 1980–7, pp. 3–72.

anti-socialist discourse. Nonetheless, this context not only influenced Mussolini's ideological evolution but also provoked a set of transformations that lay the foundations for the political manipulation of the symbol of the war veteran.

After Caporetto, a range of urgent measures was taken to motivate the soldiers once more and to maintain their discipline and commitment to the national cause; this effort would affect the mentalities and expectations of the future war veterans.[17] The military promoted the concept of a new model soldier who should be a motivated 'combatant' (*combattente*) rather than just an obedient 'serviceman' (*soldato*).[18] The authorities drew extensively on persuasive patriotic and nationalistic propaganda that demonized the enemy and glorified aggression. These discourses implied making extensive promises to the soldiers. It was said that the fatherland was enormously indebted to its saviours. Propagandists depicted a future of absolute moral recognition from the entire society. They promised to 'love', 'respect' and 'honour' the combatants. As one journal put it, 'the soldier will be the first also in rights.'[19] These promises may have helped to improve the fighting spirit of the front soldiers but surely contributed to creating unrealistic expectations for their homecoming too.

The ideal of a new self-motivated soldier found expression in the new assault troops: the *arditi*. The battle-hardened *arditi* became an elite group of soldiers who enjoyed high morale and certain concrete privileges (e.g. better food, higher pay, and more extensive rest periods). Their offensive actions would rely on a combination of the element of surprise and extreme violence. The limited *arditi* assault units (*reparti di assalto*) numbered approximately 35,000 members. As their emblem, they adopted the aggressive symbols of the skull and the sword surrounded by a laurel wreath. The *arditi* equalled the battalions of the *alpini* in prestige and reliability on the battlefield, even though their contribution to the war cannot be considered decisive. The main significance of the *arditi* was that they represented a new kind of war mentality that was elitist, violent and intransigent, thus intersecting with the wishes of intellectuals like the futurists, who stressed action and violence as means to an end.[20]

From 1917 on, while the Russian Revolution evolved, re-mobilizing measures to enhance the morale of soldiers were needed in all belligerent

---

[17] Sabbatucci, *I combattenti*, pp. 9–19.   [18] Mondini, *La politica delle armi*, p. 43.
[19] *Il giornale del soldato* (Milan), 4 November 1917.
[20] Giorgio Rochat, *Gli arditi della Grande Guerra: Origini, battaglie e miti*, Milan, Feltrinelli, 1981; Cordova, *Arditi e legionari Dannunziani*.

nations,[21] and Italy was no exception. It is true that, to some extent, patriotic discourses had also permeated the lower social classes of countries participating in the war, providing them with a sense of honour to confront a probable death on the battlefields, but the average soldier experienced the war as an unwanted imposition.[22] To generate consent among the masses of soldiers and their families, state propaganda was accompanied by social assistance and promises of material rewards. In Italy, home-front committees and new trench newspapers spread the spirit of interventionism, as well as hatred towards shirkers, 'draft dodgers' (emboscati), 'opportunists' (profittatori), pacifists and defeatists.[23] The authorities were profoundly worried about events in Russia, where soldiers fuelled the revolution by joining workers' and soldiers' councils (Soviets).

Mussolini paid close attention to all these developments. In November 1917, when Georges Clemenceau was appointed Prime Minister in France, Mussolini praised the energetic attitude of the French statesman who was committed to a greater national war effort. According to Mussolini, the democratic way of waging war would 'fatally' lead – as in Russia – 'to the regime of the Soviets, to committees of workers and soldiers, and to soldiers' assemblies that would debate and reject the generals' strategy plans'.[24] On 20 November 1917, while discussing the needs of the front soldiers, Clemenceau stated that 'they have rights over us' (ils ont des droits sur nous), a sentence that became famous among French soldiers and veterans and even generated a sense of superiority among them. Meanwhile, in Italy, Mussolini was enthusiastic about the first legislative initiatives to support the families of combatants.[25] Since peasant workers formed the bulk of the Italian army, the Italian state promised land to those who were fighting at the front. In December 1917, the Orlando government issued a decree establishing the Opera Nazionale Combattenti (ONC). This institution addressed the endemic problems of Italian agriculture and the development of the south (Mezzogiorno), as well as the reintegration of soldiers after the war. The ONC transformed the old motto 'land to the peasants' (la terra ai contadini)

---

[21] John Horne, 'Remobilising for "total war": France and Britain, 1917–1918', in John Horne (ed.), State, Society and Mobilization in Europe during the First World War, Cambridge University Press, 2002, pp. 195–211.

[22] Antonio Gibelli, L'officina della guerra: La Grande Guerra e le trasformazioni del mondo mentale, Turin, Bollati Boringhieri, 2007 (1st edn., 1991), pp. 99, 106, 115.

[23] Andrea Fava, 'Assistenza e propaganda nel regime di guerra (1915–1918)', in Mario Isnenghi (ed.), Operai e contadini nella Grande Guerra, Bologna, Cappelli, 1982, pp. 174–212.

[24] 'Il senso di una crisi', Il Popolo d'Italia, 18 November 1917.

[25] 'La patria ai combattenti', Il Popolo d'Italia, 20 November 1917.

into the catchphrase 'land to the combatants' (*la terra ai combattenti*). Also in December 1917, Minister of the Treasury Francesco Saverio Nitti created free insurance policies for the soldiers, junior officers and officers.[26]

Most importantly, like other European states in 1917, the Italian state set out to tackle the problem of disabled soldiers. These timely measures succeeded in maintaining the loyalty of veterans to the war effort. An official institution, the Opera Nazionale Invalidi di Guerra, took charge of the care of the war disabled in March 1917. At the same time, the mutilated veterans started to organize themselves to defend their interests. Several newspapers – especially *Il Popolo d'Italia* – reported the activities, meetings and statements of disabled veterans' groups. The disabled veterans set up the National Association of the War Maimed and War Wounded (Associazione Nazionale fra Mutilati e Invalidi di Guerra (ANMIG)). This association would count on the benevolence of the authorities, since it adopted a patriotic stance unconnected with the socialists or any other party. In fact, the ANMIG became the interlocutor of the government in regard to pensions. In the period of Caporetto, certain groups of disabled soldiers went further in their support of the war effort; in line with the interventionists, they showed an extreme zeal in persecuting internal enemies.[27] Thus, the government and the interventionists precluded the formation of the kind of socialist or democratically oriented disabled veterans' organizations that existed in France or Germany.[28]

During 1917, discourses and representations of the disabled veterans in *Il Popolo d'Italia* foreshadowed the mythic role that war veterans would play in Fascism. In the spring of 1917, the newspaper argued that the veterans should be offered not only pensions and assistance but also the honour and respect of the fatherland. Furthermore, whereas the newspaper admitted that the state had acquired duties in relation to disabled veterans, it also said that these men were not exempt from the obligation to contribute productively to the nation – veterans were not allowed to be 'parasites'. The interventionists were enthusiastic about the disabled veterans' commitment to the war effort.[29] The ideal that these patriotic

---

[26] Giuseppe Barone, 'Statalismo e riformismo: l'Opera Nazionale Combatteni (1917–1923)', *Studi Storici* (1984), pp. 203–44; *Il giornale del soldato*, 23 December 1917.

[27] Sabbatucci, *I combattenti*, pp. 19–30; Barbara Bracco, *La patria ferita: I corpi dei soldati italiani e la Grande guerra*, Florence, Giunti, 2012, pp. 159–81.

[28] See Prost, *Les Anciens Combattants*, Vol. 1, pp. 20–44; Whalen, *Bitter Wounds*, pp. 121–9.

[29] *Il Popolo d'Italia*, 28 April 1917, 2 November 1917.

disabled veterans represented thus became an element of Mussolini's proto-fascist worldview.

Mussolini's article 'Trincerocrazia' in *Il Popolo d'Italia* delineated the mythic role that veterans would have in the ideology of early Fascism. It is crucial to take into account the context in which Mussolini wrote that text. It happened in December 1917, after Caporetto, when zones of northern Italy still remained under enemy occupation. The ANMIG was consolidating in several cities, and groups of disabled veteran activists incited the fight against external and internal enemies through their newspapers. But sacrifices were also engendering prospects for the future. For example, in *La Voce dei Reduci*, a wounded soldier wrote that, after the war, if he would go on to become a minister, he would uphold the rights of those who were fighting: 'new rights of new people'.[30] Mussolini most probably read this publication.[31] Inspired by this spirit, he picked up the notion of *trincerocrazia*. This concept allowed him to outline the role that he attributed to veterans. Mussolini stated that a 'new aristocracy' – a concept formerly invented by Prezzolini – was being formed in the trenches: 'Trenchocracy is the aristocracy of the trench. It is the aristocracy of tomorrow.' According to him, Italy was evolving towards a division between those who had fought and those who had not. The idea of two Italies was another Prezzolinian creation. Mussolini used the activities of the disabled soldiers to support his argument. The *mutilati* were the vanguard of the great army that would soon return home. Mussolini stated that the new spirit of the returnees would grant a new sense to words now devoid of meaning, such as 'democracy' and 'liberalism'. The veterans – depicted as workers who returned from the furrows of the trenches to the furrows of the land – would synthesize notions of class and nation, thus creating a kind of 'anti-Marxist' and 'national' socialism.[32]

Historians have pointed to the article 'Trincerocrazia' as the first clear evidence of Mussolini's abandonment of socialism.[33] This turn to the right has been explained as a consequence of Caporetto and also as the result of Mussolini's perception that the war had profoundly changed the country whilst transforming the front soldiers into a completely new political force for the post-war period.[34] However, in my opinion,

---

[30] *La Voce dei Reduci* (Bologna), 9 December 1917.
[31] He mentioned the appearance of *La Voce dei Reduci* in 'Trincerocrazia'.
[32] B. Mussolini, 'Trincerocrazia', *Il Popolo d'Italia*, 15 December 1917.
[33] De Felice, *Mussolini il rivoluzionario*, pp. 399–403; see also Adamson, *Avant-Garde Florence*, pp. 257–62.
[34] De Felice, *Mussolini il rivoluzionario*, pp. 362–418; Gentile, *Le origini dell'ideologia fascista*.

'Trincerocrazia' must be considered more like a self-fulfilling prophecy than as an accurate, clairvoyant prediction of the future. The article was, indeed, an early manifestation of fascist ideology, yet, at the same time, it was the revelation of a political ambition. Mussolini was proclaiming the new style of politics that he hoped would shape the post-war order; he envisioned a new society in which the war veterans would play an essential role. He was clearly targeting the combatants as potential readers of his paper and probably thinking of them as future supporters of a new political movement. At that point in time, the legendary connection between veterans and Fascism was born. But why had Mussolini become so interested in mobilizing the veterans?

There was one crucial motivation. It is clear that the course of the Russian Revolution since the spring of 1917 pushed Mussolini to position himself violently against the Italian socialists.[35] It is important to note here that Mussolini supported intervention because he believed in the revolutionary nature of war. The Russian Revolution confirmed his belief, but with undesired consequences. Overwhelmingly supported by Russian front soldiers, the Bolsheviks were willing to bring an end to the war and make peace with the Central Powers, thereby betraying the allied countries. Having become an uncompromising nationalist, Mussolini feared this scenario. By mid-December 1917, Mussolini's disappointment must have been total. For on the same day 'Trincerocrazia' was published, the armistice between Russia and the Central Powers paved the way for peace negotiations in Brest-Litovsk. Thus, the Russian peace destroyed the myth of the revolutionary war in which Mussolini had believed. Although war did lead to revolution, revolution led to the most feared consequence for the interventionists: a peace that was not a victory. When this contradiction was revealed, Mussolini chose to support war, thus rejecting socialism and focusing on the struggle to realize the nationalist war aims. This choice required looking for a new political clientele: war veterans. In Fascism, they would represent the revolutionary, albeit nationalist, force that would reverse the ex-soldiers' role in the Bolshevik Revolution. Thus, 'Trincerocrazia' shows the broad extent to which the conception of a new political phenomenon, Fascism, was entangled with the belief in the war veterans as a new political driving force. In a sense, the nascent fascist ideology was a strategy to ensure that war veterans, in contrast to what happened in Russia, would remain loyal to the nationalist struggle to the very end. Originating in the revolutionary wing of the Italian interventionist movement, the idealized

---

[35] O'Brien, *Mussolini in the First World War*, pp. 123–40.

connection between Fascism and veterans was first catalyzed by the frustrating and unexpected outcome of the Russian Revolution.[36]

Mussolini was not alone in his ideas. At that time, for instance, the interventionist intellectual Agostino Lanzillo went as far as to argue that war had defeated socialism.[37] Lanzillo had translated the work of the theorist of revolutionary syndicalism Georges Sorel into Italian. During the war, Lanzillo had served at the front and had been wounded.[38] Lanzillo believed in the revolutionary nature of war but roundly denounced the events in Russia as a 'revolution that masked defeat'.[39] In his book, *The Defeat of Socialism*, finished in January 1918, Lanzillo affirmed that the generations who had fought at the front would come out of the war 'renewed', with a 'new mentality' and with 'improved individual qualities'. This human force would be a determining factor in future events. And in any case, the veterans' actions would take a *'national direction'*. According to Lanzillo, the returning soldiers would instinctively ascribe a positive value (*valorizzare*) to their sacrifice. Therefore, it would be improbable that veterans would adopt any 'revolutionary attitude'; instead, they would 'fight to replace the ruling class, in the name of the power and the courage they represent'.[40] Retrospectively, Lanzillo's predictions might be interpreted as correct. However, they should be considered as part of the same set of interventionist beliefs as Mussolini's *trincerocrazia*. This mind-set was the blueprint for a nascent political programme and strategy for the post-war period.

Thus, after Caporetto and confirmation of the Russian 'revolutionary' peace, the interventionists' identification with the fighting soldiers increased. *Il Popolo d'Italia* changed its line, presenting itself as the defender of combatants' rights. This shift became evident during the last phase of the war, when the polarization of Italian society became sharp, and 'defeatists' were persecuted as the 'internal enemy'. As Prezzolini put it, the biggest enemy was 'at home', but the combatants would come

---

[36] For a wider discussion of this historical process, see Ángel Alcalde, 'War veterans and the transnational origins of Italian Fascism (1917–1919)', *Journal of Modern Italian Studies*, 21, 4 (2016), pp. 565–83.

[37] Agostino Lanzillo, *La disfatta del Socialismo: Critica della guerra e del socialismo*, Florence, 1918.

[38] Lanzillo, born in Reggio Calabria in 1886, studied law and joined the Italian revolutionary syndicalist trends before the war. He also collaborated with *La Voce* and with the Mussolinian *Avanti!*. Interventionist and a founder of the Fascio rivoluzionario d'azione, he collaborated with *Il Popolo d'Italia*. He joined the fascist movement in Milan in 1919. After the March on Rome, he was elected as a Member of Parliament in 1924. However, in the 1930s, he became hostile to Mussolini and critical of the regime's economic policies. In 1944, he escaped to Switzerland. He returned to Italy after 1945 and died in 1952.

[39] Lanzillo, *La disfatta del socialismo*, p. 218.   [40] *Ibid.*, pp. 289–91.

back from war to 'renovate' the country.[41] *Il Popolo d'Italia* called for the establishment of a dictatorship that would militarize Italian society until victory. The newspaper made space for the material claims of the 'trenchmen' (*trinceristi*); junior officers found in it a forum for expressing their concerns.[42] Yet the idea of distributing expropriated land to peasant soldiers was played down.[43] Finally, in August 1918, the adoption of a new subtitle – *Journal of the Combatants and Producers* (*Quotidiano dei combattenti e dei produttori*) – symbolized Mussolini's definitive rejection of socialism. Now Mussolini distinguished his notions of 'combatants' and 'producers' from the common concepts of 'soldiers' and 'workers', which were tinged with socialism.[44]

There was not yet a coherent political programme or fully developed ideology for the veterans, but Mussolini had sewn the seeds for the subsequent emergence of the fascist veteran symbol. Some Italian veterans embraced the idea of *trincerocrazia*, and disabled veterans' leaders publically presented themselves as the 'great vanguard' of those who would return from the front.[45] Until the end of the war, Mussolini and *Il Popolo d'Italia* catered to the post-war expectations of soldiers, advocating a rapid demobilization of most troops.[46] Yet, Mussolini's group was a simple observer of the emerging veterans' movement rather than its promoter, and the question of the *trincerocrazia* remained undeveloped. After the Italian victory at Vittorio Veneto and Armando Diaz's 'Victory's Bulletin' (*Bollettino della vittoria*) on 4 November, Mussolini's enthusiastic response was that of a fully nationalistic and anti-socialist interventionist, which is exactly what he had become by virtue of the war experience.[47] The First World War ended two weeks later, yet there would be no real peace in many parts of the European continent.

Veterans and the Aftermath of War in Western Europe

The outcome of the First World War was traumatic for both belligerent and many non-belligerent European countries. National experiences differed depending on the military result of the confrontation. Regardless of whether they suffered defeat or not, all the countries who participated in the war suffered massive human losses (10 million deaths in total), and

[41] Giuseppe Prezzolini, 'Mea culpa', *Il Popolo d'Italia*, 17 January 1918.
[42] See, for example, *Il Popolo d'Italia*, 25 August 1918; 29 September 1918.
[43] *Il Popolo d'Italia*, 14 May 1918.   [44] *Ibid.*, 1 August 1918.
[45] Aldo Cingolani, 'Le due Italie', *La Voce dei Reduci*, 23 December 1917; *Il Popolo d'Italia*, 11 March 1918.
[46] Mussolini, 'Interessi dei soldati – Le vecchie classi', *Il Popolo d'Italia*, 5 August 1918.
[47] *Il Popolo d'Italia*, 4 November 1918.

their populations emerged from the war profoundly transformed. Despite victory, certain countries – including Italy – went through a long and unprecedented period of social unrest and violent conflict. In the context of defeat, the dismemberment of the Central Empires paved the way for the birth of new democratic nation-states such as the German Weimar Republic. The spectre of social revolution and civil war, like what had been happening in Russia since 1917, was omnipresent. In 1919, the international relations system struggled to find a new balance of power at Versailles, and in the economic sphere, the shift from a 'total war' to a peacetime economy was turbulent. Returning to the pre-1914 order was impossible. The ordeal of demobilizing millions of ex-combatants marked the post-war history of the belligerent nations. All these countries witnessed the emergence of very politically diverse veterans associations. The issue of reintegrating veterans was a pressing task that concerned politicians and civil society. The veterans were conspicuous as a new actor in the public sphere, one impossible to ignore after the kind of experience they had endured in the name of the nation. Many returned home hoping to turn the promises made to them during the war into a reality.

In the post-war period, cultural demobilization was a necessary task for countries aspiring to return to normality after an experience of 'total' war.[48] This process was crucial for reintegrating war veterans, as well as for pacification of the most aggressive warmongers in every country. The results of this common effort varied between countries, regions, social or age groups and gender. Yet the issue of the reintegration of veterans and the problematic process of cultural demobilization must be linked with the fact that paramilitarism flourished across Europe in the aftermath of the First World War.[49] Violence persisted in several countries, especially in Eastern and Central Europe, where the emergence of armed 'home guards' was tied to the perception of a Bolshevik threat. Ex-soldiers usually joined these quasi-military formations. But the emergence of civic guards occurred even in countries that had not fought in the Great War, such as Spain.[50] This widespread reaction was transnational; it moved beyond national boundaries and took place independent of defeat, victory or participation in the First World War.[51] This was the fertile context that provided the emergence of the fascist

---

[48] Horne (dir.), 'Démobilisations culturelles après la Grande Guerre'.

[49] Gerwarth and Horne (eds.), *War in Peace*.

[50] Eduardo González Calleja and Fernando del Rey, *La defensa armada contra la revolución*, Madrid, CSIC, 1995.

[51] Gerwarth and Horne, 'Vectors of Violence'.

movement. In this section I approach the contextual elements that are crucial to understanding how and why a link between Fascism and war veterans was established in Italy, which was later extended to other countries. I also examine the emergence of veterans organizations that became important historical actors in subsequent years (Table 1.1), with particular consideration of their relation to Fascism.

Germany

Germany was a dramatic and unique case due to its weight in both Western and Central Europe, its defeat in the Great War and its Revolution, all of which had far-reaching consequences across the Continent. The aftermath of war in Germany was shaped by a series of social, political, economic and psychological processes.[52] The chaotic return of German soldiers from the front not only created a serious economic problem but also conditioned the trajectory of the German Revolution. After the Kaiser's abdication and escape, soldiers' councils (*Soldatenräte*) quickly proliferated across Germany, with soldiers waving red flags and wearing red armbands.[53] Power fell to the Social Democrats. Many officers were appalled as the imperial army crumbled; they often ripped off their own rank badges and in some cases were publically humiliated.[54] Between November and December of 1918, while the Spartacus League was the driving force behind a Communist insurrectionary movement, 1.5 million German front soldiers (*Frontsoldaten*, commonly called *Frontschweine*) returned home. Although the population usually welcomed them, returning soldiers eventually employed violence against the revolutionaries, for example, during the violent clashes in Berlin on 24 December 1918. Many of the revolutionaries were formerly demobilized veterans, rear-guard soldiers – called *Etappenschweine* – and rebel sailors. In order to restore internal 'tranquillity and order' (*Ruhe und*

---

[52] Bessel, *Germany after the First World War*.

[53] Ulrich Kluge, *Soldatenräte und revolution: Studien zur Militärpolitik in Deutschland 1918/ 19*, Göttingen, Vandenhoeck & Ruprecht, 1975; Scott Stephenson, *The Final Battle. Soldiers of the Western Front and the German Revolution of 1918*, Cambridge University Press, 2009.

[54] Richard Bessel, 'Die Heimkehr der Soldaten: Das Bild der Frontsoldaten in der Öffentlichkeit der Weimarer Republik', in Gerhard Hirschfeld, Gerd Krumeich and Irina Renz (eds.), *"Keiner fühlt sich hier mehr als Mensch ..." Erlebnis und Wirkung des Ersten Weltkriegs*, Frankfurt am Main, Fischer Taschenbuch, 1996, pp. 260–82; Mark Jones, 'From "Skagerrak" to the "Organisation Consul": War Culture and the Imperial German Navy, 1914–1922', in James E. Kitchen, Alisa Miller and Laura Rowe (eds.), *Other Combatants, Other Fronts: Competing Histories of the First World War*, Newcastle, Cambridge Scholars Publishing, 2011, pp. 249–74.

Table 1.1 *Overview of the Main Veterans Associations and Organizations in This Book*

Italy
Population in 1914 = 36 million
6 million mobilized soldiers
4 million front-line combatants
3 million veterans demobilized
in 1918–19

ANMIG: Disabled veterans association founded in 1917. Patriotic orientation, non-political, yet progressively nationalistic. Membership in 1919 = 220,000; 1934 = 500,000. Under direct fascist rule since 1925.

ANC: Founded in 1918. Politically diverse and democratic; in June 1920 became officially non-political. Membership in mid-1919 = 100,000–300,000; 1920 = *c*. 500,000; 1929 = *c*. 400,000; 1936 = 850,000; 1940 = *c*. 1 million. Under direct fascist rule since 1925.

Associazione fra gli Arditi d'Italia: Created in January 1919 by futurist *arditi*. Initially linked to the fascist movement. Later split between D'Annunzian, anti-fascist and Mussolinian trends. From September 1922, the fascist *arditi* were organized in the **Federazione Nazionale Arditi d'Italia**. Membership in December 1928 = 10,000.

ANRZO: Founded in 1918, only strong in Turin and Piedmont. Liberal (Mazzinian) inspiration. Fused with the ANC in 1920.

UNRG: Founded in 1919. Catholic and linked to the PPI. Dissolved towards 1925.

UNUS: Anti-Bolshevik, interventionist and nationalist association created in April 1919. Membership in October 1919 = 450. Dissolved at the end of 1919.

Lega Proletaria: Founded in 1918. Socialist and pacifist. Membership in April 1919 = 50,000. Dissolved towards 1925.

France
Population in 1914 = 41 million
6.4 million mobilized soldiers
5 million veterans demobilized
in 1918–19
4 million holders of the 'veteran card' in 1937

UF: Created in 1917–18 as a federation of veterans associations. Republican, centre-left orientation. Membership in 1920 = 120,000; 1921 = 191,000; 1922 = 251,000; 1923 = 280,000; 1927 = 350,000; 1931 = 700,000; 1932 = 900,000. During the 1930s, the UF made a political turn to the right and towards authoritarianism.

UNC: Founded in 1918. Republican, conservative, anti-leftist. Membership in February 1919 = 100,000; December 1919 = 300,000; June 1920 = 510,000; 1927 = 290,000; 1932 = 850,000.

ARAC: Founded in early 1919. Pacifist, republican, leftist. Later became communist. Membership in 1930 = *c*. 20,000.

Croix de Feu: Founded as an association of decorated veterans in 1929. Membership in January 1930 = 8,922; 1932 = *c*. 23,000; 1933 = c. 28,000; February 1934 = *c*. 100,000; 1935 = c. 500,000. Conservative and

Table 1.1 (*cont.*)

authoritarian, it progressively acquired fascist and paramilitary traits, while its exclusive veteran character was abandoned.

Légion Française des Combattants: Organization created by the regime of Vichy in 1940 by fusing the main associations, UF and UNC. Membership = 1.5 million.

Germany
Population in 1914 = *c.* 65 million
13.2 million mobilized soldiers

Reichsbund der Kriegsbeschädigten, Kriegsteilnemer und Kriegerhinterbliebenen: Founded in 1917. Social Democrat association. Membership in 1921 = 639,000; 1922 = 830,000.

Reichsbanner Schwarz-Rot-Gold: Founded in 1924 as a league of Republican and Social Democrat veterans. Membership in 1925–6 = *c.* 900,000?

Rote Frontkämpferbund: Founded in 1924 as a Communist league of veterans. Later included a women's section and accepted non-veterans. Membership in early 1925 = *c.* 15,000; June 1925 = 51,000; peak in mid-1927 = 120,000; November 1928 = 106,000. Banned in 1929.

Kyffhäuserbund: Founded in 1900. Patriotic and anti-socialist association. Membership in 1921 = 2.2 million; 1929 = 2.6 million. In 1938 it was merged into the **NS Deutscher Reichskriegerbund (Kyffhäuser).**

Stahlhelm: Founded in January 1919 as a self-defence group, soon became anti-republican and later inspired by Fascism. Initial membership = 1,000?; September 1919 = *c.* 2,000; 1924 = 20,000? Since the mid-1920s, it included members without war experience. Peak membership in the 1930s = 160,000–500,000 veterans; up to 1.5 million total membership. The organization became under Nazi rule after 1933, changing its name to **NSDFB (Stahlhelm)**, with membership 500,000 in 1935, the year of its dissolution.

NSKOV: Created by the NSDAP in the early 1930s as an agency of social welfare and propaganda for war veterans.

Spain
Population in 1936 = *c.* 25 million
1.2 million mobilized soldiers in the Francoist army

DNE: Created in August 1939 as an agency of the FET-JONS for veterans from the Francoist army. Membership in 1963 = *c.* 372,000.

BCMGP: Organization created in 1937 for the control and assistance of disabled veterans from the Francoist army. Membership in 1939 = *c.* 70.000.

Sources: Berghahn (1965), Sabbatucci (1974), Klotzbücher (1964), Schuster (1975), Prost (1977), Rochat (1981), Finker (1982), Cointet (1995), Ungari (2001), Kennedy (2007), Millington (2012a, 2015), Ziemann (2013), Löffelbein (2013), Alcalde (2014).

Ordnung), to repress the revolution and to defend the Eastern borders, the Social Democratic government promoted the creation of mercenary units: the Free Corps (Freikorps). The ruthless and bloody mentality of these ultra-violent paramilitaries was firmly grounded in the imagery of the war.[55] In the beginning, the bulk of their membership came from the front soldiers. Their combat methods were employed against civilians in a context of extreme anxiety and fear.[56] In Berlin, government soldiers and volunteers participated in the assault on the socialist newspaper *Vorwärts* – occupied by the revolutionary rebels – and ruthlessly killed Spartacist leaders Karl Liebknecht and Rosa Luxemburg on 15 January 1919.[57]

Events in Germany are of crucial importance to comprehend the Italian context in which the fascist movement would be born and to connect its history with the war veterans. The shocking news of the fate of the Spartacist insurrection in Berlin soon crossed borders. In Italy, the socialist paper *Avanti!* announced that in Germany, the 'militarist danger' had been reawakened with the repression; the paper reproduced Liebknecht's last message, which recognized that the revolutionaries had been abandoned 'by the sailors and soldiers'.[58] The rumours about the gruesome end of the German Communist Party leaders were also confirmed: soldiers returning from the front, or 'governmental troops' as they were still called, had crushed the Communist insurrection. Another revolution in the Russian mould had been seemingly prevented by returning veterans.

Mussolini's perception of what had just occurred in Germany contributed to strengthening his own faith in the decisive political role of veterans, who according to him would put a stop to the expansion of the 'Asiatic' phenomenon of Leninism. Mussolini speculated that army officers from the old German regime had been instrumental in the demise of the Spartacists.[59] While events in Berlin developed, *Il Popolo d'Italia* had publicized the support that the soldiers' and workers' councils had given to the German Social Democrat government and highlighted the conservative mind-set of the soldiers who reached such a decision: 'soldiers returned from the trenches do not want, do not

---

[55] Klaus Theweleit, *Männerphantasien*, Frankfurt am Main, Verlag Roter Stern, 1977–8.

[56] Mark Jones, *Founding Weimar: Violence and the German Revolution of 1918-1919*, Cambridge University Press, 2016.

[57] Heinrich Hannover and Elisabeth Hannover-Drück (eds.), *Der Mord an Rosa Luxemburg und Karl Liebknecht: Dokumentation eines politischen Verbrechens*, Göttingen, Lamuv, 1989.

[58] *Avanti!* (Milan), 16 and 17 January 1919; *Rote Fahne* (Berlin), 15 January 1919.

[59] Mussolini, 'Liebknecht è stato fucilato', *Il Popolo d'Italia*, 17 January 1919.

tolerate disorder. They have lived through too much, in the tragic, terrible disorder of battles, to not feel disgust for internal disorder and repugnance for civil war.'[60] Thus, by the end of January 1919, the violent actions of the German Freikorps helped forge a transnational perception of the veterans as effective anti-revolutionary agents in neighbouring countries such as Italy.[61]

We should note that many right-wing and nationalistic youths, students and cadets who had not actually fought in the war soon joined these anti-revolutionary organizations; only a tiny portion of the German veterans joined them. Yet, the Freikorps military performance in the Baltic region was characterized by an intense combat experience. The short-lived Soviet Republic of Bavaria – in existence between April and May of 1919 – was also crushed by the Freikorps. Subsequently, in Hungary, Miklós Horthy formed paramilitary units with the same counter-revolutionary traits of the Freikorps. These forces smashed the Soviet Republic of Hungary, inaugurating a period of 'White Terror'. Having played this counter-revolutionary role, the Freikorps have been called the 'heralds of Hitler', although these mercenary units lacked a clear or coherent political ideology.[62]

In addition to the Freikorps phenomenon, other German veterans made significant contributions to the formation of conservative self-defence groups in 1919. The Stahlhelm ('Steel Helmet') was created by Franz Seldte in Magdeburg between November and December of 1918 as one of the organizations willing to restore tranquillity and social order.[63] While the Stahlhelm was a group exclusively for 'front soldiers' (*Bund der Frontsoldaten*), most civic guards were generally composed of civilians. In February of 1919, Wolfgang Kapp, a nationalist politician in close contact with the military and the *Junkers*, suggested that to counteract the imminent 'civil war', the wealthiest landowners of every rural district should 'buy cars, and fill them with machineguns and hand-grenades ... with young [patriotic] people ... preferably officers or students'.[64] The 'civic defence' groups were particularly important in Bavaria. Furthermore, the conservative Kyffhäuserbund, an anti-socialist

[60] 'Operai e soldati solidali con Ebert', *Il Popolo d'Italia*, 19 January 1919.
[61] Alcalde, 'War veterans and the transnational origins of Italian Fascism'.
[62] Waite, *Vanguard of Nazism*; Nigel H. Jones, *Hitler's Heralds: The Story of the Freikorps, 1918–1923*, London, Murray, 1987; Gerwarth, 'The Central European Counter-Revolution'; Dirk Schumann (ed.), *Political Violence in the Weimar Republic 1918–1933: Fight for the Streets and Fear of Civil War*, Oxford, Berghahn Books, 2009, pp. 3–53; Jones, *Founding Weimar*.
[63] Berghahn, *Der Stahlhelm*, pp. 14–15.
[64] 'Vorschläge Kapps an Prinz Udo von Löwenstein-Wertheim-Freudenberg, eine von den Großgrundbesitzern gebildete Bürgerkriegstruppe zu schaffen. O. O., Februar 1919', in

but allegedly apolitical veterans' organization rooted in the tradition of Wihelmine Germany, counted on more than 2 million members.[65]

However, some of the biggest veterans' organizations that appeared in Germany were not paramilitary leagues but welfare entities. Alongside the nationalists stood pacifist veterans' groups. The Peace League of Ex-Servicemen (Friedensbund der Kriegsteilnehmer) reached 30,000 members in 1919, although it would dissolve in 1922. A Social Democratic Reich League of Disabled War Veterans, Ex-Servicemen and War Dependants (Reichsbund der Kriegsbeschädigten, Kriegsteilnehmer und Kriegshinterbliebenen) would reach 830,000 members in 1922. German Jewish veterans created their own veterans' association in February of 1919, committed to defending the memory of their German patriotism during the war and to fight anti-Semitism.[66] The majority of German veterans did not join any political organization; 'the wartime experiences of the veterans set limits to paramilitary mobilisation rather than underpinning it', as Benjamin Ziemann has put it.[67] Yet, German veterans were an active factor in the social unrest of this period. In the cities, demobilized soldiers agitated against the authorities for compensation for their war sacrifice. The problem posed by war veterans was part of the wider question of the war victims (*Kriegsopfer*) in Weimar Germany, which included a shocking number of war widows and orphans.[68]

After June of 1919, when the Treaty of Versailles was signed and made public, the German army and many veterans perceived it as a humiliation. The treaty imposed very harsh conditions on Germany, the country that was considered to have sole responsibility for the war. In this context, the 'stab in the back' (*Dolchstoß*) myth became ingrained: the German defeat had supposedly been provoked by a bunch of – depending on the version – disloyal saboteurs, Communists or Jews, whereas the German soldiers had remained unbeaten at the front.[69] The Stahlhelm became an increasingly anti-republican group; its swelling ranks adopted the monarchist black-white-red flag and maintained contact with other nationalist groupings. Implementation of the treaty entailed a substantial reduction and disarmament of the army, as well as dissolution of Freikorps units. This measure drastically curtailed the possibility of following a military career for many young ex-soldiers

Erwin Könnemann and Gerhard Schulze (eds.), *Der Kapp-Lüttwitz-Ludendorff-Putsch: Dokumente*, München, Olzog Verlag, 2002, p. 2.
[65] James M. Diehl, *Paramilitary Politics in Weimar Germany*, Bloomington, Indiana University Press, 1977; Elliot, 'The Kriegervereine and the Weimar Republic'.
[66] Dunker, *Der Reichsbund jüdischer Frontsoldaten*; Ziemann, *Contested Commemorations*.
[67] Ziemann, *War Experiences in Rural Germany*, p. 240.
[68] Whalen, *Bitter Wounds*; Seipp, *The Ordeal of Peace*.   [69] Barth, *Dolchstoßlegenden*.

who had learnt no other profession. The Weimar Constitution, promulgated in August of 1919, furthered the alienation of these military men from the Republic. Although a set of new national symbols was introduced, breaking with the monarchist tradition, the constitution allowed soldiers to use medals and decorations won through war service. Still, the anti-revolutionary military despised the new uniforms and flags. Within months, both officers and soldiers had become united in their opposition to the government.[70]

It was in this context of chaotic demobilization, revolutionary and counter-revolutionary agitation, dramatic political transformations and violence that the first Nazi organization emerged. In Munich in January of 1919, Anton Drexler created the German Workers' Party (Deutsche Arbeiterpartei). In October of 1919, Adolf Hitler, an embittered and frustrated war veteran, applied to join the party. He introduced himself as a *Frontsoldat* – though he had in fact been an *Etappenschwein* during most of the war.[71] In 1920, the party changed its name to the National Socialist German Workers' Party (Nationalsozialistische Deutsche Arbeiterpartei (NSDAP)). Hitler, who had served as an army propagandist giving anti-Bolshevik talks to the soldiers, thus began his political career.[72] The chief concern in his mind was the purportedly pernicious influence of the capitalist Anglo-American Jewry, who had imposed the humiliating peace treaty.[73] Yet, the NSDAP's first programme did not contain a word about war veterans; its main characteristics were anti-Semitism and *völkisch* nationalism. The Nazi movement remained confined to Bavaria, and it was a phenomenon distinct to German veterans' organizations.

The reaction of army officers and anti-revolutionary volunteers against the young Republic resulted in the Kapp-Lüttwitz putsch in March of 1920, which aimed to impose a military dictatorship.[74] This attempt was prevented by the mobilization of the working class through a strike that

---

[70] 'Information des Reichs- und Staatskommissars für Überwachung der öffentlichen Ordnung über Ansehensschwund der Reichsregierung' (Berlin, 8 March 1920), in Könnemann and Schulze (eds.), *Der Kapp-Lüttwitz-Ludendorff-Putsch*, p. 122.

[71] Adolf Hitler (edited by Eberhard Jäckel and Axel Kuhn), *Sämtliche Aufzeichnungen 1905–1924*, Stuttgart, Deutsche Verlag-Anstalt, 1980, p. 91.

[72] Thomas Weber, *Hitler's First War: Adolf Hitler, the Men of the List Regiment, and the First World War*, Oxford University Press, 2010, pp. 227–87; Othmar Plöckinger, *Unter Soldaten und Agitatoren: Hitlers prägende Jahre im deutschen Militär 1918–1920*, Paderborn, Ferdinand Schöningh, 2013.

[73] Brendan Simms, 'Against a "World Of Enemies": The Impact of the First World War on the Development of Hitler's Ideology', *International Affairs* 90, 2 (2014), pp. 317–36.

[74] Johannes Erger, *Der Kapp-Lüttwitz-Putsch: Ein Beitrag zur deutschen Innenpolitik 1919/20*, Düsseldorf, Droste Verlag, 1967.

saved the Weimar Republic, but subsequent violence between Communists and right-wing groups dramatically increased. In this situation, there were calls for the formation of a government of front soldiers (*Frontsoldatenregierung*) as a political option beyond the polarized 'national' and 'social' political sectors,[75] but this project remained vague. The anti-republican threat was neutralized, though it became clear that important military and paramilitary elements were utterly opposed to Weimar. In Bavaria, the putsch facilitated the imposition of a militarist government headed by Gustav Ritter von Kahr, who remained on good terms with the paramilitary organizations and who would sponsor commemorations to honour the veterans and the fallen soldiers.[76] Hence, Munich would become the centre of anti-republican agitation. The Reichsbund, one of the biggest veterans' organizations, clearly condemned the putsch,[77] but anti-republican groups such as the Stahlhelm would continue to grow and consolidate in its aftermath. Shortly after the putsch, militaristic circles were also displeased by the National Pension Law (Reichsversorgungsgesetz) promulgated in April of 1920 as it meant the full demilitarization of the care of veterans and war victims. Yet, the disabled veterans were not completely satisfied with the public assistance and pensions they were awarded.[78] The Weimar Republic was superficially consolidating, but important groups of veterans had not been fully reintegrated into the system.

All these events in Germany, however, do not imply that German veterans were precursors of fascism; neither were they harbingers of Hitler or the Nazi movement. By 1920, certain army officers and groups of demobilized soldiers joined the anti-revolutionary armed volunteers as the most active and flamboyant wing of the unreservedly anti-republican German extreme right.[79] Nevertheless, the reactionary, defensive political projects and programmes of these groups cannot be defined as fascism. There were no plans for the transformation of war veterans or front soldiers into a political vanguard either. And the NSDAP was still a very small organization, struggling to gain membership and an audience and not focused on the veterans as its primary target. Finally, despite the fact that the symbol of the ex-soldier was increasingly linked to right-wing

[75] *Vossische Zeitung* (Berlin), 18 April 1920.
[76] Adam R. Seipp, '"Scapegoats for a Lost War": Demobilisation, the Kapp Putsch, and the Politics of the Streets in Munich, 1919–1920', *War & Society*, 25, 1 (May 2006), pp. 35–54.
[77] *Reichsbund. Organ des Reichsbundes der Kriegsbeschädigten, Kriegsteilnehmer und Kriegshinterbliebenen* (Berlin), 3 April 1920.
[78] Cohen, *The War Come Home*.
[79] Gabriele Krüger, *Die Brigade Ehrhardt*, Hamburg, Leibniz-Verlag, 1971.

politics – thanks to the success of the Freikorps in smashing the Communists – it is clear that the German veterans did not act as a group committed to one political orientation – either left or right, revolution or counter-revolution. This diversity in veteran politics was also present in France.

France

In France, 1918 was neither a year of defeat nor of revolution but rather victory, and the history of its 6.4 million war veterans provides a sharp contrast to that of the German veterans in the aftermath of the war. France had been invaded by the enemy and suffered considerable destruction. While the war was still being fought, French disabled veterans, like their counterparts in Italy, were the first to forward their interests by creating associations with the aim of improving their lives through legal means. During 1919, the French veterans created a constellation of associations drawing on the associative tradition of the French Republic. The main two veterans' associations expanded quickly. The republican, centrist Union fédérale (UF) was founded in February of 1918, with Henri Pichot as its main leader. Charles Bertrand led the conservative Union nationale des combattants (UNC), created in November of 1918. The loyalty of these groups to the Republic contrasts with the lukewarm attitude that many German veterans' associations displayed towards the Weimar Republic.[80] But the French Republic had won a great victory, whereas the Weimar Republic was the outcome of defeat.

Different political movements in France developed their own programme for the returning soldiers. The posture of the French Left regarding the veterans was embodied by writer Henri Barbusse, whose best-selling novel *Le Feu* (1917) had described the war experiences of the *poilus*. Barbusse had claimed during the war that the soldiers fought against nationalism, against militarism, and for the republican ideals of liberty and justice. He criticized the French warmongers and initially supported the project of the League of Nations. Barbusse founded a small Communist veterans' association, the Association républicaine des anciens combattants (ARAC), ready to defend the material interests of the disabled veterans. Furthermore, Barbusse intended to participate in politics, aiming to achieve social justice and international peace.[81] At

[80] Prost, *Les Anciens Combattants*; Robert Soucy, 'France: Veterans' Politics between the Wars', in Ward (ed.), *The War Generation*, pp. 59–103.
[81] Nicolas Beaupré, *Écrire en guerre, écrire la guerre, France, Allemagne 1914–1920*, Paris, CNRS, 2006; Jean Relinger, *Henri Barbusse: Écrivain combattant*, Paris, PUF, 1994; Henri Barbusse, *Paroles d'un combattant: Articles et Discours (1917–1920)*, Paris, 1920; *Le Populaire* (Paris), 8 January 1919.

the beginning of 1919, the Italian socialists echoed these ideals.[82] In contrast, the French anti-republican extreme right, the Action Française led by Charles Maurras with men such as Léon Daudet and Georges Valois among his collaborators, was interested in compensating the veterans. Their programme was fundamentally based on the idea of giving veterans their 'share of the victory' – 'the veterans' share' (la part du combattant) – to which they were entitled.[83] This concept of the 'veterans' share' had been in development since 1916 and was maintained after victory, although to make it real – it was said – the Germans should pay the reparations in full. Thus, the indemnity to the veterans should come directly 'from the hands of the aggressor': Germany.[84] In any case, during 1919, the political stance of the French veterans was far from unambiguous: whilst some groups wanted tougher governmental action against Bolshevism, others heralded the creation of the 'international of the veterans' (l'internationale des combattants) that would carry out the revolution.[85]

In general, apart from their growing discontent about their social and economic situation and their opposition to politicians, the French veterans commonly felt that the war had transformed them into new men with a new spirit, who should be charged with guiding the country morally. According to Antoine Prost, in the long term, the leitmotif of the French veterans' movement would be the attempt to create a large unified association, which would be apolitical and committed to the maintenance of internal and international peace.[86] This commitment is not surprising, since the Treaty of Versailles had been very favourable to the French interests. Yet, the two main associations had clear political divergences.[87] The UNC, in contrast to the UF, distrusted the League of Nations and feared the threat from Germany. In order to defend their interests on the Continent, the UNC created the Fédération interaliée des anciens combattants (FIDAC) in November of 1920, an inter-allied organization of veterans with Charles Bertrand as its first president (the UF would later create its own international entity – the Conférence internationale des associations de mutilés et anciens combattants (CIAMAC) – in 1925).

---

[82] Avanti!, 15 January 1919.
[83] Charles Maurras, La part du combattant, Paris, 1917; Georges Valois, La réforme économique & sociale, Paris, 1918, pp. 54–5.
[84] L'Action française, 19 January 1919.
[85] Report to the Président du Conseil des Ministres (Paris, 11 March 1919), and report on the Fédération ouvrière des mutilés des Bouches-du-Rhône (Marseille, 25 August 1919), AN, F7/13243, 'Associations de Mutilés et Victimes de la guerre', 'Notes générales sur les dites associations'.
[86] Prost, Les anciens combattants.   [87] Millington, From Victory to Vichy.

Correspondingly, the ARAC maintained early international contacts with other leftist veterans' associations. The deeply rooted conviction that veterans constituted a group with a shared identity and shared interests quickly led to international contacts among veterans with similar ideologies.

The Other Allies and Spain

To complete this picture of the early post-war period, it is necessary to mention other countries that, after the First World War, either had to deal with post-war demobilization or suffered the social and economic crisis of 1918–21. Canada, for example, was faced with the re-integration of some 500,000 veterans, who formed associations as early as 1916. The Canadian government soon created an agency to ease the rehabilitation of the 70,000 disabled veterans, and the veterans would start imposing some of their aspirations through the activities of their organizations.[88] Canadian veterans sought to unify, and in 1925, they would create the Canadian Legion, which mirrored the American Legion. Likewise, in the United States, the veterans, displeased by what they encountered after returning from Europe, started to organize themselves in 1919 to protect their interests and reaffirm their identity. In the United States, the veterans had traditionally been venerated civic figures; after the war, new associations became influential political platforms that made it easier for veterans to move into traditional American politics. In both these extra-European countries, Canada and the United States, veterans created active organizations as they did in Europe; the American Legion was staunchly anti-Bolshevik.[89] However, fascist movements would not emerge to woo veterans, who unified their associations more easily and integrated relatively peacefully into the political system and civil society.

The situation in Britain was somewhat similar. During the war itself, four different organizations were set up to defend the disabled veterans' cause, obtaining some victories in their struggle. In the elections of December of 1918 – the so-called khaki elections, as the khaki soldiers' uniforms symbolized the relevance of post-war issues – the veterans' ticket obtained poor results. Only one ex-servicemen's representative was elected, probably because most soldiers, still not discharged, could

---

[88] Desmond Morton and Glenn Wright, *Winning the Second Battle: Canadian Veterans and the Return to Civilian Life 1915–1930*, University of Toronto Press, 1987.

[89] William Pencak, *For God & Country: The American Legion, 1919–1941*, Boston, Northeastern University Press, 1989.

not participate in the voting. When demobilization took place, the returnees did not find the 'land fit for heroes to live in', which had been promised by Lloyd George during the electoral campaign. Soldiers rioted, and veterans protested vehemently. In 1919, they created new associations, the National Union of Ex-Servicemen and the International Union of Ex-Servicemen, though no clear political programme emerged. At the height of unrest, they boycotted the national peace celebrations of July 1919. Finally, in late 1919, the government sponsored a set of measures in favour of veterans, so the agitation decreased: the widespread fear of 'brutalization' proved largely unfounded. Finally, in 1921, the merger of different veterans' groups resulted in the formation of the British Legion; under Field Marshal Earl Haig's leadership, it would be a collaborative, prestigious and respectable organization to mediate between veterans and the state.[90]

In the Iberian Peninsula, in contrast, the veterans' question had only an indirect impact on politics during 1919–21. Nevertheless, Portugal and Spain experienced the turbulence of the period. Portugal had participated in the First World War on the Allied side and sent a small contingent of soldiers to the Western Front. A veterans' association formed very late, in 1921, when the League of the Great War Veterans (Liga dos Combatentes da Grande Guerra) was created.[91] Spain had not participated in the First World War, but its internal politics during this time were profoundly influenced by what happened on the Continent. During the war, there was an acute division between supporters of the Allies (aliadófilos) and supporters of the Central Empires (germanófilos). In 1917, serious military, social and economic disturbances pushed the country into a political crisis.[92] The period between 1917 and 1923 in Spain was marked by social unrest, parliamentary crisis, syndicalism and violence, which were particularly destructive in Barcelona.[93] Furthermore, armed conflict broke out once more in the Spanish protectorate

---

[90] Stephen R. Ward, 'Great Britain: Land Fit for Heroes Lost', in Ward (ed.), *The War Generation*, pp. 10–37; *id*, 'The British Veterans' Ticket of 1918', *Journal of British Studies*, 8, 1(1968), pp. 155–69; Wootton, *The Politics of Influence*, pp. 203–10; Lawrence, 'Forging a Peaceable Kingdom'; Niall Barr, *The Lion and the Poppy: British Veterans, Politics, and Society, 1921–1939*, London, Praeger, 2005.

[91] Silvia Correia, 'The Veterans' Movement and First World War Memory in Portugal (1918–33): Between the Republic and Dictatorship', *European Review of History/Revue européenne d'histoire*, 19 (2012), pp. 531–51.

[92] Francisco J. Romero Salvadó, *Spain 1914–1918: Between War and Revolution*, London, Routledge, 1999; *id.*, *The Foundations of Civil War: Revolution, Social Conflict and Reaction in Liberal Spain, 1916–1923*, London, Routledge, 2008.

[93] Eduardo González Calleja, *El máuser y el sufragio: Orden público, subversión y violencia política en la crisis de la Restauración (1917–1931)*, Madrid, CSIC, 1999, pp. 11–253.

of Morocco in 1919: the struggle against the tribes of the Rif led to a severe military disaster for Spanish troops in Annual in July of 1921. This scandal further undermined the fragile liberal political system despised by the 'Africanist' (*africanistas*) officers. The Africanists, a corporatist military group forged in the Moroccan war, had a bitter rivalry with the officers of Peninsular Spain, who organized 'military councils' (*Juntas*) and were opposed to promotions based on combat experience.[94] All these conflicts marked later political developments, as we will see.

Notwithstanding the transnational nature of the historical challenges of this period, the only Western European country in which the post-war crisis ended with consolidation of a fascist movement was Italy. Italian Fascism was the first fascist movement capable of establishing a dictatorship and destroying a liberal democracy in a European country during the interwar period.[95] Fascism appeared as an ideology in Italy in 1919, and the Fasci di combattimento developed as a mass movement during 1920 and 1921, transforming into a political party – the Partito Nazionale Fascista (PNF) – in November of 1921. As early as October 1922, after the so-called March on Rome, the liberal democratic legal order had been crushed in Italy. Italian Fascism was the first, the original and the most influential European fascist movement during the twenties, and its origins are rooted in the legacies of the First World War experience.

Veterans and the Birth of Italian Fascism

Despite victory, 1919 was a year of deep crisis throughout Italy.[96] After forty-one months of total war, the country had to confront the further shock of the sudden end of the hostilities. Over the course of the first year of peace, while Europe was trying to settle down in the new context, Italy engaged in the demobilization process.[97] This task was carried out while the cost of living significantly increased. Peasants began occupying land by themselves, whilst workers' strikes, disturbances and protests traversed the peninsula. Meanwhile, the complicated international peace negotiations developed in Paris. Italian society was far from morally unified by the achievement of November 1918. The bitter confrontation between the interventionists and the pacifists, intertwined with the class struggle, intensified. Both fascist and veterans' movements appeared in

[94] Sebastian Balfour, *Deadly Embrace: Morocco and the Road to the Spanish Civil War*, Oxford University Press, 2002.
[95] Julián Casanova, *Europa contra Europa 1914–1945*, Barcelona, Crítica, 2011, pp. 61–71.
[96] Roberto Bianchi, *Pace, pane, terra. Il 1919 in Italia*, Rome, Odradek, 2006.
[97] Mondini and Schwarz, *Dalla guerra alla pace*, pp. 23–113.

this year. With the prospect of demobilization, the time had come for the would-be fascists to test their predictions about the veterans. In this section I will analyze the origins of the fascists' engagement with the war veterans.

The Italian War Ministry dealt with the burdensome demobilization of approximately 3.7 million front soldiers. Between November and December of 1918, the oldest classes (those born between 1874 and 1884) were sent home. Demobilization of the rest of the conscripts (those born between 1885 and 1900) underwent a noticeable slowing down between January and March of 1919. By March, almost 2 million soldiers had returned to civilian life, but the ongoing demobilization process would come to a stop between March and June due to the tortuous peace negotiations that were taking place in Paris.[98] The deceleration of the demobilization process, together with the problems of reintegration for ex-soldiers in the labour market, was the motive of embitterment for many veterans.[99]

It was during the first half of 1919 that the veterans' movement began to acquire a concrete shape, something that happened under the close observation of Mussolini and his collaborators. When the Armistice came, the ANMIG issued a 'Manifesto to the Country' (*Manifesto al paese*) detailing a moral, socio-economic and political programme for renovation of the nation and declaring the foundation of a larger veterans' association which would be called Associazione Nazionale Combattenti (ANC).[100] *Il Popolo d'Italia* supported this idea and under-lined that the veterans considered every old party to be defunct; at the same time, the paper insisted that the nation should welcome workers who returned from the front.[101] However, it did not explicitly express agreement with the veterans' democratic and reformist program,[102] so the newspaper soon began to outline its own policy regarding the returning veterans.

Il Popolo d'Italia started preparing the homecoming of the so-considered 'leaders of the new Italy' (*I quadri della nuova Italia*), namely, the officers and junior officers, who were named 'trenchorarchs' (*trincerarchi*) on the newspaper pages. The new concept of *trincerarchi* was an evolution of the earlier *trincerocrazia* and seemed to have been conceived to praise the young men who had commanded troops during the war. It was said

---

[98] Giorgio Rochat, *L'esercito italiano da Vittorio Veneto a Mussolini (1919–1925)*, Bari, Laterza, 1967, pp. 17–37.
[99] Cf. Cabanes, *La victoire endeuillée*, pp. 277–358.
[100] Sabbatucci, *I combattenti*, pp. 52–61.   [101] *Il Popolo d'Italia*, 7 and 9 November 1918.
[102] *Ibid.*, 25 December 1918 and 14 January 1919.

that these leaders had slowly matured during the war, acquiring consciousness of new rights and opening their minds to new horizons. Whilst
nobody in the country seemed to defend their interests, *Il Popolo d'Italia*
presented itself as the advocate of 200,000 officers whose particular
aspirations were equated with the national interest. The newspaper called
on society to 'make space for the *trincerocrazia*'. By collecting and collating
the grievances of these men, a programme demanding a fast and efficient
demobilization was produced. Veterans' aspirations were connected with
the project of a 'Constituent Assembly' (*la Costituente dei Combattenti*).
As the *trincerarchi* had been the men who had led the troops to the
victory (*inquadratori della vittoria*), they must be the leaders of new Italy,
and for this reason, it was necessary to discharge them quickly. This
kind of discourse was predominantly adopted by certain officers and *arditi*,
who viewed themselves as *trincerarchi* and understood the *trincerocrazia* as a
government made of veterans. For instance, Italo Balbo, in those days
still a young lieutenant of the *alpini*, was one of those veterans who wrote
to *Il Popolo d'Italia*, making their support for the *Costituente* explicit.
However, this *Costituente* never took place; Mussolini's plans in line with
the interventionist and nationalist groups remained unrealized.[103]

At this stage, the elitist *arditi* were the only defined veterans' group
that adhered to Mussolini's movement. Mussolini had enthusiastically
paid tribute to the *arditi* during the victory celebrations organized on
10 November 1918 in Milan. He said they represented the 'marvellous
young warriors of Italy'.[104] In September of 1918, the *ardito* Mario
Carli[105] and writers Marinetti and Emilio Settimelli founded the futurist
review *Roma futurista*. Spurred on by the futurist revolutionary discourse
that proclaimed the 'supremacy of the combatant',[106] discharged *arditi*
roamed uncontrolled around Milan and other northern regions, exerting

---

[103] *Il Popolo d'Italia*, 4, 8, 9, 10, 13, 14, 20, 27 and 30 December 1918 and 7, 14, 16 and 17
January 1919. Italo Balbo, following his Mazzinian convictions, interpreted the
initiative as potentially capable of 'rejuvenating' Italy; cf. Claudio G. Segré, *Italo
Balbo: Una vita fascista*, Bologna, Il Mulino, 1988, pp. 37–63. The failure of the
project of the *Costituente* in De Felice, *Mussolini il rivoluzionario*, pp. 470ff.

[104] *Il Popolo d'Italia*, 11 November 1918.

[105] Mario Carli, born in San Severo (Foggia) in 1889, was active in the Florentine avant
garde before the war. Along with other futurists, he joined the interventionist movement
and volunteered with the *arditi*. He reached the rank of captain, was wounded and
decorated. Since September of 1919, Carli participated in the occupation of Fiume.
Later he became a faithful follower of Mussolini, leading the Mussolinian branch of the
arditi up to the March on Rome. Linked to Farinacci's fascist trend during the mid-
1920s, he held several political positions during the fascist dictatorship. In the 1930s, he
became Italian Consul in Brazil and Greece. He died in 1935.

[106] *Roma Futurista: Giornale del Partito Politico Futurista* (Rome), 20 November 1918.

violence against civilians, particularly against the socialists.[107] In January of 1919, the Italian Arditi Association (Associazione fra gli Arditi d'Italia) was created as an expression of the spirit of these assault troops. On 11 January 1919, the *arditi* provoked disturbances at La Scala theatre in Milan, which marked the disintegration of the interventionist bloc. Mussolini's group attacked those interventionists – such as Bissolati – who renounced certain territorial aspirations. Ferruccio Vecchi, one of these ex-*arditi* maladjusted to civil life, defined their aggressive and daring mind-set and behaviour as *arditismo*.[108] The symbol of the *arditi* was already a prominent element of the interventionist, anti-socialist mythology.

Following its own agenda, in the first half of 1919, the veterans' movement started to grow and expand. While discontented demobilized soldiers demonstrated in central and northern Italian cities, the ANC extended geographically and set up a dense network of local veterans' newspapers from provincial and local sections.[109] The foundation of both ANC and ANMIG cells, their assemblies and the incipient activity of social assistance were mentioned and briefly commented on in *Il Popolo d'Italia*.[110] Simultaneously, other veterans' associations appeared, displaying a wide range of ideological orientations and an uneven territorial presence.[111] In Turin, the Operational Zone National Veterans Association (Associazione Nazionale Reduci Zona Operante (ANRZO)) was set up with a vaguely Mazzinian programme; its members employed a revolutionary but anti-Bolshevik rhetoric.[112] Predominating in rural and traditionally Catholic zones such as the Veneto, the National Union of War Veterans (Unione Nazionale Reduci di Guerra (UNRG)) was close to the new Italian Popular Party (Partito Popolare Italiano (PPI))

---

[107] Gentile, *Storia del partito fascista*, pp. 20–1; Fabio Fabbri, *Le origini della guerra civile: L'Italia dalla Grande Guerra al fascismo, 1918–1921*, Milan, Utet, 2009, pp. 11–16.

[108] Ferruccio Vecchi, 'Arditismo', *Roma futurista*, 9 (2 March 1919). Vecchi, born in Sant'Alberto (Ravenna) in 1894, became a captain of the *arditi* during the war. As a futurist ex-*ardito*, and along with Mario Carli, he founded the Associazione fra gli Arditi d'Italia and the journal *L'Ardito*. He was one of the most violent activists of the early fascist movement and one of the leaders of the assault on the *Avanti!* offices in Milan in April of 1919. Briefly imprisoned in December of 1919, after his release, he continued to be active in the pro-fascist *arditi* movement. However, in December of 1920, he was forced to step down from his positions in the association and the journal. He abandoned all political activity to become a novelist and an artist, practicing sculpture and painting during the fascist regime.

[109] Sabbatucci, *I combattenti*; id., *La stampa del combattentismo*.

[110] For example, *Il Popolo d'Italia*, 28 January, 22 February and 15 March 1919.

[111] Sabbatucci, *I combattenti*, pp. 86ff.

[112] *A Noi!* (Turin), 20 January, 20 February and 1 March 1919; *Il Popolo d'Italia*, 1 February 1919.

and represented the social and pacifist inclinations of the Catholic Church.[113] In the mountainous northern regions, the Alpini National Association (Associazione Nazionale Alpini), based on the *alpini* military units, displayed a rather conservative discourse. All these entities emerged from the widespread optimistic belief in the veterans' potential to change the country but also amidst worries and conflicts due to the worsening social and political situation.

Most importantly, the phenomenon of veterans' associations expanded in the context of growing fear about the spread of Bolshevism, which affected the Italian middle and upper classes. At the end of the war, the maximalist trend of the PSI, inspired by the Russian Revolution, became hegemonic. Simultaneously, a socialist organization for disabled veterans and ex-soldiers was created: the Proletarian League (Lega proletaria fra mutilati, invalidi, orfani e vedove di guerra), tied to the socialists.[114] This association was determined to defend the veterans' interests from a class-oriented point of view and tended to treat them as war victims – with the same consideration as war disabled, orphans and widows – rather than as heroes or as ex-servicemen. Therefore, the Lega Proletaria employed a pacifist and anti-militarist discourse that emphasized the horrors of warfare: war was represented as a useless massacre, as fratricidal madness. Its membership grew, especially in the socialist strongholds of the north, reaching more than 50,000 affiliates by the spring of 1919. The examples of Henri Barbusse and the French ARAC were an inspiration for its activities.

Within this agitated context of the proliferation of veterans' groups, Fascism emerged as a formal organization. The call for the foundation of the Fasci di combattimento at the beginning of March 1919, published in *Il Popolo d'Italia*, was specially directed at the veterans – 'combatants and ex combatants' (*combattenti, ex combattenti*). Assertions about the veterans' potential to oust the old ruling classes followed the announcement. Agostino Lanzillo appealed to ex-combatants to 'intervene and take over the government of the state', establishing an 'energetic regime' that would confront the current critical moment.[115] The initiative of *Il Popolo d'Italia* was not very successful, however. Only some local groups

[113] Livio Vanzetto, 'Contadini e grande guerra in aree campione del Veneto (1910–1922)', in Isnenghi (ed.), *Operai e contadini*, pp. 72–103.

[114] Gianni Isola, *Guerra al regno della guerra: Storia della Lega proletaria mutilati invalidi reduci orfani e vedove di guerra (1918–1924)*, Florence, Le Lettere, 1990; *id.*, 'Socialismo e combattentismo: la Lega proletaria. 1918–1922', *Italia contemporanea*, 141 (1980), pp. 5–29.

[115] Agostino Lanzillo, 'L'ora dei combattenti', *Il Popolo d'Italia*, 20 March 1919; *id*: 'L'ora dei combattenti: Politicanti e soldati', *Il Popolo d'Italia*, 21 March 1919.

of veterans pledged their support in response.[116] As is now well known, the 'picturesque' foundational fascist meeting in the Piazza San Sepolcro of Milan on 23 March 1919 passed almost unnoticed.[117] It was attended by three or four hundred people, including revolutionary interventionists, students and journalists. Perhaps half the attendees were war veterans, but they were mostly *arditi* such as Ferruccio Vecchi, along with Marinetti's futurists. The radical and contradictory nationalist claims and anti-Bolshevik diatribes aside, no clear fascist programme emerged, yet it is worth noting that the first point raised by Mussolini was supporting the demands of the associations of *combattenti*.

Over the course of the spring of 1919, several events demonstrated that officers and ex-soldiers could constitute a reactive force against the left, even if the overwhelming majority of the Italian war veterans was not interested in joining nationalist demonstrations. News about the Hungarian and Bavarian Soviet Republics, established, respectively, on the 21 March and 6 April, was circulating throughout Europe. Meanwhile, in Italy, veteran journals and organizations proliferated independent of each other. For instance, the minuscule but overtly anti-Bolshevik Officers and Soldiers' National Union (Unione Nazionale Ufficiali e Soldati (UNUS)), led by nationalist officers such as Giovanni Giuriati, launched a manifesto on 7 April.[118] Mussolini criticized this dispersion of forces: a few days after the meeting of San Sepolcro, he called for unification of all the 'national' veterans' forces in one all-powerful body, which would confront the internal socialist danger.[119] In Rome, the socialists held a general strike on 10 April, but the same day an anti-socialist counter-demonstration took place, with the participation of many army officers. The futurist ex-*ardito* Mario Carli ventured that in this anti-Bolshevik demonstration, all kinds of combatants had taken part, showing a unified spirit.[120] On 15 April 1919, following a similar dynamic of strikes and demonstrations in Milan, the fascist *arditi* assaulted and destroyed the office of the socialist newspaper *Avanti!*. The use of firearms and knives in these clashes left four people dead. This has been considered the first instance of squadrist violence.[121] The

---

[116] Particularly from Tuscan cities (Siena, Livorno); see *Il Popolo d'Italia*, 15 and 31 March 1919.

[117] *L'Idea Nazionale* (Rome), 25 March 1919.

[118] Andrea Ungari, 'Tra mobilitazione patriottica e suggestioni eversive: La vicenda dell'Unione Nazionale Ufficiali e Soldati nel primo dopoguerra', *Nuova Storia Contemporanea*, 5 (2001), pp. 41–76.

[119] Mussolini, 'Convergere gli sforzi!', *Il Popolo d'Italia*, 9 April 1919.

[120] Mario Carli, 'Lo sciopero dello stento', *Roma futurista*, 15–16 (13–20 April 1919).

[121] Fabbri, *Le origini della guerra civile*, pp. 38–49; De Felice, *Mussolini il rivoluzionario*, pp. 519–21.

destruction of the *Avanti!* offices had fateful repercussions; it was followed by a set of violent attacks by *arditi* against socialists in different places.[122]

However, it should be underlined that the perpetrators of the assault on the *Avanti!* premises in Milan were part of a very small radicalized – if exceptionally active – minority of Italian veterans. In this context, the fact that a single notion of 'veterans' was becoming exclusively associated with a marginal group is paradoxical, albeit understandable. For while the war veterans were an extremely diverse and heterogenic group of individuals, contemporaries had a limited range of concepts at hand to make sense of this variety. The diverse members of the huge Italian army held very disparate political opinions, and the experiences of demobilization sharpened the contradictions between the expectations of the common soldiers, on the one hand, and the mentalities of the command and the officers, on the other.

Many professional military and bourgeois ex-officers expected to maintain privileges obtained during the war and to receive the respect and honour of the country. They also expected that the peace conference would satisfy the national objectives for which the army had fought. Soon they were very disappointed, for the nation seemed cold and hostile towards them.[123] Since the end of the war, interventionists had demanded that the promises of the Pact of London be fulfilled, and the 'Italian' city of Fiume added to Italian territorial gains. Ardent interventionists such as Mussolini and the *Il Popolo d'Italia* group, the ex-*arditi*, and the nationalist officers of the UNUS virulently scorned politicians who 'renounced' certain territorial claims. The Italian representatives at the Peace Conference defended the interventionist aspirations (Pact of London and Fiume), although these claims contradicted the Wilsonian spirit that underpinned the conference. The result of the negotiations, therefore, was disappointing for the Italians, who would receive neither Dalmatia nor Fiume. This diplomatic failure took place at the end of April 1919 and shattered the hopes of fervent nationalists and irredentists such as D'Annunzio, who felt that the victory had been lost. In reality, the emerging myth of the 'mutilated victory' was actually a half-truth.[124] However, rumours about a military coup started to circulate.

These elevated patriotic preoccupations only shaped the mentalities of educated middle-class veterans and officers, young men who had been the promoters of intervention. Meanwhile, the common ex-soldiers

---

[122] Fabbri, *Le origini della guerra cvile*, pp. 54–9.   [123] Mondini, *La politica delle armi*.
[124] H. James Burgwyn, *The Legend of the Mutilated Victory: Italy, the Great War, and the Paris Peace Conference, 1915–1919*, Westport, CT, Greenburg Press, 1993.

returned to civil life were instead concerned about the material promises the Italian state had made to them. Peasants who suddenly found the promise of land unfulfilled showed little patience. The masses of *contadini ex combattenti* played a major role in mutinies against the high cost of living (*carovita*) between June and July of 1919 in the Mezzogiorno and especially in Sardinia.[125] Since the beginning of 1919 in Lazio and during the summer and the autumn in several provinces of the south (Puglia, Calabria and Caltanissetta), there were land occupations by veterans who aspired to a more just redistribution of land, if not to a social revolution.[126] Although at those demonstrations it was not rare to see proletarian ex-soldiers still wearing military clothes, it is true that the socialists did not systematically mobilize the symbol of the veteran to legitimate these protests. In contrast, as the nationalists declared their readiness to materially reward the soldiers' service, they also denounced the socialists' attempts to foment the feeling that answering the call of duty had been pointless.[127]

What were the positions of the fascist movement and the ANC regarding the masses of veterans? As historian Giovanni Sabbatucci pointed out, the Fasci di combattimento, despite the efforts of Mussolini's collaborators, were unable to attract many ex-soldiers; it was the ANC that absorbed the greatest number of them.[128] The ANC would reach around 300,000 members in the autumn of 1919. The popular base of this veterans' movement was in the Mezzogiorno, and thus was composed of peasants, whilst the middle-class veterans from the northern and central cities usually dominated the ranks of the leadership. Although the dominant political discourse within the ANC lacked a clear and defined orientation, the organization attempted to crystallize politically. All the ANC veterans seemed to share an instinctive anti-governmental attitude and a sense of patriotism, fused into the idea of 'renovation' (*rinnovamento*). The leaders and representatives of sections from all over Italy met at the first ANC Congress in Rome between 23 and 28 June 1919: over the course of six days of heated discussions, the key issue was whether the organization should adopt a political or an apolitical stance. It was very difficult to agree on a political standpoint shared by all sides. In the end, they approved a very abstract program written by Renato Zavataro. It was indicative of the pacifist and democratic preference of

[125] Bianchi, *Pane, pace, terra*, pp. 205–20. See, for example, in Puglia, Simona Colarizi, *Dopoguerra e fascismo in Puglia (1919–1926)*, Bari, Laterza, 1971, pp. 11–26.

[126] Sabbatucci, *I combattenti*, pp. 184–203; Roberto Vivarelli, *Storia delle origini del fascismo: L'Italia dalla grande guerra alla marcia su Roma*, Bologna, Il Mulino, 2012, Vol. 1, pp. 436–60.

[127] *L'Idea Nazionale*, 18 June 1919.   [128] Sabbatucci, *I combattenti*, p. 70.

the majority of members but also a symptom of the inexperienced leaders' lack of competence and a proof of the impossibility of defining a clear political ideology for the *combattenti*.[129]

The most interesting aspect of the veterans' Congress of Rome is that the fascists tried to impose their political orientation on the ANC. In the days leading up to the congress, it was claimed that Mussolini and D'Annunzio would attend (in reality, only Mussolini was in Rome). The political atmosphere in the capital was quite heated, since a new government headed by Nitti had just been formed, following the Italian failure at Versailles. As early as the first session of the congress, Francesco Giunta, an interventionist, fascist-friendly ex-officer representing the ex-combatants from Florence, championed violent action against the recently formed government. Standing on a table, he defended a radical motion (*ordine del giorno*) demanding the organization of a large insurrectional movement.[130] Despite this attempt, which had aimed to organize a veterans' demonstration on the spot with the objective of toppling Nitti, moderation prevailed. Moreover, just after this failure, the *ardito* Ferruccio Vecchi was forcefully expelled from the sessions due to his inflammatory declarations. For his part, Agostino Lanzillo argued that the veterans should use their force to seize power and establish 'instead of the dictatorship of the proletariat, the dictatorship of the combatants' (*in luogo della dittatura del proletariato, la dittatura dei combattenti*). But the majority of delegates received this statement rather coldly. In the end, seeing the ANC leaders' lack of sympathy for these seductive attempts, Mussolini's posture was to stress the common features existing in the fascist and veterans' programmes: 'their oneness is absolute.'[131] Likewise, the *arditi* also pointed out the similarity of their program to those of the ANC and the Fasci and advocated collaboration.[132] Despite these overoptimistic assessments,

---

[129] An exhaustive account of the congress in *ibid.*, pp. 98–119.

[130] Cf. Francesco Giunta, *Un po' di fascismo*, Milan, 1935, p. 66. Giunta, born in Florence in 1886, was an interventionist student and reached the rank of captain during the war. A founder of the ANC in Florence, he imposed a nationalist and anti-socialist stance onto the Florentine veteran movement. He would officially join the fascist movement in October of 1919. Transferred to Trieste in 1920, he founded the journal *Il Popolo di Trieste*. An active squadrist, he participated in the March on Rome. He held the position of Secretary of the Gran Consiglio del Fascismo until 1929. Between October 1923 and April 1924 he was also Secretary of the PNF. Between 1927 and 1932, he was Subsecretary to the Presidenza del Consiglio. After some years without political activity, he became a leader of the Camera dei Fasci e delle Corporazioni and, in 1943, governor of Dalmatia. He joined the Repubblica Sociale Italiana (RSI). After the war, he was absolved of charges and retired from political life. He died in Rome in 1971.

[131] *Il Popolo d'Italia*, 25 June 1919.   [132] *L'Ardito* (Milan), 29 June 1919.

the truth was that the ANC had reaffirmed its autonomy, differentiating itself from other organizations, particularly from the Fasci. The symbol of the veterans was still far from being the preserve of the fascists.

The Anti-Bolshevik Veterans: A Symbolic Appropriation

The first half of 1919 showed that the symbol of the veteran was not yet politically defined. During the second half of this year, following the signing of the Versailles Treaty, a process of symbolic appropriation took place, leading to the final consolidation of a transnationally forged and widely spread representation of the ex-soldier: that of the anti-Bolshevik veteran. In Italy, this cultural construction played a role in conditioning the origin of Fascism. However, this result was far from inevitable. Here I will argue that the alleged anti-socialist orientation of the Italian veterans was a contingent and constructed phenomenon, the product of a long evolution of discourses and representations, in which Fascism played a crucial role. I will show that the adhesion of the Italian veterans to Fascism was only a relative phenomenon; it was above all a cultural construction, the outcome of a process of symbolic appropriation, in which the summer of 1919 was a key moment.

The fascists, despite their lack of success at the ANC Congress of June of 1919, did not scale back their efforts to attract veterans to their organization. They were interested in recruiting war veterans to their movement for ideological and political reasons. Since 1917, Mussolini had based his projects on the mobilization of ex-combatants. Historian Emilio Gentile has explained that young lower-middle-class Italians influenced by the myth of the war experience, especially those who had fought in elite corps like the *arditi* or had been junior officers, had experienced the war as an initiation into politics and had returned from the trenches convinced that 'they had a mission to complete in the name of the nation'.[133] Therefore, men such as Giuseppe Bottai (interventionist, war volunteer and ex-*ardito*) joined the Fasci. They believed in the myth of the 'two Italies', one of revolutionary interventionists and combatants and the other of neutralist traitors, deserters, *profittatori*, liberal politicians and Bolsheviks, who were perceived as the internal enemy. These mentalities pushed them to embrace the fascist movement, considered as an 'anti-party' (*antipartito*). All these ideological elements had been developed by the Florentine avant-gardists before the war and were later recycled by Mussolini. It is interesting to note

---

[133] Gentile, *Le origini dell'ideologia fascista* (quoting English edition: New York, Enigma, 2005, p. 54); cf. Mosse, 'Two World Wars'.

that Florence was the city where fascists, futurists and veteran leaders were most interconnected.[134] However, the ANC Congress of Rome had revealed that these radicalized veterans were an eccentric minority in the country.[135] The Italian veterans as a mass were not the anti-Bolshevik, national-revolutionary men of action that the fascists imagined.

However, when the Versailles Treaty was being signed, the nationalist bourgeois sectors intensified the struggle to take possession of the symbol of the veteran. Their anger against Nitti's government and their frustration with the 'mutilated victory' led to moments of great tension. On 30 June 1919, after a nationalist protest meeting in the Augusteo theatre of Rome, there were violent confrontations between police and demonstrators. Among the most aggressive protesters, there were many young officers in uniform, some of whom were arrested or injured in the struggle. The next day, the nationalist journal *L'Idea Nazionale* passionately claimed that the reprehensible government had attacked the 'veterans' (*combattenti*).

Referring to these groups of officers and nationalist students as 'the veterans' was manipulative. They were men, for example, like Giovanni Giuriati and Nino Host-Venturi,[136] who, in contact with D'Annunzio, had started to drum up support for a voluntary military force to occupy Fiume. These ex-combatants were very different from the veterans' representatives who had met in their congress one day before. Even so, members of the ANC and the ANMIG condemned the government and joined the nationalist outrage about the state aggression against 'the veterans'. Even D'Annunzio, in an accusatory article against the government, depicted the stylized image of the protesting one-legged disabled

---

[134] Adamson, *Avant-Garde Florence*, p. 227.

[135] Giuseppe Bottai, 'Combattenti', *Roma futurista*, 27 (6 July 1919) and 29 (20 July 1919).

[136] Both men would reach important political positions during the fascist regime. Giuriati, born in Venezia in 1876, was a lawyer and an active irrendentist before the war. He was a war volunteer and reached the rank of captain. He was wounded and decorated. After the Fiume adventure, he joined the fascist movement, becoming an MP in 1921. After the March on Rome, he took up ministerial positions in Mussolini's regime. He was Secretary of the PNF in 1930–1. He became a senator but later withdrew from politics and refused to take up any position in the RSI. He died in Rome in 1970. Host-Venturi, born in Fiume in 1892, was also a war volunteer and a captain of the *arditi* and the *alpini*. After the Fiume adventure, he joined the ANC, as well as the fascist movement, and after 1922 worked to integrate the Fiuman fascists within the regime. A member of the ANC National Board, he was elected Provisional President of the ANC in 1924. Secretary General of the Fiuman federation of the PNF between 1925 and 1928, he also held other ministerial and party positions during the 1930s, becoming Minister of Communications between October of 1939 and February of 1943. He later joined the RSI, yet without taking up any other relevant role. He left Italy after the Second World War to die in Buenos Aires in 1980.

soldier beaten by the police.[137] D'Annunzio's literary recourse to this indignant representation of the veteran served as an appeal for the disobedience of the army. Thus, before the socialists were able to develop policies and discourses regarding the return of the soldiers, the nationalists and the fascists were already violently fighting over the symbol of the veteran. Yet, the frustration of the nationalist aspirations was only one factor of the attempted monopolization of the veteran symbol; the other ground was anti-Bolshevism.

At this early stage, the adhesion of ex-officers and *arditi* to the fascist movement must be understood as part of the burgeoning anti-socialist and anti-government reaction. The young fascist movement strived to readdress politically the seemingly prodigious veterans' force,[138] for veteran activism still lacked a clear political orientation. In Rome, several army officers still wearing uniforms attended the assemblies of the Fascio, where the *arditi* agitated to provoke violent anti-Bolshevik and anti-governmental action.[139] Yet, this climate of unrest also saw the emergence of anarchist ex-combatants, 'subversives' (*sovversivi*) who conspired against the government. In July of 1919, the anarchist *ardito* Argo Secondari organized a failed plot against Nitti in the Roman fortress of Pietralata.[140] And in Verona, for instance, anarchist workers joined a group of veterans and ex-*arditi* to found the Fascio.[141] According to the authorities in Florence, the combined agitation of veterans, fascists and *arditi* was 'impressive'.[142] In this city, veterans set up the Fascio in the local headquarters of the ANC.[143] But this case can be considered exceptional.

There was no general pattern dictating the proximity of veterans to the fascist movement. This relationship was still limited to the northern and central Italian regions. But even in a town such as Ferrara, the veterans shared their loyalties between the ANC and the socialists; only some local *arditi* were favourable to Mussolini.[144] In Bologna, divergences among the veterans led to a split; some of them joined the ANC and an anti-Bolshevik local league, and some officers

[137] Sabbatucci, *I combattenti*, pp. 144–6; ACS, MI, PS (1920), box 105, files 'Fascio Romano di Combattimento' I and II; *L'Idea Nazionale* (Rome), 30 June and 1 and 2 July 1919.
[138] Giuseppe Prezzolini, 'Il compito dei combattenti', *Il Fascio* (Milan), 30 August 1919.
[139] ACS, MI, PS (1920), box 105, file 'Roma. Fascio di combattimento'.
[140] ACS, MI, PS (1919), box 84, file 'Movimento sovversivo Roma II'.
[141] *Il Fascio*, 20 September 1919.
[142] ACS, MI, PS (1921), box 89, file 'Firenze', document dated on 1 July 1919.
[143] *Il Fascio*, 15 August 1919.
[144] Paul Corner, *Fascism in Ferrara, 1915–1925*, London, Oxford University Press, 1975, pp. 56 and 68.

remained within the Fascio.[145] In light of these complications, the fascist leaders opted not to recruit combatants exclusively but also sought members among the non-combatants. According to its organizer, Umberto Pasella, the Fascio was 'a very different thing from the veterans' association',[146] but the very fact that he had to express this distinction is significant.

By mid-1919, the veterans' movement had attracted the interest not just of the fascists and nationalists but also of the left. In this explosive situation, in which all sides used the motif of the *combattenti* in their political rhetoric, it is not surprising that the representatives of democratic interventionism – such as Gaetano Salvemini – tried to mobilize the veterans in order to motivate a wide movement of social and political renovation, particularly in the Mezzogiorno. Although many socialists were sceptical about such strategies,[147] the Lega proletaria held its own national congress, in which demobilization and amnesty were the chief slogans. The fear that men released from the army would fall prey to Bolshevik agitators was widespread in Germany and other European regions at that time.[148] Italian military authorities were conscious of this problem, as well as of the role of volunteers and ex-officers in the German forces of reaction.[149] As a result, Italian military propaganda for the soldiers stressed that the combatants (*combattenti*) desired 'peace, work and order' and that the disturbances were provoked by 'masses of working class people who did not fight in the war', while 'combatants, officers and soldiers' were confronting them.[150] Meanwhile, the socialists believed in the sharp divide that existed between proletarian soldiers and bourgeois officers; the revolutionary instinct of the former contrasted with the conservatism of the latter. And news of the counter-revolutionary reaction – directed by military

---

[145] ACS, MI, PS (1920), box 104, file 'Bologna. Associazione Nazionale dei Combattenti'; *Giornale del Mattino* (Bologna), 10 April 1919.

[146] Letter of U. Pasella to G. Maggi (1 September 1919), quoted by Gentile, *Storia del partito fascista*, p. 38.

[147] *L'Unità* (Florence), 17 July and 7–14 August 1919.

[148] See, for example, 'Bericht des Reichswehrgruppenkommandos 1 an den Reichswehrminister Noske über mögliche Folgen der bevorstehenden Entlassung von 90.000 Offizieren und Mannschaften, Berlin' (July 1919) and 'Anonyme Denkschrift über die Notwendigkeit eines Umsturzes' (12 August 1919), in Könnemann and Schulze (eds.), *Der Kapp-Lüttwitz-Ludenforff-Putsch*, pp. 19–23. For the Balkans, see John Paul Newman, *Yugoslavia in the Shadow of War. Veterans and the Limits of State Building, 1903–1945*, Cambridge University Press, 2015, pp. 136–8.

[149] Report 'Situazione militare della Germania' (Berlin, 5 August 1919), AMAE, Affari Politici 1919–30, Germania, box 1125.

[150] [Sezione 'P' del Governo della Dalmazia], *Battute di propaganda. Per i giovani Ufficiali nelle conversazioni coi soldati*, Ancona, 1919.

officers – against the Hungarian Soviet Republic seemed to confirm this interpretation.[151]

It is clear that the antagonism between the socialists and the military heightened as a consequence of the war, but did the broad group of the war veterans also become enemies of the Italian socialists and therefore inclined towards Fascism? The retrospective evaluations in this sense made by socialists such as Giovanni Zibordi, Pietro Nenni and Angelo Tasca, assumed as accurate by many historians,[152] should be taken with a certain degree of scepticism.[153] Zibordi pointed out that the ex-military element, young ex-junior officers and ex-officers who felt displaced and economically threatened, was inclined towards Fascism; however, according to him, the fault lay with the socialists, who had done nothing to 'demobilize' that attitude.[154] He was forgetting his own speeches celebrating returning disabled veterans and his early publicized calls to 'demobilize the brains' of the people.[155] Assuming that the socialists were against 'the veterans' implies obscuring and simplifying a crucial part of the story. In reality, by the summer of 1919, even the prominent socialist thinker Antonio Gramsci was arguing that the experience of the trenches had positively transformed the masses of Italian peasant-soldiers into potential agents of a revolution similar to that which had taken place in Russia.[156]

The post-war myth of socialist attacks on the 'veterans' (reduci) is still approached rather uncritically by historians.[157] Angelo Tasca affirmed that the Lega proletaria practiced sectarian maximalist politics which drove away the combattenti: the call 'down with war!' (abbasso la guerra!) would have been interpreted as 'down with the veterans!' (abbasso i combattenti!).[158] The combattenti would have reacted – as the army did – in defence of the victory, protecting an honourable version of the war

[151] Avanti! (Turin), 1–4 July 1919.

[152] For example, De Felice, Mussolini il rivoluzionario, p. 428; Sabbatucci, I combattenti, p. 47; Mondini, La politica delle armi, passim.

[153] Cf. Salvatore Lupo, Il Fascismo: La politica in un regime totalitario, Rome, Donzelli, 2000, p. 49.

[154] Giovanni Zibordi, Critica socialista del fascismo, Bologna, Cappelli, 1922, pp. 15–28, now in Renzo De Felice, Il Fascismo: Le interpretazioni dei contemporanei e degli storici, Rome, 1998, quote p. 41.

[155] G. Zibordi, 'La smobilitazione dei cervelli', Avanti!, 22 January 1919; 'L'ord. D. G. politico' (undated but probably December 1918 or January 1919), ACS, MI, PS (1919), box 84, file 'Reggio Emilia. Movimento sovversivo'.

[156] L'Ordine Nuovo (Turin), 2 August 1919.

[157] Sabrina Sgueglia della Marra, 'Le aggressioni agli ufficiali nel primo dopoguerra', Nuova Storia Contemporanea, 3 (2012), pp. 117–34.

[158] Angelo Tasca, Nascita e avvento del fascismo, Milan, La Nuova Italia, 2002 (1st edn. 1950), p. 195.

experience, and therefore against socialism and in favour of Fascism. There is a degree of truth in this explanation, but it remains a simplification. It uncritically accepts the concept of the 'veteran' as it was constructed at that time. Not supported by comparative research, this interpretation criticizes the socialist approach to veteran politics as essentially inappropriate and diminishes the offensive role that anti-socialist veterans and fascists had played from the very end of the war. In reality, the socialist anti-militarist campaign stepped up after the socialists had been victims of the attacks from the fascist *arditi* and military officers. And most importantly, the symbolic construction of the anti-Bolshevik veteran, a consequence of the counter-revolutionary reaction in Germany and Hungary, had started earlier. And yet, the anti-militarist campaign was not directed against the Italian ex-combatants. If the anti-socialist groups affirmed the contrary, they were misappropriating the symbol of the veteran.

It is true that the socialists' disdain for war, linked to the unrealistic appeal for a social revolution, outraged the military and the interventionists, who saw in the socialists the hated enemy within. Publication of the inquiry about the military responsibilities for Caporetto, just when press censorship was lifted, fuelled the socialist campaign against militarism in the summer of 1919. Through the pages of *Avanti!*, the socialists argued that the war had been a horrific deception, that it had only benefitted a few bourgeois capitalists while impoverishing, mutilating and killing millions of people.[159] The extreme repressive conduct of officers towards their own soldiers (punishment and executions) was thoroughly denounced. All the horrors of war were 'unmasked'.[160]

It is important to note that whereas the socialists insulted and scorned the army officers, this campaign – as its promoters stated – did not intend to 'denigrate either the soldiers, or those who fought, convinced that they were fulfilling an honourable or sacred duty'.[161] It was directed against those who 'desired the war, against those who conducted it badly, and against those who, even worse, glorified it'.[162] Instead of attacking the soldiers, the socialists condemned the terrible experience of the trenches and contrasted it with the distorted image that the nationalist war propaganda had constructed.[163] They suggested that the warmongers had quickly forgotten the soldiers after the war, in contradiction to the adulation and deference offered to the soldiers in 1915.[164] The socialists deplored the fact that whilst the officers did not fight in the trenches, they

[159] *Avanti!*, 4 August 1919.   [160] *Ibid.*, 14 August 1919.
[161] *Ibid.*, 19 August 1919. See also *Il Soviet* (Naples), 7 September 1919.
[162] *Avanti!*, 4 August 1919.   [163] *Ibid.*, 24 August 1919.   [164] *Ibid.*, 17 August 1919.

now enjoyed high pensions; in contrast, the conscripted had been suffering at the front and now suffered persecutions and imprisonment.

In general, the exposure of these realities was not particularly offensive to most veterans. Neither did these representations of the veterans' experiences substantially differ from those of certain French veterans' groups that carried out their propaganda in order to obtain material benefits.[165] The Italian nationalists envied the successful French celebration of the victory on 14 July 1919, but the French left was very critical of this commemoration and employed anti-militaristic terms close to those of the Italian socialists.[166]

However, the anti-militarist campaign in Italy provoked indignation not only among army officers but also among certain leaders of the veterans' movement. *Arditi* such as Ferruccio Vecchi felt outraged and clearly took the side of the army officers in articles in *L'Ardito* and *Il Popolo d'Italia*. They planned new aggressions against the socialists[167] and distributed pamphlets inviting supporters to attack those parties or persons who conducted the campaign to discredit 'those who desired the war and those who *made* it'.[168] Different press organs of the ANC published harsh condemnations of the socialists,[169] who were depicted as 'ravens' that stirred the memory of the dead for partisan objectives. The socialists were 'defeatists' who tried to 'devalue the victory'.[170] The fascists and the veterans' organization converged in their use of these representations.[171] Moreover, as the investigation of the defeat at Caporetto resulted in some administrative measures against generals and thousands of men accused of desertion were amnestied, the army's loyalty to the government weakened.

The deterioration of the neutrality and discipline of the armed forces facilitated, on 12 September 1919, the poet and war hero D'Annunzio's

---

[165] *Journal des mutilés et reformés des anciens combattants et des victimes de la guerre* (Paris), 14 June and 19 July 1919.

[166] Annette Becker, 'Du 14 julliet 1919 au 11 novembre 1920: Mort, où est la victoire?', *Vingtième siècle, Revue d'histoire*, 49 (1996), pp. 31–44; Report about the ARAC (11 July 1919), AN, F/7, c. 13243, 'Associations de Mutilés et Victimes de la guerre'.

[167] Document from the *prefetto* of Milan (9 September 1919), ACS, MI, PS (1920), box 104, file 'Milano. Associazione segreta fra combattenti e arditi di principi rivoluzionari'.

[168] Police report (22 August 1919), ACS, MI, PS (1920), box 104, file 'Associazione fra gli "Arditi' d'Italia"' (emphasis added).

[169] *La Libera Parola* (Parma), 5 July 1919.

[170] Priamo Brunazzi. 'Bisogna chiudere il becco ai corvi!', *I Combattenti* (Genoa), 30 August 1919.

[171] Cf. *Il Fascio*, 15 August 1919. Significantly, *Il Maglio: Giornale Settimanale degli ex Combattenti e Smobilitati* (Varese) changed its subtitle to *Settimanale dei Fasci di Combattimento della Lombardia*, in 15 (16 August 1919).

mobilization of troops and volunteers to occupy the city of Fiume. With this action, D'Annunzio became the point of reference for the national revolutionary veterans, *arditi* and *futuristi*, who answered his call.[172] Among the Fiuman legionaries were some who would play an important role in the fascist regime such as Giovanni Giuriati and future fascist ANC leaders such as Nino Host-Venturi. Some fascist veterans even left their home cities to join the venture, and the ANC newspapers generally supported D'Annunzio.[173]

This action aimed to provoke the fall of Nitti's government, but it was unsuccessful in this objective.[174] The Prime Minister denounced this case of 'sedition' (*sedizione*) but at the same time closed the debate about the responsibilities for Caporetto by highlighting the inevitability of the war and the righteousness of the army.[175] Later, Nitti moderated his position and showed sympathy for the veterans. Yet, his policy on the Fiume problem was repugnant to the Italian ultra-nationalists and unsatisfactory to the veterans' leaders. Mussolini did not miss the opportunity to praise the predominant orientation of the veterans' organizations in favour of D'Annunzio and against Nitti.[176] The occupation of the Adriatic city lasted until the end of 1920, and during that time, D'Annunzio's forces received the support of interventionists and elements of the veterans' movement. Furthermore, the Fiume episode would lay the foundation for Fascism in areas such as political aestheticization and ritualization.[177] Thus, the symbol of the veteran became engendered with a set of implicit meanings that the fascist movement would later exploit.

In the critical situation provoked by the occupation of Fiume, it is understandable that Nitti did not promote any official commemoration of the victory of 4 November, as was demanded by the nationalists and elements of the ANC.[178] It is not certain that an official celebration would have helped appease the interventionist groups, but its absence did not relieve the frustrations of army officers and nationalists. An opportunity for

---

[172] Cordova, *Arditi e legionari Dannunziani.*
[173] *Il Fascio,* 4 October 1919; *I Combattenti,* 21 September 1919.
[174] Mondini, *La politica delle armi,* p. 42.
[175] For example, *La Stampa* (Turin), 14 and 17 September 1919.
[176] Sabbatucci, *I combattenti,* pp. 158–61; *Il Popolo d'Italia,* 21 September 1919.
[177] Michael A. Ledeen, *The First Duce: D'Annunzio at Fiume,* Baltimore, Johns Hopkins University Press, 1977.
[178] Marco Mondini, 'La festa mancata: I militari e la memoria della Grande Guerra, 1918–1923', *Contemporanea,* 4 (2004), pp. 555–78. *id.*, *La politica delle armi,* pp. 28–51; Victor Demiaux, 'Dov'è la vittoria? Le rôle de la référence interalliée dans la construction rituelle de la sortie de guerre italienne (1918–1921)', *Mélanges de l'École française de Rome - Italie et Méditerranée modernes et contemporaines* (on-line), 125/2, 2013, available at http://mefrim.revues.org/1426 (accessed 22 February 2014).

them to express their discontent was fast approaching: the Italian elections of November 1919. The ANC was ready to participate in the electoral struggle so that a veterans' political group would enter Parliament.[179]

Both the failed occupation of Fiume and the political tensions of the electoral campaign had decisive consequences: they amplified the transnational process of symbolic appropriation of the war veteran. By this point, foreign observers regarded the Italian veterans as a homogeneous part of the overall militaristic, anti-government and anti-socialist reaction. On 4 October 1919, a report sent from Italy to the French Ministry of Foreign Affairs depicted a bipolar political panorama in which the veterans (combattants), the fascists and almost the entire army were opposed to Nitti, whereas the socialists supported the Prime Minister: 'the socialists organise demonstrations against the veterans'.[180] A report from the British embassy to the Foreign Office mentioned that there was 'considerable confusion' over the ANC, the ONC and 'the Fascii di Combattenti or local groups of ex-fighting soldiers', but the report itself failed to make a proper distinction between the veterans' movement and the fascist movement.[181] Weeks later, one of the few journals that could be read in Paris during the newspaper strike in November 1919 published a report on the Italian situation that mentioned the violent fights between socialists and the 'Fascio of the combattants', 'arditi' and nationalists.[182] The leftist journal L'Humanité mentioned that the ANC veterans' programme was devoid of political ideals but also that the ANC's statements were clearly hostile to the socialists.[183] It is interesting to note that in the same issue of L'Humanité, a call by Henri Barbusse and Anatole France to vote for the socialists in the French elections made no reference to veterans. The transnational symbol of the anti-Bolshevik veteran was growing in prominence.

However, there were important symbolic differences in the way fascists and combattenti tackled the Italian electoral process. In discursive terms, the political position of the ANC veterans – as suggested by their leader Renato Zavataro – was against those who had desired the war but had not

[179] For a detailed account of the elections, see Sabbatucci, I combattenti, pp. 203–23.
[180] MAE-AD, Europe 1918–1929, Italie, 58, 'Politique intérieure. Dossier général. Aout-Dec 1919', pp. 65–6.
[181] 'Memorandum by Mr Rodd on the Nationalist Party in Italy' (25 October 1919), in Documents on British Foreign Policy 1919–1939, First Series, Vol. IV: 1919, London, Herr Majesty's Stationery Office, 1952, pp. 130–4.
[182] La Presse de Paris. Édition du soir (Paris), 16 November 1919. This newspaper was published in collaboration by fifty-six different newspapers, including Le Temps, Petit Journal, Action Française, Paris-Midi, La Victoire, Intransigeant and La Croix, amongst others. Therefore, the article must have been widely read.
[183] L'Humanité (Paris), 6 November 1919.

fought it (i.e. the interventionist and nationalist elites) and against *those who had not desired the war and sabotaged it* (i.e. the 'anti-national' leftist forces). Implicitly, the veterans' movement represented *those who had not desired the war but loyally fought it* – the majority of soldiers. The ANC's participation in the electoral struggle was obstructed by the socialists, criticized by the fascists and seen with hostility by other political sectors, even the interventionists.[184] This was a matter of rivalry: in Milan, the fascists presented a list of nineteen candidates headed by Mussolini, in which almost all members were introduced as veterans. The fascists intended to represent *those who had desired the war and also fought it.*

Apart from a very vague programme aiming for renovation of the political elites, the actual alignment of veterans varied much depending on the region and the electoral alliances they established. The self-representations they chose to identify their candidacies bear testament to a certain diversity. Most of them adopted the helmet as a symbol, which remained as the identifying veterans' icon for the elections of 1921. The helmet mirrored an essentially defensive understanding of the role of the soldiers.[185] Different veteran tickets from the south, in contrast, chose a ladder as the representation of their aspirations for social improvement. The fascists' identifying symbol was the *fascio*, which was rather rooted in the interventionist experience, though this symbol was also employed by the veterans' ticket formed by members of the ANRZO in Turin. In any case, by the time of the elections, the veterans were symbolically confronting the left. The electoral tickets of the socialists were marked by the hammer and sickle; they, in contrast, intended to represent war victims, widows, orphans and bereaved people.

The elections would be another major disappointment for veterans, fascists and interventionists. The *combattenti* had harboured hope that their moral authority over the nation would be enforced by the popular vote, but the veterans' tickets obtained very poor results almost everywhere. The two very clear winners of the elections were the socialists – who obtained 156 seats – and the Catholic *popolari*. The ANC-promoted veteran parliamentary group, a heterogenic platform without a clear political direction, had only obtained 232,923 votes (4.1 percent) – twenty seats in the Parliament.[186] The fascists' results were even more disappointing. This outcome contrasted with the victory of the

---

[184] For example, see Mussolini, 'Rilievi elettorali', *Il Popolo d'Italia*, 16 October 1919.
[185] *Il Combattente* (Capitanata), 2 November 1919.
[186] Pier Luigi Ballini, *Le elezioni nella storia d'Italia dall'Unità al fascismo: Profilo storico-statistico*, Bologna, Il Mulino, 1988, pp. 186–7. The best results were obtained in Sardegna and Puglia, where Gaetano Salvemini was influential.

conservative Bloc national in France: 44 percent of the membership of the so-called Chambre bleu horizon were veterans. The Italian Camera dei Deputati was composed of 27.97 percent ex-servicemen. Ironically, the Italian Socialist Party was the group with the highest percentage of veterans among its parliamentary representatives (47.4 percent), who placed no stress on their veteran status.[187] To make matters worse, it was clear that most Italian veterans, even members of the ANC, had voted for anti-militarist and revolutionary options. However, many in Italy understood this situation as a victory of pacifist socialism over the veterans, who now were represented as embittered and *defeated* (Figure 1.1). In fact, in certain veterans' journals the results were presented as a new 'general rehearsal for the Bolshevik revolution'.[188]

The situation for the fascists after the elections may have been critical, but the symbol of the veteran acquired further anti-socialist meanings. The day the new Parliament resumed its sittings, a demonstration of monarchist military officers in Rome provoked clashes with groups of socialists. The 'patriotic' demonstrators punched at least one socialist MP. Outraged, the socialists immediately called a general strike. Subsequently, in many cities, such as Rome, Milan, Turin, Florence, Bologna and Mantua, socialist strikers violently attacked officers in uniform.[189] This fierce left-wing reaction highlighted the wide support enjoyed by the socialists, but the news of attacks against officers fuelled the bourgeoisie's feelings of anxiety and hatred against the left. As a result, the anti-socialist myth of the 'abused veteran' started to circulate. Meanwhile, fascist leaders were arrested, accused of threatening public order. The combination of these events helped feed the image of 'veterans' – significantly symbolized as *arditi* – being brought into jail, while deserters entered Parliament (Figure 1.2).[190] Although the nationalist veterans and fascists had to come to terms with the short-term practical consequences of the debacle, they had actually achieved a crucial victory: the symbol of the war veteran had become associated with them as individuals and as organized groups essentially opposed to the political left.

The socialists, however, conscious that they had gained the support of many ex-soldiers, were delighted and thought that the revolution was within reach. In October, the socialist party had confirmed its maximalist

---

[187] Andrea Baravelli, *La vittoria smarrita: Legittimità e rappresentazioni della Grande Guerra nella crisi del sistema liberale (1919–1924)*, Romae Carocci, 2006, p. 183.
[188] *I Combattenti*, 6 December 1919.
[189] *La Stampa*, 2, 3 and 4 December 1919; *Corriere della Sera* (Milan), 2 and 3 December 1919; *Avanti!*, 2, 3, 6 and 7 December 1919.
[190] *I Combattenti*, 21 December 1919. Among others, Ferruccio Vecchi and Mussolini were arrested; see De Felice, *Mussolini il rivoluzionario*, pp. 574–5.

— Allora lo sconfitto sono io!   (Dal « Pasquino »).

Figure 1.1 'So, it's me who is defeated!' On the banners carried by the
socialists: 'Long live Lenin!', 'He who does not work should not eat',
'Hurrah for the strike!', 'Hurrah for the defeat!', 'Down with war!'.
I Combattenti, 6 December 1919 (from the illustrated journal *Pasquino*).
(Image courtesy of Ministero dei beni e delle attività culturali e del turismo /
Biblioteca Nazionale Centrale di Firenze. Further reproduction prohibited.)

orientation, aiming at establishment of the dictatorship of the proletariat;
the socialists had considered the possibility of using violence against the
bourgeoisie. They planned to conquer the local councils (*comuni*)
through the provincial administrative elections of 1920, and the veterans
and war victims would have to play a role.[191] Although the socialists

---

[191] *Spartacus. Organo della Lega Proletaria* (Milan), 15 January 1920.

Contrasti

I disertori a Montecitorio.....   ..., ed i Combattenti al Cellulare.
                                                                    (dal *Pasquino*)

Figure 1.2 'Contrasts' 'The deserters to Montecitorio . . . and the
veterans to the police van', *I Combattenti*, 21 December 1919 (from the
illustrated journal *Pasquino*).
(Image courtesy of Ministero dei beni e delle attività culturali e del turismo /
Biblioteca Nazionale Centrale di Firenze. Further reproduction prohibited.)

lacked a coherent programme to create a 'red army',[192] some of them
attributed a revolutionary mission to the veterans.[193] The Lega proletaria
would organize them: the apparent revolutionary nature of this organization seems clear even from the title of its newspaper, *Spartacus*. This
name was not only a reference to the German Communist faction but
also an allusion to the slave of the first century BC, who, after being
forced to fight as a gladiator, broke his chains to organize a rebellion
against his masters. This symbol of emancipation figured on the front
page of the paper and was representative of the socialist understanding of
the soldiers' war experience (Figure 1.3).

Yet, the suggested parallel with the Italian proletarian soldier was never
translated into action. In fact, Lega proletaria activities during 1920
remained non-revolutionary. Moreover, internal divisions between communists and socialists weakened the organization, particularly after 1921.
In reality, the political right and the nationalists had practically monopolized the symbol of the veteran. At the beginning of 1920, when the Italian

---

[192] Giorgio Rochat, 'Antimilitarismo ed esercito rosso nella stampa socialsita e comunista
del primo dopoguerra (1919–1925)', *Il movimento di liberazione in Italia*, 76 (1964),
pp. 3–42.
[193] *L'Ordine Nuovo*, 22 November 1919.

Figure 1.3 *Spartacus* (Milan, 15 January 1920).
(Image courtesy of Ministero dei beni e delle attività culturali e del turismo / Biblioteca Nazionale Centrale di Firenze. Further reproduction prohibited.)

maximalists launched the project of creating revolutionary soviets, this strategy was not based on the old example of 'soldiers' and workers' councils' that had marked the origins of the Russian and German Revolutions. The age of the ideal socialist revolutionary veteran had passed.

In short, the year 1919 witnessed a transnational process of symbolic appropriation of the notion of the veteran. The veteran became politically and ideologically charged as an anti-leftist symbol. By the end of 1919, veterans were primarily seen as a group to be employed against the internal Bolshevik threat. If at the end of 1918 the masses of soldiers were often considered a kind of new proletariat with socialist inclinations – a consequence of the Russian Revolution – subsequent events such as the smashing of the central European revolutions and the seizure of Fiume seemed to demonstrate the counter-revolutionary and nationalist potential of ex-combatants. Different right-wing groups strived to impose such a perception. Mussolini and the early fascists were probably the most radical among them. Although a public image of veteran organizations as bulwarks against the 'reds' existed in places as diverse as Germany and the United States, it was in Italy that the process of symbolic appropriation had the most important consequences. Although Italy came under the political domination of anti-militarist socialists and pacifist Catholics, the symbol of the veteran was becoming the sole preserve of nationalist groups. As we will see in Chapter 2, the fascist manipulation of the symbol of the anti-Bolshevik veteran was crucial for the rise of Italian Fascism.

2 War Veterans and the Rise of Italian Fascism, 1920–1922

If there was some form, even limited, of historical fusion between fascism and veterans, its foundations must be sought in Italy. Since fascism was born in Italy, the link between veterans and fascism was first established in Italian Fascism. This link determined the overall relationship that transnational fascism would maintain with veterans. In this chapter I will begin with an assessment of the extent to which fascist veterans – particularly the *arditi* – gave rise to squadrism, a violent fascist political strategy that overturned the unsuccessful version of Italian Fascism started in San Sepolcro. I will then examine the process whereby two different historical phenomena – the fascist movement and the veteran movement – interweaved in Italy between 1920 and 1922, showing how this complex relationship contributed to the rise of Fascism. My explanation is based on a simultaneous analysis of both movements, the Italian veteran movement led by the ANC and the ANMIG, on the one hand, and the fascist movement and party, on the other. I will contrast their respective organizational and discursive features, highlighting their commonalities and intersection points, to assess the nature and depth of their amalgamation until the Fascist conquest of power in October 1922.

In the third section I argue that the consolidation of the 'fascist veteran' stereotype was one of the most important consequences of the amalgamation between the fascists and the Italian ex-soldiers. Historical actors widely employed this constructed image, helping to disseminate the interpretation of Fascism as a veteran phenomenon. As we will see, at the beginning of 1921, external observers, such as diplomats and journalists, transmitted this stereotypical representation of the members of the fascist movement to other geographical spaces in Europe. This cross-border dissemination justifies questioning whether the perception of the fascist veteran stereotype influenced the development of the early NSDAP in Germany. I will discuss whether Italian Fascism, encapsulated in the symbol of the fascist veteran, was an inspiration for the early Nazi movement.

To conclude, the last section of this chapter will explore the transnational impact of the March on Rome. I will ask how the symbolic link between the war veterans and Fascism established in October 1922 was perceived, interpreted and employed in other countries. To answer this question, I will recreate the complex and multilayered European context, showing how discourses on and representations of the fascist veterans influenced politics in France, Spain and Germany. The March on Rome was the fascist founding myth, and in a sense, it can be considered the birth date of transnational fascism. As we will see, the war veterans had an important symbolic role in this foundational event.

From *Arditismo* to *Squadrismo*

After the November 1919 elections, both the veteran and fascist movements entered into deep crises. In 1920, the veterans' parliamentary group was relatively inactive.[1] It was in the streets that the veteran movement was most effective, organizing protests to obtain an extension of the policies and to secure a greater number of jobs reserved for disabled veterans from the Nitti government. The fascists supported this campaign.[2] The ANC reached approximately 500,000 members that year (the ANC absorbed the ANRZO); the association was very active in the organization of agricultural cooperatives. But bitter internal divisions drove different leaders of the movement apart. Some of them made their opposition to the socialists clear.[3] The workers' movement uncovered anti-patriotic tendencies when militants attacked the tricolour national flag or – more often – replaced it with the red one.[4] Throughout the country, at the local level, there were occasional conflicts related to how to commemorate dead war soldiers.[5] Even if the bourgeois ex-officers, horrified by the rebellion of the masses, knew that strikers and protestors were often ex-soldiers they had commanded in the trenches, the ex-officers appropriated the symbol of the 'veteran', complaining that 'veterans received not only indifference and oblivion, but also sarcasm and acrimony.'[6] The anti-socialist reaction would slowly take shape, and the symbol of the veteran would play an important role.

[1] Sabbatucci, *I combattenti*, pp. 255–81.
[2] See, for example, *Il Popolo d'Italia*, 1 January, 29 February and 4 March 1920.
[3] Ugo Grasso, 'Noi e i socialisti', *I Combattenti*, 24 April 1920.
[4] *I Combattenti*, 27 March and 3 April 1920.
[5] Gianni Isola, 'Immagini di guerra del combattentismo socialista', in Diego Leoni and Camillo Zadra (eds.), *La Grande Guerra: Esperienza, memoria, immagini*, Bologna, Il Mulino, 1986, pp. 519–43.
[6] Discourse of Piero Calamandrei at the University of Siena, 29 May 1920, in Piero Calamandrei, Silvia Calamandrei and Alessandro Casellato (eds.), *Zona di Guerra: Lettere, scritti e discorsi (1915–1924)*, Rome-Bari, Laterza, 2006, pp. 315–24.

For its part, the ANMIG concentrated on obtaining legal improvements for disabled veterans from the government, but with limited results. Its leadership was completely overhauled: rightist men such as Giuseppe Caradonna[7] and Carlo Delcroix[8] became more influential. The new leaders insisted that the ANMIG maintain a non-political position, although the anti-government attitude was clear. They adopted a rigid *apoliticità* (non-political stance) as a precondition for any kind of action, and liberty of thought for ANMIG members was preserved. Nevertheless, the fascists maintained interest in the activities of disabled veterans.[9]

Inside the ANC, efforts to constitute a real political party of veterans were unsuccessful and, in fact, led to a double scission of the association. During both the ANC and Partito del Rinnovamento (the projected veterans' party) congresses in Naples in August 1920, no precise political project was able to gather consensus. Firstly, a group of leaders from northern Italy – the fascists Agostino Lanzillo and Edoardo Malusardi among them – abandoned the sessions because they endorsed the ANC's apolitical nature (*apoliticità*).[10] Subsequently, some southern and Sardinian representatives separated from the congresses and opted for their own political project, which resulted in creation of the autonomist Sardinian Action Party (Partito Sardo d'Azione (PSdA)) in

---

[7] Caradonna, born in Cerignola (Foggia) in 1891, studied law and was a war volunteer. He attained the rank of captain during the war; he was wounded and decorated. He joined the disabled veterans' movement in Foggia and in the region of Capitanata. In November 1920 he founded the *Fascio* of Cerignola and later became a prominent squadrist leader in Puglia. He was elected MP in 1921. He was an organizer of the March on Rome, after which he joined the Ministry of the Post. He held several other political positions during the fascist regime. He was condemned to prison after the fall of the fascist regime and freed in 1946. He died in Rome in 1963.

[8] Delcroix, born in Florence in 1886 of a Belgian father and an Italian mother, was an interventionist and war volunteer. He attained the rank of lieutenant during the war and became instructor of *arditi* troops. In 1917, he lost both hands and both eyes in an accident, after which he worked as a propagandist among soldiers and the wounded. He became known for his patriotic oratory and poems. After joining the ANMIG in Florence, he maintained an ambiguous attitude regarding Fascism. He consolidated his leadership role during the first years of fascist rule, overcoming his differences with Mussolini. An MP since 1924, he confirmed his loyalty to Mussolini during the Matteotti affair. This enthusiasm for the Duce ensured his own position as president of the fascist ANMIG, which he kept until the demise of Fascism in 1943. After the liberation, he continued his political activities in the Italian Monarchist party and as a writer. He died in Rome in 1977.

[9] *Bollettino mensile, Associazione Nazionale fra Mutilati e Invalidi di Guerra, Sezione di Modena* (Modena), 8 May and 10 June 1920; *Il Bollettino. Organo Mensile dell'Associazione Nazionale Mutilati e Invalidi di Guerra* (Rome), 1 September 1920; *Il Popolo d'Italia*, 29 June 1920.

[10] E. Malusardi, 'Ricostruire l'Associazione su basi apolitiche', *Il Popolo d'Italia*, 4 September 1920.

1921.[11] Significantly, the PSdA would be the only example of a successful democratic party of veterans across the country. The southern ANC leaders remained isolated, and thus the 'political' phase of the nationwide veterans' movement culminated in a blind alley. As explained in a very judgmental article written by an ANMIG leader, the veterans' pretension of making politics had been completely unfruitful; this kind of 'veteranism' (*combattentismo*) – a term that was coined at that time – was considered a thing of the past.[12]

The attempt to transform the mass of veterans into the basis of a new democracy by introducing profound reforms into social and political life and enacting a complete change of the ruling classes was definitely extinguished by the autumn of 1920. This failure, according to Giovanni Sabbatucci, contributed to deepening the political void that made fascist success possible.[13] In fact, the fascist movement took advantage of the political and organizational conflicts of the Italian veterans. Furthermore, as we will see, the fascists largely benefitted from the symbolic construction of the anti-Bolshevik veterans. The alleged anti-socialist proclivity of the veterans was an idea embedded in the minds of many people. The fascists were going to exploit this symbolic construction.

In 1920, Fascism embarked on a path towards the extreme right, pushed by a series of events at home and abroad that helped transform the relationship between the fascists and the veterans. Given the paltry results that fascists had obtained in the elections by highlighting their status as veterans and taking into account the modest electoral performance of veterans themselves, a revision of the fascist programme and strategy was needed. As social unrest and the strikes of the workers escalated, the veterans' movement simultaneously developed its own protest campaigns. Whereas the fascists opposed the workers' protests, displaying a violent anti-socialist attitude, *Il Popolo d'Italia* observed the veterans' vindications benevolently.[14] But the fascists were far from having a dominant influence on the veteran movement. At that time, the failure of the Kapp putsch in Germany mirrored the widening gap between left-wing workers, on the one hand, and the people allegedly shaped by the experience of war, on the other. As events in Germany developed in March 1920, Mussolini had been well informed about the participation of Freikorps soldiers who returned from the Baltic area in

---

[11] Lorenzo Del Piano and Francesco Atzeni, *Combattentismo, fascismo e autonomismo nel pensiero di Camillo Bellieni*, Rome, Edizioni dell'Ateneo, 1986.
[12] Priamo Brunazzi, 'L'Italia dei combattenti: gli insegnamenti di un congresso', *Il Bollettino*, 1 October 1920.
[13] Sabbatucci, *I combattenti*, pp. 343–51.
[14] For example, *Il Popolo d'Italia*, 29 February and 4 March 1920,

72   War Veterans and the Rise of Italian Fascism, 1920–1922

the anti-republican coup.[15] However, the German working class – almost mirroring the Italian reality – emerged victorious once more in its conflict with the army and the nationalists. This source of disappointment, however, was less disturbing than the problematic occupation of Fiume. The city was not being annexed to Italy, and the politics of D'Annunzio were advancing towards a kind of revolutionary syndicalism. Furthermore, futurists such as Marinetti disliked the increasingly anti-popular fascist stance and preferred to return to a non-political position.[16] How was Fascism going to reconstruct its veterans' politics?

In the bleak situation of 1920, Fascism resorted to *arditismo*, a war mentality that was a specific element of the veterans' world. In 1920, *arditismo* was conveniently wielded and transmitted, and its use would contribute to the recovery of the fascist movement. At the beginning of 1920, the political isolation of the fascists and the *arditi* was acknowledged in the pages of *L'Ardito*: the elitist ex-officers had been incapable of attracting the masses of veterans, who were left in the hands of the Bolshevik enemy. Yet, Ferruccio Vecchi argued that they were not yet tired of the struggle. In fact, he pointed to youth as a group that was not only available but also willing to continue the fight because they had not been able to do so in the war. According to Vecchi, *arditismo* – adapted to civilian life as *arditismo civile* – could be the tool to educate this new Italian generation, and all hopes were placed on them. Based on values such as courage, fatherland, victory and genius, 'schools of *arditismo*' would help instil energy and war knowledge in very young Italian men (between fifteen and twenty years of age) for the country's progress.[17]

In practical terms, this project implied the transmission of discourses and practices of violence to younger generations, and the result would be the revitalization of the fascist movement. The targets of the violent reaction were the socialists, labelled 'defeatists' and 'deserters'. Although the aims and mechanisms of this 'educational' project seemed very vague and clumsy, Mussolini fully endorsed it in the pages of *Il Popolo d'Italia*, and actual 'schools of *arditismo*' were opened for the youth in the offices of the *arditi* association in Milan.[18] As one of those newly recruited young fascists described in his diary, in the *Fascio* of Florence – situated

---

[15] Mussolini, 'Ersatz', *Il Popolo d'Italia*, 14 March 1920.
[16] Günter Berghaus, *Futurism and Politics: Between Anarchist Rebellion and Fascist Reaction, 1909–1944*, Oxford, Berghahn Books, 1996, pp. 150–5; Francesco Perfetti, *Fiumanesimo, sindacalismo e fascismo*, Rome, Bonacci, 1988, pp. 37–60.
[17] Ferruccio Vecchi, *Arditismo civile*, Milan, 1920; *L'Ardito*, 4, 11, 18 and 25 January, 22 February, and 14 and 28 March 1920.
[18] Cf. Mussolini, '"Arditismo civile" di Ferruccio Vecchi', *Il Popolo d'Italia*, 14 March 1920.

in the ANC offices – older ex-*arditi* instructed them how to throw bombs and attack with daggers to quash demonstrations of the 'reds'.[19] Meanwhile, fascist ex-*arditi* such as Giuseppe Bottai and Piero Bolzon furthered the politicization of their association.[20] The boundaries between these *arditi* and the fascists had been blurred since the end of the war, but now the ethos of *arditismo* was systematically injected into young Italians who joined the fascist movement.

The fascist aestheticization of political violence as *arditismo* may have been a new discursive and symbolic strategy, but on the ground in Italy, the social and political struggles were actually becoming increasingly violent.[21] The agitation and multiple strikes of the working class were sometimes aggressive. State repression was bloody and produced a considerable number of deaths among the protesting workers and peasants, particularly from the spring of 1920 on. As we know, in some areas, such as Lazio, ANC veterans occupied the land,[22] but others formed bourgeois armed guards to confront disorder throughout Italy. For example, in Palermo, in April 1920, a group of ex-NCOs suggested that local ANC leaders create a force to protect 'public order' against the 'subversive parties'; they would act together with the police, even participating in expeditions to trouble spots.[23] On one occasion, a group of '*arditi* and citizens' from Naples wrote a letter to Italian Prime Minister Giolitti – who had been called to replace Nitti – to virulently express the 'necessity of combating the internal enemies even with violence'.[24] Faced with the workers' occupation of factories in August 1920, the Fascio of Venice offered the services of 'around two hundred young veterans from the trenches' to the *prefetto*, claiming that they would follow the orders of the authorities.[25] Although among the so-called subversives, there were men

---

[19] Mario Piazzesi, *Diario di uno squadrista toscano 1919–1922*, Rome, Bonacci, 1980 (with a Foreword by Renzo de Felice), pp. 73–4 (entry of 14 June 1920).

[20] Manifesto authored by Giuseppe Bottai (12 May 1920); ACS, MI, PS (1920), box 104, file 'Associazione fra gli "Arditi" d'Italia'; *Le Fiamme* (Rome), 24 May 1920; Piero Bolzon, *Fiamma nera*, Milan, 1921. As we will see, both Bottai (born in Rome in 1895) and Bolzon (born in Genoa in 1883) became relevant political figures in the fascist regime.

[21] Fabbri, *Le origini della guerra civile*, pp. 151–226.

[22] For example, see the note of the *prefetto* of Rome (27 September 1920) about the occupation of land by veterans in Ciampino, ACS, MI, PS (1920), box 78, file 'Agitazione agraria'.

[23] Note of the *prefetto* of Palermo (28 April 1920), ACS, MI, PS (1920), box 104, file 'Palermo. Sezione della Federazione Nazionale fra sottufficiali smobilitati'.

[24] Letter from Naples (1 July 1920), ACS, MI, PS (1920), box 105, file 'Anonimi'.

[25] Quoted by Giulia Albanese, *Alle origini del fascismo: La violenza politica a Venezia 1919–1922*, Padua, Il Poligrafo, 2001, p. 51.

who had fought in the war, only the defenders of 'order' characterized themselves as 'veterans' (*combattenti*) or as *arditi*.

Meanwhile, Mussolini was pushing the fascist movement towards the political right, a transformation that alienated important groups of *arditi*. Whilst relying on a few veterans and on the discursive tool of *arditismo*, the fascists appealed to new social groups, namely, well-off young Italians and any citizen ready to employ violence against the left. Thus, Mussolini made clear that to join Fascism, there was 'no need to have been a combatant'.[26] Fascism was set on a new path, one that was fully anti-leftist and ultranationalistic. Due to the fact that the ex-*arditi* were not a monolithic block, a crisis broke out in the key Roman section of the *arditi* association. Revolutionary and futurist *arditi* abandoned Fascism, turning to the left. Ferruccio Vecchi himself would be expelled from the association and from the Fascio. The *arditi* splintered and diverged in their political tendencies.[27] D'Annunzio had been Mussolini's rival in leading nationalist veterans, so when Giolitti decided to put an end to D'Annunzio's Fiume adventure (as a consequence of the Rapallo treaty) in the 'Bloody Christmas' of 1920 (*Natale di Sangue*), the fascists did not do anything to impede it. In November 1920, Mussolini had finalized a pact with the Prime Minister Giolitti that marked the definitive stance of Fascism in defence of the social order.

The fascist turn to the right provoked an abrupt transformation of the rank and file of the fascist movement on the basis of the myths of *arditismo* and of youth. Whereas many syndicalists, interventionist social-ists and anarchists fled the Fasci they had joined in 1919, it is interesting to note that 'veterans' (*combattenti*) usually maintained their allegiance to the movement. Now, many young men and students adhered to Fascism. This phenomenon began as early as October 1920 in Bologna and Ferrara, where the reconstituted Fasci composed of veterans at its core, acquired a distinct anti-leftist character.[28] Likewise, in Sesto San Giovanni, near Milan, the 'board' (*direttorio*) of a new fascist section was completely composed of veterans. This *Fascio* also included one ex-Fiuman legionary as well as enthusiastic young people.[29] This new

---

[26] *Il Popolo d'Italia*, 3 July 1920.

[27] Rochat, *Gli arditi*, p. 140; Cordova, *Arditi*, pp. 64–72; Marco Rossi, *Arditi, non gendarmi! Dalle trincee alle barricate. Arditismo di guerra e arditi del popolo (1917–1922)*, Pisa, BFS, 2011. ACS, MI, PS (1920), box 104, file 'Associazione fra gli "Arditi" d'Italia'.

[28] Corner, *Fascism in Ferrara*, p. 107; Fiorenza Tarozzi, 'Dal primo al secondo Fascio di combattimento: note sulle origini del fascismo a Bologna (1919–1920)', in Luciano Casali (ed.), *Bologna 1920 le origini del fascismo*, Bologna, Cappelli, 1982, pp. 93–114; note of the *prefetto* of Bologna (18 October 1920), ACS, MI, PS (1920), f. 'Bologna. Associazione Nazionale dei Combattenti'.

[29] *Il Fascio*, 11 December 1920.

element of middle-class youngsters who had not fought in the war formed the ranks of the movement.[30] They were sons of land proprietors and urban bourgeois families who were ready to obey the orders of admired men with military experience. They only had a mythical perception and indirect knowledge of the reality of war but were influenced by the fascist discourse that exalted youth and action, and they sought to emulate the way of life of the daring *arditi*. Thus, as a few fascist veterans had anticipated, many Fasci became schools of *arditismo*.[31]

From the end of 1920 on, Fascism fostered the development of what would historically become its most decisive political instrument: 'squadrism' (*squadrismo*). Squadrism would provide a very important cultural reference for the rest of Fascism's history, easing the way to totalitarianism.[32] Above all others, landowners in the central and northern agrarian provinces promoted and financed this form of political violence, which was also supported by the petty bourgeoisie. Squadrism was employed to ruthlessly destroy socialism and its network of civic and political centres, since socialist agitation was believed to constitute a revolutionary threat to the dominant social classes.[33] Apart from being a by-product of *arditismo*, squadrism was connected in other ways to the constructed symbol of the veteran. An example of this is provided by the violent events of Palazzo D'Accursio in Bologna on 21 November 1920, which are considered the starting point of agrarian squadrism. During this incident, a nationalist veteran – a city councillor – was presumably killed at the hands of socialists. This event was an excuse for the Fascist squads – composed of many ex-servicemen – to launch a wave of violent reprisals against 'Bolsheviks'.[34]

After the Bologna events, the ANMIG officially condemned the violence and made a public call for calm. Carlo Delcroix poetically talked about love and forgiveness. At the same time, though, the association had entered into a dynamic of anti-governmental radicalization and was preparing a wide protest campaign to obtain material improvements for disabled veterans. The anger against the socialists had spread. In an ANMIG meeting in Milan, the mere suggestion of collaborating with

---

[30] The non-fascist press used to note this reality; see *Il Fascio*, 6 January 1921.

[31] See also Paolo Nello, *L'avanguardismo giovanile alle origini del fascismo*, Bari, Laterza, 1978.

[32] Emilio Gentile, *Il culto del Littorio: La sacralizzazione della politica nell'Italia fascista*, Rome, Laterza, 1993, pp. 39–60.

[33] For example, see Frank M. Snowden, *The Fascist Revolution in Tuscany 1919–1922*, Cambridge University Press, 1989; Anthony L. Cadorza, *Agrarian Elites and Italian Fascism: The Province of Bologna 1901–1926*, Princeton, NJ, Princeton University Press, 1982, pp. 290–454; Corner, *Fascism in Ferrara*.

[34] Cadorza, *Agrarian Elites*, pp. 306–15; *Il Popolo d'Italia*, 19 December 1920.

the socialists during the protests was met with an overwhelming response of hostility from a majority of the 2,000 attendees; after that, the disabled veterans organized a demonstration that ended in a fight against the Royal Guards. Three days before, in a meeting of the Milanese Fascio (where Mussolini discussed accepting the Rapallo treaty), Piero Bolzon had called for support for the protests of the 'glorious disabled veterans' (*gloriosi mutilati*); consequently, the Fascio decided to provide the veterans with any kind of resources they would need. There were more similarly aggressive protests of disabled veterans during December 1920. Finally, they demonstrated in Rome, in front of the Parliament. On the same day, in the Chamber, some socialist, liberal and *popolari* MPs came to blows in a quarrel motivated by news of the aggressions against the socialists in Bologna. As the disabled veterans violently threatened to invade the Chamber, a draft bill to reform the pension system was urgently approved. The socialists voted favourably, as proof of their recognition of the disabled veterans, but they shouted 'Down with war!' during the session, while the MPs of the veterans' group yelled back 'Long live the war!'. As we see, the disabled veterans' campaign combined with the initiation of the fascist offensive of violence, and in both conflicts the socialists were seen as the enemy of the veterans.[35]

By the end of 1920, the Fiume occupation had been terminated, and the veterans' movement was divided and lacked a clear political orientation; but Fascism had another opportunity to gather the support of veterans through the use of violence against their constructed enemy: the socialists. Initially, while some ANC leaders blamed the socialists for the 'devaluation' (*svalutazzione*) of the victory, they saw another evil phenomenon in the fascist reaction. Later, opinions inside the ANC increasingly turned in favour of the fascists. Fascist violence was considered a spontaneous rebellion against the previous socialist violence and 'anti-national' attitude. Pride for having fought the war, in addition to sorrow stemming from 'devaluation' of the victory, made it likely – according to those commentators – that 'unremorseful veterans' would join the fascist movement. This violent phenomenon was believed to be a 'noble and legitimate reaction'.[36]

---

[35] *Il Bollettino*, 1 November 1920, 1 January and 1 February 1921; Telegram of the *prefetto* of Milan (5 December 1920) and other documents, ACS, MI, PS (1920), box 104, file 'Milano. Associazione mutilati e invalidi di guerra'; telegram of the *prefetto* of Milan (9 December 1920), ACS, MI, PS (1921), box 102, file 'Milano. Fasci di Combattimento. 1 Fascicolo'; *La Stampa*, 19 December 1920.

[36] Rodolfo Savelli, 'La svalutazzione della vittoria', *I Combattenti*, 6 November 1920; Ferruccio Lantini, 'Il fenomeno fascista', *I Combattenti*, 3 January 1921

The symbol of the veteran offered the fascists a justification and also a pretext to carry out their squadrist actions. Fascists justified the use of violence against the socialists because, according to them, the socialists had previously brutalized army officers and disturbed veterans' meetings and commemorations of fallen soldiers and because they had dishonoured the national flag.[37] However, in fact, the emerging fascist movement was not just a reaction against previous socialist abuses, even if many contemporaries understood it as such. Very few veteran leaders realized that Fascism was something more: a very serious threat to the authority and stability of the state.[38]

Squadrism, the key to fascist success, has been widely studied by historians who have assessed the real and symbolic role war veterans played in its success.[39] In fact, the overwhelming majority of provincial fascist leaders who commanded the *squadre* had fought in the First World War (70 percent), comparatively more often in the *arditi* (22 percent). This was the case for Dino Grandi, Italo Balbo, Roberto Farinacci, Cesare Maria De Vecchi, Giuseppe Bottai, Achille Starace, Augusto Turati and several other future politicians of the Fascist regime. Many of them had been officers and junior officers. Certain squadrist leaders – such as Aurelio Padovani in Naples – had already played a political role in the ANC. Local studies show that within the *squadre* the percentage of people who had been conscripted during the war fluctuated between 56 and 68 percent; these figures may be considered a high involvement of veterans, thus confirming the statements of the fascists themselves and the perceptions of the authorities.[40] It was, above all, the youngest front generation (born as of 1890 onwards) that was most prone to become squadrists. In Sven Reichardt's opinion, this was because the younger men, who had a stronger need to give meaning to their war experience, had probably been more highly influenced by the patriotic war propaganda, particularly developed after Caporetto. In addition to this, since the *squadristi* did not typically come from a proletarian

---

[37] Fascist manifesto to the country, quoted by the *prefetto* of Milan (20 December 1920), ACS, MI, PS (1921), box 102, file 'Milano. Fasci di Combattimento. 1 Fascicolo'; see also C. C. dei Fasci Italiani di Combattimento, *Barbarie rossa : Riassunto cronologico delle principali gesta commesse dai socialisti italiani dal 1919 in poi*, Rome, 1921, *passim*.

[38] Rodolfo Savelli, 'L'autorità dello Stato', *I Combattenti*, 21 February 1921.

[39] See Roberta Suzzi Valli, 'The Myth of Squadrismo in the Fascist Regime', *Journal of Contemporary History*, 35 (2000), pp. 131–50; Reichardt, *Faschistische Kampfbünde*; Mimmo Franzinelli, *Squadristi. Protagonisti e tecniche della violenza fascista. 1919–1922*, Milan, Mondadori, 2003.

[40] Reichardt, *Faschistische Kampfbünde*, pp. 366–7; 'The fascists are almost all war veterans', a government inspector wrote in Porderone, 1921, quoted in Mondini, *La politica delle armi*, p. 127.

background and attained officer status during the war, they had experienced war in a less horrifying way, even though it had scarred them deeply.[41] It should also be noted that these younger men had waited longer than others to be demobilized during 1919, thus remaining under the influence of the army and its officers for an extended period of time.

Whilst Fascism unleashed the squadrist offensive, the divided ANC made some halting attempts to reorganize and reunify. The fascist leadership was not interested in interfering in the ANC leaders' quarrels but rather in maintaining the *apoliticità* of the association as long as possible so that it would not hinder the campaign against the left. It was not by chance that the *northern* ANC leaders wanted to consolidate the apolitical essence of the association, since Fascism was growing as a mass movement in the north. Paradoxically, some of those northern ANC leaders were either fascists or fascist friendly (e.g. Agostino Lanzillo in Milan).[42] Yet the ANC did not wish to become a victim of what was actually a civil war situation. In fact, many anti-fascist veterans were members of ANC sections, and even more of them would join it later, seeking refuge from fascist aggressions. Not all the fascist *ras* (local fascist leaders) were tolerant of veterans. In Cremona, the intransigent fascist Roberto Farinacci, whose veteran credentials were even less heroic than those of Mussolini, had his first dispute with the veterans at the end of February 1921: he accused them of being the combatants of the bourgeoisie.[43]

The rise of the fascist movement paved the way for quarrels between fascist and non-fascist veterans of the ANC. While playing the card of *apoliticità* in the north, in other southern regions fascist veterans exerted pressure to debilitate and disband the leftist or democratically oriented ANC sections. This was the case in Puglia, where ex-interventionist socialist Gaetano Salvemini, a member of the parliamentary veterans' group, led the veteran movement. The fascists labelled him as a 'renouncer' (*rinunciatario*) in relation to the Dalmatian question. Within the space of a few months, the fascist Araldo di Crollalanza succeeded in expelling Salvemini from the ANC section.[44] In Naples, in March of

---

[41] Reichardt, *Faschistische Kampfbünde*, pp. 368–73.

[42] Lanzillo, editor of the Milanese veteran's review *La Nuova Giornata*, was criticized for his fascist credentials, which he tried to deny at that time; see *La Nuova Giornata* (Milan), 31 August 1921. Lanzillo had actually abandoned the fascist movement at the beginning of 1920 due to its turn to the right, but later in 1921 he would collaborate again on the pages of *Il Popolo d'Italia* as an ideologue of Fascism as a middle-class party.

[43] *Il Combattente* (Cremona), 5 and 19 March 1921; Cf. Matteo di Figlia, *Farinacci: Il radicalismo fascista al potere*, Rome, Donzelli, 2007, p. 47.

[44] *Il Popolo d'Italia*, 1 October 1920; *Il Fascio*, 5 February 1921; for the context, see Colarizi, *Dopoguerra e fascismo*, pp. 15–26. Crollalanza, born in Bari in 1892, was an interventionist journalist. A war volunteer, he attained the rank of lieutenant and was

1921, fascists were also victorious in the local ANC elections for a new board.[45] Fascist infiltration of the ANC was a route for Fascism to expand in the Mezzogiorno. Conversely, some veteran leaders of the ANC opted to join the Fasci; this was the case for Giacomo Acerbo in Abruzzo province.[46] Fascists and veterans walked on the streets of Teramo chanting patriotic and fascist hymns together, having just inaugurated the new local ANC section with a speech by Acerbo.[47] In Florence, the collaboration of the ANC section was clearest; squadrists were seen leaving the local ANC offices before committing their attacks.[48] The criminal actions of the Florentine fascists led to a popular uprising in the city between late February and early March 1921, which was reported in numerous international newspapers. The fact that the ANC and its members had an ambiguous stance towards the fascist movement was one reason why the fascists were able to appropriate the symbol of the anti-Bolshevik veteran.

Contacts between disabled veterans and the fascists contradicted the ANMIG's official non-political stance. During the spring of 1921, the disabled veterans launched a set of actions in main cities pressuring authorities to favour the employment of veterans in different administrations, especially the state railway (Ferrovie dello Stato). Disabled veterans assaulted and occupied the state railway offices in Rome, obstructing the work of women they wanted to replace. Although the left argued that this conflict was another example of the class struggle, the disabled veterans did not adopt this discourse and expelled the communist agitators from their demonstrations. In contrast, in many cities the disabled veterans required the help of the fascists, and thus, the turmoil increased. Their actions succeeded in Rome, Florence, and other northern cities. In Brescia, for example, a group of ex-combatants and disabled veterans, along with fascists and ex-Fiuman legionnaires, occupied the post offices, expelling all the women working there. In Padua, a similar action ended with the hoisting of the Italian flag (*tricolore*) over the occupied offices building – a gesture that contrasted with the use of

---

wounded. He was instrumental in the founding of the ANC in Bari, and he joined the fascist movement in 1919. In 1922 he would participate in the March on Rome.

[45] *Il Fascio*, 5 March 1921.

[46] Giacomo Acerbo, *Fra due plotoni di esecuzione. Avvenimenti e problemi dell'epoca fascista*, Bologna, Cappelli, 1969, pp. 165–74. As proof of the conservative, religious and moralist discourse for veterans employed by Acerbo, see Giacomo Acerbo, *Tre discorsi politici. Chieti (1920): Teramo, Aquila (1923)*, Florence, 1923, pp. 9–26.

[47] Note of the *prefetto* of Teramo (2 May 1921), ACS, MI, PS (1921), box 89, file 'Teramo'.

[48] Phonograms from the *prefetto* of Florence (26 and 28 January 1921), ACS, MI, PS (1921), box 96, file 'Firenze. Fasci di combattimento I'.

the red flag in the socialist *comuni*. In Milan, the fascists and disabled veterans erected barricades and fought against the Royal Guards (Guardia Regia). All this upheaval actually pushed the authorities to discuss new measures in favour of disabled veterans, who therefore considered the fascists their successful defenders. An ANMIG message regarding the agitation alleged that it had not required the help of any organization, but, in fact, cooperation between fascists and disabled veterans had been widespread.[49]

The initial goodwill of some veterans towards the fascists can be traced to the process of appropriation of the war memory that the fascists undertook as squadrism was coming into force. In this endeavour, the fascists took advantage of the difficulties of the Italian state in developing a commemorative settlement. Finding a shared symbolic framework for a national commemoration of the Italian victory was an extremely onerous mission[50] firstly because in all countries that had participated in the war, the construction of a war memory was always marked by contradictions, struggles, negotiations and fractures.[51] In this sense, the boycotts organized by the Italian socialists and revolutionaries against several patriotic celebrations should not be considered a characteristic exclusive to post-war Italy. Furthermore, celebrating victory in Italy was more controversial than in other countries because the persistent divisions between interventionists and neutralists made the war memory a conflict-ridden issue. The disappointing outcome of Versailles had prevented the Italian state from emulating the celebrations of the Allies in 1919. Nonetheless, during 1920, as in other victorious nations, the Italian state offered a variety of symbolic rewards to veterans, and medals were created and bestowed on them. The Commemorative Medal of the Italian-Austrian War was created in July 1920 for almost all Italian ex-soldiers. The Interalleate Medal was created in December 1920 and given to many veterans of the victorious nations. Italy celebrated the war victory for the first time in 1920. Although the ANC had been an interlocutor of the authorities in the development of many of these initiatives, the veterans still did not have a central role in the official ceremonies. ANMIG leaders bitterly lamented that the celebrations came too late.[52]

---

[49] ACS, MI, PS (1921), box 88; *Il Bollettino*, 1 May 1921; *Corriere della Sera*, 13, 14, 15, 17, 20, 21, 23 and 30 April and 4 May 1921; *Il Popolo d'Italia*, 13, 16 and 17 April 1921; *Avanti!*, 17 and 20, April and 8 May 1921; *I Combattenti*, 21 April 1921; *Il Bolscevico* (Novara), 28 April 1921.

[50] Maurizio Ridolfi, *Le feste nazionali*, Bologna, Il Mulino, 2003, pp. 145–58.

[51] Daniel J. Sherman, *The Construction of Memory in Interwar France*, University of Chicago Press, 1999.

[52] *Il Bollettino*, 1 December 1920 and 1 November 1921.

The fascists took full advantage of the gaps in the symbolic approach to the war memory, and in fact, the set of symbols linked to veterans constituted the first elements they misappropriated. The *squadre* adopted militaristic pennants as a sign of their unity and faith.[53] Since so many members of the *squadre* were ex-soldiers, the veterans' most recognizable identifying symbols, the soldiers' helmet and medals, overlapped with the symbolic squadrist garments – the black shirt and the black beret. By examining photographs of the squadrists and fascist leaders, it is possible to confirm that fascist veterans frequently attached the commemorative medals created in 1920 to their black shirts. Using the helmet during a squadrist action was less a physically protective measure than a means for fascists to self-identify as veterans.

The blending between the veterans and the fascists, whose power became overwhelming in certain provinces – especially in the Po Valley – raised concerns among some of the veterans' leaders. The fascists, however, were proud to highlight the supposed general sympathy and fraternity between both entities owing to the common points in the political programme. The fascists patronizingly reassured the veterans, clarifying that they 'never had the whim ... to reduce the ANC sections to anything more than local branches of the Fasci di combattimento'.[54] This arrogance was possible because the national elections in May 1921 had given Fascism an important victory. After the first squadrist wave, the fascists entered Parliament, walking hand-in-hand with the conservatives of Giolitti's National Bloc. In the new legislature, the fascist group was composed of thirty-five MPs, of which twenty-eight (80 percent) were war veterans. This time – a lesson learnt after the failure of the November 1919 elections – the veterans' credentials were exhibited with moderation. In contrast, the Nationalist parliamentary group was composed of nine MPs, of which eight were veterans. The so-called Partito dei combattenti still survived, but with only ten seats. The number of paliamentary seats occupied by veterans was 135 out of 524 (~26 percent).[55]

The Fascist Veterans: A Travelling Stereotype

Fascism was booming, and violence was the key to its success; the violent symbolic appropriation of the veteran by the fascist movement produced a stereotype: the 'fascist veteran'. Once this emblematic figure became recognizable to foreign observers, a perception of fascism as a movement

[53] Reichardt, *Faschistische Kampfbünde*, pp. 563–6.   [54] *Il Fascio*, 9 July 1921.
[55] Baravelli, *La vittoria smarrita*, p. 186.

made of veterans started to be transferred to other geographical spaces. The agents of these transfers were, above all, diplomats and journalists from different countries; they were witnesses who chose to accentuate the veteran element of Fascism as a defining element. Since France and Germany were adjacent countries with an enormous number of war veterans, they were highly exposed to Fascism.

The French government was well informed about the Italian disturbances through its ambassador in Rome. At the end of October 1920, for example, the ambassador described the Italian nationalist reaction as something produced by the *arditi* associations and by '*fasci di combattimento*' that 'grouped war veterans and nationalist militants'.[56] On 22 March 1921, having sent a number of reports about the fascist anti-revolutionary, violent reaction, Ambassador Barrère wrote to the Ministry of Foreign Affairs suggesting that it would be 'convenient' to publish a newspaper article about Fascism in the French journal *Temps*.[57] The French diplomats had a very positive opinion of the movement[58] in part because of the perceived importance veterans played in it. The fascist violent acts attracted the attention of French journalists as well. Among the first foreign explanations about Fascism was an article published in the Parisian *Le Figaro* at the end of March 1921. In it, it was highlighted that the '*fascio di combattimento* [was] constituted after the war by veterans who wanted to safeguard their interests. They soon took on the task of fighting all the saboteurs of the victory.'[59] Thus, a hegemonic interpretation of the origins and causes of Fascism, which was related to the Italian veterans, was consolidated in France.

Biased French journalists were not the only people who believed that 'veterans' had created Fascism in order to restore victory. In April 1921, after the Italian Parliament had been dissolved and new elections had been called, the Swiss ambassador in the capital city transmitted the following description of Fascism:

The word comes from 'fascio', *faisceau* or league. In the aftermath of the war, leagues of war veterans were constituted everywhere with the aim of maintaining solidarity among the veterans and defending their interests. These leagues very

---

[56] Report of the French ambassador in Rome (26 October 1920), MAE-AD, Europe 1918–29, Italie, 60, Politique intérieure: Dossier general, October 1920–July 1921, pp. 51–4. Two days later, a similar description of the *fascisti* was published in *The Times* (London), 28 October 1920.

[57] Barrère to the Ministry of Foreign Affaires, MAE-AD, Europe 1918–29, Italie, 60, Politique intérieure: Dossier général, October 1920–July 1921, p. 142.

[58] William I. Shorrock, 'France and the Rise of Fascism in Italy', *Journal of Contemporary History*, 10, 4 (1975), pp. 591–610.

[59] Jacques Roujon, 'La contre-révolution en Italie', *Le Figaro* (Paris), 28 March 1921.

quickly took on a political character as a consequence of the violent antimilitaristic campaign unleashed in the country by the socialists and the frequent attacks against officers and other soldiers. In small villages, for example, there were cases where the local socialists refused to honour with a monument the memory of the fallen soldiers. Decorated military or junior officers during the war were insulted or relegated by the socialists to some form of public contempt. These facts would produce a reaction, which was very slow to take shape.[60]

This document and the above-mentioned press article show two things (apart from containing a misleading simplification of the veterans' role in the origin of the fascist rise). Firstly, they demonstrate that by the spring of 1921, the fascists had been successful in imposing a perception of Fascism as the reaction of the war veterans against the pacifist and anti-militarist socialists. Secondly, they provide evidence that this constructed image started to transcend national boundaries. In addition, these French and Swiss examples illustrate the widespread satisfaction in conservative circles regarding fascist violence, understood as just a reaction against the revolutionary leftist 'excesses'. The reality rather was that Fascism was attacking the same alleged internal enemy of the war period: pacifists, neutralists and *rinunciatari*, whose annihilation was a necessary step to resume the fight for the nationalist objectives. The veterans who were protagonists of this reaction were violent, although their numbers were very limited in overall terms: only those who, apart from believing in the expansionist aims, saw the left as their primordial class enemy. Most foreign spectators did not capture the complexity of the origin of Italian Fascism.

Through reports by journalists and other witnesses, the stereotype of the fascist veteran began to circulate outside Italy, influencing extreme-right and veterans' associations in other countries. Giving credence to the dominating belief that the Italian First World War veterans were a seamless nationalist and anti-Bolshevik collective,[61] observers were ready to uncritically accept the characterization of the fascist as a war veteran. This assumption might have also been a conscious discursive strategy of right-wing groups to conveniently convince the public that veterans were inclined to conservative and counter-revolutionary positions. In any case,

---

[60] 'Le Ministre de Suisse à Rome, G. Wagnière, au Chef du Département politique, G. Motta' (7 April 1921), in Commission Nationale pour la Publication de Documents Diplomatiques Suisses, *Documents diplomatiques suisses/Diplomatische Dokumente der Schweiz/Documenti diplomatici Svizzeri 1848–1945*, Bern, Benteli Verlag, 1988, pp. 178–80.

[61] As the *Gazette de Lausanne* (Lausanne), 23 March 1921, put it, the Italian fascists were 'anti-bolshevik organizations composed of war veterans, young men from all the anti-bolshevik parties'.

the example of Italian Fascism contributed to make the inclination of veterans towards conservative and reactionary politics relevant. In other words, it furthered the symbolic appropriation of the veterans by the right in other countries. In France, some nationalist students and ex-officers belonged to existing rightist groups, but after the example of Fascism, the fact that they were veterans was increasingly highlighted and compared to the Italian case.

Paradoxically, the left was also considering the veterans' participation in the fascist movement relevant. Maurice Pottier, a war veteran and member of the leftist French group Clarté, founded by Barbusse, realized that the Italian veterans had quite diverse political orientations but that 'a certain number' of them, 'above all ex-officers', had sided with the 'conservative elements'. Pottier believed that this phenomenon was also happening in France and in other countries. He thought that the 'conservative and violently anti-proletarian attitude' of some veterans was a 'dangerous aberration'.[62] But whilst casting doubts on the authenticity of such veterans, this article actually admitted the alleged socialist errors that allowed the veterans to be inclined to anti-socialist reaction and fascism.

Leftist Italian observers also detected the participation of war veterans in the fascist movement, and this perception contributed to the European circulation of the prototypic image of the fascist veteran. As the primordial target of fascist violence, the Italian socialists were among the first people who rationally analyzed the origins and nature of Fascism. One of them was the moderate socialist intellectual Giovanni Zibordi. Like other Marxists, Zibordi sought the causes of the fascist reaction in the economic and social contradictions of the post-war period, yet without under-estimating the role of the war experience. At the beginning of April 1921, Zibordi's article on the 'elements and motives' of Fascism, published in the magazine *Critica Sociale*, discussed the participation of 'professionals of violence' within the fascist movement. He wrote that these people, 'maladjusted from war', were young men who had gone to war at less than twenty years old, and now they were unable to resume their studies or jobs.[63] He claimed that during the war, the petty bourgeoisie had experienced the capacity to give orders, as well as the adventure of combat, and now they were reluctant to return to their humble civil occupations. Later on, analyses by socialists of the fascist violence in different regions insisted on the role of ex-*arditi*, ex-officers, and

---

[62] *Il Paese* (Rome), 2 July 1921.

[63] Gianni Zibordi, 'Il fenomeno del giorno: Elementi e moventi del Fascismo', *Critica Sociale. Rivista quindicinale del socialismo* (Milan), 7 (April 1921), pp. 1–15.

ex-combatants in the movement.[64] These leftist perceptions were likely to be transferred outside Italy.

In Germany, socialists and communists paid attention to what was happening on the Italian left, particularly at the beginning of 1921.[65] German newspapers of every political hue transmitted information about important Italian events. As early as January 1921, the social-democratic paper of Munich, *Münchener Post*, reproduced an article about Fascism that had been recently published by the Austrian *Arbeiter-Zeitung*. It was a first-hand report about fascist violence, in which it was noted that the fascists' support was 'based on the returning soldiers and on their discontent'.[66] However, the author argued that the fascists were responsible for having forced the Italian Parliament to discuss and approve a new benefits law for disabled veterans. This misapprehension proves that veterans and fascists were sometimes undistinguishable to foreign observers. Shortly after, a communist paper in the Bavarian capital mentioned the existence of the 'white guard terrorist organization of the fascists'.[67] *Die Rote Fahne* explained that the Fasci's main programmatic point was the 'glorification of the front combatant'.[68] Reports about fascist violence followed in other leftist papers and later in liberal ones as well.[69] At the beginning of May 1921, an article written by a *Vorwärts* correspondent in Italy vividly described the fascist violence that had disturbed the normal electoral process.[70] Some days later, a German translation of Zibordi's aforementioned article about the components of Fascism was published in *Vorwärts*. The editors of this socialist paper suggested that the political phenomenon could be found not only in Italy but also in Germany.[71] Revealing the veterans' input to the fascist movement, these kinds of

---

[64] Aldo Oberdorfer, 'Il fascismo nella Venezia Giulia', *Critica Sociale*, 11 (June 1921), pp. 1–15; Critica Sociale, 'Il terrore bianco in provincia di Ferrara', *Critica Sociale*, 12 (June 1921), pp. 16–30.

[65] Karl-Egon Lönne, *Faschismus als Herausforderung: Die Auseinandersetzung der 'Roten Fahne' und des 'Vorwärts' mit dem italienischen Faschismus 1920–1933*, Köln, Böhlau-Verlag, 1981, pp. 30–58 and 163–89.

[66] 'Die "Fascisten"', *Münchener Post* (Munich), 5 January 1921; cf. *Arbeiter-Zeitung* (Vienna), 31 December 1920.

[67] *Neue Zeitung* (Munich), 11 January 1921.

[68] G. F. G., 'Der Faszismus in Italien', *Die Rote Fahne*, 22 February 1921.

[69] 'Die Fascistenunruhen in Italien', *Vorwärts* (Morgen-Ausgabe, Berlin), 3 March 1921; these perceptions were not very different from those of the French left; cf. 'Le règne de la violence en Italie', *L'Humanité* (Paris), 3 March 1921. See also 'Der Bürgerkrieg in Italien', *Neues Montagblatt* (Vienna), 21 March 1921; 'Nach dem Fascisten-Überfall: Die Lage in Südtirol', *Berliner Tageblatt* (MA, Berlin), 30 April 1921.

[70] O. L. [Oda Olberg-Lerda], 'Italien im Wahlkampf', *Vorwärts* (MA), 11 May 1921.

[71] 'Was ist Fascismus?', *Vorwärts* (MA), 21 May 1921.

articles contributed to simplifying the German perceptions of Fascism, which would thereafter be based on recognizable stereotypes.

Thus, the German public became aware that Fascism was a phenomenon of young ex-combatants and ex-officers, which were groups of individuals also widely present in Germany. As the German anti-republican terrorist organizations led by ex-officers, such as the Orgesch and the Organisation Consul, committed deadly attempts to assassinate politicians in mid-1921, German left-wing opinion classified these actions as 'fascist'.[72] In turn, Italian Fascism was sometimes called the 'Italian Orgesch'.[73] At the same time, perceiving the outrage that the fascists provoked on the German left, the anti-republican extreme right might have tended to stress the common features with Italian Fascism – namely, the veteran factor.

The hypothesis that early German perceptions of Italian Fascism may have played a crucial role in the evolution of the Nazi movement has been under-explored by historians. The NSDAP, as we know, came into existence later than the Fascist movement, and its growth as a mass movement was posterior to the expansion of squadrism in Italy. I have demonstrated that the violent practices of Italian Fascism were known in Bavaria at least since the beginning of 1921; hence, it is reasonable to believe that Italian Fascism did influence the evolution of the early Nazi movement, even if this influence was not based on direct contact. While taking into account that Nazism was a product rooted in extreme-right traditions in Germany and that the German post-war experience was of paramount importance to the origins of Nazism, I will assume that the early Nazi movement was also influenced by its predecessor, Italian Fascism. In particular, I will explore the role of veterans played in the transfer of the fascist political example into Germany. As the stereotype of the fascist veteran had reached Germany in January 1921, at the very latest, it is important to observe how the Nazi movement's stance regarding the war veterans changed around this time.

By January 1921, the NSDAP had around 3,000 members, most of them inhabitants of Bavaria attracted by Hitler's oratory during his propaganda tours.[74] Although veterans might have made up a substantial part of the membership and leadership, the party did not have any

---

[72] For example, 'Landstagsabgeordneter Gareis ermordet: Eine faschistische Mordtat', *Münchener Post*, 10 June 1921; Paul Kampffmeyer, 'Vom deutschen Fascismus', *Sozialistische Monatshefte* (Berlin), 1 (1923).

[73] *Arbeiterville* (Graz), 29 January 1921; *Rote Fahne* (Vienna), 30 September 1921.

[74] Dietrich Orlow, *The History of the Nazi Party*, Vol. I: *1919–1933*, Newton Abbot, David & Charles, 1971 [1st ed. 1969], pp. 24–5.

particular programme regarding them. In the *Völkischer Beobachter*, there had been invocations that the youth (*Jugend*) would be the last heroic resort to save the fatherland.[75] At the end of 1920, when this journal became the official organ of the Nazi movement, veterans' issues were rather absent from its pages. At that time, in a brief description of the veterans' organizations published in their paper, the Nazis just showed preference for the so-called Frontkriegerbund, a small veterans' group from Munich that was opposed to the socialist, communist and Jewish veterans' associations.[76] But there was no direct connection between both organizations yet.[77] Hitler obtained control of the NSDAP in July 1921. He immediately took the initiative to reform the party's 'sports section' to create what would later be known as the Sturmabteilung (SA). Even though it is difficult to give empirical evidence, it is plausible that Hitler, who used to read the Munich press, was inspired by descriptions of the squadrist's violence to create the SA. Would veterans in the early SA play the same role as they did in Italian Fascism?

Although the Bavarian context determined the lower inflow of war veterans into the Nazi movement, the circulating stereotype of the 'fascist veteran' most probably contributed indirectly to shaping the membership of Hitler's party. According to NSDAP sources, the first group of the SA was composed of twenty-five men, but only eight of them were veterans or disabled veterans.[78] However, in June 1921, the government took the decision to dissolve the Bavarian Einwohnerwehren. Apparently, many of the members of this paramilitary organization, as well as returning volunteers of the dissolved Freikorps Oberland, flocked to the SA.[79] At that time, Freikorps members (such as Rudolf Hess and Ernst Röhm), as well as other ex-soldiers, trained and directed the younger men of the SA.[80] Yet, Nazi calls for membership were still directed towards the youth rather than towards veterans.[81] It is true that veterans were given free entrance to some Nazi meetings[82] and were invited to join the party, but this does not mean that they were the primary target of the NSDAP mobilizing discourse. The Nazi party was still a minor anti-Semitic

---

[75] K. Bratzier, 'An die Jugend!', *Völkischer Beobachter* (Munich), 17 April 1920.
[76] 'Kriegsteilnehmerorganisationen', *Völkischer Beobacther*, 1 January 1921.
[77] 'Frontkriegerbund-Reichsbund', *Völkischer Beobachter*, 20 January 1921.
[78] 'Deutschlands erste S. A. Turn - und sportabteilung 1921', BArch (Berlin), NS 26, 300.
[79] Georg Franz-Willing, *Die Hitlerbewegung: Der Ursprung 1919–1922*, Berlin, Deckers Verlag G. Schenk, 1962, p. 140.
[80] Peter Longerich, *Die braunen Bataillone. Geschichte der SA*, Munich, C. H. Beck, 1989, pp. 15–32.
[81] *Ibid.*, p. 25.   [82] Löffelbein, *Ehrenbürger der Nation*, p. 120.

organization without any special interest in war veterans. Therefore, even though some German veterans joined the NSDAP in the Bavarian context, it was less the result of a conscious political strategy than the consequence of the German and Bavarian situations. Still, as has been said, the Italian image of the 'fascist veteran' was an element that already circulated and was part of such a political environment.

Foreign policy was another factor that predisposed the Nazi movement towards Italian Fascism. In general, among the German extreme-right groups, the perception of Italian Fascism was not positive, given the fascist aggressions towards the German minority in Südtirol, which had outraged the German nationalists.[83] In contrast, Hitler had shown his preference for an alliance between Germany and Italy as early as in 1920.[84] As he explained in a meeting of war veterans, this rapprochement would drive a wedge between Italy and France, thus debilitating the status quo reached at Versailles.[85] The *Völkischer Beobachter* usually expressed support for the Südtirol Germans, but in November 1921, when the violent actions of the Italian fascists that took place in Südtirol were mentioned for the first time, the paper emphasized the 'patriotism and spirit of sacrifice' of the fascists to defend the fatherland from Bolshevism, as a positive facet of the movement. Yet, no particular relevance was given to the participation of veterans.[86]

The NSDAP of 1920–1, therefore, was neither a simple imitation of the Italian fascist movement nor a party that oriented its politics and programme towards veterans. It is very difficult to know when exactly Hitler knew about Fascism and how this knowledge influenced his political conduct. In the first half of 1921, the stereotype of the 'fascist veteran' had started to circulate in Germany and Bavaria, and it is likely, albeit difficult to prove, that it became an inspiration for the early Nazis. At any rate, during 1921, the example of Italian Fascism was not yet a decisive factor in the trajectories of the German extreme-right and war veterans' paramilitary organizations. However, as Italian Fascism continued its violent and successful path towards power, this political model, conveyed by the symbol of the fascist veteran, would become crucial to understand future German developments.

[83] 'Mussolinis Kampfansage gegen das deutsche Volk', *Gewissen* (Berlin), 16 May 1921.
[84] Walter Werner Pese, 'Hitler und Italien 1920–1926', *Vierteljahrshefte für Zeitgeschichte*, 2 (1955), pp. 113–26.
[85] 'Rede auf einer Versammlung des Bundes Deutscher Kriegsteilnehmer'(Nürnberg, 1 August 1920); Hitler, *Sämtliche Aufzeichnungen*, pp. 167–9.
[86] Rupprecht Stimer, 'Das vergessene Deutsch-Südtirol', *Völkischer Beobachter*, 2 November 1921.

Italian War Veterans and the Fascist Seizure of Power

Despite the symbolic appropriation of the veteran by the fascist movement, we should not believe that most Italian veterans were either fascists or sympathizers of Fascism. In fact, the armed confrontation between fascists and socialists can be seen as a civil war between veterans. Lega proletaria centres and meetings, which were a part of the socialist network, were systematically attacked.[87] The fascists made no distinctions between socialists and communists, even though in January 1921 an important scission in the PSI had taken place, from which the Italian Communist party emerged. Veterans also set up leftist defence organizations (*guardie rosse*). The Arditi del Popolo, at the initiative of the anarchist ex-*ardito* Argo Secondari, appeared in the summer of 1921 and were ready to defend the working class from fascist aggression. This anti-fascist organization spread quickly, reaching 20,000 members in the summer, most of them in the region between Rome and Ancona, Lazio, Umbria and Le Marche.[88] Despite being immediately persecuted by the authorities and attacked by the fascists, the achievements of the anti-fascist organization cannot be overlooked. In discursive terms, for a short period, this leftist reaction was successful in snatching the symbol of the *arditi* and the ethos of *arditismo* from the fascist dominion. Among Italians, the notion of *arditismo* would become a category used to make sense of the violence used by both the fascists and the left.[89]

In this increasingly worrying situation, the ANC officially welcomed the so-called pact of pacification (*patto di pacificazione*) between fascists and socialists in the summer of 1921, which had been promoted by Acerbo, among others.[90] At the local level, sections of the ANC worked to reach an agreement, though during these attempts they blamed the socialists for their 'hate propaganda'; the conditions proposed for the pacification meant concessions to fascist objectives.[91] Soon the official 'pact of pacification' became a dead letter. Fascist violence did not stop, but rather increased in the autumn of 1921 and in 1922, beyond Mussolini's control.

Amidst this turmoil, the northern ANC group, endorsed by the fascists, was able to impose the idea of the *apoliticità* of the ANC on the

---

[87] Isola, *Guerra al regno della guerra*, p. 144.
[88] Eros Francescangeli, *Arditi del Popolo: Argo Secondari e la prima organizzazione antifascista (1917–1922)*, Rome, Odradek, 2000.
[89] Benedetto Migliore, *Le convulsioni dell'arditismo*, Milan, 1921.
[90] *La Nuova Giornata*, 14 August 1921.
[91] Documents about Navaccio (Pisa), July 1921, ACS, MI, PS (1921), box 107, file 'Pisa. Fascio di Combattimento, fascicolo 2'.

organization, thereby marginalizing the dissident ANC splinter groups. Through a series of internal struggles, the fascists gained a presence in the veteran organization.[92] In Rome, Adolfo Schiavo, an ex-officer from an aristocratic background and a member of the Fasci di combattimento, took over the ANC provincial section and launched a series of actions to debilitate the national directing board of the ANC situated in Rome.[93] When the Third Congress of the ANC was organized in the Augusteo of Rome in November of 1921, the old board of directors was expelled, and the association reconfirmed its non-political nature. It is significant by itself the fact that, just a few days after this declaration, the fascist congress that also took place in Rome transformed the fascist movement into a party: the PNF. Fascism had neither absorbed nor subjugated the veteran movement. However, there had been a palpable displacement of the centre of gravity of the political action of Italian war veterans.[94] In other words, Fascism had become the main expression of veteran politics.

The reason why the ANC and the fascist congresses coincided in Rome in November of 1921 is that on that date, Italy performed the transnational ceremony of the entombment of the Unknown Soldier (*Milite Ignoto*) in the Roman Vittoriano (*Altare della Patria*).[95] The ANMIG was very critical of the government because it (the ANMIG) thought the celebration came too late.[96] Although the entombment ceremony of the *Milite Ignoto* had the potential to transcend political divisions, the fascists presented themselves as defending the commemorative process from the attacks by 'subversives'. After this celebration ended, Mussolini took the opportunity to declare (at the fascist congress) that the *Milite Ignoto* rested in peace thanks to the fascist movement. Thus, in November of 1921, the fascists took a further step in the appropriation of the symbolic representation of veterans. Fascism had decided to impose its own version of the victory, and it would not allow the country to transform the next celebration of 4 November into a day of national reconciliation.

Throughout 1922, the PNF continued its efforts to receive the support of veterans, while the ANC increased its protests to obtain benefits and privileges from the government. In April 1922, the national council of the

---

[92] Sabbatucci, *I combattenti*, pp. 351–60.
[93] Federico Gabelli, *Adolfo Schiavo e la 'Romana combattenti' dall'apoliticità al fascismo*, Rome, 1930; ACS, MI, PS (1921), box 89, file 'Roma. Associazione Nazionale fra gli ex combattenti'.
[94] Sabbatucci, *I combattenti*, pp. 357–8.
[95] Bruno Tobia, *L'Altare della Patria*, Bologna, Il Mulino, 1998, pp. 61–86.
[96] *Il Bollettino*, 1 November 1921.

PNF made a request to the Fasci that veterans, 'mutilated' veterans and the mothers of fallen soldiers be given the highest honours in every national celebration: the fascists were allowed to employ 'any means' to force the authorities to fulfil this measure.[97] At the time, in many cities, the ANC veterans were expressing their determination to make their aspirations real once and for all; it was time, they said, to give justice to the 'heroes of yesterday, atrociously mocked today'; they announced a wide protest campaign.[98] The fascists tried to offer the veterans the recognition they craved. In order to widen the gap between the veterans and the left, *Il Popolo d'Italia* used the misleading image of the heroic but crippled war veteran.[99]

This discursive and symbolic dynamic, fostered above all by Fascism, served to exacerbate the frustrations of the veterans. The fascist position, which defended a patriotic and nationalist version of the war memory, together with their defence of special rights sought by ex-soldiers, helped the fascist movement recruit veterans. Most likely the PNF's stance in favour of social order also contributed to expanding its affiliation. By May 1922, the PNF would reach 322,310 members, the majority from the centre and the north of Italy. The middle classes were predominant. Workers composed 40 percent of PNF membership, and 24 percent were agriculture workers; these groups were probably attracted to the party as war veterans imbued by myths like that of the peasant-soldier. Eighty-eight of 136 national and provincial fascist leaders were war veterans, and among these, thirty-two had been war volunteers, seventy-three had been officers, thirty-one held silver medals and forty held bronze medals.[100] Many Italian men who considered themselves veterans and who – for this reason – felt moved to political action joined the PNF, thereby supporting squadrism.

However, violence was the factor that contributed the most to the consolidation of the symbolic link between the fascists and the veterans. From the summer of 1922 on, veterans literally assaulted the offices of public and private institutions where they wanted to be employed, expelling women from their jobs. In an echo of the disabled veterans' protests of the spring of 1921, the fascists joined the veterans' demonstrations, threatening the authorities and trying to impose the veterans' will. In August of 1922, this strategy was especially successful in cities where the

[97] *Il Popolo d'Italia*, 6 April 1922.
[98] *Ordine del giorno* of the ANC (9 April 1922), ACS, MI, PS (1922), box 99, file 'Massa e Carrara'.
[99] *Il Popolo d'Italia*, 27 May 1922.
[100] These data are from Gentile, *Storia del partito fascista*, pp. 556–7, 562–3.

fascists had a bigger influence on the veterans: Bologna, Florence, Pisa and Rome.[101] In Genoa, the veterans' ringleader stated that if their energetic action – the occupation of offices – yielded no results, they would 'also have recourse to violent means, requiring the participation of the fascists and nationalists'.[102] Still, in many other provinces, particularly in the Mezzogiorno, the fascist tactics found no followers.

Not only was violence the key to forging a sense of community among veterans and fascists, but violence also served to destroy the leftist veterans' organizations. The Arditi del Popolo offered strong resistance to the fascists in Livorno, Genoa and Ancona; they were largely involved in the combats on 24 May 1922 in Rome, and in the defence of Parma from fascist assault in August 1922.[103] Yet, the connivance of the army and the police with the fascists made resistance hopeless. After the failure of the leftist strike movement in August of 1922, the organization of the Arditi del Popolo faded. Furthermore, the squadrists attacked any organization that challenged their monopolization of 'patriotic' politics and symbols: even the headquarters of the Catholic ex-servicemen association, the UNRG, linked to the PPI, were vandalized and its members brutalized.[104] This strategy foreshadowed what would happen in the following years to the whole of the ANC.

Considering the influence that several fascists had attained inside the ANC, it does not seem a mere coincidence that while rumours and comments about a fascist March on Rome (*Marcia su Roma*) had been freely circulating since August 1922,[105] the veterans decided to increase their agitation. Special veterans' committees were formed, and violent actions continued, for example, the occupation of bank offices. A large demonstration of ex-servicemen teachers took place in Rome.[106] In Tuscany, Ancona and other places, action squads (*squadre di azione*) of veterans appeared decked out in helmets and green-grey shirts.[107] At the end of September 1922, the national board of the ANC planned to launch simultaneous demonstrations across Italy to draw attention to the problem of veteran unemployment.[108] On 2 October 1922, the ANC (in

---

[101] ACS, MI, PS (1922), box 99, files, Bologna, Firenze, Pisa, Roma; Gabelli, *Adolfo Schiavo*, pp. 83–108.
[102] Note from the *prefetto* of Genoa (2 August 1922), ACS, MI, PS (1922), box 99, file 'Genova'.
[103] Francescangeli, *Arditi del Popolo, passim*.
[104] Gentile, *Storia del partito fascista*, pp. 513–14.
[105] Giulia Albanese, *La marcia su Roma*, Rome-Bari, Laterza, 2006, pp. 58–65.
[106] *L'Idea Nazionale*, 22 and 24 September 1922.
[107] Notes of the *prefetto* of Livorno (7 and 23 October 1922), ACS, MI, PS (1922), box 99, file 'Livorno'; *Il Combattente* (Mantova), 21 September 1922.
[108] ACS, MI, PS (1922), box 99, file 'Affari Generali'.

accordance with the ANMIG) sent a memorandum to its members giving instructions to prepare a wide, coordinated demonstration that should take place at some point after 20 October 1922. This document was signed, in the name of the ANC national board, by the secretary Angelo Zilli, and by Nino Host-Venturi, both members of the fascist movement.[109]

Although there was no direct connection between the veterans and fascists in their plans to carry out the March on Rome (they started to take shape later in mid-October), the veterans' unrest contributed to destabilizing public order. The veterans were, at the same time, seizing upon the state crisis to push for special privileges. In doing so, they did not refrain from replicating fascist methods. In some places, veterans directly asked the fascists for help. Furthermore, the veterans' public presence in tandem with the fascists helped to consolidate the perception that the fascists had the support of the Italian veterans. Undoubtedly, however, the masses of Italian ex-soldiers had very diverse opinions about Fascism, ranging from opposition to indifference and full support. But the struggle of the veterans and the fascist campaigns were combining and mixing in the symbolic realm.

During the fascist mass meeting in Naples prior to the March on Rome, the fascists publicly clarified their political plans in relation to veterans. Giacomo Acerbo was in charge of detailing this programme. (As we know, Acerbo was a provincial ANC leader.) Firstly, he declared that the problems of the veterans had a substantial importance for the PNF because, according to him, the great majority of the veterans were fascist militants and because Fascism placed the valuation (*valorizzazione*) of war ideals and victory at the core of its doctrine. Acerbo said that Fascism would definitely resolve the problems veterans faced. Fascism would not place veterans in syndicates, since the PNF actually was 'the true party of the Italian veterans'. He said that Fascism was the only movement capable of enforcing veterans' rights. He predicted that soon all the Italian veterans would flock to Fascism. In the subsequent discussion, several veteran leaders who were present raised more precise questions. It was predicted that the ANC would soon constitute one of the PNF's biggest forces. It was also suggested that the PNF contact the organizations of veterans abroad because veterans regarded Fascism as the 'purest interpreter of their feelings'. Another attendee, Vittorio Arangio Ruiz, a northern ANC leader, stated that the ANC wanted to come into contact with the PNF to ensure that the ANC remained free of 'antinational' members and to avoid

---

[109] Copy of ANC memorandum, transmitted by the *prefetto* of Rome (17 October 1922), ACS, MI, PS (1922), box 99, file 'Roma'.

conflicts with the fascists.[110] After each side made these promises, the expected veterans' protest campaign did not take place.

The involvement of certain groups of veterans, sometimes as an emanation from ANC sections, in preparing the final fascist assault on the state seems unquestionable. Not only the myth of the war experience and the squadrist ethos but also the military training acquired during the Great War by the squadrist veterans transmitted to younger fascists paved the way for the March on Rome. For example, in Florence, a group of thirteen members of the local ANC section led by fascist veteran Fernando Agnoletti had been responsible for squadrist actions in the Tuscan countryside since 1920. This group had grown in numbers and formed the so-called Cesare Battisti squad (named after the irredentist martyr). By September of 1922, this veteran group was equipped with military gear (grey-green shirts), and in October they participated in the March on Rome.[111] The ANC federation of Bologna, where veterans like ex-*alpino* Angelo Manaresi[112] and nationalist Umberto Guglielmotti[113] were influential, also participated in the operation with a group of men.[114] For their part, the *arditi* of the Federazione Nazionale Arditi d'Italia – created by Mario Carli that month to gather the fascist *arditi* – declared their interest in finding agreement with the PNF to further their collaboration prior to the March on Rome.[115] Similarly, the ANC section of Naples decided to join the fascist action, even if the fascist leaders would not need their help in the end.[116] In total, they were a few small veterans' groups, but their important symbolic presence cannot be overlooked. The inaction of the army in the face of the fascist challenge was partially due to the perception that veterans were a substantial part of the fascist movement.

Meanwhile, the official *apoliticità* of the ANC made the members of the association bystanders in the conquest of power of October of 1922.

---

[110] *Il Popolo d'Italia*, 27 October 1922.

[111] Associazione Nazionale Combattenti, Federazione Provinciale di Firenze, *Relazione Morale e Finanziaria. Ottobre XIV*, Florence [1935], pp. 37–9.

[112] Manaresi, born in Bologna in 1890, was a lawyer and ex-officer. He was present at the violent events of Palazzo d'Accursio in November 1920. In 1921, he was elected MP as a representative of war veterans.

[113] Guglielmotti, born in Perugia in 1892, was a journalist in *L'Idea Nazionale*. A war volunteer, he attained the rank of captain, was wounded and decorated. After the war, he joined the ANI, in which he held leading positions.

[114] Note of the *prefetto* of Bologna (1 January 1923), ACS, MI, PS (1923), box 75, file 'Associazioni excombattenti, sf. Bologna'.

[115] *Il Popolo d'Italia*, 25 October 1922; reports from the *prefetto* of Bologna (14 and 16 October 1922), ACS, MI, PS (1922), box 96, file 'Arditi d'Italia Bologna'.

[116] Report 'Al Direttorio del Fascio Napoletano di Combattimento', ACS, Mostra della Rivoluzione Fascista, box 106.

The guarantors of *apoliticità* within the ANC boards exhorted the rest of the veterans to remain silently outside the struggle, invoking the veterans' loyalty to King Vittorio Emanuele III.[117] We have seen that despite the official neutrality of both the ANC and the ANMIG, a certain rapprochement and collusion between important groups of veterans and the fascists had already started before the March on Rome.[118] What historically was far more decisive, however, was that in the symbolic realm, the veterans had become an imaginary subject that was not clearly differentiated from the fascist phenomenon.

Veterans and the Transnational Impact of the March on Rome

The emblematic images of the fascist regime's founding myth, the March on Rome, are of tough men dressed in a militaristic manner, wearing the black shirts of the squadrists, their chests ostentatiously covered with medals, martially parading along the streets of Rome and other Italian cities. The four men who led the March on Rome (Michele Bianchi, Emilio De Bono, Cesare Maria De Vecchi and Italo Balbo), clearing the way for Mussolini, could be perceived as victorious war veterans imposing their will to rescue the country from the hands of decadent liberal politicians and from the revolutionary communist threat. Photographs and illustrations of this kind slowly flowed into the European information networks after the fascist seizure of power[119] (Figure 2.1).

In fact, the fascists self-represented themselves in their proclamations as 'mostly the combatants of the Carso and the Piave who wanted to liberate Italy'.[120] When the seizure of power was celebrated in several Italian cities, war veterans joined the fascist parades.[121] Observing the paramilitary processions of the fascists and their 'patriotic chants', people recalled the 'glorious ranks of our valorous combatants'.[122] The fascists claimed to have achieved victory on behalf of the fallen soldiers (*caduti*).

---

[117] *La Nuova Giornata*, 1 November 1922.

[118] This fact introduces nuances to the conclusion of Sabbatucci (*I combattenti*, p. 360) that the March on Rome surprised the veterans' organizations by being 'absent and substantially passive'.

[119] See, for instance, *Zeitbilder: Beilage zur Vossischen Zeitung* (Berlin), 44 (5 November 1922), where significantly the squadrists groups are referred to as the 'fascist Freikorps' (*Fascisten-Freikorps*). In France, see *L'Illustration* (Paris), 4 November 1922.

[120] Document from the Fascio of Cervignano (28 October 1922), ACS, MRF, box 146.

[121] ACS, MI, PS (1922), box 106, file 'Aquila, Chieti'.

[122] Note of the *prefetto* of Cosenza (1 November 1922), ACS, MI, PS (1922), box 106, file 'Consenza'. See also François Charles-Roux, *Souvenirs diplomatiques: Une Grande Ambassade à Rome, 1919–1925*, Paris, 1961, pp. 194–5.

Figure 2.1 The Fascist Coup in Italy, *Wiener Bilder*.
(*Illustriertes Familienblatt*, Vienna, 5 November 1922, Österreichische
Nationalbibliothek.)

An illustration in *Il Popolo d'Italia* showed the squadrists raising their
arms in Roman salute to the resurrected corpses of the trenches, who are
responding with a military salute (Figure 2.2).

In reality, the March on Rome had not strictly taken place: the
fascist seizure of power was due to Mussolini's double strategy of
violence and political intrigue, and the entry of the fascists in Rome

Figure 2.2 Comrades, *Il Popolo d'Italia*, 7 November 1922.
(Image courtesy of Ministero dei beni e delle attività culturali e del turismo/
Biblioteca Nazionale Centrale di Firenze.)

was a violent dramatization to convince the public that the blackshirts had conquered power through their march on the capital.[123] Besides, the manly icon of the *quadrumviri* represented squadrism, not the veteran movement. On 30 October, the king appointed Mussolini to be the new Prime Minister (Presidente del Consiglio). Mussolini broadly presented himself as representative of the Italy of Vittorio Veneto rather than as the voice of the war veterans. In the government he formed together with other political parties, two-thirds of the members were military personnel or veterans. Half the undersecretaries of state, nine in total, were fascists. But there were only three fascist ministers, plus Mussolini, who took control of both Interior and Foreign Affairs Ministries. In any case, the war and the victory were the shared legitimizing symbols of the coalition.[124]

Despite the symbolic role of war veterans in the rise of Italian Fascism, practically none of the main contemporary commentators interpreted the March on Rome as solely a 'revolution' or coup d'état of the Italian

[123] Woller, *Rom, 28. Oktober 1922*, pp. 7–19.
[124] *L'Idea Nazionale*, 31 October 1922.

veterans. Indeed, some ANC leaders were sceptical about the fascist 'revolution'; they did not consider the triumph of Fascism to be a product of the veterans' will. They intelligently realized that – as historians nowadays confirm – Fascism was able to succeed because of the opposition's errors, because of the Italian liberal state's weaknesses and because Fascism had enjoyed the benevolence and support of the Italian armed forces.[125] At that time, inquisitive observers such as Antonio Gramsci identified in the original Fasci the same 'petty bourgeois character of the veterans' associations'. During the Fourth Congress of the Communist International, held shortly after the March on Rome, the Italian representative Bordiga explained that 'Fascism assembled all the discharged soldiers who could not find their place in society after the War and put their military experience to work.'[126] Yet, the internal debate about Fascism among the Italian and international left was focused on the class struggle and around the interpretation of Fascism as the 'white guard' (*guardia bianca*) of capitalism instead. Other analysts recognized the role in the fascist movement of the war-experienced petty bourgeoisie, but this factor was just part of a broader and much more complex phenomenon.[127] German socialist journalist Oda Oldberg put it clearly: without the war, Fascism would have been unthinkable, but this relationship was not in the sense the fascists intended: 'Many of today's fascist leaders' had not fought in the trenches; 'the ratio of combatants and shirkers in Fascism should coincide on the whole with the overall national average.'[128] For the Italian people, and for some intelligent external observers, the veterans' participation in squadrism and in the March on Rome did not constitute the explanatory key of the phenomenon but only a constituent element of its wider origins. Yet, from outside Italy, commentators often highlighted the veteran presence at the core of the movement when they explained Fascism to a non-Italian public.

The symbol of the victorious war veteran was a powerful means to spread the idea of Fascism in Europe, but the multiple perceptions of this myth were conditioned and modelled by those to whom it was communicated. As we will see, the impact of the March on Rome was deeply felt by the public and political forces in France, Germany and Spain. In these

---

[125] For example, Rodolfo Savelli, 'La rivoluzione fascista', *I Combattenti* (Genova), 15 September 1922, and *Il Combattente* (Bologna), 1 October 1922.
[126] John Riddel (ed.), *Toward the United Front: Proceedings of the Fourth Congress of the Communist International, 1922* (trans. by John Riddell), London, 2012, p. 408.
[127] Luigi Salvatorelli, *Nazionalfascismo*, Turin, 1923; Hanns-Erich Kaminski, *Fascismus in Italien*, Berlin, 1925.
[128] Oda Olberg, *Der Fascismus in Italien*, Jena, 1923, p. 11.

and other countries, awareness of the veterans' role in Fascism manifested at different levels and in different ways, shaped by the prism of the various domestic situations, thus contributing to different political consequences over the course of 1923. We already saw how, very soon, external observers characterized fascism as a veteran phenomenon and as a reaction against the left. Thus, in Belgium, for example, the March on Rome was seen positively by all Belgian political groups except the socialists, because it had been carried out by a 'party created by the veterans of the common war in order to annihilate the Bolshevik efforts dangerous for the whole Europe', as the Italian diplomatic representative transmitted to Rome.[129] These perceptions were relevant even in Portugal, where eminent personalities immediately visited the Italian ambassador to consult with him on the possibilities of creating a Portuguese fascist party.[130] I will discuss how these discourses and symbols circulated through France, Spain and Germany.

France

In France, the public generally believed that the Italian veterans were the precursors of the fascist movement. This opinion was consolidated when Fascism obtained its violent victories against the left, which provoked reflections about whether fascism was also possible in France. The conservative French press appreciated Fascism basically as a reasonable reaction against leftist excesses.[131] In *L'Action Française*, Léon Daudet wrote that in Italy there was a wide middle class 'comprising numerous war veterans' who resisted the socialist threat; it was said that the same social dynamic could be found in France.[132] In fact, after the March on Rome, Action Française member Georges Valois started to contact economic lobbies that were searching for a French Mussolini.[133] For his part, the French ex-socialist Gustave Hervé – who since 1914 had gone through an ideological and political evolution parallel to that of Mussolini[134] – also considered that the fascists were Italian war veterans

---

[129] Ministero degli Affari Esteri, *I documenti diplomatici italiani* [hereafter DDI], Settima serie, 1922–1935, Vol. I (31 October 1922–26 April 1923), Rome, 1953, p. 13.

[130] Ibid., p. 15.

[131] Pierre Milza, *L'Italie fasciste devant l'opinion française 1920–1940*, Paris, Armand Colin, 1967.

[132] Léon Daudet, 'La leçon du Fascisme', *L'Action Française*, 14 August 1922.

[133] AN, Police Générale, Relations Internationales, F/7 13454, Italie 1921–22, 'CGT: Les fascistes' (Paris, 25 November 1922).

[134] Michael B. Loughlin, 'Gustave Hervé's Transition from Socialism to National Socialism: Another Example of French Fascism?', *Journal of Contemporary History*, 36, 1 (2001), pp. 5–39.

organized against the left. According to Hervé, in the elections of 1921, the fascists contributed to the victory of the Italian national bloc, the 'brother' of the French *Bloc national*.[135] During the March on Rome days, Hervé again praised the nation-saving fascists: 'They were militarily organized with a strong discipline … Between the workers – who remained during the war in the factories, completely castrated by the bleating pacifism of defeatists – and the legions of veterans who had stood during four years in the infernal trenches, the street battle did not last long.'[136] Hervé stated that the lesson of Fascism should not only be taken by the weakly governed Germans but also by the French government, which had to strengthen its internal politics.[137] The perception that the Italian veterans were involved in Fascism inspired sympathy among different rightist sectors in France. This awareness made the French right believe that a similar movement was possible in France as well.

By 1922, the powerful and diverse French veterans' movement could not ignore the ostensible involvement of Italian veterans in the fall of democracy. When the dust of the March on Rome had settled, serene commentators in the French veterans' press still affirmed that Fascism had been 'originally, the veterans' armed protests against the antinational forces that wanted to "sabotage the peace"'.[138] This view was also sustained by the accounts of writers such as Paul Hazard, a traveller who had gone to Italy in 1921 and 1922. Hazard had seen the rise of Fascism first hand. His depictions of the Italian fascists included reflections on the particular fascist psychology and style.[139] According to him, the fascists were 'young people full of vehemence or war veterans', whereas the 'extremists' – meaning the leftists – were recruited among the 'bad soldiers, deserters and cowards'. For this author, the March on Rome was a positive and youthful achievement and a characteristically Italian phenomenon.[140] Would the French veterans and extreme-right groups feel pushed to follow this Italian model?

The attitude of the large numbers of French veterans and their vigorous associations remained unchanged. Despite the sympathy of many veterans, the main organizations, the UNC and the UF, kept their distance and preferred to point out that Fascism was a purely Italian product, which would not resonate in the French environment. They thought that Fascism was not something to 'export' or 'import'. The

---

[135] *La Victoire* (Paris), 18 May 1921.   [136] *La Victoire*, 28 October 1922.
[137] *La Victoire*, 30 October and 1 November 1922.
[138] *La France Mutilée* (Paris), 17 June 1923.
[139] Paul Hazard, 'Psychologie du fasciste', *L'Illustration*, 11 Novembre 1922.
[140] Paul Hazard, *L'Italie vivante*, Paris, 1923, pp. vi, 28, 47, 243–81.

main reason for this detachment was to avoid frightening the authorities, as French veterans were protesting to get material improvements. Furthermore, the French veterans were initially suspicious of Fascism because they were striving to uphold international peace and the status quo of Versailles. This concern dominated the FIDAC congress of November 1922.[141] In this situation, Mussolini soon appeared as a potentially destabilizing revisionist weight in the international relations system. Following the March on Rome, the resignation of the Italian ambassador in France, Carlo Sforza, hated by the fascists, was controversial. The Italian fascists were a very different and aggressive force in the international sphere. In November of 1922, the opening of the Conference of Lausanne made the allied statesmen believe that Mussolini could be a gentleman, but in the summer of 1923, the Italian occupation of Corfu revealed the real fascist impulses. From October of 1922 onwards, Mussolini tried to achieve his imperial goals, though he did not follow the most direct path to achieving his dreams of empire.[142]

Hence, at the beginning, Fascism was a controversial label from which the French veterans needed to dissociate. Paul Vaillant, administrator of the UF, clearly stated, 'We shall not wear the black shirt.'[143] Subsequently, over the course of the first year of the fascist dictatorship, the French veterans' movement became accustomed to referring to Fascism as a point of reference in the political debate. For instance, Henri Pichot employed it in a negative way to criticize the veterans' inclination towards political action. Nevertheless, on other occasions, fascism was wielded as a veiled menace to exert pressure on the French authorities.[144] As the Italian example proved, discontented veterans could be the harbingers of a dictatorship, but the French veterans did not expect this outcome.

The extreme right, Action Française, did not change its old approach to veterans either. The theme of the veterans' right to a 'share of the victory' (*la part du combattant*) – allegedly unrecognized by the Republic – continued unchanged.[145] Veterans' representations were not transformed.[146] In Action Française meetings, when Georges Valois addressed the bourgeois students, he mentioned that the veterans should

---

[141] *La Voix du Combattant* (Paris), 5 and 19 November 1922; *La France Mutilée*, 7 January and 17 June 1923.

[142] H. James Burgwyn, *Italian Foreign Policy in the Interwar Period 1918–1940*, Westport, Praeger, 1997.

[143] *La France Mutilée*, 7 January 1923.

[144] *La France Mutilée*, 1 July and 29 December 1923.

[145] Charles Maurras, 'La part du combatant: Hier et aujourd'hui', *Action Française* (Paris), 4 November 1922.

[146] See *L'étudiant français* (Paris), November 1922.

impose their spirit of victory onto the state, but he did not employ any powerful mobilizing discourse.[147] The fascist model for the veterans' political mobilization against the internal enemy – the left – was not being adopted in France yet. For many, some actions of the Camelots du Roi (the paramilitary branch of Action Française) in 1923 mirrored fascist violent techniques,[148] but, as was noted in a confidential report to the French Ministry of Foreign Affairs, 'violence had been always the line of conduct of the Camelots du Roi', and the political agenda of Action Française remained very different from that of the PNF.[149]

Spain

If in France the myth of the fascist veterans did not provoke any consistent reaction mimicking the Italian model over the course of 1923, in Spain, any threat to the liberal order lacked a mass base of veterans to mobilize. Yet, the March on Rome did play a catalyzing role in Spanish politics.[150] When Fascism took power in Italy, Spain had not yet overcome the post-war crisis. Violent confrontations between anarchists or syndicalists and 'civic guards' such as the Somatén or Acción Ciudadana persisted during 1922. In this context, the news of the rise of Fascism was interpreted through the lens of the Spanish conflicts. For the Spanish left, the 'Italian fascists were nothing more than the *somatenistas* or civic guards from that country.'[151] It is not by chance that at the end of 1922 the first rumours about a military coup started circulating in Madrid, and in Barcelona, politics by the pistol (*pistolerismo*) resumed as a symptom of the crisis that lasted throughout 1923.[152]

In this period, the Spanish press captured the connection between the veterans' agitation and the rise of Fascism. A concerned Spanish observer witnessed and reported on the assaults to institutional headquarters by the fascist veterans in Rome in a Spanish newspaper.[153] At the same time,

---

[147] *Action Française*, 30 November 1922.
[148] Joel Blatt, 'Relatives and Rivals: The Responses of the Action Française to Italian Fascism, 1919–1926', *European Studies Review*, 11 (1981), pp. 263–92.
[149] Report 'Le Fascisme à Paris' (31 August 1923), MAE-AD, Europe 1918–29, Italie, 214, 'Propagande italienne en France, I', sheets 31–4.
[150] Francisco J. Romero Salvadó and Angel Smith (ed.), *The Agony of Spanish Liberalism: From Revolution to Dictatorship, 1913–23*, New York, Palgrave, 2010; Manuelle Peloille, *Fascismo en ciernes: España 1922–1930, textos recuperados*, Tolouse, Presses Universitaires du Mirail, 2005, pp. 37–46.
[151] *La Acción* (Tarrasa), 3 November 1922.
[152] Cf. González Calleja, *El máuser y el sufragio*, pp. 216–40, 260.
[153] Andrenio, 'Los ex combatientes', *La Vanguardia* (Barcelona), 6 September 1922.

there were correspondents in Italy transmitting a very positive image of the fascist movement to the Spanish newspapers. Journalist Rafael Sánchez Mazas, writing for the conservative and monarchist paper *ABC*, was enthusiastic about the fascists; he vividly depicted the fascist acts of aggression and parades as festivals and described the fascists as disciplined anti-communist men, 'virile, funny and generous'. During the March on Rome, Sánchez Mazas wrote about the Italians as cheering a cohort of '100,000' fascist volunteers, along with 'war disabled veterans and athletes' who were 'recreating the blood fraternity of the dark days of the trenches'.[154] Although the relevance given to the veterans' responsibility in the fascist movement was smaller than in France, the Spanish press did not overlook this reality. In fact, the impression that Fascism was mainly a veterans' movement would become commonplace among Spaniards. Some years later, a regional republican paper continued to explain the 'incredible fascist rise' by saying that 'the capitalist strongboxes had been opened to arm thousands of unemployed veterans who – just by the fact of having taken part in the war – believed they were supermen.'[155]

In Spain, as in Italy, the relationship between the military and the liberal state experienced a period of crisis. The Spanish army remained profoundly divided between *junteros* and *africanistas*. In 1921, to recover from the military setback of Annual, the army had created an elite corps, the Legión; its promoters were the Africanist officers José Millán Astray and Francisco Franco.[156] The Legión was based on the French Foreign Legion model. Its members largely mirrored the Italian *arditi*, often ex-convicts or adventurers. And the young Franco, who possessed 'heroic' combat decorations, became an idol for the colonialist and rightist political sectors.[157] The Legión became a patriotic reference for nationalist groups who were antagonistic towards the peninsula-based military officers (*junteros*). In November–December of 1922, General Picasso's report on the responsibility for the disaster of Annual raised bitter discontent among the *africanistas*. At that time, the extreme right backed Millán Astray and portrayed him as the Spanish Mussolini. In November of 1922, whilst Millán Astray's legionnaires paraded in the metropole, he lobbied the government to

---

[154] Rafael Sánchez Mazas: 'ABC en Italia: La victoria fascista y la marcha sobre Roma', *ABC* (Madrid), 15 November 1922. See also *id.*, 'ABC en Roma: La revolución a paso gentil', *ABC*, 28 October 1922.
[155] *La Acción*, 9 September 1927.
[156] José Luis Rodríguez Jiménez, *¡A mi la Legión! De Millán Astray a las misiones de paz*, Barcelona, Planeta, 2005, pp. 81–140.
[157] Laura Zenobi, *La construcción del mito de Franco: De jefe de la Legión a Caudillo de España*, Madrid, Cátedra, 2011, pp. 21–58.

resolve the military crisis in favour of the *africanistas*. He was able to gather support among students, and after a series of riots, the government agreed to dissolve the Juntas.[158] The tough legionnaires were not war veterans, and Spanish soldiers returning from Morocco played no role in these developments; but the political use of the soldiers mirrored the Italian case. Philosopher Miguel de Unamuno affirmed: '[T]he bare-chested men of Millán Astray are like the blackshirts of Mussolini.'[159]

Furthermore, the March on Rome provoked other anti-liberal reactions in Spain. At the end of 1922 and in 1923, the first attempts to create a Spanish fascist movement inspired the foundation of the obscure group La Traza and the one-single-issue magazine *La Camisa Negra*. These short-lived organizations were promoted by army officers and supported by employers, but they only recruited a small number of petty bourgeois students. Some evidence suggests the direct involvement of Italians in these political manoeuvres: in December of 1922, a fascist military officer gave a conference in the House of Italians based in Barcelona, for an audience composed of many Spanish sympathizers.[160] Yet, the fascist leadership did not promote this type of dissemination. They said that Fascism was not transplantable. The rumours that Mussolini would visit Madrid were not confirmed.[161] The Spanish fascist cells would soon disappear.

In any case, social unrest preceded the final collapse of the Spanish liberal state. In mid-1923, liberal politicians planned to foster a decisive reform, diminishing Spanish military involvement in the Moroccan Protectorate. General Miguel Primo de Rivera's coup d'état on 13 September 1923 put an end to these detrimental changes for the Spanish *africanistas* military.[162] As in Italy, dictatorship was imposed with the connivance of the king. A few weeks later, in November of 1923, the king and the new dictator paid a visit to Fascist Italy; by then, many

---

[158] José Luis Rodríguez Jiménez, 'Una unidad militar en los orígenes del fascismo en España: la Legión', *Pasado y Memoria: Revista de Historia Contemporánea*, 5 (2006), pp. 219–40.

[159] Miguel de Unamuno, 'El fajismo en el reino de España', *El Socialista* (Madrid), 28 November 1922. 'Bare-chested men' (*despechugados*) was a sarcastic description of the Legion's soldiers, whose exacerbated manliness reflected the violent ethos of these troops. See John H. Galey, 'Bridegrooms of Death: A Profile Study of the Spanish Foreign Legion', *Journal of Contemporary History*, 4, 2 (1969), pp. 47–64.

[160] *El Debate* (Madrid), 6 December 1922.

[161] *Corriere della Sera*, 28 December 1922; Ernesto Marchiandi, 'Spagna e Fascismo', *Il Popolo d'Italia*, 4 January 1923.

[162] Pablo La Porte, 'The Moroccan Quagmire and the Crisis of Spain's Liberal System, 1917–23', in Romero Salvadó and Smith (eds.), *The Agony of Spanish Liberalism*, pp. 230–54.

considered the Spanish regime as a reflection of the Italian example.[163] Dictator Primo de Rivera initially seemed interested in getting support from La Traza, but the more conventional Somatén, and later a party created from above – the Unión Patriótica – would finally represent the much more conservative Spanish version of the blackshirts and the PNF during the 1920s.[164]

All these events, according to historians, demonstrate that a 'real' fascism was unable to take root in Spain, though conditions for the imposition of an authoritarian nationalist regime existed.[165] The predominance of Catholicism, the receding revolutionary menace, the influence of conservative militarism and, indeed, the absence of a strong veterans' movement have been suggested as the main causes of the failure of the first wave of Spanish fascism.[166] Moreover, it should also be mentioned that the arrival of the intellectual and cultural trends that fermented in all Western European countries before 1914 had not been galvanized in Spain by the cathartic 'total' war experience. The Spanish literary elites did not undergo the initiation to politics that intellectuals in other countries had gone through because of their involvement in the First World War. The artistic vanguards came to Spain belatedly and devoid of the political inclinations of the Italian *futuristi* and *arditi*.[167] But the question of the veterans needs further analysis.

In the arid cultural ground of Spain, there were writers and intellectuals who had gone through an experience of war in Morocco. Some of them developed a set of discourses that represented in Spain the protofascist veterans' worldview by 1922–4. This was the case for writers Luys Santa Marina and Ernesto Giménez Caballero, who would be promoters of the Spanish fascist party Falange Española during the 1930s. Poet Luys Santa Marina published *Tras el águila del César*, a book whose violent aesthetics served the purpose of singing the praise of the troops of the Legion and reminds one of the prose of the *ardito* Mario Carli.[168] It was his experience as a soldier in Morocco that

---

[163] Giulia Albanese, 'Alla scuola del fascismo: la Spagna dei primi anni venti e la marcia su Roma', in Mario Isnenghi (ed.), *Pensare la nazione: Silvio Lanaro e l'Italia contemporanea*, Rome, Donzelli, 2012, pp. 111–22.

[164] González Calleja and Rey, *La defensa armada*, pp. 169–77.

[165] Alejandro Quiroga, *Making Spaniards: Primo de Rivera and the Nationalization of the Masses, 1923–30*, New York, Palgrave, 2007, p. 22.

[166] Romero Salvadó and Smith (eds.), *The Agony of Spanish Liberalism*, p. 19; Peloille, *Fascismo en ciernes*, p. 46; González Calleja and Rey, *La defensa armada*.

[167] Carlos Serrano and Serge Salaün (eds.), *Los felices años veinte: España, crisis y modernidad*, Madrid, Marcial Pons, 2006.

[168] Luys Santa Marina, *Tras el águila del César: elegía del tercio*, Duero, 1924; cf. Mario Carli, *Noi arditi*, Milan, 1919.

motivated Ernesto Giménez Caballero, a student born in 1899, to compose his first important literary work, *Notas marruecas de un soldado*. In the last pages of this account, written in Madrid during December of 1922, he offered a manifesto to other ex-soldiers. He could not have been unaware of the agitation of those days in the Spanish capital. Giménez Caballero rejected the possibility of a silent reintegration because he and his comrades had 'common tasks in the new civilian life'. He wrote that the veterans should influence national opinion about Morocco, and they should get rid of those responsible for the 'thousand errors and dirty tricks' they had seen in the protectorate.[169] As we see, writing in the wake of the March on Rome, Giménez Caballero launched a clear call to veterans to intervene in Spanish politics.

By the end of 1922, the image of Fascism in Spain was that of a nationalist anti-leftist and anti-democratic movement whose members were first and foremost war veterans, characteristics that endowed Fascism with a popular and revolutionary facet. However, the immediate imitative attempts to develop a Spanish fascist movement did not take root owing to the absence of a large enough group of veterans to form a mass membership or perhaps due to the impossibility of fully manipulating the symbol of the veteran. Primo de Rivera's regime was rather conservative and Catholic. The dictatorship did not permit the diffusion of the nationalist books by Giménez Caballero and Santa Marina due to their subversive potential.[170] Yet, the Italian and Spanish dictatorships shared many features. Fascism continued to influence Spain, and the symbol of the fascist war veterans would play a role in the future. Furthermore, as in Italy, the events taking place in Spain during 1923 also had an impact on Germany. It is not unimportant that the Nazis understood the imposition of the military dictatorship in Spain as a 'fascist solution of the Spanish crisis' just two months before their own attempted putsch took place.[171] The anti-democratic thrust after the March on Rome affected different European regions, and Bavaria was one of the most alarming cases.

---

[169] Ernesto Giménez Caballero, *Notas marruecas de un soldado*, Madrid, 1923, pp. 247–52. Sixty years later, in a new edition of this book (Barcelona, Planeta, 1983), Giménez Caballero wrote in the Preface that in 1923 he still did not know about the 'social nationalism' of the war veterans from different European countries.

[170] Dionisio Viscarri, *Nacionalismo autoritario y orientalismo: La narrativa prefascista de la guerra de Marruecos (1921–1927)*, Bolonia, Il Capitello del Sole, 2004.

[171] *Völkischer Beobachter*, 15 September 1923.

Germany

In Germany, the March on Rome exacerbated the already tense politics. As of January 1923, the increasing problem of hyperinflation, the French occupation of the Ruhr and the war reparations issue all became intertwined. Thus, the difficult conditions in the country worsened. As a reaction, there was a powerful revival of German nationalism. This situation represented a blow to the republican and pacifist groups, which had neither been able to consolidate an organizational network nor fully establish a pacifist discursive framework for the war remembrance.[172] As in other countries, the public had attentively observed the March on Rome, perceiving the potential turn in international relations that it implied.[173] The situation of the German population in South Tirol (Südtirol or Alto Adige) was especially worrying, for the fascists had shown their intentions to pursue Italianization.[174] Whereas the Weimar authorities distrusted Fascism, which was the new political actor, the German nationalists now praised the fascist achievement as potentially beneficial for themselves.[175] The fascist rise to power in October of 1922 also led to a reassessment of the anti-parliamentarian threat in Germany. This threat was conceptualized as a fascist phenomenon that had taken its first steps in 1919.[176]

It is very clear that the March on Rome became the admired model that the German extreme right wanted to imitate in order to overthrow the Weimar Republic.[177] This longing was captured by the Latin expression 'Italia docet' ('Italy teaches') employed by the radical conservative review *Gewissen*.[178] These anti-Semitic, *völkisch* nationalists wondered whether fascism was possible in Germany and considered its causes. As they stressed the fact that Italian young men had made a profound transformation of the Italian state's 'spirit' (*Staatgeist*) possible, they consequently appealed to young Germans to follow the same goal of a

---

[172] Ziemann, *Contested Commemorations*, pp. 36–9.
[173] See, for example, *Vossische Zeitung*, 28–30 October and 1 November 1922; *Münchner Neueste Nachrichten* (Munich), 28, 30 and 31 October and 3 November 1922.
[174] Alfons Gruber, *Südtirol unter dem Faschismus*, Bozen, Verlagsanstalt Athesia, 1974; *Akten zur Deutschen Auswärtigen Politik 1918–1945, Serie A: 1918–1925, 1 März bis 31 Dezember 1922*, Göttingen, Vandenhoeck & Ruprecht, 1988, pp. 428–31.
[175] DDI, *Settima serie*, Vol. I, p. 12.
[176] Paul Kampffmeyer, *Der Fascismus in Deutschland*, Berlin-Stuttgart, 1923.
[177] Wolfgang Schieder, 'Fatal Attraction: The German Right and Italian Fascism', in Hans Mommsen (ed.), *The Third Reich between Vision and Reality: New Perspectives on German History 1918–1945*, Oxford, Berg, 2002, pp. 39–57; Klaus-Peter Hoepke, *Die deutsche Rechte und der italienische Faschismus*, Dusseldorf, Droste Verlag, 1968.
[178] Claudia Kemper, *Das 'Gewissen' 1919–1925: Kommunikation und Vernetzung der Jungkonservativen*, Munich, Oldenbourg Verlag, 2011, pp. 389–91.

conservative reaction. This counter-revolution would reinforce the state, order and discipline.[179] It was the young people who were represented as the protagonists of Fascism rather than the veterans. Nevertheless, in Germany, the anti-republican stance was already hegemonic in the galaxy of veteran associations. The March on Rome surprised the members of Stahlhelm in a moment of disorganization due to the government's preventive ban after Rathenau's murder (June 1922), but by the end of January 1923 the association regained its freedom and continued its progression, establishing close contacts with the military circles that were preparing a coup.[180] Different anti-revolutionary combat leagues such as the Stahlhelm and Jungdeutscher Orden (Order of Young Germans) were rivals in their common fight against the communists. These multifaceted confrontations provided the backdrop for Hitler's putsch in November 1923.

Hitler was among those who saw in Fascism, and Mussolini an example to follow. Common features between both movements were clear. In April and May of 1922, the Nazis had organized special propaganda meetings for veterans, where Hitler decried the fact that returning soldiers had been dishonourably treated at the end of the war.[181] Although the Bavarian press had pointed to the similarities between the fascists and the Nazis, the Nazis preferred to stress their own anti-Semitism as a singularity, regretting that the fascists did not undertake the fight against the Jews.[182] Nonetheless, at the end of September 1922, Hitler sent an emissary to Milan, Kurt Ludecke, who made Mussolini aware of the NSDAP. According to Ludecke's memoirs,[183] in their conversation, the Duce appreciated the common anti-Marxism of both the fascists and the Nazis but was intransigent regarding the Alto Adige question and unconcerned about the Jewish 'problem'. Even so, once he had returned to Munich, Ludecke confirmed to Hitler the many commonalities existing between both movements and, in fact, mentioned that both Mussolini and Hitler were war veterans as a motive for an understanding between them.[184] Hitler was probably delighted.

---

[179] Viktor Wagner, 'Die Schule des Fascismus', *Gewissen*, 9 October 1922; 'Italia docet', *Gewissen*, 6 November 1922. Arthur Moeller Van den Bruck was the author of this text. At that time, Moeller Van den Bruck also invented the term 'Third Reich'; see Moeller Van den Bruck, *Das Recht der Jüngen Volker: Sammlung politische Aufsätze*, Berlin, 1932.
[180] Berghahn, *Der Stahlhelm*, pp. 39–53.   [181] *Völkischer Beobachter*, 3 and 18 May 1922.
[182] 'Fascismus und Nationalsozialismus', *Völkischer Beobachter*, 2 August 1922; see also 'Fascismus und Judenfrage', *Völkischer Beobachter*, 23 December 1922.
[183] Roland V. Layton, Jr., 'Kurt Ludecke and *I Knew Hitler*. An Evaluation', *Central European History*, 12, 4 (1979), pp. 372–86.
[184] Kurt Lüdecke, *I Knew Hitler*, London, 1938, p. 80.

After the March on Rome, the Nazi imitation of the fascist style became all too evident for increasingly anxious republicans in Munich.[185] Both the German and Bavarian left and some leading Nazis saw a 'Bavarian' Mussolini in Hitler. As the Nazis saw how the resolute fascists finally imposed their will, Hitler's speeches pointed to the exemplary Italian 'fascist fight'.[186] Hitler's notion of heroism developed at that point, and he started to highlight the example of the front-line soldiers to his SA men.[187] Furthermore, the Italians' alleged 'national rebirth' (*nationale Wiedergeburt*) pushed Hitler to reinforce his ideas for an agreement with Italy. He was even ready to abandon the Südtirol question in order to construct a relationship with Mussolini, even if this attitude raised criticism among his Austrian followers.[188]

Although the Nazis wanted to walk the same path as their successful Italian counterparts, their strategy and praxis were conditioned by a different context – that of Bavaria during 1923.[189] The symbol of the March on Rome, mixed with Hitler's obsessions and prejudices, shaped the developments leading to the Beer Hall putsch. For many rightist circles in Europe, the March on Rome made clear that officers mobilizing anti-Bolshevik youth could build an imitation of the Italian fascist reaction.[190] Accordingly, old German officers offered themselves as instructors for the Nazi assault troops. Yet, Hitler preferred 'instinctive young men, who possess recklessness and idealism'. For Hitler, Mussolini's example simply meant 'willingness for action', since fighting was necessary to reach victory.[191] Despite this insistence on mobilizing youth and the differentiation from the army, the adoption of uniforms and symbols for SA members, who publicly paraded in Munich at the end of January 1923 during the Day of the NSDAP (*Parteitag*), clearly emulated the fascist style.[192]

Whilst the Nazi movement grew in this fashion, external observers identified it as a part of a German fascist movement composed of war

---

185 *Vorwärts*, 11 (MA) and 18 (Abends-Ausgabe) November 1922; *Münchener Post*, 20 November and 11 and 16 December 1922; Werner Maser, *Frühgeschichte der NSDAP: Hitlers Weg bis 1924*, Frankfurt am Main, Athenaeum Verlag, 1965, p. 356.
186 Hitler, *Sämtliche Aufzeichnungen*, pp. 712–13; 'Männer und Waschweiber', *Völkischer Beobachter*, 1 November 1922.
187 Sabine Behrenbeck, *Der Kult um die toten Helden: Nationalsozialistische Mythen, Riten und Symbole 1923 bis 1945*, Vierow bei Greisfald, SH Verlag, 1996, pp. 81–95.
188 Hitler, *Sämtliche Aufzeichnungen*, p. 728; DDI, *Settima serie*, Vol. I, p. 12.
189 Harold J. Gordon, Jr., *Hitlerputsch 1923: Machtkampf in Bayern 1923–1924*, Munich, Bernard & Graefe Verlag, 1978.
190 For example, in Sweden, 3 November 1922, army officers published a call to the young to follow the fascist example; see DDI, *Settima serie*, Vol. I, p. 22.
191 Hitler, *Sämtliche Aufzeichnungen*, p. 729; cf. Lüdecke, *I Knew Hitler*, pp. 102–4.
192 Maser, *Frühgeschichte*, pp. 326–7.

veterans and people who adopted their image. This perception was predominant in Spain, where newspapers of every hue noted the uneasiness produced by the nationalistic groups in Bavaria parading with their 'Prussian helmets' and 'wearing the uniform of the German trench soldier'; the political manoeuvres of Hitler and Ludendorff were labelled as the 'fascist plot in Germany'.[193] Certainly, like the fascist movement of 1921 and 1922, the protagonists of the Bavarian unrest were mostly young men, many of them veterans, trained and armed by military officers. In Spain, it was explained that Hitler's party was composed of veterans (*excombatientes*), employees and students.[194] In Italy, it was known and particularly reiterated that anti-Semitism was the main characteristic of the NSDAP.[195] Yet, the Italian left understood this phenomenon as fascism: as in Italy, German fascism recruited – apart from a few idealists – many opportunists, 'injudicious youngsters' and 'war detritus'.[196] Again, the stereotype of the fascist veteran, which now also included association with the Nazi movement, circulated.

In contrast, French veterans did not fully take the symbolic presence of veterans in the German reaction into consideration. Focused instead on the question of reparations, the veterans of the UF longed for peace and rejected any imperialistic inclination; but at the same time they required that the peace be built on France's right to compensation.[197] These French veterans avoided expressing support for or rejection of the occupation of the Ruhr. Their first timid contacts with German veterans completely stopped with the crisis.[198] They seemed unaware of the nationalist agitation that spurred on their German counterparts. When Hitler held his putsch, veterans of both the UNC and UF were absorbed by the 11 November celebrations of the French victory and paid little attention to the events in Germany.

At the beginning, this coup d'état was conceived as a March on Berlin. For this reason, by November of 1923, the Italian public was expecting an event similar to the March on Rome.[199] In actual fact, such action did not take place: the military organizers understood that there had been insufficient preparation in northern Germany and that the army's

---

[193] *ABC* (Madrid), 30 January and 26 March 1923.   [194] *ABC*, 4 October 1923.
[195] *La Stampa*, 19 February 1923.   [196] *Avanti!*, 5 July 1923.
[197] *La France Mutilée*, 8 April 1923; cf. *Corriere della Sera*, 4 April 1923.
[198] Christian Weiß, '"Soldaten des Friedens": Die pazifistischen Veteranen und Kriegsopfer des "Reichsbundes" und ihre Kontakte zu den französischen anciens combattatns 1919–1933', in Wolfgang Hardtwig (ed.), *Politische Kulturgeschichte der Zwischenkriegszeit 1918–1939*, Göttingen, Vandenhoeck & Ruprecht, 2005, pp. 183–204.
[199] *Avanti!*, 1 November 1923; *Corriere della Sera*, 3 November 1923.

cooperation was uncertain. Despite this hesitation, the pressure of Hitler's fanatic followers, the SA brown shirts, precipitated a move in Munich.[200] A Nazi leader guaranteed to the *Corriere della Sera* that they would be successful.[201] But the putsch failed, and the press across Europe did not hold back in its depiction of this shameful adventure as a tragicomedy. This abortive imitation also embarrassed the Italian fascists, who consequently abhorred the disastrous Nazi venture.[202] The fascists distanced themselves from the Nazis, stressing the important differences between them. They said that Fascism was an essentially Italian phenomenon, and likewise, the Spanish example of the Primo de Rivera dictatorship was another proof of this differentiation.[203] However, it is difficult to deny that the fascist movement had liberated forces that did not respect national boundaries. Even if the November 1923 German attempt to overthrow a democratic regime in the fascist manner ended in deadlock, the idea of a March on Berlin would remain present among the Nazis and anti-republican groupings such as the veterans' Stahlhelm as a notion that synthesized their fight for power until 1933.[204]

---

[200] Diehl, *Paramilitary Politics*, pp. 149–50.   [201] *Corriere della Sera*, 8 November 1923.
[202] Renzo De Felice, *Mussolini e Hitler: I rapporti segreti (1922–1933)* (2nd edn.), Florence, Felice Le Monnier, 1983, p. 23.
[203] Silvio Delich, 'Italia e Spagna', and W. Cesarini Sforza, 'Socialnazionalismo', both in *Critica fascista* (Rome), 15 November 1923.
[204] *Der Marsch auf Berlin*, Berlin, 1932.

Part II

Fascism and Veterans during the 1920s

3   Veterans under Fascist Rule, 1923–1925

In previous chapters the stereotypical construction of the fascist veteran and the myth-making process surrounding the veterans' March on Rome were explained. It is now necessary to assess the ways and extent to which Italian veterans were truly transformed into fascists. A detailed analysis of the relationship between veterans and Fascism is needed in order to understand the deep cleavage between reality in Fascist Italy and the mythologizing discourses that circulated in Europe at that time. This chapter analyzes the phenomenon already referred to at the time as the 'fascistization' *(fascistizzazione)* of war veterans that took place in Italy roughly between 1923 and 1925. This term referred to the process by which Fascism progressively infiltrated, co-opted and assimilated various social groups and institutions, which willingly or forcibly adopted, or acquiesced to, ideological and organizational fascist principles and commodities.[1]

Fascism's impregnation and co-optation of Italian veteran politics must be understood in the historical context of 1923–5. In Italy, things did not change suddenly after the fascist takeover of October 1922. Although the legal political order had been broken, this shift was, above all, a compromise between Fascism, the king, liberals and conservatives to form a coalition government. The construction of the dictatorship was slow paced, and the transformations that affected Italian war veterans evolved progressively from late 1922 to early 1925.[2] This was a period of many paradoxes, full of contradictory situations, internal tensions and struggles. The eventual outcome – the establishment of a fully fledged dictatorship that displayed totalitarian traits and that would lead again to war – was not determined from the beginning, although forces that pushed steadily towards political radicalization did exist.

---

[1] Cf. Kallis, '"Fascism", "Para-fascism" and "Fascistization"'.
[2] Adrian Lyttelton, *The Seizure of Power: Fascism in Italy 1919–1929*, Princeton, NJ, Princeton University Press, 1987 (1st edn. 1973); Salvatore Lupo, *Il fascismo*, pp. 115–80.

In the first year of Mussolini's government, two main impulses sought to shape the agenda: the projected 'normalization' of the fascist movement struggled against pressure from radical fascist sectors that wanted the implantation of a full fascist state. Farinacci was the most important representative of the radical fascists. While the Chamber functioned precariously with the Sword of Damocles hanging over it, the squadrists continued exerting violence in several provinces. In December of 1922, the bloody events in Turin (*fatti di Torino*) demonstrated that it would be very complicated to appease Fascism. Unrestrained violence could endanger the order-restoring ambitions of the recently formed fascist government. In response, Mussolini and his close collaborators created the Milizia Volontaria per la Sicurezza Nazionale (MVSN) in January of 1923. This kind of partisan army inside the state was an attempt to bring squadrism under control, overcoming the resistance of intransigent provincial leaders.[3] Thus, many Italian veterans who had been squadrists now became MVSN members. Seventy percent of MVSN officers were between twenty-four and thirty-eight years of age, came predominantly from central northern Italy and had experienced the war as junior officers or NCOs.[4] This institutionalization of squadrism can be understood as a demobilization of veteran groups but did not imply their disarmament: the tasks assigned to the MVSN (i.e. the persecution and surveillance of the internal enemy) precluded the demobilization of the practices and discourses of violence rooted in the war experience.

Another step in the 'normalization' of Fascism was the creation of the Gran Consiglio del Fascismo (Great Council of Fascism) as the new supreme organ of Fascism at the end of 1922. Amongst its first members were the four *quadrumviri* of the March on Rome – Balbo, Bianchi, De Vecchi and De Bono – and men such as Giacomo Acerbo, Achille Starace, Nicola Sansanelli[5] and Piero Bolzon, all of whom were fascist veterans. This decision-making institution remained one of Mussolini's instruments of power, though its influence over the regional fascisms was reduced. In order to extinguish both the opposition and resistance of dissident fascists, Mussolini relied on new *prefetti*, who represented the state in the provinces.

---

[3] Matteo Millan, *Squadrismo e squadristi nella dittatura fascista*, Rome, Viella, 2014.
[4] Camilla Poesio, *Reprimere le idee: Abusare del potere. La Milizia e l'instaurazione del regime fascista*, Rome, Quaderni della Fondazione Luigi Salvatorelli, 2010, p. 21.
[5] Nicola Sansanelli would go on to become a key figure in fascist veteran politics. Born in Sant'Arcangelo (Potenza) in 1891, he fought in the Lybian War and in the Great War. A lawyer and journalist, he was active in the early fascist movement in Naples, commanding groups of blackshirts during the March on Rome.

The political left, persecuted by both the fascists and the state authorities, was not the only victim of this situation. Catholics would soon meet
a similar fate. The process of absorption of the Italian Nationalist Association by the PNF, especially relevant in the south, was not free of
violence until its conclusion in February of 1923. However, voluntarily
fusing with the powerful PNF yielded many advantages for nationalist
politicians. 'Normalization' was desired by political sectors that were
ready to collaborate with Mussolini's government in the restoration of
social order. These groups were called *fiancheggiatori* ('supporters'), and
they intended to collude with Fascism without losing their own political
identity or autonomy. Having absorbed these elements, the PNF saw its
ranks swollen with new members.

Meanwhile, towards the summer and autumn of 1923, 'revisionism'
emerged as a new ideological fascist current, represented by Giuseppe
Bottai and the magazine *Critica fascista*. The revisionists tried to develop
a new fascist doctrine, adjusted to the social and political changes insti-
gated by the March on Rome. They considered the violent revolutionary
phase to be over and saw a need for the creation of a new state and an
intellectual fascist class. The leading figure of the revisionist trend,
Bottai, was himself an ex-*ardito* and now advocated fascist attitudes that
were far from the virulent *arditismo*. Bottai's insistence on discipline,
obedience and hierarchy symbolized the 'normalization' process because
it implied the transformation of former fascist values. With this shift, the
militaristic ethos of Fascism did not vanish. As Bottai said, discipline and
hierarchy made Fascism similar to a marching victorious army.[6] Revisionism still faced active opposition from squadrism and intransigent
fascists, including Farinacci and ex-*arditi* such as Mario Carli and his
publication *L'Impero*.[7] In 1925, in the wake of the Matteotti crisis, this
intransigent trend would contribute to the imposition of the dictatorial
fascist regime under the rule of Mussolini and the PNF.

It was against the background of this ideological and political ferment
that the main Italian veteran organizations first sought to collaborate with
Mussolini's government, thus becoming progressively fascistized. I will
analyze the process of organizational and political negotiation between
the ANMIG, the ANC and the PNF which led to Fascism's permeation
of these veteran organizations and, in response, to the appearance of anti-
fascist veteran trends. Concurrently, ideological and discursive developments also interweaved and escalated in the context of the Matteotti
crisis during the summer of 1924, leading to a drastic resolution in

[6] Giuseppe Bottai, 'Disciplina', *Critica fascista*, 15 July 1923.
[7] Gentile, *Le origini della ideologia fascista*, pp. 323–96.

1925. It was this year that saw the culmination of the process of *fascistizzazione* of the Italian veterans.

The Beginnings of a Relationship: Veterans and Mussolini's Government

Just after the March on Rome, the veteran associations celebrated the Victory of 4 November. *Il Popolo d'Italia* stated that Mussolini had made the celebration possible.[8] However, it was in fact the last liberal government that some weeks before had declared 4 November as a national holiday, following a petition by the ANC. At that time, there had been plans for a demonstration of disabled veterans, with the participation of D'Annunzio and the collaboration of Aldo Rossini – ANC member and Undersecretary for War Pensions in the last liberal government – and ANMIG leaders such as Delcroix.[9] This was a pacifying and reconciling initiative aimed at pre-empting the imminent fascist assault on Rome and allowing the veteran movement to have a key role in government. It might have been another steppingstone towards a nationally shared war memory, since D'Annunzio intended to talk about 'peace, labour and faith' (*di pace, di lavoro, di fede*). But the March on Rome came too soon, allowing the fascists to appear as the main patrons of the celebration of 4 November 1922. The disabled veterans relinquished their plan to challenge the fascist rise. In the end, many ANC and ANMIG leaders were equally enthusiastic about having the fascists in the government as the promoters of the 4 November anniversary.[10] But Italian politics had changed dramatically.

The disabled veterans of the ANMIG were the first to experience the down side of a close relationship with Fascism.[11] Beyond a common patriotism and nationalism, the particularities of fascist ideology disturbed the political harmony that the veterans envisioned. When the time came to transform promises into concrete concessions, conflicts arose. A revision of the Pensions Law for maimed veterans had long been

[8] *Il Popolo d'Italia*, 5 November 1922.
[9] Ugo Pavan Dalla Torre, 'L'Anmig fra D'Annunzio e Mussolini (ottobre 1922): Note e prospettive di ricerca', *Italia contemporanea*, 278 (2015), pp. 325–52.
[10] Antonino Répaci, *La Marcia su Roma*, Milan, Rizzoli, 1972, pp. 448, 794–5, 947–52; *L'Idea Nazionale*, 28 October 1922; *Il Combattente Romagnolo* (Ravenna), 1 November 1922; *Il Combattente* (Bologna), 4 November 1922; *Bollettino della Sezione Provinciale fra Mutilati ed Invalidi di Guerra* (Rovigo), 31 October 1922; *Bollettino della sezione provinciale di Ferrara fra mutilati e invalidi di guerra* (Ferrara), 1 (January 1923); Emilio Lussu, *Marcia su Roma e dintorni*, Turin, Einaudi, 2002 [1945], pp. 51–2.
[11] For a local account of this process, see Francesco Zavatti, *Mutilati ed invalidi di guerra: una storia politica. Il caso modenese*, Milan, Unicopli, 2011, pp. 101–60.

demanded by the ANMIG and studied by government experts such as Rossini in collaboration with the association. A project to change the law, led by Camillo Peano (Minister of the Treasury), was already under discussion in October 1922.[12] This new law intended to refine the levels of pensions granted, not according to military rank (although some progressive percentage concessions were maintained according to rank), but in relation to the seriousness of the wounds. Furthermore, disability caused by actual combat service – caused by enemy weapons – was to be better rewarded than disabilities resulting from non-front-line service. The ANMIG played an important role in the discussion of these stipulations, which largely corresponded with the wishes of the organized disabled veterans. The dramatic arrival of the fascists in government jeopardized this process.

In fact, the fascist seizure of power made the fate of disabled veterans' issues unclear. One of the fascist *quadrumviri*, Cesare Maria De Vecchi, was appointed as the new State Undersecretary for War Pensions. De Vecchi was a military man and a squadrist, but despite his 'heroic' record, he was not an appropriate candidate for managing the sensitive and complex problems of disabled war veterans. De Vecchi was more interested in setting up a militia from squadrism, and he would later become a general of the MVSN. Initially, he declined Mussolini's offer, but finally, according to his account and in honour of his monarchism, he accepted the post at the request of the king. He followed the instructions of Mussolini and worked together with experts in furthering pension reform. The main aims of the reform were the removal of the alleged 'demagogic principles' of the previous law, a revision of the categorization of disability on the basis of war sacrifice and a reduction in the interference of the ANMIG in pension affairs. Mussolini pointed to the scandalous situation of many deserters who were now presumably living at the expense of the state.[13]

It is interesting to analyze how De Vecchi as Undersecretary for War Pensions approached disabled veterans after the fascist seizure of power, as this examination underlines how Fascism's ideology, discourse and organizational projects regarded veterans by the end of 1922. In his first message to all Italian veterans, De Vecchi began by evoking Italy's fallen soldiers, subsequently introducing himself as 'an artilleryman, a bomber, an

---

[12] *Il Mutilato* (Cremona), 2 (November 1922).
[13] Cesare Maria De Vecchi di Val Cismon and Luigi Romersa (eds.), *Il Quadrumviro scomodo: Il vero Mussolini nelle memorie del più monarchico dei fascisti*, Milan, Mursia, 1983, p. 86; De Vecchi's letters to Mussolini (31 October and 1 November 1922), ACS, SPD, CR, box 4, file 'Sen Prof Cesare Maria De Vecchi di Val Cismon'; *Il Popolo di Trieste* (Trieste), 2 November 1922.

infantryman, an *ardito'* – a discourse that reflected the basic characteristics of the fascist approach.[14] As we will see next, this new paradigm supposed a radical shift from the old discourse of the *trincerocrazia*, originally directed towards disabled veterans who in 1917 were said to be the 'vanguard of those who returned' and who supposedly bore the right to lead the new Italy. Mutilated veterans had not forgotten Mussolini's speeches in 1919, in which he had demanded increased recognition of their sacrifices, along with appropriate levels of material reward.

Now, the fascists considered the state to be a superior entity, to which disabled veterans owed obedience and service. The state, in De Vecchi's words, was like a father and a master that had a 'duty' to assist his sons. Thus, the disabled would conserve their 'right to live', whilst their potential to continue giving and donating to the fatherland would be encouraged. The state had a moral duty but not an obligation: pensions should not be considered to be a compensation for suffering. The state was not an employer but a father. Hence, the state had the right to ask its sons to sacrifice their lives, while the sons had the duty of cheerfully giving their lives for the fatherland's salvation and grandeur. On this basis, De Vecchi announced a full revision of all pensions, which would include an unremitting battle against profiteers such as *disertori, autolesionisti* and *imboscati*, who supposedly abused the system. Pensions thus would recover their moral and integrative function. In pursuing these objectives, De Vecchi called for the consolidation and unification of the various entities that offered assistance. In doing so, he suggested that spirit-corrupting organizations that represented the disabled (supposedly the ANMIG) would not be exempted from the reform.[15]

The debate among interest groups and specialists on the matter developed in December of 1922. It was said that the revision would not yield many savings and that it should be avoided, as it would sow discord among the affected persons.[16] De Vecchi had to clarify his position. He reaffirmed the three guiding principles of the government: reform and revision of the pensions and unification of services. Moreover, he pointed out that according to the fascist conception of the state, all citizens had the 'absolute, natural and indispensable obligation to offer themselves to the defence of the fatherland'; 'therefore, [they had] no right to indemnity'.[17] The disabled veterans' leaders met this radical position with outrage. Since the fascist Undersecretary of War Pensions ignored their complaints, ANMIG leaders – particularly Delcroix – personally visited

---

[14] De Vecchi's message can be read in *Il combattente romagnolo*, 30 November 1922.
[15] *Ibid.*   [16] *Corriere della Sera*, 6 and 14 December 1922.
[17] *Corriere della Sera*, 19 December 1922.

Mussolini to inform him of their displeasure (*rammarico*) with regards to De Vecchi's outlook. This situation provoked the first serious clash between Mussolini and De Vecchi: Mussolini decided to yield to the pressure exerted by disabled veterans. Momentarily leaving fascist principles to one side, Mussolini said to De Vecchi that he considered it inconvenient to ignore the disabled veterans association and that representatives of the disabled veterans should be allowed to attend discussions on the law project. Significantly, De Vecchi justified his stance by saying that he wanted to precipitate the 'purification' of the ANMIG in a 'national' sense.[18] The fascist undersecretary was willing to resign his position, but he remained in his post despite satirical criticisms from disabled veterans and the reproaches of some fascists.[19]

And yet, the ANMIG leaders, particularly Delcroix, reaffirmed their confidence in Mussolini and the national government whilst criticizing De Vecchi's views and technical ignorance.[20] Disabled veterans' leaders wrongly differentiated between Mussolini and his subordinate in the government. This contradiction was possible because, in reality, the orientation of the ANMIG was, on some ideological points, not so different from that of the fascists. The association rejected the charitable character – labelled as 'socialist' – of material benefits, even if the ANMIG wanted these advantages to be increased. During this period, the ANMIG section of Milan expelled 500 of its 5,000 members because they had not fought on the front line or because they lacked a clean record.[21] In any case, what seems evident is that Mussolini and most fascists highly valued the symbolic support of disabled veterans. The material and discursive negotiation between fascists and the disabled veterans can be seen as a step in the process of fascist permeation of the Italian veterans' movement.

Mussolini was very interested in stressing the common interests of his government and disabled veterans. He resorted to the concession of material rewards in order to obtain the support of disabled veteran leaders and thus transmit fascist ideology to them. In March of 1923, Mussolini inaugurated the new ANMIG Headquarters in Rome. This ceremony concluded with an embrace between him and Delcroix, who meaningfully stated that 'sacrifice' was the first duty of every citizen.

---

[18] Mussolini's and De Vecchi's letters (18 and 19 December 1922), ACS, SPD, CR, box 4, file 'Sen Prof Cesare Maria De Vecchi di Val Cismon'; see also Romersa and De Vecchi di Val Cismon (eds.), *Il Quadrumviro scomodo*, pp. 90–1.

[19] *Corriere della Sera*, 22 December 1922; *L'Idea Nazionale*, 23 February 1923.

[20] *Il Popolo di Trieste*, 6 December 1922; *Il Popolo d'Italia*, 3 January 1923; *Corriere della Sera*, 24 February 1923.

[21] *Corriere della Sera*, 20 February and 1 March 1923.

Mussolini, after introducing himself as a trench comrade, stressed that he admired and respected the 'mutilated' veterans and that he considered all ex-combatants and the families of fallen soldiers to be the aristocracy of the new Italy, whose rights would never expire.[22] This symbolic union marked the beginning of a definitive collusion between the ANMIG and Mussolini's government: in June, the ANMIG was institutionalized as an *ente morale*, the official Italian disabled veterans' organization.

Soon after, in July of 1923, the new pensions law was finally promulgated. By then, Mussolini had defenestrated De Vecchi for political reasons. In any case, as stated by Mussolini, the position of Undersecretary for War Pensions could be abolished without concern.[23] The task of drafting the pensions law was assigned to nationalist lawyer Alfredo Rocco, and the final text, supported by the veterans' associations, remained firmly grounded in the legislative tradition of provision for veterans.[24] The only significant novelty in the law was the distinction between combatants and non-combatants: to receive a pension, individuals had to either have suffered physical injury at the hands of the enemy, fallen ill in a zone of combat or suffered injury in a non-combat zone by the effect of weapons – as long as they had actually fought in a combat zone at some point or another. It was rather a broad definition of who was to be considered a *combattente*.[25] The Fiuman legionaries were also included in the benefits system. After this law was published, the position of the Undersecretary for War Pensions was abolished. In this period, war-blind poet and ANMIG leader Carlo Delcroix was publicly honoured and well treated in the salons of Milanese high society.[26] He had cemented an amicable relationship with Mussolini, and the ANMIG had become fully integrated into the early fascist regime. Something similar was also happening to the ANC.

The ANC engaged in negotiations with Mussolini's government during this early period as well, establishing a relationship that initially seemed easy going and straightforward. Shortly after the March on Rome, on 9 November 1922, the ANC leaders – namely, Giulio Bergmann – expressed to Mussolini their desire for a concord between Fascism

---

[22] *Il Popolo d'Italia*, 13 March 1923; *Corriere della Sera*, 13 March 1923.
[23] Mussolini's letter (1 May 1923), ACS, SPD, CR, box 4, file 'Sen Prof Cesare Maria De Vecchi di Val Cismon'.
[24] *Corriere della Sera*, 5 July 1923.
[25] Giuglielmo Pocaterra, *La pensione di guerra nella sua legge base (R. Decreto 12 luglio 1923 n. 1491) e successive integrazioni, modifiche e aggiunte (preparazione a un testo unico)*, Rome, 1936.
[26] *Corriere della Sera*, 6 and 8 July 1923; *Il Popolo d'Italia*, 6 July 1923.

and war veterans.[27] They requested that the government define the ANC as an *ente morale* (i.e. an official entity). This quality would mean recognition of the ANC's specific role in the moral and economic management of war veterans and in their 'education' in relation to patriotic cults.[28] The ANC leaders were interested in safeguarding their clientele faced with a potential competitor – Fascism – while simultaneously hoping to take advantage of Fascism's position in power. The association boasted that it had expelled certain groups of veterans since 1921. At the beginning of 1923, the main ANC regional sections, Lombardy and Liguria, unified their press organs in one single newspaper that would often show satisfaction with the fascist government.[29] With the expectation of a positive response, ANC representatives (Bergmann, Savelli, Host-Venturi and Zilli, amongst others) visited Mussolini to specify their demands. Giacomo Acerbo, who had been an ANC provincial leader and now was a member of the government as Undersecretary of the Presidency, introduced them to the Prime Minister. The veteran representatives requested that the ANC be officially defined as an *ente morale*. If this was secured, the ANC would work in the fields of pre-military and post-military education, popular cultural education, production cooperatives and social assistance, particularly regarding migrants and agricultural zones. Mussolini agreed to pursue this transformation and predicted that the ANC would become a sourcing ground for state officials.[30] In fact, different legislative measures were undertaken during 1923 to promote war veterans' privileges, reserving vacant positions for them in the state administration.[31]

The ANC National Congress of Naples in February 1923 saw important steps taken towards the political alliance between veterans and the fascist government. A new directing board was appointed, joined by fascists such as former Fiuman legionnaire Nino Host-Venturi and Mario Ponzio di San Sebastiano, Gold Medal holder and former Fiuman legionnaire. A government representative, the moderate fascist Giovanni Giurati – also a former Fiuman legionnaire – was also included in the ANC national committee. The leaders asserted the ANC's 'loyal, devoted, powerful and dignified adhesion' to the fascist government. All these enthusiastic adjectives sharply contrasted with the declaration, at the same time, of the ANC's non-political stance (*apoliticità*).

---

[27] *Il Combattente* (Bologna), 15 December 1922; *La Nuova Giornata*, 30 November 1922.
[28] *La Nuova Giornata*, 30 November 1922.
[29] *I Combattenti. La Nuova Giornata* (Genoa), 18 January 1923.
[30] *Il Bollettino dell'Associazione Nazionale Combattenti* (Rome), 1–2 (15–30 January 1923).
[31] Giuseppe Colonna (ed.), *Raccolta delle disposizioni di legge a favore degli ex combattenti*, Siena, 1954.

Nevertheless, this *apoliticità* was understood purely as a non-partisan position, neither 'agnostic' nor neutral.[32] Despite the contradictions of the ANC position regarding the fascist government, it was very clear that there existed a compromise between Fascism and the veterans.

This mutual rapprochement was facilitated by Mussolini's discursive abilities in dealing with ex-soldiers. The president addressed them in a very flattering way, and he *always* introduced himself as a comrade (*camerata, commilitone, compagno*). In January of 1923, when Mussolini received some Gold Medal (*Medaglia d'oro*)–holding veterans at Palazzo Chigi, he called them the 'highest aristocracy of the Nation'. Additionally, he evoked the notion of a future 'second victory' and 'second Italian mission'. This endeavour would come in the form of Italian expansion in the world, in which the veterans would, once more, be the craftsmen. After the ANC congress in Naples, Mussolini received the veterans' leaders again and confirmed to them that he would deal with their demands. He also declared that he desired the *combattenti* and *mutilati* to be at the head of the Fasci. The ANC leaders were very satisfied with the resolution of the pensions crisis in favour of disabled veterans. Mussolini predicted that he and the veterans still had 'further to go together'. Likewise, the aristocratic veterans of the Istituto del Nastro Azzurro (an association of highly decorated veterans) paid a visit to Mussolini and avowed their devotion to him. While visiting a workhouse for the war blind, Mussolini paid tribute to them by stating, '[T]he Government will guard your sacred rights: it will meet your legitimate desires ... and as a trench comrade I exhort you to be confident in what the government will do for you.' Fascist propaganda depicted Mussolini constantly stressing his war accomplishments, with his war diaries published as a volume in 1923.[33] The target of these discourses was the veterans' elites and maimed veterans, who theoretically composed the aristocracy of the nation in the fascist worldview.

The period of mutual courtship between the ANC and the fascist government concluded with the decision, taken in April of 1923, of institutionalizing the ANC as an *ente morale*. The same measure was taken regarding the ANMIG and the ad hoc creation of the Families of Fallen Soldiers Association (Associazione fra le famiglie dei caduti). ANC leaders such as Giulio Bergmann were satisfied, since they believed

---

[32] *Il Bollettino dell'Associazione Nazionale Combattent*, 3–6 (February–March 1923).

[33] Benito Mussolini, *Mussolini ai combattenti d'Italia*, Rome, 1923, *passim*; *Corriere della Sera*, 2 May 1923; Mussolini, Edoardo and Duilio Susmel (eds.), *Opera Omnia*, Vol. XIX, *passim*; Luisa Passerini, *Mussolini immaginario: Storia di una biografia 1915–1939*, Bari, Laterza, 1991, pp. 15–32.

the ANC had acquired significant strength, assuring its own autonomous role and rights.[34] With a decree on 24 June 1923, this transformation became definitive. The conversion of the ANC into an *ente morale* meant granting official recognition of the ANC's exclusive activity in the realm of social assistance. Tasks of this nature previously developed by the ONC were transferred to the ANC. However, in reality, the control of the three associations was handed to the Presidenza del Consiglio, namely, Mussolini. Furthermore, recognition of the ANC and the ANMIG as the only official veteran associations implied the marginalization of others, such as the Catholic UNRG, and marked the death knell for the Lega proletaria. Any political orientation of the ANC was also omitted. It was clear that veteran leaders were politically satisfied with Mussolini's government because, after a succession of unpopular liberal prime ministers, there was at last a war veteran at the head of the government.[35]

During this time, the partial neutralization of the PSdA can be considered to be another achievement for Mussolini and Fascism with regards to veterans. This Sardinian party had been the only successful outcome of the veterans' failed attempt to set up a democratic party. Yet, the party had remained limited to its autonomist aims defended by leaders such as Camillo Bellieni and Emilio Lussu. Although veterans had also set up the first Fasci of Sardinia (Cagliari and Sassari), most Sardinian veterans had manifested a predominantly anti-fascist attitude until the March on Rome. After October of 1922, the Sardinian fascists insisted on attracting the veterans from the PSdA to their own ranks with renewed vigour. A first attempt to fuse the PNF and the PSdA took place in January of 1923 but remained incomplete. Lussu continued to direct the original PSdA as an active political movement. Later, Mussolini himself visited the island in June of 1923 to praise the Sardinian people with his speeches, emphasizing that they had demonstrated their patriotism in the trenches of the Great War.[36] In the end, a combination of the dominant trend amongst veterans towards *apoliticità*, squadrist harassment and the political manoeuvres of the *prefetto* designed by Mussolini allowed the gradual subjugation and fascist co-optation of veterans in Sardinia.[37]

---

[34] Giulio Bergmann, 'L'Associazione dei Combattenti verso la sua nuova potenza', *I Combattenti. La Nuova Giornata*, 12 April 1923; also in *Il combattente* (Cremona), 1 May 1923.

[35] Cf. Sabbatucci, *I combattenti*, pp. 362–3.   [36] *Il Popolo d'Italia*, 11 and 12 June 1923.

[37] Sabbatucci, *I combattenti*, pp. 365–6; Del Piano and Atzeni, *Combattentismo, fascismo e autonomismo*; Luigi Nieddu, *Dal combattentismo al fascismo in Sardegna*, Milan, Vangelista, 1979; Eugenia Tognotti, *L'esperienza democratica del combattentismo nel*

The next steppingstone in Fascism's gradual permeation of the veterans' movement was the symbolic staging of the faithful relationship between the veterans and the government. Veterans' parades in some cities had marked the celebration of 24 May (day of Italy's intervention in the First World War). Later, on 26 June 1923, in Rome, a great demonstration of an estimated 30,000 war veterans commemorated the Piave River battle. It was the first time that veterans had the exclusive leading role in a ritual of this nature, but it was Mussolini who actually occupied the centre stage. He stated that it was an honour for him to be amongst his trench comrades.[38] Even if during the ceremony the anti-fascist veterans' group L'Italia Libera showed its first signs of existence,[39] this occasion represented the fascist government's peak in popularity amongst Italian war veterans.

Despite fissures in the allegedly indissoluble link between Fascism and the veterans, the principal ANC leaders continued to firmly endorse Mussolini. These leaders, filo-fascists and fascists – including Savelli, Ponzio di San Sebastiano and Arangio Ruiz – faithfully expected that the normalization and depuration of Fascism would be completed. They hoped that Fascism would be fully integrated into a reinvigorated Italian state. Some veterans' leaders saw the Acerbo electoral law, discussed since the summer of 1923, as another step in this direction. At the same time, though, there were concerns about the dictatorial thrust of the regime and the persistent squadrist intimidation and violence.[40] From the summer of 1923 to the fascist victory in the elections of April 1924, the history of the ANC was marked by ideological debates and internal struggles. On the one hand, the ANC aspired to obtain high returns for its loyalty to Mussolini. On the other, Fascism progressively absorbed the ANC; the ANC suffered a loss of identity, influence and agency in favour of the PNF.[41] In the next two sections I will focus on organizational, discursive and symbolic developments that marked the relationship between veterans and Fascism in this period and which played a key role in determining its future.

Mezzogiorno: Il movimento degli ex-combattenti e il Partito Sardo d'Azione a Sassari (1918–1924), Cagliari, Edizioni Della Torre, 1983.

[38] *Corriere della Sera*, 9 and 25 May 1923; *I Combattenti. La Nuova Giornata*, 21 and 28 June 1923; *Il Combattente* (Cremona), 30 June 1923. Initially organized for the 17 June, the celebration of the Piave battle was postponed to coincide with the publication of the decree transforming the ANC into Ente Morale.

[39] Luciano Zani, *Italia Libera: Il primo movimento antifascista clandestino 1923–1925*, Bari, Laterza, 1975, p. 3.

[40] See, for example, *I Combattenti. La Nuova Giornata*, 2 August 1923.

[41] Sabbatucci, *I combattenti*, pp. 361–9.

The Struggle for Organization: The ANC and the PNF

While the solid discursive harmony between the fascist government and the veterans was very clear in the first half of 1923, the relationship between the ANC and the PNF had to be articulated in social and political practice as well. Veterans from the Italian provinces demanded solutions for their problems by visiting Mussolini directly.[42] The president appeared to the veterans as an approachable and brotherly leader. Yet, on a daily basis, the real issues that affected veterans had to be tackled by dealing with the provincial fascist authorities. And within this less visible sphere, the relationship between the ANC and the PNF proved to be far more problematic. The first documented contact established between ANC and PNF cells, particularly between the Lazio federations of both organizations, date from the end of April 1923.[43] At the beginning of May, there were meetings in Rome and Milan between the ANC spokespersons, namely, Arangio Ruiz, and PNF leaders, most notably the fanatical fascist Michele Bianchi, secretary general of both the PNF and the Ministry of Internal Affairs.[44] They approached the issue of the relationship between the ANC and the PNF. They knew that some clashes between fascists and *combattenti* had taken place, and the leaders wanted to prevent such cases occurring in the future, enforcing the decisions adopted at the last ANC congress. Stressing that Mussolini's government was that of the *combattenti* and the *valorizzazione* of the victory, the fascist and veterans' leaders planned a closer collaboration. With this accord, the fascists secured a commitment from the veterans to effectively stop their activities in the sphere of syndicalism, transferring that task to Fascism. It was agreed that both organizations should cooperate at the local level, and Bianchi announced that he would propose that all fascist federations make their veterans become members of the ANC.[45]

The fascists named these agreements the 'trench pact' (*patto della trincea*). Taking into account the idea that 'the best' members of Fascism were veterans and that Mussolini's government had enhanced the victory, the fascists considered it logical that veterans identified with Fascism; their commonality of ideals would lead veterans to giving Mussolini their loyal and unshakeable support.[46] These views were

---

[42] *Il Popolo d'Italia*, 20 May, 29 June 1923.
[43] They probably took place as a result of an ANC proposal; see Archivio della Camera dei Deputati, Archivio Ettore Viola, Corrispondenza, box 3, file 70.
[44] *Il Popolo d'Italia*, 1 and 2 May 1923.
[45] *Il Popolo d'Italia*, 8 May 1923; *L'Idea Nazionale*, 8 May 1923.
[46] 'Il patto della trincea', *Il Popolo d'Italia*, 8 May 1923.

widespread amongst the fascists. A member of the PNF argued that Fascism, having emerged from the war, was closely related to the veterans; through them, Fascism should permeate the whole nation.[47] ANC leaders also thought that this link existed, but they rather implied that it was Fascism that should be integrated into the nation instead of the nation being converted to Fascism.[48] Furthermore, some veterans warned that any kind of collaboration with the fascist government should be based on two conditions: the purging of undesirable individuals from fascist ranks and a respect for personal liberties.[49] Despite the mythologization of the trench community, which formed the basis of the 'trench pact', there existed certain differences in opinion that complicated the relationship between the ANC and the PNF.

It is not surprising that relations between fascists and veterans turned sour, even violent, if we take into account the agitation of the fascist movement in the Italian provinces. The party was riddled with internal disputes, such as the crisis in Alessandria, where Nicola Sansanelli was sent to impose order amongst the fascists.[50] New cases of fascist violence against veterans emerged in the province of Cremona, where Farinacci had harassed veterans since 1921.[51] In some southern provinces, such as Agrigento in Sicily and Terra di Lavoro in northern Campania, confrontations between fascists and veterans also became a thorny issue.[52] In Palermo, where the numerous *mutilati* and *combattenti* functioned independently from the few fascist militants, the veterans buttressed Mussolini because they considered him their equal rather than a fascist.[53] Furthermore, outright opposition to any 'trench pact' with the fascists appeared in September of 1923 because it was perceived that these pacts were actually subordinating the ANC sections to the Fasci.[54] Despite this violence, the veterans' leaders – dazzled by the fascist 'revolution' – would usually ignore these problems, downplaying them as 'little disputes' (*piccole beghe*).

It was often said in the press at the time that the fascists attacked the veterans because the ANC had, in some places, become a refuge for antifascists. There was a certain element of truth to this claim. However, the ANC grew in numbers during this time not merely due to the flow of

---

[47] *I Combattenti. La Nuova Giornata*, 19 July 1923.
[48] Arturo Codignola, 'Ciò che è stata e ciò che rappresenta l'ANC, II', *I Combattenti. La Nuova Giornata*, 5 April 1923.
[49] *I Combattenti. La Nuova Giornata*, 2 August 1923.
[50] ACS, MI, PS (1923), box 75, file 'Alessandria'; *Il Popolo d'Italia*, 5 July 1923.
[51] *Il Combattente* (Cremona), 31 May and 21 June 1923.
[52] ACS, MI, PS (1923), box 75, files Girgenti, Roma and Caltanissetta.
[53] *La Stampa*, 4 June 1923.   [54] *I Combattenti. La Nuova Giornata*, 23 September 1923.

anti-fascist and non-fascist veterans[55] but also thanks to the planned introduction of fascists into the ANC cells, which was probably more significant. Joining an organization whose national leaders collaborated with the PNF and were publicly connected to the fascist government was no safe option for anti-fascists; becoming a member was only possible in isolated localities or on certain occasions. In some cases, anti-fascist veterans detached themselves from the ANC and tried to create their own organizations, but the *prefetti* immediately moved to disband them. In contrast, in newly founded ANC sections, the fascists seemed to be predominant.[56]

In this context, on the first anniversary of the March on Rome, the fascists managed to ensure the participation of the veterans' associations. For the fascists, it was very important to be on good terms with the veterans during the commemorative celebrations of the March on Rome and 4 November. The veterans' involvement was possible thanks to the political leadership of individuals such as Arangio Ruiz and Delcroix. The memorandum sent by the ANC to its veterans provides an insight into their underlying reasoning. For them, the celebration of the March on Rome transcended the mere partisan ritual; it was supposedly an exaltation of the values that had 'emerged from the dual work of war and peace'. Therefore, veterans should solemnly partake in the rite, although this should not be understood as a challenge to the 'untouchable political independence' of the association. In fact, it was not by chance that this message included greetings to the 'youth that carried out the March on Rome and achieved the vibrant national renovation emerging from the indestructible glory of the trench'.[57] This ambiguous sentence in the ANC message implied that – from the veterans' point of view – it was not the veterans who had carried out the March on Rome but rather young people more generally, even if their inspiration had been the trench soldiers' wish for a renovation of the fatherland.

For the following celebration of 4 November in Rome, the ANC and the ANMIG invited Mussolini to take part in the commemoration that they organized in the Augusteo, after the customary homage to the *Milite Ignoto*.[58] In his speech, Delcroix justified the recent participation of disabled veterans in the March on Rome celebration. The presence of 'mutilated' veterans had given a colourful symbolic prominence to the

---

[55] Cf. Sabbatucci, *I combattenti*, p. 364. The ANC reached perhaps 500,000 members by December of 1923.

[56] ACS, MI, PS (1923), box 75, files Lecce, Potenza and Livorno.

[57] *Il Popolo d'Italia*, 19 October 1923.   [58] *Corriere della Sera*, 3 November 1923.

fascist celebration.[59] Delcroix associated the 4 November victory with the 'historical necessity' of intervention. In his view, veterans had the role of transmitting 'new forces' to the Italian people and the mission of safeguarding the fatherland's conquests.[60] Beneath the high-flying rhetorical flourishes, Delcroix had established a symbolic link between interventionism, the victory and the March on Rome and had bestowed upon veterans the role of transmitting Fascism to the wider public. Rather than Mussolini, it was a more publicly neutral figure, Delcroix, who was in charge of making such discursive connections. Meanwhile, anti-fascist veterans commemorated this date separately[61] but with limited impact, since the principal national symbolic spaces, Altare della Patria and the Campidoglio in Rome, were occupied by the official ceremony and by veteran associations sympathetic to Fascism. The Istituto del Nastro Azzurro held its first national congress in the Campidoglio over those dates.[62] The most prestigious military men, including Badoglio, stood alongside royal and governmental representatives at the celebration, whereas a public appearance by Cadorna – the figure held responsible for Caporetto – around the same time in Florence was associated with the anti-fascist demonstrations.[63]

It was in Cremona that the incomplete integration of veterans into the commemorative fascist celebrations provoked virulent reactions by Farinacci.[64] His intransigent attitude deserves attention because this approach would ultimately be imposed on the ANC during 1925, as we will see. Farinacci presumed that the ANC section of his city was mainly composed of anti-fascist veterans despite the fact that the ANC section had approved of the March on Rome commemoration and had shown that it was keen to establish a cordial relationship with the PNF in line with ANC national directives. The fascist *ras* proposed that the ANC local leaders should dissolve the section, reconstructing it later without 'antinational' (*antinazionali*) elements. Thus, the fascists would ensure that the section took a truly 'national direction' (*indirizzo veramente nazionale*). As the circumstances in Cremona demonstrated, the ANC was forced to maintain an unstable dual position, balanced between Mussolini's government, on the one hand, and Mussolini's party, on the other.

---

[59] *Cremona Nuova* (Cremona), 1 November 1923.
[60] *Corriere della Sera*, 6 November 1923.   [61] *Avanti!* (Milan), 4 and 6 November 1923.
[62] *Il Popolo d'Italia*, 4 November 1923.
[63] *Cremona Nuova*, 6 and 8 November 1923; Cf. *Corriere della Sera*, 9 November 1923.
[64] ACS, MI, PS (1923), box 75, file 'Cremona'; *Cremona Nuova*, 10 November 1923; *Avanti!*, 11 November 1923.

The situation was serious enough to warrant the urgent reopening of the debate within the ANC and the fascist Gran Consiglio in order to find a clear settlement for the ANC-PNF relationship.[65] At the meetings between the main leaders of both sides, a new agreement was reached, although it now implied a set of important symbolic and discursive concessions made by the ANC under the fascist pressure. The ANC *recognized* that the 'fascist revolution' had been the 'concrete and definitive revaluation and re-consecration of the victory'; for this reason, the ANC loyally collaborated with Mussolini's government.[66] For its part, the PNF merely *recalled*, if proudly, that Fascism had emerged from the war experience. The party merely expressed 'sympathy' towards the ANC. In conclusion, it was agreed that both organizations would cordially continue developing their activities, and in case of conflict, they would try to reach new agreements and to establish normality as soon as possible. However, the different tasks of the ANC and PNF were not demarcated, and it was unclear how they would resolve future disputes. Farinacci bluntly stated that his fascist veterans would simply obey the orders of his party. Meanwhile, within the ANC, the 'trench pacts' were ridiculed, since they would never lead to any genuine agreement at the local level.[67] What attitude would the *fascist* members of the ANC adopt?

Later, when the intention of creating a 'fascist veterans' association' emerged from the intransigent fascist circles, the ANC had to yield again to fascist pressure.[68] In mid-December of 1923, the ANC national board (Arangio Ruiz) decided to expel the Italia Libera dissident group, which became an independent anti-fascist organization.[69] Moreover, the ANC reaffirmed once more its collaboration with Mussolini's government and 'therefore, with the PNF, of which the government is an expression'.[70] In the newly elected ANC national board there was a significant fascist presence, including Host-Venturi, Schiavo and Ponzio di San Sebastiano. Still, this was not enough for Farinacci, who went as far as a physical duel with Arangio Ruiz, resulting in injury of the ANC leader. In Turin, the provincial ANC leaders said that implementing collaboration with the PNF was extremely difficult, since they lacked precise instructions.[71] Meanwhile,

---

[65] *Avanti!*, 14 November 1923.   [66] *Corriere della Sera*, 15 November 1923.
[67] *I Combattenti. La Nuova Giornata*, 18 and 26 November 1923 and 2 December 1923; *Avanti!*, 15 November 1923; *Il Combattente Maremmano* (Grosseto), 5 December 1923.
[68] *Corriere della Sera*, 16 November 1923; *La Stampa*, 23 December 1923.
[69] *L'Italia Libera. Organo dei gruppi combattenti 'Italia Libera'*, 8 January 1924.
[70] *Il Primato. Settimanale dei Combattenti* (Turin), 27 January 1924.
[71] *Il Primato*, 25 May 1924.

in the south, where the ANC-PNF pacts had never really functioned, antagonism increased.[72] In Lucca, Tuscany, fascist leader Carlo Sforza pushed the fascist veterans to abandon the ANC *en masse*, creating an independent federation that only recognized the Duce's orders.[73] The alleged reason for these fascist steps was that, under the cover of the ANC *apoliticità*, the veteran organization did not fully collaborate with the fascist government. These astute manoeuvres furthered the fascist impregnation of the Italian veterans' movement.

With the elections of April 1924 fast approaching, a resolution of the crisis was needed. In the end, Arangio Ruiz was removed from his leading position in the ANC, and the fascist Host-Venturi was installed as the association's provisional president.[74] Host-Venturi stressed the ANC's assisting role in purely social and economic terms, whilst the political debates among veterans abated or moved into the press of veterans' groups that had separated from the ANC (as had happened in Florence).[75] Nonetheless, the drawing up of the 'big' fascist 'electoral list' (*listone*) was another method by which the fascist authorities hoped to attract suitable veteran leaders to their project while marginalizing others. As some commentators noted at the time, mere inclusion on this *listone* represented a direct pass into the Chamber, thanks to the particularities of the Acerbo law.[76] The inclusion of several ANC and ANMIG leaders, such as Delcroix, on the *listone* can be considered to be the result of a long negotiation process between veterans and fascists. Veterans obtained a seat in the Chamber, but their associations lost their autonomy and political dimension. The elections were an overwhelming success for the fascists, and the new Chamber was at last full of war veterans, who occupied 264 of 535 seats (49.34 percent).[77] These electoral results persuaded many Italian veterans to consider Mussolini as the president 'who made real the promises and aspirations of the trenches'.[78] Furthermore, many veteran leaders most certainly believed that a process of political 'normalization' of Fascism would definitely begin.

---

[72] *I Combattenti. La Nuova Giornata*, 6 January 1924
[73] *L'Intrepido* (Lucca), 24 December 1923.
[74] *Volontà* (Rome), 15 March 1924; *I Combattenti. La Nuova Giornata*, 14 March 1924.
[75] *Fanteria* (Florence), 1 (January 1924).
[76] Giovanni Sabbatucci, 'Il "suicidio" della classe dirigente liberale: La legge Acerbo 1923–1924', *Italia contemporanea*, 174 (1989), pp. 57–80.
[77] Andrea Bavarelli, *La vittoria smarrita*, pp. 187–8.
[78] *Battaglie: Libera voce dei combattenti della provincia di Alessandria* (Alessandria), 3 March 1924.

The Struggle for Ideology: *Combattentismo* and *Apoliticità*

Until now I have avoided employing the concept of *combattentismo* ('veteranism') when referring to the Italian veterans' movement, although previous scholars have commonly identified this phenomenon as typical of the Italian post-war period and early fascist ideology. In current historiography, *combattentismo* has been described as a 'state of mind' – characterized by dissatisfaction and discontent – that found expression in the rhetorical exaltation of war as a school for life. The term also refers to the belief that veterans constituted a privileged category of citizen with special rights and virtues and that ex-combatants would form an autonomous political force. These mentalities and ideals supposedly converged into Fascism, as did *arditismo*.[79] However, if Fascism soon absorbed the ideology of *arditismo* as a codification of the *arditi* war mentality and demeanour, the word *combattentismo* appears just once in historical sources before 1923. This absence does not mean that the concept *combattentismo* would not serve, from 1923 onwards, to *represent* events that actually took place earlier. As I will demonstrate throughout this work, *combattentismo* had an extremely important role in the history of Fascism. Here, however, I will approach *combattentismo* as a discursive device that historical actors developed and used to interact with their context. I will historicize the notion of *combattentismo* to understand how a connection between this cultural element and Fascism was established and what the consequences of that conjunction were.

The paradigm of the veterans' *apoliticità*, which restricted ANC agency to the realms of social assistance and commemorative ceremonies, was in crisis after the March on Rome. Earlier, as we have seen, the initial ANC ideological project of completely renovating Italian politics had failed by 1920. While the veterans' movement went through its non-political phase, the fascist movement grew and took power. This alleged *apoliticità* became a blatant contradiction when the ANC collaborated with the fascist government and with the PNF. The institutional changes and the agreements between both organizations were part of the process of fascist permeation of the Italian veterans' movement, which raised concerns among veteran leaders across the country. Since the ANC was constantly performing political actions, it was absurd to define the association as a non-political entity. For this

---

[79] Roberto Berardi, *Dizionario di termini storici politici ed economici moderni*, Florence, Felice Le Monier, 1976, *ad nomen*.

reason, some leaders suggested that the ANC should limit its activity to social assistance.[80] This current of thought was increasingly adopted by the fascists inside the ANC, and it would be imposed in the spring of 1924 during Host-Venturi's temporary presidency.

However, at the beginning of 1923, a different line of thinking also emerged: the development and adoption of *combattentismo* as the ideology of the veterans' movement. The origin of this notion is not clear; its first mention in written sources dates from 1920, when it was employed by Priamo Brunazzi. Apparently, after the March on Rome, people started to use *combattentismo* in a pejorative way to refer to the veterans' new relevance in Italian politics, which was a product of Mussolini's government and was noticeable in the disabled veterans' agitation against De Vecchi's pensions project.[81] During 1923, as the decrees and laws granting veterans special privileges in the sphere of public employment proliferated, many professional bureaucrats considered such measures an injustice, employing the term *combattentismo* when highlighting their concerns.[82] The notion of *combattentismo* therefore had materialistic and negative connotations.

Nonetheless, the first codification of *combattentismo* as an ideology for Italian veterans can be found in the spring of 1923, sometime after the ANC had declared its adhesion to the government in the congress of Naples. Lio Rubini, a war veteran writing in the pages of the most important veteran organ, tried to clarify the position of the ANC. He positioned the veterans' association within a tradition emerging from 1848, based on service to the nation. According to him, the ANC had 'a spirit, a mind-set, a political base, an ideal' that he would call *combattentismo*. He connected historical individuals such as the hero of the *Risorgimento* Garibaldi, the poet Carducci and the irredentist martyr Oberdan with the interventionist students of 1915. The 'religion' of *combattentismo* was 'the style of Italy', the guardians of which were veterans. As a religion, *combattentismo* could be adopted by any party or government. *Combattentismo* represented the nation with a human face; it was as 'popular' as the Italian 'saints' Garibaldi, Mazzini and even Mussolini and the king. The ANC was the idea of *combattentismo* incarnate. For all these reasons, the fascist party should be 'loyal to *combattentismo*, feeling the blood of *combattentismo* coursing through its veins'.

---

[80] Arturo Codignola, 'Ció che è stata e ciò che rappresenta l'Associazione Nazionale Combattenti. I', *I Combattenti. La Nuova Giornata*, 29 March 1923.

[81] *I Combattenti. La Nuova Giornata*, 1 March 1923.

[82] See 'Burocracia e combattentismo', *La Vittoria. Organo dell'Associazione Nazionale Combattenti di Palermo* (Palermo), 17–18 (16 November–1 December 1923).

In other words, it was argued that the ANC should not be dissolved into the fascist party.[83]

Having coined this notion – *combattentismo* – it was possible to open a debate among the veterans' educated elite. The new concept spread successfully, and the discussions that ensued were tinged with controversy concerning the ANC-PNF relationship. The correlation between *fascismo* and *combattentismo* was the predominant question tackled by many commentators, some of whom came from the Salveminian veteran sector of the PSdA.[84] Yet, regardless of some generic assumptions, a single, uncontested definition of *combattentismo* as the war veterans' ideology par excellence was not reached. The meaning of *combattentismo* varied widely according to the context in which it was used and depending on the political aims that the argumentation pursued. Thus, this concept became a symbolic framework used to focus discussion around the relations between the PNF and the ANC.

At the beginning of 1924, the debate was intense.[85] The anti-fascist veterans of L'Italia Libera denied that Fascism emerged from *combattentismo*, whereas fascists within the ANC adopted the intransigent position that Fascism was the only possible faith for patriotic Italians. As one member of the Italia Libera wrote, the topic of *combattentismo* had been obfuscated, and *combattentismo* as an expression of ideals of liberty and justice had never crystallized. Instead, a different *combattentismo*, which was a continuation of the war, had clearly been consolidated: Fascism. This connection was in no case positive, for Fascism had made use of the warlike characters of *combattentismo* to pursue a fratricidal fight. Unjustifiably naming its struggle as *combattentismo*, Fascism had obtained power and improperly defined itself as the government of the veterans. The Italia Libera veterans resented the fact that the fascist *combattentismo* had nothing to do with the fight for liberty, justice and the end of the military oligarchies that had animated soldiers during the Great War.[86] Anti-fascist veterans highlighted that the origins of *combattentismo* were pure, arguing that Fascism had abused it. They argued that the democratic spirit of *combattentismo* had been removed from the ANC and confined to a few independent

---

[83] Lio Rubini, 'Combattentismo', *I Combattenti. La Nuova Giornata*, 5 April 1923.

[84] For example, 'Polemica interna: Combattentismo e Fascismo', *I Combattenti. La Nuova Giornata*, 10 November 1923.

[85] Unfortunately, due to a gap in the historical sources, it is possible to know only indirectly the content of the speech by Umberto Mancuso, 'Il Combattentismo: sua origine, sua essenza, suoi limiti, sua funzione politica', delivered in the National Council of the ANC in December of 1923, see *I Combattenti. La Nuova Giornata*, 6 January 1924.

[86] *L'Italia Libera*, 8 January 1924.

veterans' journals.[87] The maturing of *combattentismo* as an ideology of veterans came too late, when it was already in fascist hands.

Since *combattentismo* became a discursive device likely to be employed in Fascism's favour, some critics endowed *combattentismo* with a completely negative meaning. The magazine *Volontà*, in which veterans such as Camillo Bellieni had given life to their autonomist and reformist political projects, resumed publication at this time. In March of 1924, this magazine published a very critical examination of *combattentismo*. The key to the phenomenon – it was said – was the veterans' claim to an allegedly essential role in the national political life, which had an appalling set of implications. In contrast to the veterans' conceited pretensions, the actual political input of *combattentismo* was very marginal and was limited to a certain political-military jargon: any political discussion ended in a brawl and the launching of hand grenades. The article denounced veterans for holding a deceitful political stance, ignoring the actual destruction of liberties. Lamentably, *combattentismo* was the sole political patrimony of those who had gone to war without a previous moral and ideological background; these young people had been transformed into both combatants and political men during a single spiritual process: war. In this way, *combattentismo* became their only political ideology. But it was a very flimsy ground from which to lead the country. *Combattentismo* was an expression of ingenuity and political virginity. The only form of *combattentismo* in force was Fascism, and the fascists had taken advantage of this in order to obtain power. Now, veterans had to choose between joining Fascism and constructing their own political path.[88]

Alongside the aborted conception of *combattentismo* as a veteran ideology differentiated from Fascism, the reawakening of a political consciousness of the veterans themselves was silenced by the fascist victory in the elections of April 1924.[89] At this stage, the ANC preferred to underline its primordial role in the realm of social assistance. As Fascism seemed to be consolidating itself with a Chamber full of veterans, the notion of *apoliticità* gained renewed importance for different sectors of veterans. In June 1924, a new ANC/ONC monthly magazine, *Problemi d'Italia*, was created. This publication was devoted to technical and generic patriotic issues, where ideological and political debates were absolutely absent.[90] The lack of public controversies in this journal suggested that a stable political settlement for the complex veterans-Fascism relationship had been reached. On the left, anti-fascism had renounced *combattentismo*.

---

[87] Luigi de Grazia, 'Combattentismo', *Fanteria*, 27 January 1924.
[88] *Volontà*, 31 March 1924.   [89] See *Il Primato*, 20 April 1924.
[90] *Problemi d'Italia. Rassegna mensile dei combattenti* (Rome), 1 (June 1924).

In the hypothetical centre, the ANC had been emptied of political meaning. In power, Fascism framed the activity of all veterans willing to take part in politics. The intransigent fascists seemed content with this balance. Would this standstill allow the final 'normalization' of Fascism? A new crisis would prevent this.

The assassination of Giacomo Matteotti, a socialist MP who maintained a critical line of opposition to Fascism, badly affected the process of fascist 'normalization'.[91] Historians have had much to say about the crisis that opened at this point. Its resolution would imply the definitive establishment of the fascist dictatorship, with Mussolini's infamous speech of 3 January 1925.[92] In the following pages I will analyze how cumulative discursive contradictions and organizational tensions in the veterans' sphere found a difficult and drastic resolution.

Evidently, the Matteotti crisis had a great impact on the relationship between Fascism and veterans. This crime outraged many of the ANC veterans who had fully supported Mussolini until this point. Although some ministers resigned and Mussolini yielded the Ministry of Interior to the moderate nationalist Federzoni, many veteran leaders became cognizant of the impossibility of a 'normalization' of Fascism within the existing state structure. Fascism – it was said – seemed finished, and the fascist conceptions about the veterans came under harsh criticism. Anti-fascist veterans convincingly argued that the mere fact of being a veteran did not imply the right to exert political power; decorations and wounds, as glorious as they might be, were not titles of professional or political competence; the 'profession of veteran' had to disappear.[93] Camillo Bellieni, disheartened, wrote a famous article in which he argued that the original project of the ANC – that of a renovation of Italian politics – had painfully failed.[94] In contrast, within the ANC, few leaders were in favour of definitively withdrawing their political support from the government; some of them, such as Manaresi in Bologna, were confident that Mussolini's government could recover its prestige and restore order.[95] Although ANC leaders such as Savelli or Giulio Bergmann

---

[91] Matteotti, in fact, had repeatedly denounced fascist violence that affected war veterans as well; see Giacomo Matteotti, *Un anno di dominazione fascista*, Sala Bolognese, Arnaldo Forni, 1980 (1st edn. 1923), *passim*.

[92] Renzo De Felice, *Mussolini il fascista. I. La conquista del potere 1921–1925*, Turin, Einaudi, 1966, pp. 619–730; Lyttelton, *The Seizure of Power*, pp. 237–68; Mauro Canali, *Il delitto Matteotti: Affarismo e politica nel primo governo Mussolini*, Bologna, Il Mulino, 1997.

[93] G. Pierangeli, 'Le due Italie', *La Critica Politica* (Rome), 25 July 1924, pp. 291–5.

[94] Camillo Bellieni, 'L'Associazione dei Combattenti (Appunti per una storia politica dell'ultimo quinquennio)', *La Critica Politica*, 25 July 1924, pp. 301–15.

[95] *Cremona Nuova*, 19 July 1924.

expressed severe criticisms of fascist illegality and violence, they did not join the Aventino opposition group in abandoning the Parliament.[96]

The ANC Congress of Assisi at the end of July 1924 would serve to clarify the veterans' hypothetical stance in this state of affairs. Members of the Aventinian opposition such as Giovanni Amendola hoped that veterans would align at Assisi against the anti-democratic drift.[97] There was also much expectation and nervousness amongst fascists regarding the congress. Many fascists, Dino Grandi among them, went to Assisi to be present at the sessions. The discussions were heated and tumultuous, with an especially bitter confrontation between the outgoing leaders Arangio Ruiz and Ponzio di San Sebastiano. Despite substantial fascist presence, Giulio Bergmann presented a crude motion of condemnation of the government that attracted the support of various representatives. In contrast, the representative of Udine, Luigi Russo,[98] calmly talked about maintaining confidence in Mussolini. Finally, the convention passed a compromising 'conciliatory resolution' (ordine del giorno), proposed by Ettore Viola – a former officer of the arditi, a fascist MP and holder of the Gold Medal. The ordine del giorno of Assisi stressed the ANC's autonomy above all else; support for the government was implicitly suspended pending the re-establishment of legality and state sovereignty. In the end, Viola took over the presidency, together with four other fascists, including Luigi Russo. The presence of these fascist individuals in the Comitato Centrale was counterbalanced by four anti-fascists such as Livio Pivano, a republican from Alessandria. The main leaders of the new Comitato Centrale were also members of Parliament. The Aventinian opposition interpreted the ordine del giorno of Assisi as a symptom of veterans' anti-fascism. The fascists showed disappointment with its cold and distant tone. Farinacci stated that it was necessary to come out of this ambiguous situation.[99]

When, some days later, the National Council of the PNF met, Mussolini very clearly declared that he did not like the ordine del giorno of Assisi: 'l'ordine del giorno di Assisi non mi piace.' This reaction bore

---

[96] I Combattenti. La Nuova Giornata, 22 June and 17 July 1924.

[97] Giovanni Amendola, L'Aventino contro il fascismo: Scritti politici (1924–1926), Milan, 1976, pp. 56–9.

[98] Luigi Russo would go on to become a key figure in fascist veteran politics. Born in Verona in 1882, he was a decorated ex-officer and a leader of the ANC in the region of Friuli.

[99] Il Popolo d'Italia, 27, 29, 30 and 31 July and 1 August 1924; Cremona Nuova, 29, 30 and 31 July and 1 August 1924; Problemi d'Italia, 2 (September 1924), 3 (October 1924); Il Giornale dei Combattenti. Organo dei Combattenti Nazionali del Piemonte (Turin), 26 July and 2 August 1924; Ettore Viola, Combattenti e Mussolini dopo il congresso di Assisi, Florence, 1975, pp. 13–20.

testament to the political turn experienced by Fascism at the time, which was linked to the ascension of Farinacci and the intransigent fascists. Importantly, Mussolini argued that the ANC owed a lot to him and that it had been only after the March on Rome, during 1923, that 'political manifestations of *combattentismo*' had taken place; earlier, there had not been such a phenomenon in Italy. The Duce's argumentation claimed that only Fascism's arrival into power had made *combattentismo* possible by supporting veterans and the ANC.[100] This animosity between Mussolini and the veterans of Assisi did not lead yet to an absolute rupture, but the relationship between veterans and the PNF became extremely tense. Furthermore, the most radical sector of Fascism aggressively jumped into veterans' debates through the pages of new fascist newspapers. *Roma fascista* directly attacked the opposition by clearly affirming that Fascism equalled veterans and veterans equalled Fascism: there was no difference between the two.[101] The Roman Fascio made clear that over 3,000 of its 9,000 members were veterans, some of them Gold Medal holders, such as Amilcare Rossi.[102] A big demonstration of veterans in Rome exhibited their confidence in Mussolini.[103] In other words, the fascists were mobilizing resources to preserve their monopoly over the symbol of the veteran.

Thus, the discursive struggle escalated. The term *combattentismo*, lacking any concrete definition, became polyvalent and a source of dispute between anti-fascist veterans, the ANC and fascist veterans. The anti-fascist veterans of L'Italia Libera, expelled from the ANC, opted to continue their attacks on the idea of *combattentismo*, accepting that it was already a concept married to Fascism. As it was believed that anti-fascist *combattentismo* was not different from fascist *combattentismo*, L'Italia Libera veterans renounced to the notion. By this time, they had come to understand this veteran ideology not as positive political action but merely as a vehicle for demanding rewards in the name of the war experience. L'Italia Libera veterans sought to carry out anti-fascist political activities, but paradoxically, they shared the fascist view that the ANC should recover its *apoliticità* and its exclusive function of social assistance.[104]

---

[100] *Cremona Nuova*, 5 August 1924; *Il Popolo d'Italia*, 5 August 1924.
[101] A. F. Proja, 'Il Fascismo è Combattenti: I combattenti sono il Fascismo', *Roma fascista. Settimanale politico* (Rome), 2 August 1924.
[102] *L'Idea Nazionale*, 6 and 7 August 1924; *Roma fascista*, 9 August 1924. As we will see, Amilcare Rossi, a lawyer born in Lannuvio (Rome) in 1895, became the most important fascist veterans' leader in Mussolini's regime.
[103] *Il Popolo d'Italia*, 8 August 1924.
[104] G. Golinelli, 'Il "combattentismo"', *L'Italia Libera*, 4 August 1924; G. Golinelli, 'Critiche sul 'combattentismo'', *L'Italia Libera*, 16 August 1924.

Meanwhile, some fascists also disowned the notion of *combattentismo*, disregarding it as a degeneration of patriotic values and arguing that having fought the war did not give rise to rights but rather to duties.[105] This complex discussion is evidence of the unclear position held by veterans at the time of the Matteotti crisis. Unsurprisingly, the Duce was hesitant and appeared to prefer to wait until the general situation became clearer before deciding which measures to take.[106]

In 1924, as had happened the year before, the two symbolic dates of 28 October and 4 November served to test the level of veterans' commitment to Fascism. The commemoration of the March on Rome revealed profound divisions amongst Italian veterans. Correctly judging it to be a partisan celebration and for the sake of *apoliticità*, the ANC Comitato Centrale refused to join the fascist celebration. Confronting the ANC withdrawal, the fascist response was solemnly bitter. In *Critica fascista*, it was argued that veterans were acting 'outside of their historical function'. Fascists considered the hostile attitude of veterans very disappointing because 'the historical function of so-called *combattentismo* has been incarnated by Fascism'. They stated that Fascism would complete its celebrations even without the participation of veterans.[107] The veterans, disappointed with Fascism, argued the contrary: 'the historical mission of Fascism – which was not a party but a state of mind – was completely finished.'[108] In the days prior to the March on Rome anniversary, the fascists made important efforts to convince veterans to join the celebration. Paradoxically, now the fascists attacked the concept of *apoliticità*.[109]

In reality, important sectors of veterans throughout the Italian provinces joined the ceremonies for the March on Rome regardless, as was the case in Rome and in several northern towns.[110] Mussolini obtained endorsement from veterans' associations other than the ANC, namely, the war volunteers and *arditi*. It came as no surprise that Delcroix maintained his loyalty to him.[111] Forty-four bearers of the Gold Medal publicly declared their full support to Mussolini.[112] Likewise, many other *combattenti* wanted to reinforce the links with Mussolini instead of breaking with the government. Their decision to disobey the ANC was

---

[105] Nicola Moscardelli, 'Combattentismo e pescecanismo', *La Conquista dello Stato* (Rome), 1 October 1924.
[106] *La Stampa*, 15 August 1924.
[107] Nino Sammartano, 'I "combattenti" fuori della loro funzione storica', *Critica fascista*, 15 October 1924.
[108] *Il Primato*, 7 December 1924.   [109] *Il Popolo d'Italia*, 21 October 1924.
[110] *Roma fascista*, 8 November 1924; *Il Combattente Maremmano*, 31 October 1924.
[111] *Il Popolo d'Italia*, 1, 7, 16, 19 and 24 October 1924.
[112] *Cremona Nuova*, 9 and 11 November 1924; *Il Popolo d'Italia*, 11 November 1924.

justified by the view that its Comitato Centrale practiced an ambiguous *apoliticità*.[113] In other words, the decision not to participate in a celebration because of the *apoliticità* of the ANC was criticized precisely as a *political* reaction. Furthermore, the belief in the mythical link between Vittorio Veneto and the March on Rome was widespread. And many were convinced that the veterans had actually been 'pioneers of the fascist gospel' through their participation in war propaganda, and that Fascism was a phenomenon that had emerged from the war.[114] But, in general, veterans who joined the 28 October celebration were moved by their fascist membership rather than by their status as veterans. In any case, the fascists were disappointed.[115] In the end, violence broke out in many Italian cities between fascists and veterans who performed the 4 November commemoration separately.[116] The commemorative celebrations of October–November 1924 provoked a violent conflict that revealed the deadlock at which the veterans' ideological evolution had arrived.

In conclusion, the two fundamental discursive elements that entered into the veterans' ideological worldview at this time – *combattentismo* and *apoliticità* – did not lead to a widely and uniformly shared political position either for veterans' organizations or for their members and leaders. Yet, at the same time, both ideas favoured Fascism's progressive impregnation of the social and cultural realm. The original 1919 project of *rinnovamento* was now long since forgotten; the ideologies of the 'anti-patriotic' left had been rejected; the republican (L'Italia Libera) and the Salveminian trends (PSdA) had been marginalized.[117] Therefore, by October 1922, Fascism was the main ideological and discursive framework left for veterans who wished to take part in political action. Soon dissatisfied with the totalitarian impulses of fascist ideology – already present in De Vecchi's project – most veterans tried to maintain themselves in an idiosyncratic discursive framework, or strived to find a new one, while they negotiated with Fascism. It was necessary to define an ideological position for veterans to safeguard their organizational independence. *Combattentismo* and *apoliticità* were two tools for this discursive negotiation, which would allow for the accommodation of veterans

---

[113] *Il Popolo d'Italia*, 18 and 21 October 1924.

[114] *Il Combattente d'Italia*, 5 September and 3 November 1924.

[115] Leo Polini, 'Combattenti e fascisti', *Il Popolo d'Italia*, 2 November 1924.

[116] *La Stampa*, 3 November 1924; *I Combattenti. La Nuova Giornata*, 9 November 1924; Cf. *Cremona Nuova*, 6 November 1924; Marco Baldassari, 'La memoria celebrata: La festa del 4 novembre a Lucca tra dopoguerra e fascismo', *Italia contemporanea*, 242 (2006), pp. 23–43.

[117] In the south, veterans who wanted to pursue a reformist programme had to become independent from the ANC, creating their own press organs; see *Il Combattente. Politico indipendente dell'Italia Meridionale* (Naples), 20 October 1924.

into Fascism. However, in reality, Fascism did not aim to accommodate but rather to assimilate. *Combattentismo* and *apoliticità* did not help militate against the fascist impregnation of veterans' political culture. Instead, between 1923 and 1924, both discursive tools permitted the final consolidation of Fascism as the perceived real political manifestation of the veterans' spirit and voices, even if this discursive bond did not translate into reality.

The *Fascistizzazione* of the ANC, 1924–1925

Understanding the final stage of Fascism's co-optation of Italian veterans is crucial, as it was integral to the imposition of the fascist dictatorship in 1925. Both the establishment of the dictatorship and the process of assimilating veterans into Fascism should be understood in the context of both the political ascension of Farinacci – who would go on to become the general secretary of the PNF on 15 February 1925 – and the 'second wave' of fascist violence.[118] Most importantly, Mussolini's infamous speech on 3 January 1925 made resistance from non-fascist veterans highly difficult given Italy's formal conversion to dictatorship. Thereafter, any opposition could be deemed illegal or completely marginalized. Despite the relevance of the fascist co-optation of Italian war veterans to the process of establishing the dictatorship, until now, historiographical studies have provided only limited accounts of Italian veteran politics in this period. Veterans' memoires of this crucial time are usually contradictory and tend to be self-justifying in nature.[119] In this section I will provide a new and more detailed analysis of this process, offering a view from below and focusing on its discursive and symbolic features. This analysis will allow us to reassess the role played by veterans in the consolidation of the fascist dictatorship during 1925.

Unleashing Fascistizzazione

The aforementioned events of 4 November 1924 represented a symbolic breaking point that unleashed the definitive fascist offensive to absorb the ANC. In the following weeks, some ANC leaders, such as Ponzio di San Sebastiano, broke off their relationship with the PNF; some of

---

[118] Adrian Lyttelton, 'Fascism in Italy: The Second Wave', *Journal of Contemporary History*, 1 (1966), pp. 75–100.

[119] Sabbatucci, *I combattenti*, pp. 371–5; De Felice, *Mussolini il fascista. II. L'organizzazione dello Stato fascista 1925–1929*, Turin, Einaudi, 1968, p. 76; Arturo Codignola, *La resistenza de 'I combattenti di Assisi'*, Modena, 1965.

them made moves to collaborate with the anti-fascist parliamentary opposition.[120] To reverse this situation, some fascists suggested infiltrating the ANC gradually and peacefully. They recommended that fascist veterans, seizing on their superiority in numbers, enrol in the veterans' association, frequent its headquarters and make themselves known; the objective was not to 'conquer' (*conquistare*) the ANC sections but to make their ideals prevail within the association.[121] Farinacci, in contrast, was in favour of a far more intransigent way of resolving the veterans' issue. As we know, in Farinacci's Cremona the confrontation between veterans and fascists was particularly hostile.[122] According to the radical *ras*, there was no space for intermediate positions; the veterans should either be with Fascism or against it. As we will see in this section, fascists not only pursued a strategy of silent infiltration but also employed violent, ruthless methods to finally 'fascistize' the veterans organization.

Using propaganda and local political manoeuvres, the fascists launched a campaign aimed at discrediting the ANC. For this purpose, they set up an alternative veteran platform, the Unione Nazionale Combattenti (UNCi). The UNCi emerged in Turin at the end of October 1924, promoted by the fascist veteran Aldo Bertelè, who was part of a group of fascists expelled from the ANC.[123] The new association emanated from some local Fasci and tried to attract veterans who were unhappy with the political attitude of the ANC Comitato Centrale.[124] Thus, during November and December of 1924, the first sections of the UNCi appeared on the initiative of certain fascist leaders in the province of Turin and in some villages near Florence; shortly after, UNCi cells emerged in Palermo and Rome.[125] In the capital, Adolfo Schiavo reaffirmed the ANC section's loyal collaboration with Mussolini's government – 'donor of the greatest value to the Victory' (*valorizzatore della vittoria*) – during a meeting attended by influential bearers of the Gold

---

[120] *Cremona Nuova*, 8 and 9 November 1924; *Il Popolo d'Italia*, 9 November 1924; *L'Impero* (Rome), 9 November 1924; *L'Idea Nazionale*, 11 November 1924.

[121] See Rino Landi's articles in *Il Fascio*, 4, 11, 18 and 29 November and 20 December 1924.

[122] Arturo Codignola, *La resistenza de 'I combattenti di Assisi'*, p. 114; *Cremona Nuova*, 22 October and 7 November 1924; also in Roberto Farinacci, *Andante mosso, 1924–25*, Milan, 1929, pp. 125–32 and 140–2.

[123] *La Stampa*, 29 October 1924.

[124] According to Sabbatucci, *I combattenti*, p. 373, the UNCi had scant success, but I will demonstrate that the whole political move was successful.

[125] *L'Idea Nazionale*, 7 November 1924; *Il Giornale dei Combattenti. Organo Ufficiale dell'Unione Nazionale Combattenti* (Turin), 25 November and 28 December 1924; *Il Popolo d'Italia*, 16 November 1924; *Cremona Nuova* 16 November 1924; Cf. *Il Primato*, 7 December 1924.

Medal such as Amilcare Rossi.[126] Meanwhile, sections of the UNCi started to appear in many other Italian regions from January of 1925, though it was a phenomenon confined to small towns. According to a circular sent by a fascist organizer in the Sicilian province of Caltanissetta, this strategy had to be very subtle, but the objectives were straightforward. The fascists saw that due to the uncertainty of veteran leaders' political positions, ordinary veterans were in a 'state of mind' that could be exploited 'in the interests of the consolidation and development of the PNF'. In principle, the key issue was to depoliticize these veterans and to direct them towards welfare tasks only, and for this reason, the UNCi veterans had to keep very weak links with the PNF sections. In reality, however, veterans were not expected to continue being 'agnostic' in the political realm.[127] Veterans across Italy had to submit to the fascist will.

Spaces

Fascism launched a countrywide campaign in January and February of 1925 to debilitate the ANC and to reinforce the position of Mussolini, whose fully fledged dictatorship had recently been installed on 3 January. Subsequently, most groups of L'Italia Libera were swiftly repressed and dismantled.[128] Having broken the anti-fascist veterans' platform, the rest of Italian veterans would also be brought under the control of the regime. This process can be seen not just as a fascist mobilization against a neutral ANC but also as the first campaign to gather support and manufacture consent for Mussolini's dictatorship. However, the presence of fascist veterans was far from widespread throughout the country. It is therefore interesting to carefully examine the geographical distribution of the fascist support among the Italian veterans.

The pages of *Il Popolo d'Italia* and other fascist journals testified to the creation either of local UNCi sections or of sections that were independent from the ANC Comitato Centrale. The newspapers divulged the veterans' declarations of fidelity to the Governo Nazionale, even if the sections remained linked to the ANC. In local meetings, the ANC sections decided to adopt an official position relating to whether a scission would take place. The information reported in *I Combattenti* and *Il Popolo d'Italia* regarding the ANC sections loyal or not to the Comitato Centrale and the reports from the *prefetti* to the Ministry of

---

[126] *Il Giornale dei Combattenti*, 28 December 1924.
[127] ACS, MI, PS (1925), box 107, file 'Associazione Nazionale Combattenti, sf. 'Caltanissetta'.
[128] Zani, *Italia Libera*, p. 125.

Interior – Federzoni, a figure opposed to radical fascism – help us to gain an overall view of the extent of the fascist veterans' campaign by the end of February 1925.[129]

Two poles of fascist agitation among veterans were especially important: one in Tuscany, between Florence and Pisa, and another around Milan. In addition, fascist strongholds in Emilia-Romagna were violently opposed to the ANC Comitato Centrale. Unsurprisingly, fascist veterans were powerful in these zones, where the fascist movement had been born and first flourished. These pro-governmental groups often mushroomed in medium-sized localities around urban centres. For example, in the case of Tuscany, fascists controlled the veterans' movement as early as 1919 or 1921 in cities such as Siena, Pisa and Florence. In the latter, the first fascist reactions against the ANC had started around December of 1924 in certain neighbourhoods. From there, the fascists expanded their control to the urban centre, physically attacking rival veteran centres and then intervening in other villages. Veterans from Lucca also came under fascist control, thanks to the aggressive actions of squadrist leader Carlo Scorza. In the rest of the Tuscan region, the spread of Fascism amongst veterans also depended on squadrist coercion. In Farinacci's province of Cremona, the process was similar.[130]

These fascist offensives were directly related to the existence of previous conflicts between veterans and fascists. Such quarrels had arisen as early as 1922–3, especially in Farinacci's province. In other northern regions, there was a smaller need to mobilize veterans against the ANC, since the masses of veterans had already been brought under fascist control. For example, in Veneto, there was less agitation, as Fascism had already dismantled the previously dominant Catholic UNRG. In Brescia, the Catholic veterans of the countryside mostly remained loyal to the fascist government, whilst veteran leaders in the city remained loyal to the ANC Comitato Centrale; Augusto Turati – the fascist *ras* of Brescia – preferred to wait until the decree of 2 March (see below) to dissolve this ANC section.[131] All these cases (Tuscany, Cremona and Brescia) show that the fascist reaction against the ANC was not spontaneous; instead, it depended on the personal initiative of fascist leaders to mobilize veterans.

---

[129] *Il Popolo d'Italia*, 20, 22–25 and 27–31 January and 1, 3–5, 7, 10, 14, 15, 17, 25 and 26 February 1925; *L'Idea Nazionale*, 27 January and 4 and 6 February 1925; *I Combattenti*, 25 February 1925.

[130] *Cremona Nuova*, 21, 23, 24 and 25 January 1925; ACS, MI PS, 1925, box 107, Ass. Naz. Combattenti, sf. 'Cremona'.

[131] Paolo Corsini, *Il feudo di Augusto Turati: Fascismo e lotta politica a Brescia (1922–1926)*, Milan, Franco Angeli, 1988, pp. 243–50, 682–4.

Seemingly, some zones remained only slightly affected by the fascist drive, especially in the centre and south of Italy. Veterans from Lazio and the Marche may have shown little sympathy for Fascism for several reasons. In these zones, veterans had been involved in agrarian activism during the *bienio rosso*, and both the Arditi del Popolo and L'Italia Libera organizations were well rooted. Further south, the same causes for a less significant fascist penetration can be pointed out. In the Mezzogiorno and in Sicily, fascist veterans tried to drum up support in a generally hostile environment. In Sardinia, the masses of veterans of the PSdA most certainly remained unconvinced by Fascism. Anti-fascist veteran leaders such as Lussu were still influential. Several ANC federations from Campania, Calabria and Sicily declared their loyalty to the *ordine del giorno* of Assisi. However, in these regions, fascists made efforts to mobilize veterans in different local sections, confronting non-fascist groups.[132]

In reality, fascist veterans were present in the south as well. Several ANC section leaders from Lazio were among the promoters of the pro-fascist agitation in Rome.[133] In the province of Lecce (Puglia), a local section adhered to the government on the grounds of rejecting 'faction ideologies' and denouncing the 'disintegrating action of subversive forces'. At the end of February 1925, in this provincial federation, sixteen of thirty-six local sections supported the fascist government, which received 3,762 votes.[134] In the case of Trapani (Sicily), the veterans' assembly had divided into four groups: fascists (69 votes), pro-fascists (140 votes) and two anti-government groups (134 votes in total).[135] In Catanzaro, too, down on the sole of the boot-shaped Italian peninsula, a division between two trends was reported: one favourable and the other critical of the ANC.[136] In Cagliari (Sardinia), there was a significant inclination towards Fascism amongst veterans: 105 of 115 sections (containing 12,000 of 15,000 veterans) supported Fascism.[137] In general, in the south, whereas some urban squadrism-connected veteran elites underpinned Fascism, the large numbers of peasant ex-soldiers did not.

---

[132] *I Combattenti*, 15 February 1925; cf. *Il Giornale dei Combattenti*, 21 February 1925.
[133] *L'Idea Nazionale*, 3 February 1925.
[134] ACS, MI PS, 1925, box 107, Ass. Naz. Combattenti, fascicles by provinces, file 'Lecce'.
[135] ACS, MI PS, 1925, box 108, Ass. Naz. Combattenti, fascicles by provinces (II), file 'Trapani'.
[136] ACS, MI PS, 1925, box 107, Ass. Naz. Combattenti, fascicles by provinces, file 'Catanzaro'.
[137] ACS, MI PS, 1925, box 108, Ass. Naz. Combattenti, fascicles by provinces (II), file 'Cagliari'.

In the north, inversely, Fascism was a mass movement, but there were places with a predominantly anti-fascist tendency amongst veterans (Alessandria and Genoa). For instance, writing from Imperia, on the Ligurian Coast, the *prefetto* reported that the ANC provincial section had voted in February in favour of an anti-fascist position, gathering 860 votes against 460 votes and 330 abstentions, though seven pro-fascist sections decided to create their own independent federation.[138] On some occasions, the decision of the provincial or local section just depended on the personal choice of the leaders. Most veterans were indifferent or incapable of discerning any real differences between either supporting the Comitato Centrale or stating loyalty to the fascist government. In Reggio Emilia, for instance, during a meeting in mid-February, a new pro-ANC committee prevailed over the fascist list of candidates by a difference of around 400 votes, but the *prefetto* noted that there were names common to both lists.[139] It is difficult to discern the local political controversies that swayed the ANC sections to tilt towards the fascist government or towards the ANC Comitato Centrale. Beyond a superficial division between north and south, many other factors divided Italian veterans.

Discourses and Symbols

The kind of reasoning and discourse with which veterans legitimized their support for Mussolini's government is easier to understand. As they launched their campaign to fascistize the ANC, the fascists again took advantage of the *apoliticità* motif, which was deeply engrained within the veteran discursive framework. Veterans were, in the fascists' view, bound to the future task of safeguarding superior national interests; for this reason, they should be controlled, tamed by the idea of *apoliticità*, until that moment arrived. In the fascist discursive strategy of the time, it was only the attitude of the ANC Comitato Centrale and the *ordine del giorno* of Assisi that were considered perniciously political, whereas adhering to the Governo Nazionale and Mussolini as Presidente del Consiglio was considered a wholly national and patriotic (non-political) position. Naturally, any real war veteran was expected to support Mussolini. For the fascists, 'the *combattenti* worthy of this name should not forget and should maintain their supportive help, their recognition and fidelity to the PNF and to its great leader.'[140]

---

[138] ACS, MI PS, 1925, box 107, Ass. Naz. Combattenti, fascicles by provinces, file 'Imperia'.
[139] ACS, MI PS, 1925, box 108, Ass. Naz. Combattenti, fascicles by provinces (II), file 'Reggio Emilia'.
[140] *Il Popolo d'Italia*, 8 January 1925.

The manipulated notion of *apoliticità* and mythologized narratives concerning the fascist seizure of power explain why many veterans' sections sided with Fascism and stood against the ANC Comitato Centrale. The statement by veterans in La Spezia on 2 February 1925 illustrates this point.[141] According to them, members of the Comitato Centrale, such as Ettore Viola, had abused the right to carry out political action in the name of veterans, thereby discrediting and dividing the ANC. By forgetting the statutory principle of *apoliticità*, the Comitato Centrale had favoured the victory-sabotaging political groups. In order to save unity, veterans disavowed their leaders. In contrast, they stressed that Mussolini's government had 'always been a jealous guardian and defender of their moral and economic rights' and that 'only after the coming of the fascist government [did] the veterans [see] their heroic sacrifice recognised.'[142] For them, the national government had made the victory real and given meaning to the heroic sacrifice of soldiers.[143] This kind of declaration proves that the fascist discourse had to a certain extent permeated the veterans' movement. Such statements also reflected the positive reception of the measures taken by Mussolini's government and demonstrate how the discourse of *apoliticità* was bene-fitting Fascism.

The fascists were the victors of the discursive and symbolic struggle of this period. At a moment when Fascism and anti-fascism were the only available political options, the pitfall of *apoliticità* was detrimental for the veterans.[144] The ANC leaders were less successful than the fascists in employing the narrative of the veterans' political neutrality. The veterans wrongly thought that impartiality would lead to the end of the fascist 'revolution'. As a cartoon published in the ANC main newspaper shows, the veterans tried to represent themselves as independent spectators in the 'theatre of Italian politics'; they over-emphasized the typical veteran attributes, the grey-green uniform, the helmet and the medals strip as something very different to the fascist model of squadrist political actor with the black shirt and the black beret.[145]

However, after 3 January 1925, the anti-fascist veterans' leaders had a very low probability of winning the symbolic and discursive struggle, given that the independent veteran press constantly suffered attacks

---

[141] ACS, MI PS, 1925, box 107, Ass. Naz. Combattenti, fascicles by provinces, file 'Spezia'.
[142] ACS, MI, PS 1925, box 107, Ass. Naz. Combattenti, fascicles by provinces, file 'Spezia'.
[143] ACS, MI PS, 1925, box 107, Ass. Naz. Combattenti, fascicles by provinces, file 'Ascoli Piceno'.
[144] Cf. *L'Idea Nazionale*, 4 February 1925.   [145] *I Combattenti*, 22 February 1925.

and confiscations.[146] Indeed, the fascists now appropriated the same neutral symbolic representation of the veterans. Fascist publications also represented the veterans without fascist traits, as well-behaved soldiers whose loyalty was bound to the government and not to the vile, self-interested ANC leaders.[147] Thus, during this process, a shared representation of veterans was consolidated: that of loyal soldiers. It was a symbol rather typical of the nationalist patriotic discourse. But now this symbol remained tied to Fascism in power.

Actors, Practices and Strategies

Who exactly were the agents of the process of veterans' co-optation by Fascism? Sociologically, this phenomenon was in essence the same as the fascist reaction of 1920–2. It differed from squadrism in the nature of the actions performed, although violence was eventually used. As mentioned earlier, the first pro-fascist veterans' sections appeared in January of 1925 in the centre-north of Italy.[148] There is evidence to demonstrate that the protagonists were stereotypical fascist veterans: officers, young junior officers and ex-*arditi*. For instance, in Trieste, three former lieutenants and one frigate captain established the UNCi cell on 25 January.[149] In Pavia, on 5 February, a colonel, a lieutenant colonel, a captain, a major and some professors, lawyers and doctors set up the local UNCi cell recruiting 200 members.[150] Some groups of *arditi* were also involved in the UNCi associative operation.[151] The anti-Bolshevik veterans of 1919 were again in action.

Nevertheless, the fascist veterans did not rely on violent squadrist practices during the campaign against the unbowed ANC. They made their voices heard, but they did not assault the ANC headquarters in the same way as they had previously attacked socialist centres. In Turin, on 19 January, after an assembly in the Fascio headquarters, there was a demonstration of fascist veterans in front of the ANC premises, which were guarded by soldiers and *carabinieri*. They sang fascist and soldiers' hymns ('Giovinezza' and 'Inno del Piave'), but there were no incidents.[152] In other towns, fascist veterans publicly protested, rallied and

---

[146] *Ibid.*   [147] *Roma fascista*, 7 March 1925.
[148] ACS, MI PS, 1925, box 107, Ass. Naz. Combattenti, fascicles by provinces, files 'Firenze', 'Cremona' and 'Ancona'.
[149] ACS, MI PS, 1925, box 108, Ass. Naz. Combattenti, fascicles by provinces (II), file 'Trieste'.
[150] ACS, MI PS, 1925, box 108, Ass. Naz. Combattenti, fascicles by provinces (II), file 'Pavia'
[151] *Il Giornale dei Combattenti*, 21 February 1925.
[152] *Il Popolo d'Italia*, 20 January 1925.

demonstrated against the ANC, but there were no physical attacks yet.[153] In the biggest cities, where anti-fascist ANC leaders still controlled important provincial sections, the division between fascists and veterans was more troublesome. This was the case of Milan, where Giulio Bergmann was the main leader. On 10 February, tumultuous brawls took place during a veterans' meeting, yet without bloodshed.[154] On 15 February, the *prefetto* of Milan reported that another electrifying meeting ended with the approval of the fascist *ordine del giorno* by a narrow margin (2,165 to 2,039 votes). Giulio Bergmann defended the *ordine del giorno* of Assisi and protested, but the fascist commissaries occupied the ANC establishment without incident.[155] A common denominator of shared symbols and discourses prevented violence between the fascists and ANC veterans.

However, violence was an important vector for fascist success, eventually exploding during clashes for the control of the ANC headquarters. The ANC establishments symbolized the control of the sections and, in fact, contained the archives, funds and materials necessary to carry out assistance tasks. The fascists never wanted to destroy but rather to seize them. Nonetheless, in certain places throughout the Mezzogiorno, groups of peasant ex-soldiers either had socialist inclinations or had rivalled the fascists for the control of towns and syndicates. Here the level of violent behaviour was higher. In fact, in Puglia, squadrist violence against veterans' associations had continued after the March on Rome, and now conflicts stepped up.[156] In Bari, for example, a provisional ANC committee riddled with internal controversies tried to keep the section united. The pro-fascist leaders, however, occupied the headquarters by force and mobilized forty-three of fifty local sections in their favour. The *prefetto* of Bari believed that future violent skirmishes were likely.[157]

Perhaps the most important confrontations took place in Rome, although physical violence did not yet break out. In the capital city, the ANC central headquarters co-existed with the fascistized ANC local section. On 1 February 1925, a group of 200 veterans organized a meeting in the Teatro Argentina to declare their hostility to the ANC Comitato Centrale. After this demonstration, they moved on to the Altare della Patria to venerate the tomb of the *Milite Ignoto*, stopping

---

[153] *Cremona Nuova*, 21 January 1925.   [154] *Avanti!* (Milan), 10 February 1925.
[155] ACS, MI PS, 1925, box 107, Ass. Naz. Combattenti, fascicles by provinces, file 'Milano'.
[156] Salvatore Coppola, *Conflitti di lavoro e lotta politica nel Salento nel primo dopoguerra (1919–1925)*, Lecce, Salento Domani, 1984, pp. 92–7, 104–5; Simona Colarizi, *Dopoguerra e fascismo, passim*.
[157] ACS, MI PS, 1925, box 107, Ass. Naz. Combattenti, fascicles by provinces, file 'Bari'.

en route to protest in front of the ANC national headquarters in Palazzetto Venezia. Their attempt to invade the building was only prevented by police intervention. The following day, they gathered again in Piazza Venezia, and a group of approximately twenty of them tried to approach the ANC headquarters, again with hostile intentions. Once more, however, the police blocked their way.[158] Further north, in Forlì (Romagna), veterans suffered fascist aggressions at the end of January 1925.[159] In Pavia, fights between anti-fascist and fascist veterans took place on several occasions, whilst fascists were carrying out a campaign to affiliate veterans to the PNF.[160] In the province of Verona, the fascists attacked some veterans who were members of the Italia Libera or even ANC members.[161] However, physical attacks against persons were not common unless they took place against veterans clearly considered to be socialists or anti-fascists.

The ANC establishments were the targets of this fascist violence rather than the veterans themselves. In Tuscany, this kind of attack became more systematic than in other areas. The first violent explosion took place in Florence on 31 December 1924, when a fascist gathering ended with the destruction of several centres of the anti-fascist middle class, for example, the printing press of the combatants' weekly *Fanteria*.[162] At the end of February, in the province of Pisa, the ANC offices of at least three localities were ravaged, and this strategy continued into March, when several fascists were arrested and charged.[163] Coercion seems, however, to have worked, since many veterans joined the new UNCi sections created in Tuscany at around this time. It was in the province of Lucca that conflicts reached a peak. By the end of February, the eighty-four ANC sections registered 8,300 members in this province, whereas the fifty-five pro-fascist UNCi sections numbered 5,000.[164] On 1 March, after a UNCi meeting, there was a veterans' parade; some fights took place, and the fascists attempted to occupy the ANC headquarters. In light of these clashes, the *prefetto* opted to close them down. Finally, fascist leader Carlo Scorza demanded control of the premises, arguing

---

[158] ACS, MI PS, 1925, box 108, Roma e provincia, ex combattenti autonomi, file 'Roma città'; *L'Idea Nazionale*, 3 February 1925.

[159] *Avanti!*, 29 January 1925.

[160] ACS, MI PS, 1925, box 107, Ass. Naz. Combattenti, fascicles by provinces (II), file 'Pavia'. *Avanti!*, 5 February 1925

[161] *I Combattenti*, 23 January 1925.

[162] *Cremona Nuova*, 1 January 1925; *Fanteria*, 6 December 1924, was the last issue.

[163] ACS, MI PS, 1925, box 107, Ass. Naz. Combattenti, fascicles by provinces (II), file 'Pisa'.

[164] ACS, MI PS, 1925, box 107, Ass. Naz. Combattenti, fascicles by provinces, file 'Lucca'.

that the UNCi section had already exceeded the numbers of the ANC. In reality, the fascists had subjugated the veterans through a series of arson attacks, aggressions, occupations and robberies committed against several local ANC headquarters all throughout the province.[165] The objective was to take over the organizational structure of the ANC.

The fascists seemed to be looking for a confrontation. The ANC National Congress was arranged for 5 March in Viareggio. With this meeting, several ANC leaders headed by Viola wanted to gather veterans' support, probably in order to proclaim a strong opposition to the fascist government. However, the pro-fascist UNCi leaders called the veterans to a national congress in the same town. In the last days of February, the UNCi threateningly expanded throughout Italy; its leaders stated that they wanted 'just to show their forces'.[166] The *prefetto* and the Ministry of Interior, fearing the consequences of this showdown, disposed 400 soldiers and 200 *carabinieri* ready to intervene in Viareggio. Many interpreted the situation as a fascist attempt to silence veterans' criticism.[167] When the ANC decisive congress was moved to Rome, the UNCi correspondingly summoned their veterans to Rome.[168] It was very clear that an agreement between the two factions would not work. Luigi Russo, a pro-fascist member of the Comitato Centrale, had resigned from his position, declaring that no compromise was possible.[169] Russo and Host-Venturi blamed the Comitato Centrale for having abandoned the mission of social assistance; the ANC was not fulfilling its duties.[170] It was also said that Freemasonry had infiltrated the ANC.[171] On the basis of these allegations, some sections started to clamour for government intervention.[172] Two days before the ANC Congress in Rome commenced, this meeting was banned by the *prefetto* of Rome, and crucially, Mussolini made use of his powers to decree the dissolution of the ANC Comitato Centrale.[173]

Mussolini's decree of 2 March 1925 dissolved the central administrative organs of the ANC and entrusted a triumvirate with the temporary

---

[165] ACS, MI PS, 1925, box 107, Ass. Naz. Combattenti, Affari generali, file 'Lucca'.

[166] *Il Giornale dei Combattenti. Organo dell'Unione Nazionale Combattenti*, 28 February 1925.

[167] *I Combattenti*, 1 March 1925.

[168] ACS, MI PS, 1925, box 107, Ass. Naz. Combattenti, Affari generali; *Il Popolo d'Italia*, 6 and 28 February 1925.

[169] *Il Popolo d'Italia*, 8 February 1925.

[170] *Il Popolo d'Italia*, 20 February 1925; *L'Idea Nazionale*, 1 March 1925.

[171] *Il Popolo d'Italia*, 28 February 1925; *Roma fascista* had since 1924 suggested this connection; see also 7 and 9 March 1925.

[172] *Il Popolo d'Italia*, 26 February 1925.

[173] *Il Popolo d'Italia*, 3 March 1925. The *prefetto* of Rome also vetoed on 3 March the celebration of the UNCi Congress.

mission of administering the association. This action was the result of the previous fascist campaign of slander, coercion, disturbance and political disintegration at the local level, which encouraged groups of veterans to mobilize against the Comitato Centrale. As a foreign observer noted, this was a 'new *coup de force* of Mussolini, carried out under the pressure of the extremist elements'.[174]

The fascist manipulative manoeuvre had succeeded. When the decree came, it was alleged that more than half the veterans' sections had stated their position supporting the government and against the ANC. The leaders of the Comitato Centrale were only able to maintain certain zones under control, such as Genoa, Alessandria and Naples. Their anti-fascist reaction came far too late. By contrast, the fascists were reaping their rewards for having cultivated the support of veterans since the beginning of Mussolini's government. After the decree was passed, the symbolic and economic measures taken in relation to veterans were recalled once more in the fascist press.[175] Fascism had fostered the perception that it had placed great value on the victory (*valorizzato la vittoria*), that *apoliticità* should be the expected attitude of veterans, and that the fascists really cared about veterans.

Despite its significance as a political move, the dissolution of the ANC Comitato Centrale roused little indignation, or even interest, amongst most Italians. The *prefetti*, thoroughly questioned by Federzoni, answered in almost all cases that the population was widely indifferent. For many, the measure gave 'an inevitable, logical solution to an unsustainable situation'.[176] But veterans harboured a wide variety of feelings. In some places, they met after the decree to declare their support for the government. In Cremona, the fascist veterans were very satisfied with the resolution. By contrast, in some zones, such as Rome and Campania, veterans raised protests and remained supportive of the position of the Comitato Centrale, trying to stay united and keeping contact with politicians from the opposition. However, neither anti-fascist reorganization nor challenges to public order were in sight.[177] Throughout the rest of March, the fascist press published articles justifying the decree and introducing to the public the mission of the renewed ANC. However, the process of fascist co-optation of Italian veterans was not yet complete.

---

[174] Report of the French Special Commissary in Menton (5 March 1925), AN, F/7/13456, Italy.

[175] *Il Popolo d'Italia*, 5 March 1925,

[176] ACS, MI PS, 1925, box 107, Ass. Naz. Combattenti, Affari generali, file 'Arezzo'.

[177] ACS, MI PS, 1925, box 107, Ass. Naz. Combattenti, Affari generali; *L'elmetto. Trimensile dei combattenti di Terra di Lavoro* (Caserta), 20 March 1925.

Consolidating Fascist Rule

The *triumvirato* appointed by Mussolini was composed of Amilcare Rossi, Luigi Russo and Nicola Sansanelli. Only Luigi Russo had been a leader of the ANC before; he and Sansanelli were also MPs. During the Congress of Assisi, Russo had demonstrated his commitment to the fascist government, supporting an enhancement of the ANC social assistance tasks. Sansanelli had some experience in resolving internal disputes inside the provincial Fasci. Amilcare Rossi, the key figure in the *triumvirato*, was a war veteran, a lawyer, a professor and a holder of the prestigious Gold Medal as the result of his actions during the war. Rossi was well known in Rome's aristocratic nationalist circles, in the Roman section of the ANC and also in the PNF, of which he had been a member since 1923. His most important position was as a member of the leading *triumvirato* of the Gold Medal Group (Gruppo Medaglie d'Oro al Valor Militare d'Italia), which endorsed Mussolini. Rossi had expressed his views on the veterans' question during the summer of 1924, saying that all veterans should be disciplined and maintain their loyalty towards Mussolini.[178] With this leadership, it is not surprising that the first actions of the *triumvirato* were restricted exclusively to a very prosaic social assistance, detached from any political stance. The fascist hierarchies were satisfied. The PNF would not tolerate treachery similar to that of the dissolved Comitato Centrale; the fascists 'did not want enemies inside the ANC'.[179]

The veteran crisis of 1925 also reinforced the political position of Mussolini as dictator. After the decreed *fascistizzazione* of the ANC, a number of local veteran sections from across the country sent telegrams to Mussolini giving him their support, thus demonstrating the extent to which 'consent' towards Fascism had spread.[180] The reliability of this source is only relative, but we should concede some value to these data. In some provinces (Varese, Isernia and Bari), a large number of sections joined in the initiative, probably at the behest of the provincial fascist leaders. However, large parts of the south, the north and Sardinia still did not manifest any support for the fascist Duce. It can be argued that in some zones, the veterans' 'consent' was due to fascist coercion. In contrast, the more homogeneously spread geographical origin of these messages, which came from almost all regions of the country, also

---

[178] An insight into the character of Rossi can be found in his autobiography, Amilcare Rossi, *Figlio del mio tempo: Prefascismo, fascismo, postfascismo*, Rome, 1969; *Il Combattente d'Italia*, 5 September 1924; Nicola Brancaccio *et allii*: *Le Medaglie d'Oro (1833–1925)*, [1925].

[179] *Il Popolo d'Italia*, 7 March 1925.   [180] *Il Popolo d'Italia*, 12–14 and 20 March 1925.

suggests that Mussolini – after his apparently firm role in the crisis – had a wider popularity than the PNF among Italian veterans.

Indeed, the fascist co-optation of Italian veterans was incomplete. After the decreed dissolution of the ANC Comitato Centrale, further measures, including violence and persecution, were needed to marginalize the anti-fascist veterans' groups. In Alessandria, whose provincial section remained committed to the spirit of the *ordine del giorno* of Assisi,[181] several violent incidents were reported between April and August of 1925, until all resistance was finally extinguished.[182] In the province of Genoa, the unrepentant ANC headquarters resisted the fascist attacks until August of 1925.[183] Ettore Viola and the rest of the dissolved Comitato Centrale had been forced to transfer their powers to the new *triumvirato*, something that took place peacefully immediately after the decree.[184] Yet, during the spring and summer of 1925, Ettore Viola continued his activism, trying to create new independent veterans' organizations against Fascism.[185] He and his followers were closely watched by the police and harassed by fascists; in Parliament, according to Viola, he and the fascists Bottai and Giunta came to blows.[186] However, as the *prefetto* of Bari reported, anti-fascist veteran leaders attracted little support, and armed resistance seemed unlikely.[187]

In order to definitively submit the veterans to fascist control, different strategies were employed. For example, violent fascist attacks served as an excuse for the *prefetti* to order the closure of veteran sections. Following these closures, a fascist *commissario* took over the section. Even in Lucca, the claims of ANC leaders regarding the anti-Bolshevik, heroic and monarchist past of their sections did not serve to save them from fascist assimilation.[188] Moreover, pro-fascist leaders blackmailed veterans, threatening to leave them unprotected if they maintained an anti-government stance. In a meeting of disabled veterans in Belluno on 28 April 1925, some veterans reported the persecutions they suffered because of their political opinions, but the president bluntly answered that 'the ANMIG was able to intervene, impose respect and protect its

---

[181] *Battaglie*, 8 March 1925.
[182] ACS, MI PS, 1925, box 107, Ass. Naz. Combattenti, fascicles by provinces, file 'Alessandria'.
[183] ACS, MI PS, 1925, box 107, Ass. Naz. Combattenti, fascicles by provinces, file 'Genova'.
[184] Rossi, *Figlio del mio tempo*, p. 87; *Il Popolo d'Italia*, 4 March 1925
[185] Viola, *Combattenti e Mussolini*, pp. 31ff.
[186] *Ibid.* pp. 38–51; ACS, MI PS, 1925, box 107, Ass. Naz. Combattenti, fascicles by provinces, file 'Messina'.
[187] ACS, MI PS, 1925, box 107, Ass. Naz. Combattenti, Affari generali.
[188] ACS, MI PS, 1925, box 107, Ass. Naz. Combattenti, Affari generali, file 'Lucca'.

members only when [those] members did not adopt any charge or attitude contradictory to the politics of the government.'[189] These procedures served to enforce the veterans' submission to Fascism everywhere in Italy.

In the south, ending the veterans' crisis proved more difficult than in the north. Fascism's assimilation of the ANC was achieved through persuasive propaganda, violent tactics and a deepening of the collaboration between the state authorities and fascist veterans. A latent war between veterans took place during the spring and summer of 1925 in some places of the Mezzogiorno, where the majority of veterans were anti-fascist peasant ex-soldiers (*contadini combattenti*). Fascists behaved aggressively and were helped by the *prefetti* to bring ANC sections under control. In several places and on several occasions, fascists fired shots in veterans' meetings, causing panic among the audience; they also provoked numerous fights and disturbances.[190] These conflicts not only broke the veterans' resistance but also provided an excuse for the state authorities to dissolve the ANC sections. Thus, in Lazio, where the majority of veterans had barely supported Fascism, the *prefetto* solved the crisis: between April and June of 1925, he closed down a set of ANC sections. Later, in October–November of 1925, once the fascist ANC had been reorganized, he allowed the sections to form again, since they would now have a 'neatly national colour'.[191] In the south, the fascist discourse of *apoliticità* and the authoritarian actions of the *prefetti* were decisive in fully realizing the fascist co-optation of the ANC. Thus, the organization was transformed into a kind of annex of the PNF.

After the summer of 1925, the crisis finally ended with the rehabilitation of a profoundly fascistized ANC, which implied in many cases the transformation of veterans into PNF members. In Lecce, veterans began to meet again in the local Fascio. In Bari, the UNCi section with its sixty members decided to return to the ANC, since the association had 'recovered its initial programme of patriotism'.[192] In Caserta, near Naples, the enrolment of all veterans into the PNF section took place

---

[189] ACS, MI PS, 1925, box 111, file 'Mutilati e invalidi di guerra', sf. Belluno.
[190] ACS, MI PS, 1925, box 107, Ass. Naz. Combattenti, fascicles by provinces, files 'Avellino', 'Bari', 'Lecce', 'Palermo', 'Taranto' and 'Trapani'; file 'Arditi d'Italia', sf. 'Lecce'; ACS, MI PS, 1925, box 111, Mutilati e invalidi di guerra, files 'Bari', 'Napoli' and 'Messina'.
[191] ACS, MI PS, 1925, box 108, Ass. Naz. Combattenti, file 'Roma e provincia'.
[192] ACS, MI PS, 1925, box 107, Ass. Naz. Combattenti, fascicles by provinces, files 'Bari' and 'Lecce'.

in April of 1925.[193] In Lecce, after a long struggle, the renewed ANC section met at the end of August. In the meeting it was stated that

only Mussolini's government strived to give value to the Italy of Vittorio Veneto, and impose respect and gratitude towards veterans, who had been despised in 1919 ... that no different views or aims exist between the ANC and the PNF, and that both the qualities of veteran and fascist are compatible and possible to be held at the same time.

The members of this section declared their complete and unconditional support (*adesione*) for the PNF, and they took the decision to enrol all the veterans into it.[194] In Naples, in June of 1925, the *arditi* – duly invited by the fascists – joined the PNF and the MVSN. Many *arditi* were already affiliated with the PNF in the centre and north of Italy.[195] Converting veterans into members of the PNF was an old fascist aspiration now being realized.

By the autumn of 1925, Rossi, Russo and Sansanelli, the fascist triumvirate in charge of the ANC, were, after a few months of activity, in a position to demand complete control over war veterans in Italy. They asked the *prefetti* to ensure that all independent veterans' organizations stop their activities.[196] By the end of 1925, therefore, any real possibility of maintaining an independent veterans' movement or association had been destroyed. When in 1926 the fascist *provvedimenti per la difesa dello Stato* were approved, none of the veteran leaders who had tried to oppose the process of *fascistizzazione* dared to contradict Mussolini.[197] The dictatorship had consolidated its control over the ANC and the ANMIG, through which Fascism maintained a tight grip on Italian veterans of the First World War.

In conclusion, the process of *fascistizzazione* of Italian war veterans during 1925 was not easy; it was long and difficult. In the first phase, propaganda, local political manoeuvres and coercion created an appropriate climate for the decree of 2 March 1925. In this phase, there was also pressure from below, carried out by groups of fascist veterans in the provinces. Most likely these groups were not very large, and they emerged from the local and provincial Fasci rather than from the ANC sections. In any case, this movement was successful in gathering enough

---

[193] ACS, MI PS, 1925, box 107, Ass. Naz. Combattenti, fascicles by provinces, file 'Caserta'.
[194] ACS, MI PS, 1925, box 107, Ass. Naz. Combattenti, fascicles by provinces, file 'Lecce'.
[195] ACS, MI PS, 1925, box 107, Arditi d'Italia, fascicles by provinces, files 'Genova', 'Modena', 'Napoli'.
[196] ACS, MI PS, 1925, box 107, Ass. Naz. Combattenti. Affari generali.
[197] Viola, *Combattenti e Mussolini*, p. 53.

support to take over an important number of ANC sections, thus justifying intervention by the government. After the decree of 2 March 1925, the second part of the process consisted of the gradual isolation of anti-fascist veterans' leaders and the submission of ANC sections all over Italy to fascist rule. Propaganda, violence and the help of many *prefetti* were the key to success. This was the true nature of the relationship between veterans and Fascism between 1924 and 1925, though in other countries veterans' organizations remained largely unaware of the conditions under which fascist control had been achieved.

4   Veterans and Fascism: Consolidation and European Expansion, 1925–1929

The second half of the 1920s was marked by the transcontinental circulation of discourses and myths about fascist veterans. These years have passed into history as a period of stabilization for the European continent. After the turbulence of 1923, which had exposed the failure of the status quo orchestrated at Versailles, the international powers sought a new settlement. The United States and Britain sought to resolve the Franco-German dispute and attain the financial security that would ensure their geopolitical influence. The arrival of Herriot to the presidency in France, after the victory of the French left (*cartel des gauches*) in the elections of May 1924, facilitated an international agreement on the basis of the Dawes Plan that offered a solution to the thorny issue of reparations. At the end of 1925, the Treaties of Locarno constituted the 'real peace' settlement in post-war Europe, inaugurating a phase of political and economic stability.[1] France abandoned its intransigence around its security concerns, and Germany was integrated into the international system, joining the League of Nations in 1926. In that year, both the French and German foreign ministers, Aristide Briand and Gustav Stresemann, were awarded the Nobel Peace Prize. However, in these European countries, 'recasting bourgeois Europe' implied not only the promise of peace and the neutralization of the leftist threat but also the weakening of parliamentarianism and a shift towards corporatism. The class struggle may have lost its preponderance as a political issue, but the underlying tensions in the social structure remained unchanged.[2] This period also saw the emergence of a culture of consumption. On the fringes of Europe, authoritarianism advanced, with dictatorships established in Poland (Pilsudski) and Portugal (Salazar) in 1926.

---

[1] Patrick O. Cohrs, 'The First "Real" Peace Settlements after the First World War: Britain, the United States and the Accords of London and Locarno, 1923–1925', *Contemporary European History*, 12, 1 (2003), pp. 1–31.

[2] Charles S. Maier, *Recasting Bourgeois Europe: Stabilization in France, Germany, and Italy in the Decade after World War I*, Princeton, NJ, Princeton University Press, 1975.

In Italy, the evolution of the fascist dictatorship simultaneously responded to and exerted an influence on these historical trends. After the dictatorship was officially imposed, a series of legal and institutional measures was introduced to construct a totalitarian regime.[3] Although the moderate Augusto Turati replaced the radical Farinacci as the Secretary General of the PNF in March of 1926, the Provisions for the Defence of the State (Provvedimenti per la Difesa dello Stato, the so-called *leggi fascistissime*) in November of 1926 ensured the repression of any non-fascist political force. These legal measures institutionalized violence against political enemies. The PNF purged its ranks, and around 60,000 early fascists and squadrists were expelled from the party in 1928–9. The party was submitted to the authority of the state, and the strength of fascist syndicalism faded. The Labour Charter (Carta del Lavoro), published in April of 1927, talked about 'class collaboration' and reflected the conservatism of the corporatist system. Mussolini and the fascist leaders were determined to transform the press and the schools into 'instruments of the regime'.[4] For the fascists, these were the years of optimism, even if there were plenty of internal political struggles and intrigues in the movement, and the living standards of the Italian population did not improve considerably.

Consolidation pushed the fascists to stretch their tentacles abroad. There were important reasons for this policy. The total number of Italian emigrants in the mid-1920s probably surpassed 9 million. From the end of the war until 1926, the traditional flows of Italian emigration had not abated but rather increased due to the migration of anti-fascist political exiles (*fuoriusciti*). France was the main European destination, particularly the south-eastern regions and Paris.[5] Many Italian migrants in France and other countries deplored Fascism, but from 1921 on, and especially after the March on Rome, cells of the fascist movement had proliferated in several European (and indeed non-European) cities. Usually, their founders were Italian war veterans. These Fasci all'estero ('Fasci abroad') were officially organized into a centralized structure during 1923. By 1925, their leader, Giuseppe Bastianini, dreamed of a fascist international organization that would unite different European fascist movements. Groups such as the NSDAP in Germany were enthusiastic about this project.[6] But Mussolini was more cautious and did not

---

[3] De Felice, *Mussolini il fascista, II*; Morgan, *Italian Fascism*, pp. 96–124.
[4] ACS, SPD, CR, box 29, file 'Situazione generale interna e internazionale (1927)'.
[5] Pierre Milza (ed.), *Les italiens en France de 1914 à 1940*, Rome, École française de Rome, 1986.
[6] *Völkischer Beobachter*, 2 May 1925.

permit the establishment of contacts with any foreign movement. The Fasci all'estero enjoyed very little autonomy.[7] In all probability, it was the ANC cells in foreign countries, rather than the Fasci all'estero, that were the main link between the Italian migrant veterans and their fatherland. Well before its submission to fascist rule, the ANC had become aware of the importance of assisting Italian communities abroad.[8] The social and patriotic activities of the ANC cells represented an asset for the 'peaceful penetration and expansion of Italy'.[9] As the ANC was placed under fascist control, the Italian veterans residing in foreign countries went through the same process of *fascistizzazione* as those in the mother country.[10] Thus, the fascists gained a new and fully elaborated structure through which they could exert influence and operate outside Italy.

In this chapter I will demonstrate that war veterans were a decisive element for the dissemination of the fascist idea in Europe during the middle and late 1920s. On the one hand, in the realm of discourses and representations, different political and veteran groups abroad absorbed and reworked the myth of the fascist veterans that had been born in Italy. In the cases of France and Germany, the fascist-veteran symbolic complex was synthesized into ideologies and political parties. I will analyze the two most important expressions of this transfer: the French Faisceau and the German Stahlhelm. These organizations did not eventually succeed in their political objectives, but their influence must not be underestimated. On the other hand, with the fascist co-optation of the ANC, the fascists entered the FIDAC, an international veterans' association through which Fascism, as we will see, exerted international influence. In this context, Italian Fascism continued manipulating veteran discourses and organizations towards a totalitarian goal.

The Myth of the Fascist Veterans in France: The Faisceau

The political myth of fascism as an ideology of war veterans was most clearly adopted in France by the earliest precursors of French fascism. In France, perceptions of Italian Fascism had overemphasized the

---

[7] Luca De Caprariis, '"Fascism for Export"? The Rise and Eclipse of the Fasci Italiani all'Estero', *Journal of Contemporary History*, 35, 2 (2000), pp. 151–83; Emilio Franzina and Matteo Sanfilippo (eds.), *Il fascismo e gli emigrati: La parabola dei Fasci italiani all'estero (1920–1943)*, Rome, Laterza, 2003.

[8] Bruno Biagi, 'I combattenti all'estero', *I Combattenti. La Nuova Giornata*, 14 June 1923.

[9] *I Combattenti. La Nuova Giornata*, 11 May 1924.

[10] See, for example, the case of Barcelona in Claudio Venza, 'El consulado italiano de Barcelona y la comunidad italiana en los inicios del fascismo (1923–1925)', *Investigaciones Históricas*, 17 (1997), pp. 265–83.

participation of war veterans in the movement. The French extreme right was very pleased with this effective anti-leftist reaction. Yet, fascism seemed not necessary in France, since the conservative government acted firmly in foreign policy to defend the Versailles settlement. This situation changed at the end of 1923, when the quest for a more equitable international order commenced, and especially when the *cartel des gauches* won the elections of May 1924, in the context of a steep decline in the value of the French franc. The first French fascist movement, the Légion, was created in June of 1924 by a war veteran and ex-officer, Antoine Rédier. Between July and December of 1924, a group of war veterans and young men set up another organization, the Jeunesses Patriotes, led by ex-captain Pierre Taittinger. Both groups mobilized middle-class war veterans who were opposed to the politics of Herriot and the *cartel des gauches*.[11] In addition, towards the end of 1924, certain intellectuals began to propagate political theories that would become the ideological basis for the Faisceau.

How was the Italian fascist model transferred to French politics? In the first instance, the visits of French veterans to Fascist Italy in many cases reinforced pre-existing perceptions of the relationship between fascism and veterans. French veterans believed that, in theory, the formation of 'a party of veterans' might allow for the 'conquest of power', leading to the establishment of a 'nationalist dictatorship (fascism)'.[12] In January of 1924, a group of Action Française members arrived in Italy to get a first-hand impression of Fascism in action. Georges Valois – the Action Française specialist on economic matters – participated in the visit; he was introduced to Mussolini by Curzio Malaparte.[13] This contact did not immediately produce any imitation fascist movement in France; after his return from Rome, Valois continued writing about purely economic issues, such as the monetary crisis.[14] Yet, the conception of a new political force matured slowly in the mind of Georges Valois. He was a decorated war veteran, ex-junior officer who had spent twenty-five months at the front. This experience had reinforced his nationalism and anti-pacifism. The Italian example mirrored some of the thoughts that Valois had developed since the war, particularly consideration of the

[11] Robert Soucy, *French Fascism: The First Wave, 1924–1933*, New Haven, CT, Yale University Press, 1986, pp. 27–86. Rédier's Légion was incorporated into the Jeunesses Patriotes in July 1925.

[12] René Cassin, 'Les Méthodes d'Action', *La France Mutilée*, 16 March 1924.

[13] Didier Musiedlak, 'L'Italie fasciste et Georges Valois', in Olivier Dard (ed.), *Georges Valois, itinéraire et réceptions*, Berne, Peter Lang, 2011, pp. 205–14.

[14] Georges Valois, 'La crise monetaire et financière: Le problème de l'action', *L'Action Française*, 16 January 1924.

'social' organization of the army as the mould for a perfected productive and hierarchical society.[15] Similarly, another writer in the orbit of Valois, Jacques Arthuys, visited Fascist Italy in 1924.[16] That year, Valois' publishing house, the Nouvelle Librairie Nationale, translated a book by Pietro Gorgolini into French which described the 'revolutionary' work of Fascism as a movement composed of 'veterans, students, artists'.[17] However, no proto-fascist party was launched in France while Italy went through the Matteotti crisis.

Alongside political tourism in Fascist Italy and the new publications praising the achievements of Mussolini,[18] the political situation in France during 1924 and early 1925 witnessed escalation of the veterans' protests and radicalization of the right. There were contacts between the UNC and anti-communist groups such as the Jeunesses Patriotes.[19] In 1924, given the rise of the cost of living, the celebration of the Armistice in Paris was marked by a demonstration of more than 30,000 disabled veterans in favour of increased pensions.[20] Later, when the ashes of Jean Jaurès – the socialist politician assassinated in 1914 because of his pacifism – were transferred to the Pantheon at the end of November, the nationalist right was outraged. While the working class celebrated this ceremony, L'Action Française depicted the official cortege as a parade of 'anti-patriots' (*antipatriotes*) and revolutionaries with red flags 'insulting the army and the fatherland'.[21] This symbolic confrontation recalls the Italian disputes of 1919–22 around the meaning of the war and the victory. But on this occasion the situation of 1919 appeared to be inverted. In 1924, while in Fascist Italy the religion of the fatherland was imposed, and veterans entered the Chamber in significant numbers, in France the socialists dominated the Chamber, and pacifism and internationalism were publicly expressed.

In France, as in Italy, the protagonists of the outburst against non-nationalist or socialist pacifism manipulated the symbols of the dead soldiers and veterans in order to pursue radicalized political aims. In late

---

[15] Georges Valois, *D'un siècle a l'autre: Chronique d'une génération 1885–1920*, Paris, Nouvelle Librairie Nationale, 1921, pp. 263–93; Jean Norton-Cru, *Témoins*, Nancy, Presses Universitaires de Nancy, 2006, (1st edn. 1929), pp. 478–9; Allen Douglas, *From Fascism to Libertarian Communism: Georges Valois against the Third Republic*, Berkeley, University of California Press, 1992.

[16] Jacques Arthuys, *Les Combattants*, Paris, Nouvelle Librairie Nationale, 1925, pp. 13–16.

[17] Pietro Gorgolini, *La Révolution fasciste: Avec le texte intégral des principaux discours de Benito Mussolini*, Paris, Nouvelle Librairie Nationale, 1924, pp. viii, x.

[18] See also Giuseppe Prezzolini, *Le fascisme*, Paris, 1925.

[19] Millington, *From Victory to Vichy*, pp. 34–7.

[20] Prost, *Les anciens combattants*, Vol. 1, pp. 94–7.

[21] *L'Action Française*, 23 November 1924.

bES VAINQUEURS

Figure 4.1 The Vanquishers (*L'étudiant français, Organe bi-mensuel de la Fédération Nationale des Étudiants d'Action Française*, 1 January 1925) (Bibliothèque nationale de France.)

1924 and early 1925, the conservative veterans' organizations (UNC) and the extreme right stepped up their appeals to veterans to intervene in the civic and political life, talking about a 'mutilated victory'.[22] In their attacks against the leftist government, they employed an array of representations of veterans and fallen soldiers that recalled the Italian experience of 1919–22. Let us consider three examples that illustrate this point. Firstly, the image of a soldier (in this case dead) standing defeated in front of a rally of politically victorious leftists who were waving red flags was deployed in Action Française circles (Figure 4.1; compare with Figures 1.1 and 2.2).

Secondly, during the so-called battle of pensions (*bataille des pensions*), conservative veterans had recourse to the trope of the helpless and impoverished – though decorated – disabled war veteran begging on the street, an image employed by the Italian fascist propaganda in 1922.[23] And thirdly, the masses of dead soldiers in heaven, watching from above and lamenting that their sacrifice had served for nothing, were represented by supporters of an authoritarian republic – such as Gustave

---

[22] Ernest Pezet, *Combattants et Citoyens: Les Combattants dans la Cité branlante devant la Victoire mutilée*, Paris [1925].

[23] *La Voix du Combattant*, 13 December 1924; cf. *Il Popolo d'Italia*, 27 May 1922.

Hervé.[24] Although the portrayal of the masses of dead soldiers was a traditional and transnational symbolic reference that had originated in the war, now it conveyed the need of giving a new value to the victory of 1918. Among the members of the Jeunesses Patriotes, these kinds of perceptions and representations of veterans and dead soldiers served to justify their political project.[25] For many of them, fascism was the solution.

Some commentators indeed asserted that France was on the verge of disintegration and that only two outcomes were possible: Bolshevism or fascism. The first option was presented as a threat to civilization that loomed over France in 1924, as it did in Italy during 1920. Fascism, on the contrary, was depicted as the veterans' solution originating from Italy: a form of political order, the religion of the fatherland. Fascism had been 'born from the rage of the veterans'.[26] On the contrary, in France, according to this line of thought, the veterans had been swindled, and they did not enjoy the fruits of their victory, nor their right to lead the country. The Chamber of 1924 – it was argued – had expelled the veterans of 1919, giving way to a number of deserters and traitors. But now the time of the veterans had come.

Georges Valois and his group of collaborators, having broken with Action Française, took advantage of this discursive and symbolic context to develop a new political movement: the Faisceau. At the end of 1924 and the beginning of 1925, a set of publications paved the way for the movement. Georges Valois' book, La Révolution Nationale, laid the guidelines for his new ideological project. The motivation for Valois' manifesto was the decadence he saw in all sectors of French society and the menace he perceived to the very existence of the nation. The cause of this bleak situation was, according to Valois, removal of the veterans from public affairs. The victory had been nullified not just by Herriot but also by Poincaré. 'We should have assumed command of France the day of the armistice', Valois wrote. Now the solution was national revolution. Criticizing the bourgeois spirit, Valois advocated the 'heroic spirit', the 'spirit of the victory'. The veterans should expel all the deserters and shirkers who had taken the power. The veterans would organize 'the recuperation of the victory in order to lay the foundations for French greatness'.[27] The parallels between the veteran discourses and

---

[24] La Victoire, 2 November 1925.

[25] Pierre Taittinger, Les Cahiers de la Jeune France, Paris, 1926, passim.

[26] Camille Aymard, Bolchevisme ou Fascisme? . . . Français, il faut choisir!, Paris, Flammarion, 1925, pp. 188, 273–9.

[27] Georges Valois, La Révolution Nationale, Paris, Nouvelle Librairie Nationale, 1924, pp. 10, 189–90, passim. This book was written between August and September of

representations employed by the French fascists and the arguments and symbols developed since 1919 by the Italians are striking.

The next relevant publication was Jacques Arthuys' book, *Les combattants*. While Valois was a modernist inspired by fascist syndicalism, Arthuys was more of a traditionalist; but the anti-parliamentarian spirit of the 'combatants' was an important point common to both.[28] Arthuys talked about the essential differences that the war experience had engendered between those who had fought at the front and those who had not. If the soldier had become a warrior, the non-combatant had remained a simple patriot. After the war, however, the predominant notion that the veteran was a *former* combatant transformed into a civilian had facilitated the veteran associations' sole focus on material claims. Furthermore, according to Arthuys, the *cartel des gauches* had placed France in the worst situation possible; the country was exposed to every kind of danger. He said that the veterans must reverse this situation. Arthuys agreed with Valois: '[S]oon after the war, the veterans should have taken the power'; the 'veteran spirit' should dominate the state; this was their mission. The means for the seizure of power were very simple: 'organized force'.[29]

The group formed by Valois, Arthuys and other collaborators launched the newspaper *Le Nouveau Siècle* on 26 February 1925, only two weeks after the French veterans succeeded in their 'battle of pensions'. The paper benefitted from the financial support of certain industrialists. This younger generation of activists lamented the passivity of Action Française, from which they separated, progressively becoming avowed rivals.[30] Their chief ideological innovation was the full use of a new discursive and symbolic system, rooted in Italian Fascism, at the core of which were the veterans. They went far beyond the old conservative notion of 'the combatant's share'. From the beginning, they expressed the intention of enforcing the unrecognized political rights of veterans.[31] This was particularly explicit in the 'Appeal to the Combatants' ('*Appel aux combattants*'), published on 16 April 1925. This was a clear call to construct a fascist political force led by the veteran *spirit* that brandishes a sword (Figure 4.2).[32] The outcome

---

1924 and was published with occasion of the November armistice commemoration. It inaugurated the collection *Les Cahiers de la Victoire*.

[28] Samuel Kalman, 'Georges Valois et le Faisceau: un mariage de convenance', in Dard (ed.), *Georges Valois*, pp. 37–53.

[29] Jacques Arthuys, *Les combattants*, pp. 43, 143, 220, *passim*. This book appeared in January 1925, and it was number two of the collection *Les Cahiers de la Victoire*.

[30] Zeev Sternhell, 'Anatomie d'un mouvement fasciste en France: le faisceau de Georges Valois', *Revue française de science politique*, 1 (1976). pp. 5–40.

[31] *Le Nouveau Siècle. Journal de la Fraternité Nationale, veut la politique de la Victoire* (Paris), 26 February 1925.

[32] *Le Nouveau Siècle*, 16 April 1925.

Figure 4.2 '– He is resurrected!' (*Le Nouveau Siècle*, 16 April 1925).
(Bibliothèque nationale de France.)

of this movement was envisaged as the 'dictatorship of the veteran'.[33] Thus, the veterans were pitted against politicians and *embusqués* in order to restore the victory.[34] These combative representations of the veteran, appealing to his aggressive will to take power,[35] co-existed in the paper with the more conservative representation of the veterans' spirit of sacrifice and work, bulwarks against leftist revolutionaries.[36] Both representations corresponded to different manifestations of the fascist veteran myth.

After this phase of propaganda, on 11 November 1925 – Armistice Day – the Faisceau was born. However, the organization suffered financial difficulties; *Le Nouveau Siècle* was unable to transition from being a weekly to a daily newspaper. Although the Faisceau reached 10,000 members in February of 1926, and during that year several big fascist-style ceremonies were organized, the communists sabotaged many of the Faisceau activities, attacking its paramilitary branch, the Légions.[37] Despite its efforts, the movement was unable to attract many veterans from the associations. At the peak of its activity, when a meeting was organized in Reims on 27 June 1926, the UNC and the Jeunesses Patriotes for the first time sent a group of militants to hear the fascist orators.[38] Though *Le Nouveau Siècle* talked about an attendance of 14,000, in reality, the fascist sympathizers in Reims numbered no more than 4,000, and the anti-fascist counter-demonstration was equally numerous.[39] In contrast, on 11 July 1926, the French veterans' movement gathered 20,000 men in Paris during a protest against the governmental accords with the United States for the payment of French debt.[40] As the Italian fascists had previously done, the Faisceau tried to capitalize on the veterans' mobilizing potential.

Once the veterans' associations organized a giant inter-associational meeting in Versailles – *les États generaux de la France meurtrie* – on 11–13 November 1927, the Faisceau increased its propaganda and attracted new

---

[33] Georges Valois, *La politique de la victoire*, Paris, Nouvelle Librairie Nationale, 1926, pp. 16–21.

[34] Georges Valois, 'Le combattant et l'embusqué', *Le Nouveau Siècle*, 14 May 1925.

[35] Georges Valois, 'Légionnaires', *Le Nouveau Siècle*, 2 April 1925.

[36] Pierre Arthuys, 'Valeur du sacrifice', *Le Nouveau Siècle*, 21 May 1925; see also *Le Nouveau Siècle*, 30 April 1925.

[37] Allen Douglas, 'Violence and Fascism: The Case of the Faisceau', *Journal of Contemporary History*, 19, 4 (1984), pp. 689–712.

[38] Report of 1 July 1926, AN, F/7/13212, 'Notes sur le Faisceau'; see also *Cahiers des États Generaux: Première Assemblée Nationale des Combattants, des Producteurs et des Chefs de Famille tenue à Reims le 27 juin 1926 sur l'initiative du Faisceau des Combattants et des Producteurs. Compte rendu des travaux de l'assemblée*, Paris, Nouvelle Librairie Nationale, 1926.

[39] AN, F/7/13210, 'Manifestation Fasciste de Reims'.

[40] Prost, *Les anciens combattants*, Vol. 1, pp. 100–1.

members.[41] Some observers in France and even in Italy expected that this veterans' meeting would result in the creation of a kind of fascist unifying movement, but they were disappointed.[42] Still, the Faisceau leaders ordered the members of the Légions to join the veterans' associations in order to convince them to embrace the fascist ideology.[43] However, if the veterans' attempt to create a unified platform in Versailles did not completely crystallize, the Faisceau was incapable of significantly growing or imposing its doctrine on the veterans. In time, the Faisceau came to appeal not only to veterans but also to 'producers' (*producteurs*), workers, civil servants and heads of families.[44] The erstwhile preponderance of the veteran mystic was diluted in what became a more diversified fascist project. Nevertheless, when it came to the veterans' associations, many in France believed that, to quote one contemporary commentator, 'the fascist spirit, the spirit of dictatorship have [*sic*] little by little penetrated them.'[45] The emergence of right-wing paramilitary leagues in the mid-1920s even led the communist ARAC, a movement in decline, to form its own anti-fascist paramilitary squads, thus mimicking the violent tactics and combative traits of extreme-right veterans.[46] Paramilitarization can be seen as a collateral effect of the fascist influence.

Both the concrete role of Italians in these processes and their perceptions of the growing influence of fascism among French veterans merit discussion. It can be argued that the fascist discourses and representations of the veterans were transferred into French rightist political culture, whilst the fascist and ANC cells in France did not directly intervene. Although the evidence to demonstrate that members of the Parisian Fascio provided some funding for *Le Nouveau Siècle* is limited,[47] the Italian fascists were, initially, pleased to see the emergence of fascist organizations in France, the prominence of veterans and the 'politics of the Victory'. If at the end of 1923 the fascist theorists had underlined the essentially Italian character of Fascism, at the beginning of 1926 they debated its universality.[48] Valois' articles in

---

[41] Reports of 28 November and 6 December 1927, AN, F/7/13212, 'Notes sur le Faisceau'.
[42] *La Stampa*, 16 November 1927.
[43] 'Notes sur le Faisceau' (report of 8 December 1927), AN, F/7/13212.
[44] Georges Valois, *Le fascisme*, Paris, Nouvelle Librairie Nationale, 1927.
[45] François Berry, *Le fascisme en France*, Paris, 1926, pp. 41–5, quote on p. 45.
[46] Chris Millington, 'Communist Veterans and Paramilitarism in 1920s France: The Association républicaine des anciens combattants', *Journal of War & Culture Studies*, 8, 4 (2015), pp. 300–14.
[47] Report signed on 18 November 1925, AN, F/7/13208, 'Le Nouveau Siècle 1925–1926'.
[48] Alessandro Pavolini, 'Le cose di Francia e l'universalità del Fascismo', *Critica fascista*, 15 January 1926; see also Roger Giron, 'Il compito delle "Jeunesses Patriotes"', *Critica fascista*, 1 October 1926.

Le Nouveau Siècle were translated into Italian.[49] However, the Italian fascists soon realized that the Faisceau was failing to gain momentum. A very critical article published in *Roma fascista* ironically noted that the March on Paris was always in development; where was the will of action and violence required to conquest the fatherland?[50] The Faisceau lacked what was essential for the rise of Fascism: not the veterans – though Valois and his men believed they were the keystone – but political violence and the possibilities of exerting it with impunity.

In the end, the Faisceau faded as a political movement. Its collapse was mainly due to the change of government. In July of 1926, the *cartel des gauches* succumbed to the financial crisis, and Poincaré became Prime Minister. The political right in the government managed to overcome the economic difficulties. Thus, the reasons for the existence of fascism in France diminished considerably. Although the Action Française and the Jeunesses Patriotes lived on, the first wave of French fascism receded from 1927 on. This failure can be ascribed to a variety of structural, political and social factors.[51] In respect to the veterans, the power and internal diversity of their movement was another obstacle to their absorption into the fascist movement. It was in 1928 that the veterans' movement entered into a more assertive phase. But the time of exposure to fascist discourse had consequences as well, and Italian Fascism continued to be considered an example either to admire or to analyze for French veterans of different political tendencies.[52]

Clearly, the myth of the fascist veterans, originated in Italy and communicated to France, was a key factor in the emergence of the French fascists groups, especially the most important of them: the Faisceau. In the first phase, the insistence on the political role of the veterans in this party even outweighed the importance that Italian fascists had given to the veteran identity during 1919–23. Yet, the Faisceau simply reworked, adapted and applied a political discourse that had been gradually developed in Italy. This discourse and the representations it promoted would outlast the Faisceau. As we will see, myths about war veterans had a longer shelf life than political organizations.

---

[49] Georges Valois, *Il fascismo francese*, Rome, 1926, Preface by Mario Carli.

[50] Manlio Pompei, 'Cher monseiur Valois. . .', *Roma fascista*, 27 March 1926.

[51] See Soucy, *French Fascism: The First Wave*, pp. 217–32.

[52] See the first issue of *La Revue des vivants. Organe des générations de la guerre* (Paris), February 1927, devoted to the topic 'L'Italie et nous'.

The Myth of the Fascist Veterans in Germany: the Stahlhelm and the NSDAP

Developments in Germany during the mid-1920s in the realm of veteran cultures and organizations reveal some points in common with the French case, such as the influence of Italian Fascism. In the aftermath of November 1923, after the anti-republican plot had been defeated, some republican and leftist groups adopted a defensive stance. On 22 February 1924, in Magdeburg, a group of social democrats and republicans founded the Reichsbanner Schwarz-Rot-Gold. It was a republican defence league for war veterans.[53] Four days later, Hitler's trial for his involvement in the failed putsch began; in April, he was condemned to four years in prison. The NSDAP went underground, as did other paramilitary rightist organizations such as the Frontbann, founded by Ernst Röhm in May of 1924. In contrast, the KPD recovered its legal status. As violence between the communists and the extreme right continued, the communists created another defence organization theoretically composed of war veterans: the Rote Frontkämpferbund (RFB). While in the autumn of 1924 the republican Reichsbanner probably reached almost 1 million members throughout Germany, the communist veterans' group proliferated only in KPD strongholds, with 15,000 members by February of 1925, expanding substantially but more slowly. The RFB established contacts with the French ARAC.[54] Paradoxically, as in the French case, the adoption of paramilitary traits – such as uniforms and parades – by communist and socialist German veterans and their predisposition to violence were an imitation of, and a reaction to, the fascist-inspired veterans' groups.[55]

In the case of the Stahlhelm, the movement was obliged to moderate its public attitude and adopt legalist strategies. It declared its nonpartisan position (*Überparteilichkeit*) but continued to try to influence politics. The Stahlhelm was internally divided between moderate (Seldte) and radical (Duesterberg) leaders. The rivalry and competition between different anti-republican groups during this period, the Stahlhelm included, made it very difficult to create stable platforms uniting all

---

[53] Ziemann, *Contested Commemorations*, pp. 60ff.

[54] Kurt Finker, *Geschichte des Roten Frontkämpferbundes*, Berlin, Dietz Verlag, 1982, p. 139.

[55] In a sense, the 'Red Days' (*Rote Tage*) organized by the RFB between 1925 and 1928 were an alternative to the Stahlhelm's *Frontsoldatentage*; see Günter Bers (ed.), *'Rote Tage' im Rheinland. Demonstrationen des Roten Frontkämpfer-Bundes (RFB) im Gau Mittelrhein 1925–1928*, Wentorf, Einhorn Presse Verlag, 1980.

these splintered organizations.[56] They were incapable of imposing their views despite their numbers. For example, at the end of August 1924, the Reichstag ratified the Dawes Plan, which the nationalist veterans disliked.[57]

Despite this inauspicious political climate, anti-republican ideas remained popular among some German veterans and were reinforced, in part, by the perceived good health of Italian Fascism. The example of Italy roused the curiosity of travellers and scholars.[58] The conviction that Fascism had been 'constructed by Italian war veterans, by the representatives of a tragic-heroic way of life', solidified also in Germany.[59] The intellectual Oswald Spengler, author of the influential *Der Untergang des Abendlandes*, talked about the combative character of Fascism; he would visit Fascist Italy in early 1925.[60] Jurist and Stahlhelm member Rudolph Schaper travelled to Italy to gather impressions too.[61] These men reconsidered their memories from the time of the defeat and the revolution not only in light of the failures of 1923 but also in light of the Italian fascist example. It was in these circumstances that the so-called soldierly nationalism (*soldatische Nationalismus*) was developed.[62]

The case of Helmut Franke is representative. He was a Stahlhelm leader and a former Freikorps volunteer. In 1924, his book, *Staat im Staate*, collated published and unpublished writings from the years 1918–21, representing his militaristic political views as a front officer (*Frontoffiziere*). The earliest version of these writings had talked about the army as an exemplary entity, embodied by its front officers and independent from capitalists or socialists – a 'state within the state' (*Staat im Staate*). In 1921, Franke had also fantasized about a revolution initiated by front soldiers and front officers.[63] Nevertheless, in his 1924 book, he

[56] James M. Diehl, 'Von der "Vaterlandspartei" zur "Nationalen Revolution": Die "Vereinigten Vaterländischen Verbände Deutschlands (VVVD)" 1922–1932', *Vierteljahrshefte für Zeitgeschichte*, 33 Jahrgang, 4 H (1985), pp. 617–39.

[57] Berghahn, *Der Stahlhelm*, pp. 55–101; Alessandro Salvador, *La guerra in tempo di pace: Gli ex combattenti e la politica nella Repubblica di Weimar*, Trento, Università degli Studi di Trento, 2013, p. 43.

[58] See, for example, Fritz Schotthöfer, *Il Fascio. Sinn und Wirklichkeit des italienischen Fascismus*, Frankfurt am Main, 1924; Adolf Dresler, *Mussolini*, Leipzig, 1924.

[59] J. W. Mannhardt, *Der Faschismus*, Munich, 1925, p. 186.

[60] Michael Thöndl, *Oswald Spengler in Italien: Kulturexport politischer Ideen der 'Konservativen Revolution'*, Leipzig, Leipziger Universitätsverlag, 2010, pp. 108–9.

[61] Berghahn, *Der Stahlhelm*, p. 76.

[62] This ideological trend can be understood as part of the so-called Conservative Revolution; see Armin Mohler, *Die Konservative Revolution in Deutschland 1918–1932*, Darmstadt, Wissenschaftliche Buchgesellschaft, 1994 (1st edn. 1949).

[63] Helmut Franke, *Staat im Staate: Aufzeichnungen eines Militaristen*, Magdeburg, 1924; cf. the series 'Altes und neues Heer', in *Die Grenzboten, Zeitschfit für Kunst, Politik, Literatur*

introduced new political concepts previously absent from his political thought. In a letter of 16 April 1920, supposedly sent to a Stahlhelm leader and published in his 1924 book, Franke talked about the foundation of a front soldiers' party (Frontsoldaten-Partei). He wondered, '[W] hy is the formation of the party of veterans not successful in all countries, *like in Italy*, the party of those who have bled for the state, of those who have the preference before everyone else to form and to dominate the state for which they have sacrificed themselves?'[64] Even if references to a government of front-line soldiers had not been uncommon among Freikorps members and Kapp-putsch supporters in 1920, the mention of Italy was in all probability introduced later, after the rise of Italian Fascism. Furthermore, at the end of his 1924 book, Franke employed another political concept: the *Frontsoldatenstaat* ('the veterans' state'). He suggested that such a new regime must be realized by the veterans, in the name of the fallen soldiers. In line with French representations of dead soldiers at that time, Franke evoked 'The dead, the dead!', who watched from heaven and did not rest in peace, wondering, 'For what did we die?'.[65] The roused memory of the dead and the concepts of a veterans' party and a veterans-led state appeared at the same time in Germany as in France, inspired in both cases by Italian Fascism.

In the first half of 1925, Franke's ideas became the guiding 'spirit' of the Stahlhelm (*Stahlhelmgeist*). Having abandoned the violent path of 1919–23, this new stage of the struggle, aimed at realizing the state of the front soldiers (*Der Staat den Frontsoldaten*), required specific techniques and organization. Thus, the example of Fascist Italy was carefully studied through academic research and personal visits. Franke also travelled to Italy.[66] He stated that Stahlhelm members 'should hear, try, criticize, examine, learn and – most usefully – adopt' elements of the fascist model. Fascism and the Stahlhelm, despite acting in different contexts, shared a common goal: 'the seizure and penetration of the state through the front soldiers'.[67]

Ernst Jünger, a young ex-officer with an extensive record of combat experience, was the author that best represented the *soldatische Nationalismus*. His political awakening came late, but it was, as I will

---

(Berlin), 80 Jahrgang (1921), which contains the articles later republished in *Staat im Staate*.

[64] Helmut Franke, *Staat im Staate*, p. 164 (italics mine).
[65] Helmut Franke, *Staat im Staate*, p. 248.   [66] Klotzbücher, *Der politische Weg*, p. 73.
[67] Helmut Franke, 'Der Stahlhelm marschiert ...', *Der Stahlhelm. Organ des 'Stahlhelm', Bund der Frontsoldaten* (Berlin), 1 February 1925; Helmut Franke, 'Das System des Faszismus', *Der Stahlhelm*, 7 and 14 June 1925; G. D., 'Das Werden des Faschismus', *Der Stahlhelm*, 9 August 1925.

demonstrate, influenced by Italian Fascism. Jünger began his literary career writing about his own war experiences, embellished with a posteriori philosophical reflections. In *Im Stahlgewittern* (1920) he presented war as an interior experience that transcendentally transformed individuals into hardened soldiers. Reading Nietzsche, Jünger interpreted war as a way of life, as a Dionysian fight for life and death. Spengler and probably Barrès were among his other intellectual influences. He had brief contact with a Freikorps unit, but he focused on his studies. During 1923, in Munich, he heard of Hitler and Ludendorff. Thus, his first political article, talking about a *völkisch* revolution that was coming soon, was published in the Nazi newspaper *Völkischer Beobachter* in August of 1923. The failure of the putsch was surely a big disappointment for him. He did not publish another political article until April 1924, at which point he first spoke of 'we front soldiers'.[68]

It was in August of 1925 that Jünger published a new political article, 'Revolution and Front Soldiers', in the national conservative review *Gewissen*. Jünger attacked the revolution of 1918, denouncing the fact that the front soldiers had been disregarded and held in contempt. The best men, the young front officers, had been overlooked, in contrast to what had happened in the Russian Revolution of 1917. This was a result, according to Jünger, of the complete lack of ideas that underpinned the German Revolution of 1918. The revolution 'lacked the race, the martyrs, the dramatic development'. For Jünger, front soldiers were not just those men forced to serve at the front but also those who fought for ideals; therefore, the German youth who shared this spirit were accepted into the front soldiers' community. Young officers and front soldiers had joined the Freikorps, the only worthy endeavour at that time, in Jünger's view. But this service had not been appreciated either. Jünger wondered whether the front soldiers should have acted differently, as had the fascists in Italy. However, in Germany, the front soldiers did not find men like Mussolini, even if the forces were available. Jünger regretted that they lacked a 'genuine party of the front soldiers'. They had to find a political leadership in order to make a real revolution.[69]

When this article was published, the collaboration of Jünger with the *Stahlhelm* review directed by Helmut Franke had already been agreed. It is known that Jünger wrote a letter to Spengler on 7 August 1925 announcing that he wanted to write in *Der Stahlhelm* about 'the front soldier and his duty'; he wanted to make a call for a 'conscious politics'.[70]

---

[68] Helmut Kiesel, *Ernst Jünger: Die Biographie*, Munich, Siedler, 2007.
[69] Ernst Jünger, 'Revolution und Frontsoldatentum', *Gewissen*, 31 August 1925.
[70] Quoted by Kiesel, *Ernst Jünger*, p. 283.

The interest of Jünger, Franke and Spengler in Fascist Italy, as well as their perception of Italian Fascism as a state led by war veterans, is clear. In September of 1925, Jünger inaugurated a series of articles in *Der Stahlhelm*'s new ideological supplement, *Die Standarte*.[71] In these radical texts, politics was – inverting Clausewitz's aphorism – 'the continuation of war by other means'. First of all, Jünger clarified his conception of the front soldier; as already mentioned, it was not an exclusivist notion empirically based on the 'lived experience' of war (*Erlebnis*). Instead, being a front soldier was a matter of 'character' (*Charakter*). A front soldier was every man who felt himself to be so, ready to fulfil his national duties. The class of front soldiers – *Frontsoldatentum* – was a fighting community – *Kampfgemeinschaft*. Its members were not characterized by their past but by their present and future.[72] Mussolini was presented as an exemplary leader whose followers included officers and workers marching side by side.[73] The front soldiers were considered neither reactionaries nor pacifists; they harboured a revolutionary potential, but their revolution was not of the same type as that of 1918.[74] However, when it came to defining the political strategy of the war veterans, Jünger did not signal one unequivocal path; he pointed to two possible options. On the one hand was a legalist position recognizing the Weimar state. On the other hand was the revolutionary path, conquering the state and making real the 'national ideals'. Undoubtedly, the goal of both paths was 'national dictatorship'.[75]

The Stahlhelm chose to follow the legalist path.[76] Initially, in the first half of 1926, there was a period when the movement seemed inclined towards the violent seizure of power. Some of Jünger's views were implemented, for example, opening the Stahlhelm membership to men who had not experienced the war. Subsequently, however, the ideology expressed in the pages of *Die Standarte* seemed too revolutionary and disconnected from the Stahlhelm's policy at the time, so the supplement ceased publication in April 1926. From this point on, Jünger and Franke published their radical nationalist texts in other journals, such as *Arminius*, named after the Germanic hero of ancient times. This magazine adopted, as its cover, a more aggressive symbol than the Stahlhelm helmet – the

---

[71] Ernst Jünger, *Politische Publizistik: 1919 bis 1933*, Stuttgart, Klett & Co., 2001.
[72] Ernst Jünger, 'Unsere politiker' and 'Wesen des Frontsoldatentums', *Standarte. Wochenschrift des neuen Nationalismus* (Berlin), 6 September 1925.
[73] Ernst Jünger, 'Abgrenzung und Verbindung', *Standarte*, 13 September 1925.
[74] Ernst Jünger, 'Die Reaktion' and 'Der Pazifismus', *Standarte*, 1 and 15 November 1925.
[75] Ernst Jünger, 'Der Frontsoldat und die innere Politik', *Standarte*, 29 November 1925.
[76] Berghahn, *Der Stahlhelm*, pp. 91–142. See also Klotzbücher, *Der politische Weg*, pp. 72–164.

Figure 4.3 *Arminius* (*Kampfschrift für deutsche Nationalisten*, 1 May 1927). (Published by Arminius-Verlag, Helmut Franke.)

sword (Figure 4.3). The rupture with the Stahlhelm took place in terms of doctrine as well. In a bitter article, Franke resignedly stated that after seven unsuccessful years, they would never again believe in the front soldiers as the vanguard for the conquest of the state. The 'new nationalism' (*neue Nationalismus*) that they would continue to preach would target other forces, for example, young men.[77] The myth of the fascist veterans was thus abandoned.

---

[77] Helmut Franke, 'Die Tragödie der Frontsoldaten', *Arminius. Kampfschrift für deutsche Nationalisten* (Berlin), 14 November 1926.

For its part, the Stahlhelm adopted the motto, 'Inside the State' (*Hinein in den Staat*) and inaugurated a legalist strategy based on negotiations with the rightist parties, contacts with Marshal Hindenburg (the new Reich president since May of 1925, who was a venerated honorary member of the Stahlhelm), and yearly mass demonstrations, the 'Day of the Front Soldier' (*Frontsoldatentag*), which served to publicize its political programs. They talked about *Frontsozialismus*, which described an allegedly patriotic common experience of the trenches considered as the base of the *Volksgemeinschaft*.[78] At this time, the Stahlhelm's visual representation of the veteran was always that of a virile front soldier with the steel helmet, an image conveying conservative and authoritarian values.[79] However, the Stahlhelm was not politically successful, and the hypocrisy of its allegedly non-partisan nature (*Überparteilichkeit*) was evident. After the disappointing results of the 1928 elections, certain Stahlhelm sectors embraced once more an acutely anti-republican attitude.

The Stahlhelm's stance regarding Italian Fascism soon became evidently contradictory; the sustained exaltation of Fascism collided with the Südtirol (South Tyrol) question.[80] As the fascist oppression against the German-speaking minority in this region continued, the Stahlhelm was moved by its nationalism to react. The veterans combined admiration and condemnation. On 21 February 1926, the *Stahlhelm* journal published a translation, with a commentary by Franke, of the fascist syndicalist law. On the front page of the same issue, Mussolini was harshly attacked for his most recent declarations about Südtirol. This article contained at once a threat and an overture: while saying that in Germany there existed the same patriotic youth as in Italy, ready to defend the Germans of Südtirol, it was also said that Mussolini should not seek a confrontation with them but desert France and Britain, countries lacking that kind of patriotic young men, to find an understanding with the Germans.[81] This ambivalent attitude would be maintained in the years that followed,[82] whilst the attraction of authoritarianism and Fascism did not abate. In the *Stahlhelm* organ, the

---

[78] *Der Stahlhelm*, 10 October 1926.

[79] See, among others, the poster 'Stahlhelm. Hamburg 9th Frontsoldatentag', June 1928, BArch Plak 002–033-040.

[80] For a general overview on the Südtirol question from the point of view of the Stahlhelm, see BArch, R 72/891.

[81] F. W. Heinz, 'Antwort an Mussolini', and Helmut Franke, 'Ehre der Arbeit', both in *Der Stahlhelm*, 21 February 1926. See also *Nachrichtenblatt des Gaues Postdam des 'Stahlhelm' Bund der Frontsoldaten* (Postdam), 3 (March 1926).

[82] For example, see *Der Stahlhelm*, 11 March 1928.

fascist-inspired Primo de Rivera dictatorship was described with praise, and democracies were scorned.[83]

While there was a partial adoption of fascist discourses, representations and political aims among the nationalist veterans in Germany, the Nazi movement was much slower to develop a symbolic and discursive frame to approach war veterans. The Nazis were rather reluctant to appeal directly to the front soldiers. The NSDAP was re-launched in February of 1925, after Hitler's release from prison in December of 1924. Hitler abandoned the idea of a March on Berlin, inaugurating a course of legality. In fact, *Mein Kampf*, the book he conceived in prison, did not include any passage in which the veterans were clearly presented as the instrument for the conquest of the state. As is widely acknowledged, Hitler exalted the heroism of the soldiers of the First World War; he understood and occasionally depicted himself as a former soldier, and he sought to instil a fighting mentality into his SA.[84] However, Hitler did not assign any specific political role to the veterans. In *Mein Kampf*, we can only find a set of common stereotypes: the front 'heroes' versus the 'deserters' of the revolutionary soldier councils and the insulted and spat-upon veterans whose decorations were torn. These unoriginal representations justified restoration of the army's honour, but there were no evocations of a future state of front soldiers.[85]

In this period marked by growth and expansion of the NSDAP, the myth of the fascist veterans played no role. Since 1925, the *Völkischer Beobachter* had included a supplement entitled *Der deutsche Frontsoldat*, but it was largely devoted to military politics and technical questions. In NSDAP meetings, Hitler often introduced himself as a soldier who had fulfilled his duty for 'four and a half years', and he used to address the audience as though it were composed of equally self-sacrificing ex-soldiers; the target of his diatribes were the Jews and traitors of the home front, who had stabbed the heroic soldiers in the back.[86] However, there were no appeals to the veterans to seize power, nor depictions of the front soldiers as the elite of the nation. Furthermore, the leftist NSDAP group in northern Germany, represented by the Strasser brothers and Joseph Goebbels, ascribed no relevance to the veteran identity. For the Nazis, the front soldiers embodied a set of values: the 'spirit of duty',

---

[83] See the section 'Auslandrundschau' in *Der Stahlhelm*, 8 and 22 May and 12 and 19 June 1927.
[84] Sabine Behrenbeck, *Der Kult um die toten Helden*, p. 100.
[85] Adolf Hitler, *Mein Kampf*, Munich, 1936 (172nd–173rd edn., 1st edn. 1925), p. 606.
[86] Adolf Hitler, *Reden, Schriften, Anordnungen. Februar 1925 bis Januar 1933*, München et al., K. G. Saur, 1992–2006, Vol. I, p. 303, Vol. II, part 1, pp. 247–8, 258–9, Vol. II, part 2, pp. 494–6, 700, 855.

'sacrifice', 'patriotism', 'comradeship' and 'subordination', as Georg Strasser put it. But even for this ex-officer and ex-Freikorps member, neither the veterans nor the front soldiers personified the National Socialist ideology.[87] Local leaders who, still imbued by the myth of the fascist veterans, wanted to merge German *Frontsoldaten* and young men into defence organizations such as the Frontbann and instil the National Socialist spirit into them were disappointed by Hitler's and Luddendorf's disapproval of this strategy.[88]

Recently, Nils Löffelbein has argued that front soldiers and war victims (*Kriegsopfer*) were dominant themes in NSDAP propaganda before 1933,[89] but this assertion should be nuanced by taking into account chronology. From 1924, the National Socialist representative in the *völkisch* bloc in the Reichstag, Hans Dietrich, a severely mutilated ex-soldier, defended the disabled veterans and war victims in some of his public speeches, but this type of intervention was far from prominent in both the discourse and practice of the NSDAP. For the Reichstag elections of May 1928, Hitler and the Nazis invoked the front soldiers' support through speeches and electoral posters. It was even said that they represented the Germany of the future, which would be governed 'by the representatives of the front-troops'.[90] (Note that he referred to the *representatives* and not to the front troops themselves.) Yet, this propaganda was not original either discursively or iconographically.[91] The representations and slogans used scarcely differed from those formerly employed by the Stahlhelm. Propaganda posters of both the Stahlhelm and NSDAP portrayed the German soldier with his steel helmet: an image conveying ideas of strength, resilience and determination, but not aggression. In any case, the electoral returns were very poor for the Nazis. Until the early 1930s, the Nazis did not develop any substantial

---

[87] Gregor Strasser, 'Frontsoldaten', *Völkischer Beobachter*, 24–25 April 1927. Notice also the lack of any references to the veterans and front soldiers in Strasser's main discourses between 1925 and 1927: Gregor Strasser, *Freiheit und Brot*, Berlin, 1928; Georg Strasser, *Hammer und Schwert*, Berlin, 1928. For a different opinion about Strasser, but mostly based on post-1929 evidence, see Peter D. Stachura, *Gregor Strasser and the Rise of Nazism*, London, Allen & Unwin, 1983, p. 15.

[88] Document of resignation of Max Pledl as local Frontbann leader (8 May 1925), Staatsarchiv München (Munich), Polizeidirektion München, Nr. 6782, Microfilm P 102.

[89] Löffelbein, *Ehrenbürger der Nation*, p. 110.

[90] Adolf Hitler, *Reden*, Vol. II, part 2, p. 790.

[91] See, for example, the posters 'National-socialist. Otherwise the victims were for nothing', May 1928, BArch Plak 002–042-017; and '2 million dead! For nothing? Never! Front soldiers! Adolf Hitler shows you the way!', May 1928, BArch Plak 002–039-013.

doctrine around the veterans nor any precise political strategy towards war victims.

There are several reasons to explain why the Nazi movement did not absorb the myth of the fascist veterans. In Germany, as a result of the 1918 revolution, the front soldiers – rather than the veterans in general – became the group idolized by the nationalist extreme right. They were believed to have crushed the Spartacist uprising and the short-lived communist Räterepublik of Bavaria. But organizations such as the Stahlhelm, not the NSDAP, had assumed the political representation of these men. Hitler's credentials as a front soldier allowed him to state that he had fulfilled his duty, but not much more. In the case of Goebbels, it was evident that he had not served as a soldier in the First World War due to his physical disability. The Nazis were conscious that some Jews also represented themselves as front soldiers. In fact, the Nazis pointed out the difficulties in clearly defining who was a front soldier.[92] Furthermore, when the fascist veteran myth was being transferred into Germany and France during 1924 and early 1925, the Nazi movement had been dismantled. Subsequently, as it sought to recruit members, the prime target of the NSDAP was not the veterans but rather the working class, the unemployed and the youth. Meanwhile, the preponderance of the veteran mystique among the anti-republican groups generally receded. In contrast, the pacifist memory of the war persisted through the 'No more war!' (*Nie wieder Krieg!*) movement and the activities and publications of republican veterans.[93] It was not that the Nazis did not copy ideological and behavioural patterns from the Italian fascists. Despite the absence of fascist-inspired discourses about the veterans, the Nazis paid a lot of attention to Italian Fascism. However, the knowledge about Fascist Italy grew more complex and nuanced; people realized that Mussolini's regime was much more than a veterans' state.

If the Nazis progressively took an interest in the political mobilization and indoctrination of veterans, it was largely due to the precedent set by the Stahlhelm. The transmission of ideas from the *soldatische Nationalismus* to the NSDAP is beyond question in the second half of the 1920s, yet this ideological connection never came to fruition. In 1926, Ernst Jünger sent some of his works to Hitler, which the Führer read with great interest. However, a planned personal meeting between them never took place.[94] In 1927, the *Völkischer Beobachter* created a new section, 'The New Front' (*Die neue Front*), where a Nazi-inflected version of the

[92] 'Wer ist Frontsoldat?', *Völkischer Beobachter*, 17 September 1927.
[93] Ziemann, *Contested Commemorations, passim.*   [94] Kiesel, *Ernst Jünger*, p. 280.

soldatische Nationalismus ideology was relayed. In its first issue, Jünger, who had just broken with *Der Stahlhelm*, wrote an article about the 'new nationalism' (*neue Nationalismus*). In this article, the category of the front soldier was absent from Jünger's argumentation, though he did evoke the example of Mussolini and Fascist Italy. Now, meaningfully, the key protagonist was the 'class of nationalistic workers'.[95] In the late 1920s, Jünger was active in establishing these contacts with the Nazi movement, especially with its leftist branch. The preponderance of the front soldier in his writings gave way to the exaltation of the worker (*Arbeiter*).[96] As with Jünger's writings, the Stahlhelm concept of *Frontsozialismus* was also familiar to and discussed by the Nazis, but they did not adopt it.[97] Many Nazis had been soldiers or/and Freikorps volunteers; therefore, they were not impermeable to the myth of the fascist veteran conveyed by Jünger and others. Indeed, the autobiographical book of Ernst Röhm, published in 1928, was 'dedicated to the front soldiers', whom 'the SA comrades should emulate'. Röhm's declared goal was 'to give the veterans through acts of combat their due share of the state leadership, and to make sure that the real spirit of the front soldiers is politically enforced'.[98] Yet, in this period, Röhm was not taking part in the Nazi movement.[99] While the renewed SA was mainly set up by men with combat experience, the bulk of its membership was composed of younger people who had no direct knowledge of war.[100]

The myth of the fascist veteran was not transferred to the NSDAP but rather to the Stahlhelm, as I have shown. The Stahlhelm did not evolve into a political fascist party (as the Faisceau in France did), but it tried – without success – to influence German politics. This history recalls the trajectory of the ANC in Italy before it fell under control of the fascists. Also, the relationship between the NSDAP and the Stahlhelm during the second half of the 1920s resembled that of the fascist movement and the ANC in the early post-war period in Italy. The Nazis, particularly the leftist group of Gregor Strasser, showed interest in the Stahlhelm veterans, but in the end, their relationship was defined by a profound

---

[95] *Völkischer Beobachter*, 23–24 January 1927.
[96] Cf. Nikolaus Wachsam, 'Marching under the Swastika? Ernst Junger and National Socialism', in *Journal of Contemporary History*, 33, 4 (1998), pp. 573–89; Markus März, *Nationale Sozialisten in der NSDAP*, Graz, Ares Verlag, 2010, pp. 61–82.
[97] Wilhelm Weiß, 'Kameraden vom Stahlhelm!', *Völkischer Beobachter*, 8–9 May 1927; Werner Catte, 'Frontsozialismus', *Völkischer Beobachter*, 25 June 1927.
[98] Ernst Röhm, *Die Geschichte eines Hochverräters*, Munich, 1934 (1st edn. 1928), p. 10; see also a book review in *Völkischer Beobachter*, 14–15 October 1928.
[99] Eleanor Hancock, *Ernst Röhm: Hitler's SA Chief of Staff*, New York, Palgrave Macmillan, 2008, pp. 83–104.
[100] Longerich, *Die braunen Bataillone*, pp. 45–77.

rivalry.[101] However, the Stahlhelm had served as the conduit through which new political discourses rooted in the myth of the fascist veterans entered political life in Germany, circulating freely and thus influencing the Nazi movement's long-term development.

By 1927, echoes of the fascist-inspired political discourses and representations of the German veterans had reached back to Italy. In April of 1927, the new Stahlhelm demonstration in Berlin was described in Italy as a revolutionary, albeit peaceful 'march on Berlin'. This information attracted Mussolini's interest, although the Italian ambassador in Berlin told him that 'a peaceful march on Berlin without arms makes no sense.'[102] A report about the German veterans' organization was prepared for the Duce, in which the fascist inspiration of the Stahlhelm was discussed in detail. The question of the Südtirol, however, seemed an important obstacle between fascists and German veterans. In contrast, Hitler was establishing indirect contacts with Mussolini, explicitly asserting that the Südtirol would never represent a hurdle to reaching an understanding between the Nazis and Fascist Italy. In any case, the myth of the fascist veterans had facilitated the establishment of this circuit of ideological and political dialogue and exchange.

The main origin of these discourses and representations was Fascist Italy, where a set of transnational elements had first politically synthesized. The rise of Italian Fascism had been understood as the seizure of power by a party of veterans, which had restored the victory, redeemed the neglected, smashed communism and given the veterans their deserved leading role in the state. This was the myth of the fascist veteran. As I will now demonstrate, the fascists were active propagators of this legend in the international sphere.

The Fascist Veterans and the FIDAC

The Fédération Interalliée des Anciens Combattants (FIDAC) had been created by conservative French veterans in late 1920. The initial core of this association had been French, Belgian, British, American and Italian veterans, whilst Czechoslovakian, Yugoslav, Polish, Romanian and Portuguese representatives progressively signed up in the years that followed. In the beginning, the FIDAC strived to strengthen the ties between former allied veterans. By doing so, it expected to exert

---

[101] Alessandro Salvador, 'Il nazionalsocialismo e la destra nazionalista tedesca: 1925–1933', PhD dissertation, Università degli Studi di Trento, 2009, pp. 84–105.

[102] AMAE, Affari Politici 1919–1930, Germania, box 1174, file 'Congresso "Stahlhelm" "elmi d'acciaio" a Berlino'.

international political influence in order to improve social benefits for war victims and to preserve the peace. In a somewhat contradictory policy that clashed with this goal, and in contrast to other international veterans' platforms, the FIDAC openly excluded the veterans from the former enemy countries. This discriminatory position, zealously defended by the three-times-re-elected President Bertrand, was reaffirmed at the FIDAC Congress of Brussels in September of 1923, where the opinions of the French and Belgian leaders predominated. However, by this year, the instability of the international situation also began to resonate within the FIDAC. The Italian representatives were unable to join the congress because the transformation of the ANC into a state organization breached the FIDAC's requirement for political independence amongst its members.[103] However, the Italian veterans would soon regain and, subsequently, increase their influence within the group.

In 1924, when the international peace settlements were being restructured, the debates inside the FIDAC became heated. Between March and April of 1924, Mussolini and the British Legion Vice President Colonel Crosfield had arranged for the return of an Italian delegation to the FIDAC.[104] Thus, in September of 1924, the ANC took its place once more within this organization. In the wake of the London conference on the reparations issue, FIDAC representatives met in the same city. Meanwhile, Italy was in the throes of the Matteotti crisis. Ettore Viola personally headed the Italian committee, and this participation can be taken as further evidence of his intention of making the ANC an influential institution independent of the fascist government. The association did not ask the fascist government to express allegiance to the congress. Nonetheless, the Italian ambassador in London received instructions from Mussolini to observe this veterans' gathering with interest.[105]

Even though the London meeting had little impact on the British and international public, it was important for the trajectory of the FIDAC, as well as for that of Fascism. At the congress, the French veterans' intransigent viewpoint was thwarted by the more open attitude adopted by the

---

[103] *La Voix du Combattant*, 28 October 1923; Fagerberg, *The 'anciens combattants'*, pp. 202–8, 211–13; Julia Eichenberg, *Kämpfen für Frieden und Fürsorge: Polnische Veteranen des Ersten Weltkriegs und ihre internationalen Kontakte, 1918–1939*, Munich, Oldenbourg, 2011, pp. 72–83; Eichenberg and Newman (ed.), *The Great War and Veterans' Internationalism, passim.*

[104] AMAE, Società delle Nazioni, box 66, file 'Federazione interalleata ex-combattenti FIDAC'; see also Salvante, 'The Italian Associazione Nazionale Mutilati e Invalidi di Guerra', p. 169.

[105] AMAE, Società delle Nazioni, box 66, file 'Federazione interalleata ex-combattenti FIDAC'.

British representatives, who suggested that German veterans' associations be invited to join the FIDAC. Faced with the difficulties of reaching an agreement on this question, Viola's conciliatory proposal for an intermediate resolution resolved the impasse. The congress approved the Italian suggestion of permitting an inquiry about the German veterans' associations as the first step towards potential voluntary contacts between the FIDAC and the former enemies. In addition to this success, the Italian delegation used the occasion of the congress to boast about the favourable fascist legislation for disabled veterans. As a result, the rest of the national representatives agreed to urge their governments to develop similar measures. Furthermore, it was decided that the next FIDAC congress would be held in Rome, a decision to which Mussolini gave his acquiescence after being consulted from London by the Italian ambassador.[106]

Most probably, all these facts contributed to the decision of Mussolini and the fascists to push for the final imposition of fascist hegemony in the ANC. The representation of Italian veterans in the international sphere could not be left in the hands of non-fascists. The expeditious purge of the ANC and the exclusion of Viola and the anti-fascist veteran leaders (see Chapter 3) would be completed just in time for the next FIDAC congress in Rome. In April of 1925, ANC triumvirate member Nicola Sansanelli met with FIDAC international representatives in Paris and convinced them of the legitimacy of the fascist government measures regarding the ANC.[107] By September of 1925, the Italian veterans' organizations offered a fully fascist united front to the international veterans' delegates who gathered in the Italian capital. The list of the Italian representatives spoke for itself: Amilcare Rossi, Luigi Russo, Nicola Sansanelli, Adolfo Schiavo, Aldo Bertelè, Angelo Zilli, Bruno Biagi and other fascists, none of them present at the previous FIDAC congress. The fascists had so thoroughly prepared the event that the foreign veterans were delighted. Among the visitors were the FIDAC president, American Thomas W. Miller, and French veterans such as Marcel Héraud (UF), Paul Vaillant (UF), Charles Bertrand (UNC) and Jean Goy (UNC).[108]

---

[106] *La Voix du Combattant*, 4 October 1924; *La France Mutilée*, 5 October 1924; *Problemi d'Italia*, 6 (November 1924), 7 (December 1924); *I Combattenti. La Nuova Giornata*, 5 October 1924; *La Stampa*, 20 September 1924; AMAE, Società delle Nazioni, box 66, file 'Federazione interalleata ex-combattenti FIDAC'.

[107] AMAE, Società delle Nazioni, box 66, file 'Federazione interalleata ex-combattenti FIDAC'.

[108] *FIDAC. Bulletin mensuel de la Fédération Interalliée des Anciens Combattants* (Paris), 1 (January 1926); *La France Mutilée*, 27 September 1925; *Problemi d'Italia*, 9 (September

During the congress, the fascist veterans managed to steer the discussions towards topics and conclusions that matched their interests. When the question of international migration was broached, the Italians requested of the American delegates that a higher number of Italian veterans be allowed to emigrate to the United States. The fascists also asked the French delegates to ensure that Italian veterans in France enjoyed preference in employment in agricultural and construction work. When discussing organizational matters, the fascists proposed that in the hypothetical case that veterans' associations were officially recognized by a state – as had happened in Italy – no other association from that country should be admitted to the FIDAC. Regarding the sensitive issue of inter-allied debts, the Italians, backed by the Americans, stressed the necessity of finding a solution (since Italy was a debtor country). Yet, the French succeeded in subordinating the revision of the inter-allied debts to the payment of reparations by the former enemies. In the conclusions of the congress, it was stated that communist propaganda was an international threat; the FIDAC leaders defined the solidarity of their associations as 'the greatest enemy of communism'. The FIDAC, following the demands of Polish and Czechoslovak representatives, denounced German militarism, but this anti-German stance included a positive assessment of Mussolini's intransigent attitude regarding the Alto Adige (South Tyrol) question. Besides these discussions, the congress attendees visited Roman sights, paid tribute to the *Milite Ignoto*, and met fascist leaders such as Farinacci. All this propaganda paved the way for the FIDAC to send a message of support to Mussolini, calling him the 'saviour of Italy', when he survived an assassination attempt in November of 1925.[109]

The next FIDAC congress was held in Warsaw and Krakow in September of 1926, with British Colonel Crosfield serving as president of the association. Earlier, during the spring, Crosfield had travelled through Fascist Italy, visiting Genoa, Turin, Milan, Naples and other cities; he had paid visit to the *Milite Ignoto* monument, raising his arm in roman salute.[110] The FIDAC congress in Poland came only three months after Pilsudski's coup d'état, and this situation made it necessary to eliminate

1925); AMAE, Società delle Nazioni, box 66, file 'Federazione interalleata ex-combattenti FIDAC'.

[109] *Problemi d'Italia*, 10 (October 1925), 12 (December 1925); *La Voix du Combattant*, 26 September 1925; *Il Popolo d'Italia*, 12 and 16 September 1925; *FIDAC*, 2 (February 1926), 3 (March 1926); League of Nations Archives, Geneva (SDNA), 40R1595, dossier 17591, doc. 45434.

[110] *Italia Augusta: Problemi d'Italia. Rassegna dei combattenti (Roma)*, 3 (May 1926); *FIDAC*, 5 (May 1926).

certain delicate issues from the agenda.[111] The Italian committee sent to Poland was headed by Nicola Sansanelli and composed of Gianni Baccarini, Angelo Zilli and other fascists, including Mario Dessaules, leader of the ANC in France. At this congress, the division at the heart of the FIDAC was acute, given that the British position, reflecting the spirit of Locarno, contrasted with the French attitude of distrust towards Germany. The French veteran leaders who favoured a rapprochement with the Germans paid more attention to their own international conference in Geneva (CIAMAC). This was the case for the influential UF member René Cassin, a jurist and delegate at the League of Nations who had been instrumental in launching the CIAMAC with the support of the International Labour Organization one year before.[112] Cognizant of the competition posed by the CIAMAC to establish a truly international organization of veterans, the delegates at the FIDAC congress finally agreed to invite German associations to a future meeting in Luxemburg. At this point, however, some French representatives abandoned the sessions in protest.[113] Veterans of the CIAMAC, in turn, became divided over the issue of collaborating with the FIDAC, but the opinion prevailed in favour of furthering their own international collaboration to defend the ideal of peace in the spirit of the League of Nations.[114] Thus, while the real advances towards European peace took place at the CIAMAC rather than at the FIDAC, the latter organization became more and more influenced by the fascists. The fascist veterans within the FIDAC did not let any opportunity pass 'to show to their comrades how lucky their country was to have a war veteran as the head of state'.[115] As a result, international veterans in the FIDAC made for potentially easy converts to the myth of the fascist veteran.

The FIDAC review, published in English and French, became another organ for the diffusion of fascist discourse and policies regarding war veterans. The veteran organ described, for instance, Italian veterans' visits to the Duce and their mutual declarations of admiration and loyalty. It was in the pages of this journal that veterans of all the formerly allied countries learnt that the bearers of the Gold Medal in Italy were addressed by the Italian president himself as the 'flower of your race, the

[111] Eichenberg, *Kämpfen für Frieden*, p. 178.
[112] Jay Winter and Antoine Prost, *René Cassin and Human Rights: From the Great War to the Universal Declaration*, Cambridge University Press, 2013, pp. 59–61.
[113] *Il Popolo d'Italia*, 8 September 1926; *La France Mutilée*, 19 September 1926; *Journal des débats politiques et littéraires* (Paris), 23 September 1926; Fagerberg, *The 'Anciens Combattants'*, pp. 78–81.
[114] SDNA, 40R1595, dossier 17591, doc. 54386.
[115] *Il Popolo d'Italia*, 12 September 1926.

real aristocracy of the generation which on land, on sea and in the sky has achieved acts of prodigious heroism'.[116] Mentioning the circular to the *prefetti* sent by Mussolini in January of 1927, it was said that Italian veterans were considered the 'Aristocracy of the Victory'[117]:

Italy, writes Mr. Mussolini, contrary to some countries, has known how to guard in its ex-service men's associations the incomparable inheritance of victory. The mothers and widows of the soldiers, fallen on the field of honour, the Association of the Disabled and Invalids, the Gold Medals and Blue Ribbons, the National Association of Ex-Service Men, that of Volunteers and others of less importance, constitute a valuable force for the regime. They give it the disinterested and sincere approval of millions of Italians. It is these Italians who left hundreds and thousands of their glorious dead on the battlefields; it is these Italians who fought and bled during forty months; it is these Italians who bear on their bodies the irrevocable marks of sacrifices and duty accomplished.

The example of Italy radicalized the political orientation of the FIDAC. It was considered natural that the war generation of each country exerted a preponderant influence on public affairs: 'In two of our countries, Italy and Poland, this generation already holds power in its hands.' The FIDAC bulletin exalted both regimes and their 'popular' leaders, Mussolini and Pilsudski, arguing that 'under these circumstances it is difficult to speak of dictatorship.' The FIDAC undermined its pacifism by conveying the positive opinions of Mussolini about the war. The new FIDAC president, the Frenchman Marcel Héraud, travelled to Italy, receiving magnificent welcomes in Turin from Zilli, in Rome from Rossi and Russo (visiting the *Milite Ignoto*) and in Naples from Sansanelli. Héraud came back to France convinced that 'the same spirit moved all the veterans' and that in Italy veterans participated in the management of the public affairs and had 'the responsibility of power'.[118]

The culmination of this evolution was the nomination, at the Congress of London in September of 1927, of Nicola Sansanelli as the president of the FIDAC. This decisive victory was achieved in spite of the resistance of a few FIDAC members, particularly some French representatives from the UF, who disliked Fascism. The appointment of Sansanelli was also seen as another obstacle for the rapprochement between the FIDAC and the CIAMAC, still rivals in the objective of representing veterans internationally. According to a League of Nations official involved in veterans' affairs, 'the socialist elements of the [CIAMAC] seemed resolved

---

[116] *FIDAC. Bulletin of the Allied Legions* (Paris), 1 (January 1927).
[117] *FIDAC. Bulletin of the Allied Legions*, 3 (March 1927).
[118] *FIDAC. Bulletin of the Allied Legions*, 5 (May 1927).

not to reach any agreement with a fascist.[119] Having obtained the presidency of the FIDAC, the fascists had the opportunity to be the official representatives of the inter-allied war veterans in Europe as well as in the United States. In fact, the American Legion leaders who had visited fascist Rome at the end of September 1927 invited Sansanelli to their country for a propaganda trip in the spring of 1928. Needless to say, Sansanelli used his travels to publicize not only the FIDAC but also 'Fascism as a political-social doctrine and as a government system'; in passing, he denied the description of the Duce as a dictator. The loyalty and obedience of the ANC to Mussolini, as well as the alleged great achievements of the fascist regime in the realm of social assistance, were exhibited during this time through the FIDAC.[120]

However, during Sansanelli's presidency, the FIDAC international relevance in Western European affairs declined. The FIDAC Luxembourg conferences, where former enemy veterans were invited, cannot be portrayed – despite the fascist triumphalism – as successful. For example, the FIDAC had sent invitations to the Stahlhelm, but it plainly rejected the offer, on the basis of its radical opposition to Versailles and to the Dawes plan. The Jungdeutsche Orden did join the conversations with the ex-allies but defended its nationalist views with intransigency. These discussions among convinced patriots with completely opposing opinions did not reach any consensus at all. At the end of the second Luxembourg meeting, the biggest success had been simply maintaining a 'polite ambiance'. Furthermore, these meetings brought about a grave crisis in CIAMAC-FIDAC relations.[121] In a sense, as the Nazis shrewdly noted, it was a contradiction to organize an international veterans' movement if the objective was to consolidate peace. Faced with these complications, and having used the FIDAC for their interests for some time, fascist predominance inside the organization faded. In September of 1928, President Sansanelli excused his absence from the congress in Bucharest; he prioritized joining the fascist Gran Consiglio. It is not surprising that his mandate in charge of the FIDAC was not renewed.[122]

---

[119] 'Note sur la troisième conférence de la CIAMAC', Geneva, 15 October 1927, SDNA, 40R1595, dossier 17591, doc. 54386.
[120] 'Italia Augusta', 8 (August 1928); Il Popolo d'Italia, 29 September 1927; La Stampa, 26 April 1928; New York Times, 26 May 1928; AMAE, Società delle Nazioni, box 66, file 'Federazione interalleata ex-combattenti FIDAC'.
[121] Eichenberg, Kämpfen für Frieden, pp. 190–1.
[122] Der Stahlhelm, 11 March, 15 April and 30 September 1928; Le Matin (Paris), 1 April and 11, 12, 17, 18 and 21 September 1928; La Stampa, 18 September 1928; Völkischer Beobachter, 15 September 1928; SDNA, 50R3565, dossier 1085.

The Fascist ANC

During the second half of the 1920s, once the process of imposing fascist dominance on the ANC had been completed, Italian veteran politics experienced a period of relative tranquillity. There were also cultural and organizational transformations, as we will see; but the main struggles around the Italian veterans had been resolved, and obedience had been imposed by force and censure. In a journal interview, Amilcare Rossi, asked about the recent debates about the role of *combattentismo*, opined: '[T]his ugly word does not refer to any real force present in our nation: in any case, if this kind of shapeless soul existed – and I doubt it – it has forever disappeared.'[123] In October of 1925, the directors of the veterans' news review *Problemi d'Italia* were obliged, in unclear circumstances, to resign.[124] Their posts were taken over by Umberto Guglielmotti[125] and Nicola Sansanelli. These fascists changed the title and the content of the review in keeping with the regime's needs.[126] Any kind of veteran expression was subject to fascist control to such an extent that we should refer to the veterans' organization from this point onwards as the fascist ANC.

This phase was the most stable in Italian veteran politics during the interwar period. Social assistance and agricultural reform were the most common activities at this time. The ONC was also put under fascist supervision; directed by Angelo Manaresi, it sought to reclaim agricultural lands through hydraulic works.[127] At the same time, it carried out propaganda, through cultural activities such as a travelling cinema. All these projects aimed for the 'ruralisation of Italy'.[128] The ANC, enjoying direct funding from the government, conceded limited credits to veterans, distributed agricultural machinery and contributed to the 'Battles for Grain' (*Battaglie del Grano*) that the regime promoted since 1925 to spur production. The association also offered healthcare assistance to veterans and gave subsidies to the needy. Thus, it claimed to be 'an instrument for the elevation of the agricultural classes'.[129] The goal of

---

[123] *Il Combattente. Giornale letterario assistenziale apolitico organo uffciale della federazione provinciale combattenti* (Naples), 30 April 1926.
[124] *Problemi d'Italia*, 12 (December 1925).
[125] After the March on Rome and the absorption of the ANI by the PNF, Guglielmotti became a leader of the Roman Fascio and director of the weekly *Roma fascista*. In 1929, he also became a member of the fascist Parliament. In the 1930s and early 1940s, he was a very active journalist and supporter of Mussolini. After the Second World War, he joined the neo-fascist Movimento Sociale Italiano. He died in Rome in 1976.
[126] *Italia Augusta*, 1 (March 1926).   [127] *L'Opera Nazionale Combattenti*, Rome, 1926.
[128] 'Codice della terra', in *Biblioteca agraria dell'Opera Nazionale Combattenti*, Rome, 1928, p. 11.
[129] Paolo Ceci, *I Gerarchi dell'Associazione Nazionale Combattenti*, Rome, 1928, p. 94.

ruralization was part of the regenerative mission that Fascism wanted to fulfil, and thus, in order to discipline agrarian society, the ideal of the obedient 'peasant soldier' was employed. However, while there were certain technical and economic achievements, neither the ONC nor the ANC resolved important regional and class inequalities, and the problems of Italian agriculture persisted.[130]

The fascist ANC consolidated in the second half of the 1920s. Another step in this development was the adoption of a new statute in November of 1926. This reform coincided with the modification of the PNF statute, which restricted party autonomy and suppressed every kind of internal electoral process. Correspondingly, the new ANC regulations liquidated the electoral system within the ANC apparatus under the pretext of avoiding factionalism.[131] Unsurprisingly, Mussolini nominated the temporary triumvirate Rossi-Russo-Sansanelli as the new definitive directing board of the ANC.[132] In this new phase, the ANC consolidated as an effective manager of veterans' material interests, remaining focused on assistance tasks. Even though the Carta del Lavoro had made no mention of the veterans, the ANC successfully defended the rights of veterans to preference on the job market when unemployment started to steadily rise during 1927 and 1928.[133] In May of 1928, having heard the veterans' concerns, Turati sent a memorandum to the PNF federations insisting on the preferential right to work of those who had been in the trenches.[134]

The changes within the regime structure saw a major militarization of politics and a politicization of the army. It is significant that the dictatorship promoted an association of discharged officers (Unione Nazionale Ufficiali in Congedo), whose function was maintenance of the ties of retired officers with the army and the War Ministry.[135] This group was soon granted the same official status as other veterans' associations.[136] Thus, Italy was progressively assuming the 'physiognomy of a warrior nation, dynamic, spiritually and physically armed, ready and impatient to affront any challenge'.[137] According to official data, the ANC reached

---

[130] Francesco di Bartolo, *Terra e fascismo*, pp. 95–125; Gustavo Alares, 'Ruralismo, fascismo y regeneración: Italia y España en perspectiva comparada', *Ayer*, 83 (2011), pp. 127–47.

[131] *Il Popolo d'Italia*, 19 October 1926.

[132] *Il Combattente. Organo letterario assistenziale apolitico* (Naples), 27 December 1926.

[133] Ernesto Campese, *Il Fascismo contro la disoccupazione*, Rome, 1929.

[134] *Bollettino della Federazione Provinciale di Terni dell'Associazione Nazionale Combattenti* (Terni), 1 (May 1928) and 2 (June 1928).

[135] *Esercito e Nazione. Rivista per l'ufficiale italiano* (Rome), 6–7 (June–July 1926), 8 (August 1926) and 11 (November 1926).

[136] *Esercito e Nazione*, 3 (March 1927).   [137] *La Stampa*, 16 October 1926.

more than 400,000 affiliated in 1927 and continued growing. In this context, some fascist leaders advocated for the regime to stress the political function of the veterans by strengthening their military spirit. It was said that the ANC should go beyond assistance tasks and transform into a kind of reserve army in close contact with the military. This opinion was expressed by Guglielmotti, but it was contradicted by ANC leaders, who did not want to change the main role of the association yet. Even so, the expectations of some fascists that veterans would have an ever deeper involvement in the military or economic affairs endured.[138]

In general, during the second half of the 1920s, a process of concentration of power took place in Italy, not only in Mussolini's hands but also within the fascist and veterans' organizations. There was a feeling that the multiple state entities and associations should start to fuse in order to avoid duplications and to favour discipline and simplicity. This question applied particularly to the multiple veterans' groups.[139] Furthermore, since PNF members dominated ANC structures throughout Italy, these men simultaneously held several positions, as MPs, leaders of the MVSN, directing members of the fascist corporations and so on.[140] To give only the most noteworthy examples, Augusto Turati presided over the ANC federation of Brescia, Italo Balbo the federation of Ferrara and Achille Starace the federation of Lecce. Sansanelli was the head of Fascism in Naples, Rossi led the fascist federation of Terni, and Russo was appointed to be *prefetto* of Chieti. By 1928, in many provinces it was impossible to make a distinction between veterans' organization and PNF structures.[141] The veteran press, hitherto notable for its variety and diversity, progressively declined. Even the innocuous *Italia Augusta* veterans' informative magazine disappeared at the end of 1928, transformed into a purely technical and illustrated monthly publication for ONC propaganda.[142] All these steps moved the veterans' organizations closer to the totalitarian ideal.

The discourses, practices and representations of Italian veterans evolved in harmony with this drift towards totalitarianism, whilst the political rites of Fascism developed and consolidated.[143] Thus, the

---

[138] This debate, through *Roma fascista*, 12 and 19 November and 3 December 1927; *Il Popolo d'Italia*, 22 November 1927.

[139] Domenico Montalto, 'Lo Stato e le organizzazioni. III. Le associazioni minori', *Critica fascista*, 1 June 1928.

[140] Cf. the list of provincial ANC leaders annexed in Palo Ceci, *I Gerarchi dell'Associazione*, and political biographies in *Chi è? Dizionario degli italiani d'oggi*, Rome, 1936 and 1940, *ad nomen*.

[141] '*Italia Augusta*'. *Rassegna dell'Opera Nazionale per i Combattenti* (Rome), 8 (August 1928).

[142] '*Italia Augusta*', 12 (December 1928).   [143] Gentile, *Il culto del Littorio*, pp. 61–103.

official war memory was deeply infused with Fascism from 1925 on. Commemorative rituals and monuments were the two instruments for imposition of the fascist interpretation of the war and the victory. These factors reinforced the symbolic link between the intervention, the victory and the March on Rome, in which many veterans believed.

Veterans were both agents and targets of these cultural expressions. In 1926, the ANC leadership gave instructions that the veterans participate in the celebrations of the March on Rome under the aegis of the PNF and also in the local commemorations of Vittorio Veneto. In 1927 and 1928, official messages from the ANC simultaneously commemorated both concurrent dates. The association sent messages expressing loyalty to the king and the Duce on the occasion of 4 November. In 1928, the tenth anniversary (*decennale*) of the victory featured the inauguration of the Mother Home of the Disabled in Rome (Casa Madre dei Mutilati) and a big demonstration of veterans. In his address, Mussolini stated, as though it were an accepted truth, that the Italian people had desired the war, that the intervention had not been the result of unexpected foreign aggression but rather a conscious voluntary act. Mussolini addressed thousands of *combattenti* and *mutilati*, affirming that in 1922 'a handful of men issued from the trenches' had forever restored the victory. The commemoration of Italian intervention in the First World War was another important annual ritual introduced by the fascists. In this celebration of the interventionist spirit, the fascist veterans exerted a crucial role. In 1927, there was a meeting in Rome to celebrate 24 May at which not only ministers and PNF authorities were present but also ANC leaders and bearers of the Gold Medal. Turati, saluting in the Roman style, reviewed the veterans of the ANC before paying homage to the *Milite Ignoto*. Disabled veterans and decorated veterans from the Istituto del Nastro Azzurro – an association transformed into *ente morale* in 1928 – sent messages of exaltation and loyalty. And veterans abroad also celebrated these commemorations in an environment sympathetic to the fascists; for example, French *anciens combattants* attended the banquet marking the *decennale* of the victory in Paris.[144]

Inaugurations of new monuments to the memory of fallen soldiers were a constant feature in all the Italian regions during the second half of the 1920s. Probably the most famous of them was the monument to

---

[144] *Il Popolo d'Italia*, 25 May, 23 and 27 October and 4 November 1926, 29 October 1927 and 23 and 24 May, 18 September, 28 and 31 October and 4 and 6 November 1928; *Il Popolo di Roma*, 25 May 1927 and 27 October and 4 November 1928. For the *decennale* ceremonies, see the film *Giornale Luce CCXV* (November 1928), available at www.archivioluce.com (accessed 28 July 2013).

the victory in Bolzano (in the Alto Adige), finished in 1928.[145] This construction commemorated the irredentist martyrs of the Trentino region and therefore was a symbol of the oppression of the German-speaking population of Südtirol. On this occasion, the yearly congress of the ANC was convened in Bolzano too. In this period, rituals around the monuments to fallen soldiers, as well as veterans' congresses – formerly heated and tumultuous meetings where radical and disparate political discussions were held – became routine and elitist meetings that time and again declared loyalty to the king and Mussolini.[146] Publicly, the fascist veterans declared their devotion to both personalities. It is interesting to note, however, that during this period, Mussolini commenced to surpass the king as the focus receptor of veterans' and army officers' loyalties.[147]

The stylization and standardization of the fascist identity and aesthetic continued throughout these years. There was an interest in defining the model characteristics of a fascist person and in transmitting these traits to the next generation. Put simply, new Italians had to be created in the likeness of Mussolini.[148] The fascists extolled values such as faith, discipline and sacrifice and pointed at the exemplary *arditi* as the most desirable figures to imitate. Even bodily attitudes and gestures with a militaristic appearance were recommended: 'a straight and agile posture, better proud than modest. Head held high, straight back.'[149] The publication of veterans' memoirs and accounts of heroic war deeds also served this purpose. The 'trench' was represented as the 'school of schools'; young children had to learn its significance.[150] The ANC, its leaders and other fascist veterans actively supported initiatives to reinforce and transmit these models of masculinity and political attitude.[151]

This preoccupation with the fascist education of children and youths was not new[152] but was growing exponentially in this period. The fascist

---

[145] Renato Monteleone and Pino Sarasini, 'I monumenti italiani ai caduti della Grande Guerra' and Vincenzo Calí, 'Il monumento alla Vittoria di Bolzano: Un caso di continuità fra fascismo e post-fascismo', both in Leoni and Zadra (eds.), *La Grande Guerra*, pp. 631–62 and 663–70.

[146] *Numero unico per l'inaugurazione: Monumento della Vittoria*, Bolzano, 1928; *Italia Augusta*, 8 (August 1928); *Il Popolo d'Italia*, 18 September 1928.

[147] *Italia Augusta*, 1 (March 1926).

[148] Mario Carli, *Codice della vita fascista*, Rome, 1928, p. 7.

[149] Alberto Marchese, *Vademecum per l'Avanguardista d'Italia*, Naples, 1928, p. 5.

[150] Giovanni Borelli, 'Il senso della trincea', *Il Popolo d'Italia*, 19 August 1927.

[151] Francesco Pironti, *Manuale di cultura fascista: Ad uso delle scuole medie*, Rome, 1929, with a Preface by Amilcare Rossi; Arturo Gallo, *Stirpe eroica*, Naples, 1929; Ass. Naz. Combattenti Federazione Provinciale di Torino, *Canti di guerra. diretti dal Maestro Gaetano Salvadego ed eseguiti da ex Combattenti*, Turin, 1929.

[152] Tracy H. Koon, *Believe, Obey, Fight: Political Socialization of Youth in Fascist Italy, 1922–1943*, Durham, University of North Carolina Press, 1985.

youth organizations were expanding. It was an indication that a different era had begun. New generations who had not fought the war were reaching their maturity. This required the actualization of fascist identity and particularly the revision of the myths around youths.[153] Subsequently, the myth of the fascist veteran was progressively displaced, although the veterans did not lose their political relevance. As we will see, they would assume new political functions. At the end of the 1920s, a whole phase of the history of fascism closed, opening a new era for the relationship between fascists and veterans.

---

[153] Bruno Wanrooij, 'The Rise and Fall of Italian Fascism as a Generational Revolt', *Journal of Contemporary History*, 22, 3 (1987), pp. 401–18.

Part III

Fascism and Veterans during the 1930s

5   Transnational Fascism and Veterans, 1929–1935

If the 'Golden Twenties' were not an entirely happy decade for many Europeans, including war veterans, the decade that followed would be marked by decline and desolation across the Continent. The 1930s are remembered as a period of deep crisis, starting with the Great Depression. The first half of the decade was marked by an unprecedented global crisis of capitalism. Although European countries – such as Italy – had shown signs of economic distress earlier, the major shock came from the United States and the Wall Street crash of October 1929. With Weimar Germany deprived of American loans, the reparations schedule and European financial networks were severely disrupted. Industrial production slumped, and unemployment rocketed. Many countries sought to insulate themselves from the crisis by implementing protectionist measures, which led to a collapse in international trade. Syndicalism gained momentum among the working classes. Simultaneously, corporatism was further developed in Fascist Italy as an alternative economic model and was increasingly regarded as a solution by certain lobbies and by political groups abroad.

The dramatic political consequences of this economic slump led to a 'legitimation crisis' in many countries. This situation served as a breeding ground for new fascist or proto-fascist movements and parties. Furthermore, their evolution was no longer solely influenced by Italian Fascism; German Nazism also inspired them. In the context of the Depression, National Socialism grew apace in Germany. Hitler would accede to power in January of 1933. This event constituted a further shock to both international and domestic affairs in all European countries; in particular, Fascist Italy and the French Republic had to reorient their positions regarding the German Third Reich.

Far from disappearing from the political scene, the veterans of the Great War became more involved in European politics. The memory of the war did not fade; rather it was substantially transformed. New discourses and representations of the war came to the fore in the first half of the 1930s, inaugurating symbolic struggles over the meaning of the war

197

experience, in which the veterans of different countries would be heavily involved. Fascism continued to monopolize the political and cultural expression of the Italian veterans. In Germany, a process of nazification of veteran politics and discourses took place. All these developments had an important transnational dimension across the continent, as fascist and non-fascist veterans constructed international networks and were the agents of cultural transfers.

This chapter analyzes this multifaceted historical process, with a view to highlighting the role played by war veterans. In the first section I show that the years 1929 and 1930 initiated a new phase in the historical evolution of the relationship between veterans and Fascism, marked by a set of changes that took place in Italy and elsewhere. In the early 1930s, the relationship between fascism and veterans took very different forms, as an examination of Spanish and French fascist groups will reveal. In Germany, as I will discuss in the third section of this chapter, a process of nazification of the German veterans ended around 1934. In the last section I will focus on the contacts and relations between fascist, French and Nazi veterans until 1935, highlighting the consequences of this transnational process. I will argue that the fascist veterans constructed a wide and complex network that had an impact on the general evolution of international affairs. As a result, the influence of fascist ideas further expanded in Europe, heightening international tensions and increasing the likelihood of the outbreak of new wars.

New Directions: 1929–1930

For several reasons, 1929–30 can be considered a pivotal year. It was the end of one historical period and the beginning of another for both the European continent and Fascist Italy. In this section, I discuss the substantial changes that took place within fascist veteran politics. I will consider the irruption of Italian fascist veterans as active participants onto the scene of European international relations whilst also examining the emergent phenomenon of transnational entanglements in veterans' discourses and organizations in both cultural and political terms. As we will see, this transnational process also marked the beginning of the development of a National Socialist model for war veterans in Germany.

Fascist Veterans and the Leap into Europe

The consolidation of the fascist dictatorship can be said to have culminated with the Lateran Pacts of February 1929, whereby a concordat regulating the relations between the Vatican and the fascist state was reached. Taking advantage of the prestige that this accord gave to Mussolini, an electoral plebiscite took place in March of 1929. Italians were given the opportunity to say 'yes' or 'no' to the list of deputies drafted by the Grand Council of Fascism. Perhaps unsurprisingly, due to the conditions and the context of the vote, very few of the more than 8 million electors voted against the fascists. After this resounding success, the national leaders of the ANC sent a public message to Mussolini underlining how veterans had participated in the elections: 'ranged like battalions' to renovate their 'oath of loyalty' to the Duce.[1] There were many fascist veterans among the new members of the Chamber, including Amilcare Rossi himself.[2] The victory in the plebiscite can be seen as an indication of the complete stability of the regime and marked the beginning of the era of the so-called consensus (*consenso*).[3] Fascist veterans had contributed greatly to this.

Seeking to take advantage of this moment of strength for their movement, the fascist veterans and the ANC launched a new press organ in May of 1929 – *L'Italia grigio-verde* – based in Rome and directed by Ugo Trombetti, a fascist veteran from Bologna. It aspired to be the national newspaper of the Italian veterans. In the journalist's words, it was the newspaper of the 'fascist *combattentismo*' (*combattentismo fascista*).

By this time, ANC membership had reached more than 400,000 in Italy. Rates of membership varied widely between different regions.[4] This uneven regional distribution was to some extent due to unequal population density and to the greater human contribution of the northern regions to the war effort. It is not surprising that the bulk of the members came from the north of Italy and from the biggest cities. The total membership of the ANC remained a small fraction of the huge number of Italian men who fought the Great War – around 10 percent. However, if in the early post-war period the basis of the veterans' movement had been the peasantry of the Mezzogiorno, now the fascist ANC was a largely urban phenomenon, close to the centres of political and economic

---

[1] *Bollettino Associazione Nazionale Combattenti* (Pavia), 30 April 1929.

[2] *Bollettino della Federazione Provinciale di Terni dell'Associazione Nazionale Combattenti*, 1–3 (January–March 1929).

[3] Renzo De Felice, *Mussolini il duce. I. Gli anni del consenso 1929–1936*, Turin, Einaudi, 1974; Simona Colarizi, *L'opinione degli italiani sotto il regime 1929–1943*, Rome, Laterza, 1991, p. 31.

[4] Affiliation data in *L'Italia grigio-verde. Periodico di disciplina nazionale* (Rome), 24 May 1929. Cf. Ministero della Guerra, 'Ufficio stadistico', *La forza dell'esercito: Statistica dello sforzo militare italiano nella guerra mondiale*, Rome, 1927; Istituto Centrale di Statistica del Regno d'Italia, *VII censimento generale della popolazione, 21 Aprile 1931*, Roma, 1933–4. See also *Bollettino della Federazione Provinciale Valtellinese dell'Associazione Nazionale Combattenti* (Sondrio), 6 (August–September 1930).

power (Rome and Milan). The regions with the highest rate of veteran affiliation to the fascist ANC were Tuscany – above all, Pisa – and Lombardy – particularly the northern provinces. The lowest affiliation rates were in the south: Abruzzi, Campania, Puglia, Calabria and the islands. An interesting phenomenon that should be highlighted is the growth of the affiliation abroad: by 1929, the ANC counted more than 12,000 members in foreign countries.

According to the fascists, the main reason for the sharp rise in membership, reaching 500,000 at the end of 1929, was the 'spiritual factor' rather than the ANC's social assistance programme.[5] However, there undoubtedly were material motivations for the increase, given that the association reached several agreements for the preferential employment of veterans in some provinces. In the summer of 1929, whilst the deterioration of economic conditions provoked the first strikes of the period,[6] the Confindustria, the fascist industrial syndicates and the ANC decided to give preference on the labour market to veterans from fascist syndicates that were affiliated to the ANC.[7] Subsequently, the Minister of Corporations, Bottai, confirmed these benefits, which were extended to all branches of production. In addition, the president of the National Board of the ANC obtained the right to sit on the High Council of Corporations.[8] The prestige of the veterans' association increased within the regime.

Fascist veterans reinforced their presence within the state institutions. In September of 1929 a new government was formed. Fascist personalities who had fought in the Great War such as Dino Grandi (Minister of Foreign Affairs), Italo Balbo (Minister of Aeronautics), Giuseppe Bottai (Minister of Corporations), Giacomo Acerbo (Minister of Agriculture) and Michele Bianchi (Minister of Public Works) maintained their positions of power within the cabinet. They were joined by new members directly linked to the veterans' movement: Angelo Manaresi – president of the ONC until now – and Araldo di Crollalanza were nominated to the position of Undersecretary of State.[9]

When the Sixth National Council of the ANC met in Rome a few days later, Mussolini attended and outlined his vision for the political future of the war veterans. 'Fascism and *Combattentismo* – Mussolini declared – are

---

[5] *Bollettino della Federazione Provinciale Mantovana dell'Associazione Nazionale Combattenti* (Mantova), 3 (January 1930).

[6] Colarizi, *L'opinione*, p. 39.   [7] *L'Italia grigio-verde*, 15 July 1929.

[8] *L'Italia grigio-verde*, 20 January 1930.

[9] Crollalanza had become a member of the fascist Parliament in 1924. In 1930, he was appointed Minister of Public Works. He would go on to become the president of the ONC between 1935 and 1943.

two bodies and one soul, but tomorrow, when the day of the final test arrives, Fascism and *Combattentismo* shall be one body and one soul.'[10] This prophecy, as we will see, would shape the development of the veterans' organization. Its roots lay in the long-held but frustrated fascist desire that Fascism be the unique expression of veteran identity, both in ideology and in organization. In this sense, it is interesting to note that in organizational terms, a project for the fusion of all the Italian veterans' associations had previously been sponsored by Ugo Trombetti in the paper *L'Italia grigio-verde*. A debate about the possibility of forming a Green-Grey Federation (Federazione Grigio-verde) encompassing all kinds of veterans' groups extended into 1930.[11] From the point of view of the clandestine Italian communists, Mussolini's words were yet more proof of the drift towards war; the 'fascist-bourgeois regime' was the 'regime of war'.[12]

The year 1929 was also marked by a major change in the fascist stance towards the rest of Europe. Fascism began to try to expand its influence abroad. This new orientation contrasted with the previous focus on internal consolidation and with the old affirmation of the purely Italian and non-exportable nature of Fascism. The internationalization of fascism was a result of the need to give new national goals to the youth[13] and a consequence of the fascist quest for international prestige, leverage, territorial expansion and imperial domination.[14] The perceived good health of the regime inside the country allowed the fascists to dream of a fascist Europe. Over the course of 1928–9, Mussolini had moved to support the Austrian Heimwehr, a paramilitary league composed of voluntary home guards of demobilized soldiers.[15] The new will to intervene in European politics and to combat the 'democratic, communist ideas' that according to the fascists dominated the European spirit was keenly represented by the new magazine *Antieuropa*, directed by Asvero Gravelli.[16] It is true that moderation prevailed in Italian foreign policy

---

[10] *Il Popolo d'Italia*, 17 September 1929; *L'Italia grigio-verde*, 15 September 1929.

[11] *L'Italia grigio-verde*, 25 July and 25 November 1929 and 20 November and 15 December 1930.

[12] *L'Unità* (clandestine edition), 1 (1929).

[13] Michael Arthur Ledeen, *Universal Fascism: The Theory and Practice of the Fascist International, 1928–1936*, New York, Howard Fertig, 1972.

[14] Aristotle Kallis, *Fascist Ideology: Territory and Expansionism in Italy and Germany, 1922–1945*, London, Routledge, 2000.

[15] Burgwyn, *Italian Foreign Policy*, pp. 48–51.

[16] *Antieuropa* (Rome), 1 (April 1929). Asvero Gravelli, born in Brescia in 1902, experienced the Great War as a teenager and joined the syndicalist revolutionary movement. He adhered to the early fascist movement in 1919 and later joined the Fiume occupation. In 1920 he returned to Sesto San Giovanni (Milan), where he was

until 1932, but Mussolini himself would gradually enforce a more radical fascist policy in the realm of foreign affairs.[17] His brother, Arnaldo Mussolini, director of *Il Popolo d'Italia*, published a set of articles arguing that the time for the fascists to fulfil 'their responsibility' towards Europe had come.[18] Crucially for us, the fascist veterans would prove pro-active in following the new political guidelines by intensifying their foreign activities.

As part of the fascist veterans' new European mission, Amilcare Rossi devoted time to reinforcing the ANC abroad. His trip to France and Switzerland on the occasion of the 24 May celebration in 1929 served that purpose.[19] In both countries, fascist activities developed in a hostile environment where anti-fascism predominated. By 1930, three dozen members of the Fasci all'estero had been killed and 200 injured by anti-fascist actions.[20] Seemingly, only loose connections existed between the Fasci all'estero and the ANC cells abroad. The activities of the latter were characterized by a generic patriotism, and it was the figure of the king, rather than that of Mussolini, that they most exalted in their bulletins.[21] (At that time within Italy, at the inauguration of new monuments to fallen soldiers, the fascists persisted in employing the same reverential monarchical discourse.[22]) But this reality did not contradict the fact that the fascists sought to politically exploit the veterans inside and outside the country. This was particularly true in France, where more than 400 events with veterans were celebrated during 1930.[23] *Il Popolo d'Italia* published a cartoon showing a helmet in the form of a huge swinging bell, with a clapper shaped as a Fascio, symbolically suggesting that the Italian veterans served as an amplifier for Fascism.[24] The fascist co-optation of the ANC and the Italian veterans in foreign countries, which had begun as early as 1925, was unrelenting.

active in the local Fascio. A leader of the fascist youth movement, he was close to the most intransigent fascists. After the Matteotti crisis, he focused on his activities as a journalist. He became a prominent figure of the fascist regime during the first half of the 1930s. In 1936 he became a war volunteer in the Spanish Civil War. He also adhered to the RSI. He died in Rome in 1956.

[17] De Felice, *Mussolini il duce*, I, pp. 323–533.
[18] A. M. [Arnaldo Mussolini], 'Il dovere', *Il Popolo d'Italia*, 3 July 1929.
[19] *L'Italia grigio-verde*, 5 and 15 June 1929; Amilcare Rossi, *Figlio del mio tempo*, pp. 98–100.
[20] Fasci italiani all'estero, *Trentacinque morti: Duecentododici feriti*, Rome, 1930.
[21] *Bollettino dell'Associazione Nazionale Combattenti per la zona del nord (Nord, Pas-de-Calais e Somme)* (Lille), March 1930.
[22] *Le Celebrazioni della Patria, Orazioni dell'On, Nicola Sansanelli pronunziate in presenza di S. M. il Re*, Naples, 1930.
[23] *L'Italia grigio-verde*, 20 April 1931.   [24] *Il Popolo d'Italia*, 5 November 1929.

In short, during 1929, veterans acquired a decisive role in the expansion of Fascism, paving the way for a set of new contacts and transfers between actors in the international sphere. This reality transcended the previous unilateral visits and the mere circulation of tropes and myths about fascist veterans that had characterized the mid-1920s. Besides, in 1929, the fascist stance regarding the FIDAC changed, as these inter-allied meetings seemed increasingly obsolete to them.[25] Now Italy embraced an integrationist attitude towards the former enemies. Yet, the fascist veterans' propaganda inside the FIDAC persisted. In 1930, Amilcare Rossi represented Italy at the FIDAC Congress in Washington, where he tried to rebut the 'calumnies' against the fascist regime.[26] Italian veterans presented themselves more openly as fascists, and those residing abroad were required to follow the ANC programme. When French veteran leader Henri Pichot admonished the Italians, calling on them not to present themselves in the FIDAC as fascists but simply as veterans, the fascist veterans replied by restating the oneness of *combattentismo* and Fascism.[27] A new phase of fascist veteran diplomacy had begun.

Transnational Entanglements: Veteran Politics and Culture

As the fascist veterans erupted onto the international scene, they also became symbolic actors in the entangled politics of Europe. It is import-ant to note that the interest in setting up an organizational structure in foreign regions was not an exclusive feature of the Italian veterans; by 1929, the German Stahlhelm had also created cells in a dozen different countries, particularly in Latin America.[28] The Stahlhelm cell in Oporto, Portugal, was the most active; following its example, in January of 1929, the Stahlhelm sent to its branches instructions about how to carry out nationalist and anti-republican propaganda abroad.[29] Fascist and nation-alist German veterans were, by this point, ready to establish contacts. As we will see, transnational political entanglements with Italian Fascism

---

25 Telegram from Belgrade (place of the FIDAC Congress) to Rome, 3 September 1929, AMAE, Società delle Nazioni 1919–30, box 66, file 'Federazione interalleata ex-combattenti FIDAC'.

26 Amilcare Rossi, *Le tappe gloriose*, Rome, 1933, pp. 65–93; id., *Figlio del mio tempo*, pp. 101–4.

27 *L'Italia Grigio-verde*, 5 and 20 January 1931; 'Fascismo ed ex combattenti', *Bollettino della Federazione Provinciale Valtellinese dell'Associazione Nazionale Combattenti*, 4 (April 1931).

28 BArch (Berlin), R 72/250, folios 6–9.

29 BArch (Berlin), R 72/250, folios 3–9 and 11–14.

were a crucial cause of a spiralling radicalization of veterans and extreme right groups in Germany and France.

In 1929 and 1930, German veterans from the Stahlhelm came to Italy and entered into dialogue with the Italian Fascists. Many Stahlhelm members clearly sympathized with the fascists and seemed willing to set aside both the Italian participation on the Allied side during the Great War and the Südtirol question. The members of the Stahlhelm group in Venice enthusiastically heralded the appearance of a 'German Mussolini' and placed their hopes in an agreement between the Stahlhelm and the NSDAP, which had yet to be secured.[30] Within the veterans' association, however, there were sectors that criticized any rapprochement with Italy. In November of 1929, when a group of Stahlhelm members travelled to Italy, they did so in an unofficial manner. They were obliged to justify their visit by publicly stating initially that it had been just a leisure trip and then subsequently that it was necessary and useful to gain first-hand knowledge about Fascism.[31] Many members of the Stahlhelm reasonably feared that establishing political contacts with a former enemy country would discredit the organization. In fact, the satirical German review *Simplicissimus* mocked the contact between fascists and Stahlhelm members by bringing up the contradiction between this incident of German-Italian fraternization and the situation in Südtirol.[32] The Stahlhelm leadership was forced to issue an internal memorandum to clarify what the official conduct of its members who made trips abroad should be: if political contacts were to be established, they needed the prior approval of the Stahlhelm political counsellor.[33]

Important events taking place in Germany during 1930 would contribute to furthering the absorption of fascist traits by German veterans. As the social and economic conditions rapidly worsened, the anti-republican forces gathered support, presenting a united front against to the payment of reparations scheduled by the Young plan. At that time, both the Stahlhelm and the NSDAP were sincere admirers of Fascism, and both tried to be on good terms with fascist representatives in Germany.[34] In fact, since the beginning of 1929, the group of Nazi parliamentarians had been in contact with the fascist authorities in order to prepare a study trip to Italy. As Nazi MP Robert Ley explained in a

---

[30] BArch (Berlin), R 72/260, folio 3.

[31] *Der Stahlhelm*, 17 November and 8 December 1929.

[32] *Simplicissimus* (Stuttgart), 2 December 1929.

[33] 'Entwurf. Richtlinien für Reisen von Stahlhelmkameraden ins Ausland' (21 November 1929), BArch (Berlin), R 72/250, folios 15–17.

[34] 'L'Ambasciatore a Berlino, Orsini Baroni, al ministro degli esteri, Grandi' Berlin (14 April 1930), in DDI, *Settima serie*, Vol. VIII, pp. 608–9.

letter, they hoped to gain first-hand knowledge of all sorts of political, economic, social, cultural and military aspects of Fascist Italy, including the 'treatment of disabled veterans'.[35]

In March of 1930, a new German government was formed. It was headed by Chancellor Heinrich Brüning, who was a decorated ex-officer of the Great War. Two other ministers were also war veterans. Somewhat undeservedly, the new government was dubbed a 'front-line soldiers' cabinet' (*Frontsoldatenkabinett*) in some newspapers, and it was suggested that Brüning brought the soldierly spirit and mind-set into politics.[36] Seldte and other Stahlhelm leaders used such ideas to justify a strategic rapprochement with the government.[37] The Nazis, instead, maintained an intransigent position in their violent quest for power. They solemnly denied that the German government was a true representative of the front generation: it would be stupid to believe – the Nazis argued – that with Brüning's men 'anything like a takeover of political power by front soldiers would happen'.[38] Furthermore, the NSDAP prohibited its members from being simultaneously members of the Stahlhelm.[39] In the *Völkischer Beobachter*, harsh criticism against the Stahlhelm came along with approving commentaries about a speech made in Rome by Carlo Delcroix – 'the leader of the Italian veterans' – in which the strong fascist position in foreign policy was explicit.[40] As the economic crisis provoked drastic reductions in the war victims' pension system, the Nazis realized that this section of society was a potential source of NSDAP votes. The *Völkischer Beobachter* condemned the so-called 'Front combatants cabinet' (*Frontkämpferkabinett*) for purportedly humiliating the disabled veterans; the Nazis also disparaged the allegedly Marxist-inspired assistance to war victims.[41]

This tougher political stance of the Nazis was met with the approval of many German voters. In September of 1930, the NSDAP achieved great success in the elections to the Reichstag, securing 104 seats, even if Brüning retained power. In this situation, the Stahlhelm veterans, who had been supporters of Hugenberg's DNVP, radicalized themselves in order to capitalize on the Nazi breakthrough. A few weeks after the

---

[35] AMAE, Affari Politici 1919–1930, Germania, box 1181, file 'Viaggio deputati hitleriani in Italia'.
[36] *Vossische Zeitung* (AA), 2 April 1930; *Völkischer Beobachter*, 3 April 1930; *Münchner Neueste Nachrichten*, 31 March 1930; Rüdiger Robert Beer, *Heinrich Brüning*, Berlin, 1931, pp. 55–6; Herbert Hömig, *Brüning. Kanzler in der Krise der Republik: Eine Weimarer Biographie*, Paderborn, Ferdinand Schöningh, 2000, p. 156.
[37] Berghahn, *Der Stahlhelm*, p. 143.   [38] *Völkischer Beobachter*, 16 April 1930.
[39] Berghahn, *Der Stahlhelm*, p. 148.   [40] *Völkischer Beobachter*, 15 May 1930.
[41] Löffelbein, *Ehrenbürger der Nation*, pp. 142–5; *Völkischer Beobachter*, 3–4 August 1930.

elections, the Reichsfrontsoldatentag in Koblenz – situated at the Rhine River, very close to the border with France – was marked by a paramilitaristic and aggressive demonstration that shocked many Frenchmen and was the source of much interest amongst Italian fascists.[42] The ranks of veterans paraded with a fascist-like salute. That a PNF representative and other fascists joined this Stahlhelm ceremony fuelled panic about an anti-French threat.[43] This was a turning point in international veteran politics.

The Nazi success and the Stahlhelm demonstration had repercussions in France. The French associations of the CIAMAC, presided over by Henri Pichot, contacted the moderate, non-revanchist German veterans.[44] In contrast, French nationalist groups scorned any rapprochement effort. Since 1929, the Croix de Feu had taken a hard line in foreign policy.[45] Now, characterizing the demonstration of the Stahlhelm as typical of the alleged overall German threat, they abandoned all nuance and condemned any policy of rapprochement or pacifism.[46] This issue intensified the Croix de Feu dynamic of radicalization in subsequent years. However, French veterans were reluctant to establish contacts with the nationalist German organizations.

This notwithstanding, the impressive advance of German radical nationalism also paved the way for sectors of the French right to become open to a profound revision of Versailles. Gustave Hervé, after seeing the imposing Stahlhelm demonstration, suggested that the Croix de Feu and the French veterans should adopt the same attitude as the Germans. They had many things in common, such as anti-communism. Moreover, Hervé suggested that an understanding between the German and French veterans should be the first step towards the rapprochement between both nations. He publicly made an overture to Seldte and Hitler, asking their opinions about a potential bilateral agreement that would recognize many of the German nationalists' territorial claims. This accord would allegedly save Europe from war and Bolshevism. Initially, Stahlhelm leader Franz Seldte did not disregard the idea of furthering the union of veterans from different nations; he stated, 'Front soldiers of the world, unite' (*Frontsoldaten aller Länder, setz euch zusammen*). But later Seldte declined Hervé's proposal, since the French would not accept the

---

[42] *Der Stahlhelm am Rhein. 11. Reichsfrontsoldatentag am 4–5 Oktober in Koblenz*, Berlin, 1930; *Il Popolo d'Italia*, 5 and 7 October 1930.
[43] Wilhelm Kleinau (ed.), *Echo aus dem Westen: Berichte der französischen Presse über den XI. Reichsfrontsoldatentag am Rhein (Koblenz, 4–5 Oktober 1930)*, Berlin, 1930.
[44] *Journal des Mutilés et Combattants* (Paris), 7 December 1930.
[45] On the origins and development of the Croix de Feu, see the next section.
[46] *Le Flambeau. Organe des 'Croix de Feu'* (Paris), 14 (December 1930), 17 (March 1931).

abolition of the Versailles clause about German responsibility for the war. For the same reason, Hitler rejected Hervé's revisionist offers as well. Even the Croix de Feu and other French groups were hostile to Hervé's project. Besides, these debates took place at the same time as the anniversary of the March on Rome was celebrated, and Mussolini took this opportunity to express his own revisionist intentions regarding the Versailles status quo. As can be seen, in Italy, Germany and even France, tendencies towards a possible veterans-led international agreement appeared. Yet, both the Stahlhelm and the Nazis were much more inclined to reinforce their ties with Italy than with France.[47]

It is hardly surprising, then, that in November of 1930 Stahlhelm members travelled to Italy again. The trip was organized in collaboration with the Italian Chamber of Commerce in Berlin or, in other words, in contact with Major Renzetti, Mussolini's agent in Germany.[48] The Stahlhelm members laid a laurel wreath on the Altar of the Fallen Fascists (*Ara dei Caduti Fascisti*) in the Campidoglio (near to the *Milite Ignoto*) and were received on 13 November by Mussolini, to whom they gave a Stahlhelm insignia. Heinke, leader of the group, declared that the 'fascist idea' was the 'cornerstone' of his organization.[49] All these actions and statements aroused indignation and criticism not only among republicans but also among German nationalists such as those of the Jungdeutscher Orden. There were protests from Stahlhelm members, who balked at the budding friendship with the former enemy country; their memory of the war and their 'feeling of solidarity' with their 'fallen comrades' were still vivid.[50] Because of this inappropriate visit, the Stahlhelm came under attack from all sides again. Once more, the national leaders had to send an official memorandum rebuking Heinke's group and its supposedly unauthorized political manoeuvres in Italy. This reprimand was half-hearted because, after all, the Italian government seemed to adopt a pro-German stance as a consequence of the visit. In reality, as was recognized in a private letter sent to Renzetti, the Stahlhelm national leaders had considered the underlying idea of the trip 'correct'.[51] Despite the controversy, the Stahlhelm not only persisted in

---

[47] *Der Stahlhelm*, 26 October and 2 and 9 November 1930; *La Victoire*, 4, 5, 7, 14, 16, 17, 18, 20, 21,22, 24, 26, 27 and 29 October and 2, 3 and 9 November 1930; *Il Popolo d'Italia*, 25, 26 and 28 October 1930; *Völkischer Beobachter*, 18, 23, 24, 26– 29 and 31 October and 7 November 1930.

[48] Wolfgang Schieder, 'Faschismus im politischen Transfer: Giuseppe Renzetti als faschistischer Propagandist und Geheimagent in Berlin 1922–1941', in *id.*, *Faschistische Diktaturen: Studien zu Italien und Deutschland*, Göttingen, Wallstein Verlag, 2008, pp. 223–49.

[49] *Il Popolo d'Italia*, 14 November 1930; BArch (Berlin), R 72/260, folio 6.

[50] BArch (Berlin), R 72/260, folio 4.   [51] *Ibid.*, folio 45.

but even increased the frequency and importance of its contacts with the fascists; Major Renzetti would be a key person in this relationship.

Germany's weight in European affairs was increasing at a time when the international status quo was being renegotiated. By this point, there was constant communication between Fascist Italy and the Stahlhelm, and the NSDAP had established itself as the preponderant force in the German anti-republican right. At that time, the conflicts and cleavages within the Weimar Republic came to epitomize the multiple political and social fractures that riddled other European regions. The German cultural wars influenced the contested reshaping of the war memory that took place in European societies during the early 1930s. Former combatants of the First World War were active actors in this process.

Erich Maria Remarque's novel, *Im Westen nichts Neues*, was first published in serial form by the *Vossische Zeitung* between November of 1928 and January of 1929. Immediately, it was published as a book and became an overwhelming international bestseller. The English version, *All Quiet on the Western Front*, appeared simultaneously. Since then, much has been said about the crude depiction of warfare and about the pacifism – rather than anti-militarism – of the novel.[52] Remarque, a writer who had fought in the war, relayed the point of view of the common front soldier. He introduced his work neither as an 'accusation' nor as a 'confession', but just as an account of 'a generation that was destroyed by war'.[53]

In this period, the description of war through autobiographical or semi-autobiographical accounts, written by veterans who shared the sense of belonging to a generation, was a transnational phenomenon. In France, the idea of a *génération du feu* was widely diffused, as a decade seemed a proper time for many veterans to reconsider their war experiences.[54] Remarque's book also revived debates about the objectivity or subjectivity of his work and of war novels in general. This question was similarly approached in France, through Jean Norton Cru's well-known study of *Témoins* (1929). This work systematically analyzed French war literature in order to discern whether it was reliable or not. As in Remarque's case, Cru's objective was to avoid a new war by transmitting

---

[52] Elisabeth Krimmer, *The Representation of War in German Literature*, Cambridge University Press, 2010, pp. 88–104.

[53] Erich Maria Remarque, 'Im Westen Nichts Neues', *Vossische Zeitung*, 10 November 1928.

[54] Wohl, *The Generation of 1914*; Prost, *Les anciens combattants*, pp. 130–7; Bruno Cabanes, '"Génération du feu": aux origines d'une notion', *Revue historique*, 309, 1 (2007), pp. 139–50.

the reality of warfare.[55] Remarque's novel was partially responsible for the subsequent transnational wave of war literature: a great number of veterans wanted to publish their opinions and memories. This phenomenon also reached Spain. Ramón J. Sender's novel, *Imán* (1930), set during the Moroccan war and the disaster of Annual, conveyed the same pacifist message as Remarque. However, this vast literary production was not uniform when it came to the writers' opinions about war; roughly two polarized positions can be identified: on the one hand, the pacifists, and on the other hand, those who still highlighted the alleged positive values of war by employing the nationalist and patriotic discourse born of the war experience. War veterans were the only authoritative participants in this wide debate, which was not only literary but also political.[56] As a matter of fact, in Germany, the patriotic and conservative literary war accounts outnumbered the pacifist ones,[57] even if Remarque's novel was more widely read.

This controversy contributed to the rising awareness among the Nazis of the advantages of developing a more consistent and distinctive veterans' policy. The implementation of such a policy became possible after their electoral victory. In mid-November of 1930, Gregor Strasser, National Organizational Leader (*Reichsorganisationleiter*) of the NSDAP, informed all the Nazi local leaders that Hitler had decided to found a party department dedicated to this matter.[58] Disabled veterans and war victims now attracted the Nazis' attention, as they were a potential pool of votes in the context of the crisis. Hans Oberlindober, a war veteran and NSDAP member since October of 1922, was appointed head of this new organization. On 30 November 1930, in a meeting of the Kyffhäuserbund, Oberlindober made public the Nazi programme of provision for war victims, basically consisting in the rejection of Weimar's pension system.[59] But the Nazis decided to carry out their struggle for the war veterans' support also in the cultural sphere.

[55] Jean Norton Cru, *Témoins*; Leonard V. Smith, 'Jean Norton Cru et la subjectivité de l'objectivité', in Jean-Jacques Becker (dir.), *Histoire culturelle de la Grande Guerre*, Paris, Armand Colin, 2005, pp. 89–100.

[56] Brian Murdoch, 'Innocent Killing: Erich Maria Remarque and the Weimar Anti-War Novels', in Karl Leydecker (ed.), *German Novelists of the Weimar Republic: Intersections of Literature and Politics*, New York, Candem House, 2006, pp. 141–68.

[57] Ann P. Linder, *Princes of the Trenches, Narrating the German Experience of the First World War*, Columbia, Camden House, 1996.

[58] 'Organisations-Abtlg. I./Ref. Kriegsbeschädigte (Gregor Strasser) an alle Gauleitungen' (18 November 1930), BArch (Berlin), NS 22/411.

[59] 'Bericht über den Stand der deutschen Kriegsopferversorgung' (26 May 1933), BArch (Berlin), NS 22/1279; on Oberlindober, see Löffelbein, *Ehrenbürger der Nation*, pp. 91–109.

It is well known how the Nazis attacked the exhibition of the film, *Im Westen nichts Neues.*[60] Joseph Goebbels, who considered the book to be 'nasty' and 'dangerous',[61] was responsible for the series of disturbances and demonstrations that took place in Berlin in December of 1930 to protest against the screening of the American film of Remarque's novel. This Nazi campaign was above all motivated by Goebbels' political strategy regarding internal developments within the NSDAP. The movie was despised as a 'Jewish' production. The Nazi attacks were based on accusations that the film was 'insulting the honour of the German soldier and particularly the heroic youth of Langemarck'.[62] The Stahlhelm also demanded prohibition of the film. As the German government yielded to the pressure and banned the film, despite the Reichsbanner's protests, the Nazis were exultant. This victory marked the beginning of a more direct appeal to the ideal of the front soldier in Nazi political propaganda. Nevertheless, Nazi discourse around veterans still lacked a certain originality.

At the time of this anti-Remarque reaction, the similarity between Hitler's veterans-related discourse and Mussolini's long-established concept of *trincerocrazia* was noticeable. Rationalizing the Nazi fusion of Nationalism and Socialism, Hitler boasted about his own past as a front soldier. The soldiers had fought the war neither for the proletariat nor for the bourgeoisie, but for the entire nation (*Volk*). As Hitler stated in his speech on 11 December 1930, the soldiers had 'discovered in the battle-fields the synthesis between Nationalism and Socialism'.[63] Yet, this claim, possibly inspired by Hitler's readings about Italian Fascism, did not imply elevating the veterans as the aristocracy of the new Germany. Even though Hitler prefaced Hans Zörbelein's *Der Glaube an Deutschland*, this answer to Remarque did not approach the veterans as protagonists; it simply introduced patriotic justifications for the murderous reality of warfare.[64] Something similar can be said about Ernst von Salomon's autobiographical novel about the Freikorps published in January of 1930. There the returning front soldiers were aesthetically represented as hardened warriors, profoundly divorced from the non-combatant world. Von Salomon despised the 'Soldiers Councils without

---

[60] Modris Eksteins, 'War, Memory, and Politics: The Fate of the Film *All Quiet on the Western Front*', *Central European History*, 13 (1980), pp. 60–82.

[61] Elke Fröhlich (ed.), *Die Tagebücher von Joseph Goebbels: Sämtliche Fragmente*, Munich, K.G. Saur, 1987, p. 399, entry of 21 July 1929.

[62] *Der Angriff. Das deutsche Abendblatt in Berlin* (Berlin), 9 December 1930.

[63] Hitler, *Reden*, Vol. IV, Part 1, pp. 154–5, 162 (speeches on 7 and 11 December 1930).

[64] Jay W. Baird, *Hitler's War Poets: Literature and Politics in the Third Reich*, New York, Cambridge University Press, 2008, pp. 98–105.

soldiers' of the hated 1918 revolution; instead, he glorified the Freikorps, the real essence of the front soldiers.[65] This ideal of the 'eternal soldiers' (*ewige Soldaten*) was celebrated by the Nazis, but it had nothing to do with the challenges and experiences of German war veterans.

In contrast, Remarque's next novel, *Der Weg zurück*, firstly published in the *Vossische Zeitung* between December of 1930 and January of 1931 as the sequel of *Im Westen nichts Neues*, focused centrally on the experiences of war veterans. The novel restated Remarque's pessimistic and pacifist point of view.[66] In this novel, mainly set in post-war Germany in the year after the Armistice, the misfortunes and tragic fate of a group of returning front soldiers were vividly depicted and their feelings and emotions – alienation, disappointment and isolation – profoundly characterized. No clear political orientation was ascribed to them; they were essentially sceptical and mistrustful of the revolution that was taking place in their country. The central narrative of the novel was, however, grounded in the process of disintegration of the mythical 'comradeship' (*Kameradschaft*) of the trenches. While the group of veterans tried to maintain their unity, idealizing the past experience of brotherhood, the harsh reality on the ground fatally undermined their hopes. This outcome was, nevertheless, conveyed as inevitable and necessary. The surviving protagonists recovered their individual identity whilst maintaining their friendship. In the last part of the novel, probably set in the early 1930s, Remarque offered a direct criticism of the activities of paramilitary groups that were trying to militarily educate younger generations (i.e. the Stahlhelm) and thus increasing the probability of a fresh catastrophe.

In Italy, the hostility of Fascism towards the pacifist depiction of warfare conditioned the reception of Remarque. As we know, since the early post-war period, the fascists had struggled against and suppressed the representation of the war as a senseless massacre. It is not surprising that the reviews of Remarque's book published in Italy were in general negative and hostile.[67] It was said that the stunning commercial success of the novel was a 'bluff' and that the book's description of war was 'erroneous' because it ignored the alleged reality of battle as the origin of 'heroic values' and 'self-improvement'.[68] The Italian translation of *Der*

[65] Ernst Von Salomon, *Die Geächteten*, Berlin, 1935 (1st edn. 1930), pp. 26–35, 57–8.
[66] Tilman Westphalen, 'Nachwort', in Erich Maria Remarque (ed.), *Der Weg zurück*, Cologne, Kiepenheuer & Witsch, 2012 (1st edn. 1931).
[67] For example, Giuseppe Piazza, 'Il mondo di Remarque', *La Stampa*, 11 May 1929; Enrico Rocca, 'Processi letterari alla guerra', *La Stampa*, 18 July 1929.
[68] E. Servadio, 'Le insidie di un libro ("Im Westen nichts Neues")', *Esercito e Nazione*, 12 (December 1929).

Weg zurück would not be allowed to be sold in either the kingdom of Italy or its colonies.[69] The news about prohibition of the sale of Remarque's book inside Fascist Italy soon circulated in Europe.[70] Nevertheless, many people in Italy managed to read these novels, and Mussolini himself privately recognized that people were more receptive to this kind of discourse than to the patriotic accounts of officers and generals.[71]

Although pacifist war novels did not proliferate in Italy at that time, other kinds of war accounts appeared. Since 1929, for example, in the pages of Benedetto Croce's magazine *La Critica*, historian and war veteran Adolfo Omodeo earnestly analyzed a set of diaries and letters of Italian fallen soldiers of the Great War. His work, however, served as a refutation of Remarque's interpretation of the war as 'mere horror' by conveying, instead, 'the breath of poetry, of hope, of justice' that had animated the Italian soldiers at the front.[72] The transmission of positive values attributed to war was also the background theme of several war novels published in Italy at that time. Although the atrocities and some injustices of the war were recognized and explored in detail, these books made neither moral nor political judgements. On the contrary, they often celebrated the virtue of sacrifice.[73] On some occasions, as in Adolfo Baiocchi's book, *Generazioni*, the experience of the front was connected with the post-war experiences of the demobilized soldiers. The veterans' alleged reaction against revolutionaries, organized through the early fascist movement, was narrated as a continuation of the patriotic service that had secured victory in the war.[74] Fascist literary critics explicitly described this literature as '*Antiremarque*'.[75]

These kinds of literary works formed part of the cultural context in which a 'fascist art' was forged during the 1930s.[76] From this point onwards, both Italian Fascism and Nazism developed a culture in which war literature was included. The target of these accounts was not only the

---

[69] Erich Maria Remarque, *La via del ritorno*, Milan, Mondadori, 1932.

[70] For example, *La Voz* (Madrid), 25 September 1929.

[71] De Felice, *Mussolini il Duce*, I, p. 27, n. 2.

[72] Adolfo Omodeo, *Momenti della vita di guerra (dai Diari e dalle Lettere dei Caduti)*, Bari, Laterza, 1934.

[73] Luigi Bartolini, *Il Ritorno sul Carso*, Verona, 1930; Arturo Marpicati, *La coda di Minosse*. *Romanzo di guerra*, Bologna, 1931 (1st edn. 1925); Adolfo Baiocchi: *Uno dei tanti*, Rome, 1931; Imre Balassa, *Fronte: Romanzo di guerra*, Milan, 1931; Vicenzo Dini, *Dalla scuola alla trincea: Commedia in quattro atti*, Florence, 1930; Francesco Sapori, *La Trincea: Romanzo*, Milan, 1931 (1st edn. 1917).

[74] Adolfo Baiocchi, *Generazioni: Romanzo della guerra*, Milan, 1930, pp. 289–408.

[75] Valentino Piccoli, 'Antiremarque', *Il Popolo d'Italia*, 24 May 1931.

[76] Giuseppe Villaroel, 'I libri. Generazioni', *Il Popolo d'Italia*, 9 November 1930. For a monographic account about the fascist culture during the 1930s, see Ruth Ben-Ghiat, *Fascist Modernities: Italy, 1922–1945*, Berkeley, University of California Press, 2001.

literate, culture-consuming war veterans but also the younger generations. Discourses about the war experience contributed to shaping the idealized model of warrior that both Fascism and Nazism would subsequently employ.

Different Paths through the Crisis

The role of war veterans in the historical evolution of transnational fascism in Europe was far from unidirectional during the early 1930s: a simultaneous study of the cases of France and Spain helps to understand the versatility of the relationship between veterans and fascism. Although fascist and proto-fascist movements now emerged in different European countries, Italy remained the only fascist dictatorship established on the Continent until 1933. Even after Hitler's seizure of power, the main Western democracies – Britain, France and republican Spain – still resisted the fascist or authoritarian surge. However, in these countries, the presence or absence of war veterans as ambiguous or open representatives of fascism conditioned domestic politics.

In this section, I will examine the path towards totalitarianism that the Italian veterans walked during the early 1930s, contrasting it with the cases of Spain and France. In the latter countries, there were attempts to consolidate an anti-democratic, fascist-inspired reaction. In particular, I will examine the Spanish organizations that converged into the fascist party Falange Española de las JONS, as well as the case of the French Croix de Feu. I intend to demonstrate that despite the entangled nature of the fascist phenomenon in Europe, the symbolic link between veterans and fascism was established in very different – often paradoxical – ways, conditioning the trajectory and reach of different fascist movements. This analysis will facilitate an understanding of the complexity of the wide network of cross-cultural transfers and cross-border contacts in the realm of fascist veteran politics.

The Transforming Model of Fascist Italy

In Italy, fascist veterans were an integral part of the dictatorship in its sustained progression towards totalitarianism. After Achille Starace became Secretary General of the PNF in September of 1931, the institutionalization of the rites of Fascism culminated, and their aesthetics were refined.[77] The Mostra della Rivoluzione Fascista, inaugurated in

---

[77] Emilio Gentile, *La via italiana al totalitarismo: Il partito e lo Stato nel regime fascista* (3rd edn.), Rome, Carocci, 2008; Gentile, *Il culto del Littorio*; Falasca-Zamponi, *Fascist Spectacle*.

October of 1932 for celebration of the *decennale* ('tenth anniversary') of the March on Rome, was the epitome of the fascist aestheticization of politics. Accordingly, fascist veterans refined their external appearance to match the official visual displays: the use of black shirts and helmets among the veterans participating in ceremonies and parades was regulated between 1931 and 1932.[78] For the *decennale*, the ANC ensured that many war veterans were able to participate in the fascist rituals.[79] Starace attended several ANC provincial congresses during 1932, and he was in contact with fascist veteran leaders.[80] As a consequence of this evolution, a new ANC statute was published in February of 1933 whereby the association's ritualistic and commemorative functions were reinforced, without diminishing its responsibility for social assistance tasks.[81] With this transformation, the triumvirate that had controlled the ANC since 1925 was dissolved, but its members continued to serve on the new directing body: Amilcare Rossi was now the president of the new Comitato Centrale.[82] During the economic depression, the ANC's activities were dominated by a combination of fascist ceremonies and the management of benefits, with the aim not so much of enhancing the living conditions of the people but rather of reinforcing the veterans' loyalty to the king and the Duce and tightening control over the masses of veterans.[83]

If the veterans' organization kept pace with the regime's thrust towards totalitarianism, the evolution of fascist discourse about the veterans also reflected this new political orientation. The context of the economic crisis meant that traditional strategies of appealing to veterans were no longer sufficient. At the grass-roots level, the ANC offices in Italian cities were constantly crowded with veterans, their widows and orphans, who turned to the ANC for help in the face of unemployment and hardship. Veteran leaders, incapable of resolving the people's problems, encouraged them to apply the comradeship of the trench to their daily life; the

---

[78] *Bollettino della Federazione Provinciale Valtellinese dell'Associazione Nazionale Combattenti*, 10–11 (October–November 1931); *L'Italia Grigio-Verde*, 15 December 1932.

[79] *L'Italia Grigio-Verde*, 20 October 1932.

[80] *L'Italia Grigio-Verde*, 20 September–5 October and 20 November 1932.

[81] *L'Italia Grigio-Verde*, 5 January 1933; *Bollettino dell'Associazione Nazionale Combattenti. Federazione della Tripolitania* (Tripoli), February–March 1933.

[82] *L'Italia Grigio-Verde*, 20 February 1933; *Bollettino della Federazione Provinciale Valtellinese dell'Associazione Nazionale Combattenti*, January–February 1933. Other six members completed the new Central Committee: Luigi Russo, Nicola Sansanelli, Michele Barbaro, Count Gustavo Besozzi di Carnisio, Giovanni Cao di San Marco and Adelchi Serena.

[83] See, for example, Associazione Nazionale Combattenti, *Direttorio Nazionale, VIII Consiglio Nazionale, Trieste 15–21 Giugno 1932-X. Atti Ufficiali*, Rome, 1932.

fascists emphasized endurance and patience, confidence and discipline, virtues allegedly born of the experience in the trenches.[84] Whilst they vigorously defended the equation between Fascism and *combattentismo* as an unquestionable historical fact, the fascists now emphasized the need for 'iron discipline'. The economic crisis was seen as a new war, and the way to reach victory was the 'subordination of everyone to the reason of state'. Logic, it was said, dictated that Fascism absorb the spirit of *combattentismo*, and thus, it was right that Fascism should also monopolize the veterans' organization.[85]

Veterans in Fascist Italy during the early 1930s played new roles that added to the repertoire of political functions that Fascism had attributed to them since its birth. This evolution sat comfortably with the changes in the regime and in the PNF. For example, the propaganda campaign *Verso il Popolo* ('Towards the People') that sought the regime's rapprochement to the lower classes was matched by measures specifically designed for veterans, particularly in the framework of the ONC, and through the ANC sections' social activities. The same can be said about the development and consolidation of the fascist symbolic and ritualistic universe, into which fascist veterans were integrated. Yet, Italian Fascism was the exception, not the norm, in the wider European context.

During the early 1930s, the symbol of the war veteran was a shared commodity in the complex phenomenon of transnational fascism, yet there were different ways in which the fascist movements used this symbol. As Italian Fascism had already attained power, the position of fascist veterans within the Italian regime could not be simply copied and transferred by fascist movements in other European countries. These other fascist movements, often still in their infancy, had two options: they could either mimic the existing mythical role of the veterans in the rise of Italian Fascism – albeit a decade later and adapted to their own domestic national environments – or develop an idiosyncratic model for the mobilization of veterans in order to destroy the left, suppress democracy and pursue ultra-nationalistic aims. As we will see, these European fascist movements chose the second option, the development of a home-grown model, even if they could not completely ignore the Italian example. In the early 1930s, historical conditions in countries such as Spain, Germany and, to a considerably lesser extent, France seemed to present an opportunity for the destruction of the liberal order, similar to the Italian context of 1919–22. But, in the early 1930s, it was not historically

---

[84] *Bollettino della Federazione Provinciale di Terni dell'Associazione Nazionale Combattenti*, 28 September 1932; Amilcare Rossi, *Le tappe gloriose*, pp. 143–7.
[85] Angelo Amico, *Combattentismo e Fascismo*, Milan, 1932, pp. 177–96.

possible for the veterans to exert the role they had played in the Italian fascist reaction. In the Spanish case, there were no veterans of the Great War. In Germany and France, the war experience, the frustrations of the demobilization, the culture of war and other post-war elements that Italian Fascism had capitalized on lay far in the past. How, then, would they employ the symbol of the veteran?

Before delving into the specifics, a brief exploration of peripheral European fascist movements in the early 1930s is needed. This will allow us to make a preliminary assessment of the veterans' role in transnational fascism at that time. New fascist parties that were built neither on the myth of the fascist veterans nor on the direct exploitation of the First World War experience appeared in different parts of Europe. In Britain, the financial crisis had culminated in the abandonment of the gold standard in September of 1931. Oswald Mosley, an aristocratic British ex-serviceman, founded the British Union of Fascists (BUF) after a visit to Mussolini's Italy. The party would receive secret financial support from Fascist Italy. As Mosley's chief preoccupation was Britain's economic and imperial decline, his main sources of inspiration were fascist corporatism and the fascist potential to rally the youth against the 'Old Gang' of decadent politicians. Although he was a veteran and his movement attracted some ex-officers,[86] Mosley's thought was not focused on the war experience. Rather, the motivation of his followers was to avoid another bloody conflict in Europe. In the BUF program, little attention was paid to ex-servicemen.[87] On the eastern fringe of Europe, in Romania, the Iron Guard was created in 1931 by Corneliu Zelea Codreanu, building on the foundations laid by the Legion of the Archangel Michael. Yet, Codreanu had not been a soldier during the Great War, and Romanian veterans were not the main constituency for Romanian fascism. Religious and patriotic mysticism, as well as anti-Semitism and mobilization of the youth, were the key features of the Romanian fascist movement.[88] It is true that the BUF and the Iron Guard, as well as several other minor fascist organizations in other European countries, remained somewhat marginal. These movements demonstrate, however, that war veterans were not essential, either in membership and

---

[86] Jakub Drábik, "'We're of their blood and spirit of their spirit": ex-servicemen and the British Union of Fascists', in Salvador and Kjøstvedt (eds.), *New Political Ideas*, pp. 151–74.

[87] Oswald Mosley, *The Greater Britain*, London, 1931; Thomas Linehan, *British Fascism 1918–39: Parties, Ideology and Culture*, Manchester University Press, 2000; Chiara Chini, 'Fascismo britannico e fascismo italiano. La British union of fascists, Oswald Mosley e i finanziamenti stranieri', *Contemporanea*, XI, 3, July 2008, pp. 433–57.

[88] Traian Sandu, *Un fascisme roumain: Histoire de la Garde de fer*, Paris, Perrin, 2014.

organizational terms or in the discursive and symbolic sphere, for the foundation of a fascist movement.

Spain and the Falange Española

The efforts of the creators of Spanish fascism to compensate for the absence of veterans' organizations and for the non-existence (yet) of a Spanish veteran mystique are most enlightening. In Spain, the authoritarian dictatorship of Primo de Rivera had collapsed in 1929. In April of 1931, King Alfonso XIII renounced the throne, and the democratic Second Republic was established amidst the enthusiasm of a great part of the middle and working classes. Very soon, however, when the state tried to implement profound social and economic reforms, monarchists and traditionalists reorganized their opposition to democracy. At the beginning of this process, Catholic fundamentalism was the mobilizing force against the secular republic. Many military officers were involved in anti-republican activities, but as a report sent to Mussolini in March of 1930 stated, Spanish NCOs and troops stood absolutely outside of politics.[89] In this context, small fascist groupings appeared. In October of 1931, the Juntas de Ofensiva Nacional Sindicalista (JONS) were founded, adapting fascist and national socialist concepts to the Spanish context. This group was the result of a fusion between certain ultraconservative Castilian organizations – led by Catholic propagandist Onésimo Redondo – and the more radical group of the journal *La Conquista del Estado*, represented by Ramiro Ledesma Ramos – a student inspired by Italian Fascism. Ledesma Ramos had collaborated with Ernesto Giménez Caballero, an intellectual whose writings had become increasingly political after his visit to Italy in 1928.[90]

The promoters of Spanish fascism adopted a set of attitudes and ideas rooted in the Italian and German experiences. While Giménez Caballero, profoundly inspired by the imperial myth of Rome, worked to produce

---

[89] Report by the Brigadier General Maurizio [illegible] (31 March 1930), ACS, SPD, CR, box 71, file 463/R 'Spagna', sf. 4.

[90] Eduardo González Calleja, *Contrarrevolucionarios: Radicalización violenta de las derechas durante la Segunda República, 1931–1936*, Madrid, Alianza, 2011; José Luis Rodríguez Jiménez, *Historia de Falange Española de las JONS*, Madrid, Alianza, 2000; Enrique Selva, *Ernesto Giménez Caballero: Entre la vanguardia y el fascismo*, Valencia, Pre-textos/ Institució Alfons el Magnànim, 2000; Ferran Gallego, *Ramiro Ledesma Ramos y el fascismo español*, Madrid, Síntesis, 2005. In Italy, Giménez Caballero met, among others, Giovanni Gentile, Giuseppe Bottai and Rafael Sánchez Mazas; see Ernesto Giménez Caballero, *Circuito Imperial*, Madrid, 1929, pp. 37–58. In October of 1930, Giménez Caballero visited again Rome, arranging an appointment with Mussolini; ACS, SPD, CR, box 71, file 463R 'Spagna', sf. 5.

an abstract Catholic 'general theory of Fascism',[91] Ledesma Ramos was more concerned about realizing a 'national revolution' (*revolución nacional*), and Onésimo Redondo exalted the use of violence for counter-revolutionary purposes. Ledesma Ramos despised the peaceful 'electoral revolution' that had brought about the Second Republic because it had lacked 'blood' and 'audacity'.[92] Ledesma Ramos, who had studied German philosophy, particularly Heidegger, seemed to echo in the Spanish context the opinion once held by Jünger regarding the 1918 German Revolution. In all probability, Ledesma Ramos had read some of Jünger's works.[93] There were, however, no Spanish front soldiers to carry out the national revolution, and Ledesma Ramos rejected 'pseudofascist' organizations such as the Civic Guards. Therefore, he wholeheartedly embraced the myth of youth and the exaltation of violence. Even if he recognized that in Spain there was no communist threat, his appeal to the Spanish youth implied advocating a 'combative conscience, a warrior spirit, assault spirit'. Young Spanish men would give themselves to 'combat, to heroism and to war sacrifice'.[94]

Despite this kind of discourse, membership of Spanish fascist groups remained small. The anti-democratic threat growing in Spain during 1931 and 1932 took the form of a more traditional military plot, of an essentially Catholic and conservative inspiration, even if Mussolini promised support to its leaders.[95] In Spain, the main paramilitary potential was that of the traditionalists – the Carlist Requeté – rooted in the memory of the nineteenth-century dynastic civil wars. After the failure of General Sanjurjo's coup d'état in August of 1932, the republic enjoyed some months of political stability, and the Catholic opposition assumed a legalist posture. Yet, the rightist paramilitary agitation and social unrest, including armed insurrections of the revolutionary left, thwarted a more permanent stabilization. Nonetheless, it was Hitler's seizure of power in Germany that most encouraged the political right during 1933. Over the course of this year, Spanish anti-republican politicians and intellectuals

---

[91] Ernesto Giménez Caballero, *La nueva catolicidad: Teoría general sobre el Fascismo en Europa: en España*, Madrid, 1933.

[92] Ramiro Ledesma Ramos, *¡Hay que hacer la revolución hispánica!*, Madrid, 1931, p. 18.

[93] *Im Stahlgewittern* was translated into Spanish and published in Spain in 1930: Ernest [*sic*] Jünger, *Tempestades de Acero*, Barcelona, 1930. In Giménez Caballero's intellectual circles, it was known that Jünger developed the 'idea of the "warrior" as a "hero", who should be the "leader of the nation"'; see R. Kaltofen, 'La literatura alemana en 1931', *La Gaceta Literaria* (Madrid), 1 August 1931.

[94] Ramiro Ledesma Ramos, *¡Hay que hacer la revolución hispánica!*, pp. 12, 15, 17, 22, 24 and 26; see also Onésimo Redondo, *Obras completas. Edición cronológica*, 2 vols., Madrid, 1954–5.

[95] González Calleja, *Contrarrevolucionarios*, p. 118.

observed and praised the new Nazi Germany[96] while simultaneously preparing the recovery of the Spanish right in the elections of November 1933.

In October of 1933, José Antonio Primo de Rivera, son of the deceased ex-dictator, returned from a personal visit to Mussolini in Rome to create the Falange Española – another fascist party.[97] A set of journalists and writers, Giménez Caballero and Sánchez Mazas among them, constituted the entourage of Primo de Rivera. They developed a Falangist aesthetic, with symbols, hymns and rhetoric that were mainly inspired in Italian Fascism. The Falange directly sought supporters among bourgeois students and among the working class, employing violent language about 'fists and guns'.[98] It was a rhetoric full of references to military and religious topics. However, no veteran 'mystique' appeared, not even referring to the war experience of Morocco.[99] This element was not necessary for Spanish fascism. As a Spanish book about Italian Fascism suggested, the veterans – particularly ex-officers – had been important in the origins of the movement. However, many of the members of the *squadre* – it was argued – had been 'younger than twenty years old'. This fact showed that no impediment existed for the emergence of a fascist movement if similar political circumstances should occur. Only 'moral factors' were needed: 'vigour, audacity, spirit of sacrifice, submission to a discipline of iron, patriotism, desperation'.[100] As this example demonstrates, the ethos of the fascist paramilitary fighters, rooted in the symbolic appropriation of the anti-Bolshevik veteran, had been transferred to Spain as part of a longer and wider process of circulation throughout Europe.

For the increasingly 'fascistized' monarchist sectors, represented by the party Renovación Española and the magazine *Acción Española*, the lack of war veterans to achieve the conquest of the state had to be counterbalanced as well. As the leader, José Calvo Sotelo, wrote in February of 1933, Italy, Germany, Portugal and Poland had been able to get rid of parliamentarianism thanks to a 'visceral factor: the war

---

[96] See, for example, Vicente Gay, *La revolución nacional-socialista: Ambiente, Leyes, Ideología*, Barcelona, 1934.

[97] Ismael Saz, *Mussolini contra la II República: Hostilidad, conspiraciones, intervención (1931–1936)*, Valencia, Edicions Alfons el Magnànim, 1986, pp. 109–18.

[98] Monica Carbajosa and Pablo Carbajosa, *La corte literaria de José Antonio: la primera generación cultural de la Falange*, Barcelona, Crítica, 2003; José Antonio Parejo Fernández, *Señoritos, jornaleros y falangistas*, Sevilla, Bosque de Palabras, 2008.

[99] See Agustín del Río Cisneros (ed.), *Obras completas de José Antonio Primo de Rivera. Edición Cronológica*, Madrid, 1959.

[100] Nazario Cebreiros, *El Fascismo: Su origen, organización, doctrina, lucha y triunfo de Mussolini en Italia (1919–1922)*, Madrid, 1933, p. 145.

veterans'. The veterans were a 'mass, and also a spirit, capable of everything, even dying while killing, against the enemy of the Fatherland, either external or internal'. Calvo Sotelo argued that Spain had lacked *excombatientes* until 1931, when the Second Republic had started – according to him – to victimize the people. Now, organized 'in phalanxes, in disciplined and courageous human bundles' (*haces humanos*), these outraged Spaniards would be, in Calvo Sotelo's words, the combatants necessary to conquer the state against democracy and Marxism.[101] It is crucial to note that Calvo Sotelo had visited Fascist Italy in the same month, trying to obtain financial support from Mussolini and Italo Balbo; thereafter, he wrote press articles exalting Fascism.[102]

It was the Catholic political option that emerged with the greatest number of parliamentary seats from the elections of November 1933; the fascist and monarchist tickets suffered poor results, even if Primo de Rivera and Calvo Sotelo were elected to Parliament. The subsequent trajectory of Falange was marked by its fusion with the JONS in February of 1934, but the resulting party, Falange Española de las JONS, was no more successful. Even so, the diffusion of fascist newspapers inaugurated a spiral of street violence. By September of 1934, a report written for the fascist regime by an Italian observer said that the falangist action squads numbered around 6,000 members, including some veterans of the Moroccan war.[103] (Poet and veteran of the Morocco war Luys Santa Marina became leader of the Catalan Falange.) The Spanish political left, faced with a broader process of paramilitarization of the right, was on the defensive. The socialist insurrection of Asturias in October of 1934 must be understood in this context. The Spanish army, with its anti-democratic, 'Africanist' officers and generals (i.e. Franco), intervened to crush this revolutionary uprising. Thus, rather than the young Spanish fascists, who were, essentially, groups of combat-inexperienced employees, professionals and students who assisted the army during the repression, it was the military that was viewed by the upper social classes as the bulwark to whom they could turn to neutralize the left and eventually dissolve the Second Republic.[104]

---

[101] Speech of José Calvo Sotelo, quoted by Miguel Herrero García, 'Actividades Culturales', *Acción Española* (Madrid), 1 March 1933, pp. 654–5. It should be noticed that the Spanish word *haces*, plural of *haz*, is the most direct translation of the Italian *fasci*.

[102] González Calleja, *Contrarrevolucionarios*, pp. 119–20; Alfonso Bullón de Mendoza, *José Calvo Sotelo*, Barcelona, Ariel, 2004, pp. 382–4.

[103] González Calleja, *Contrarrevolucionarios*, p. 222.

[104] *Ibid.*, 173–245; Javier Jiménez Campo, *El fascismo en la crisis de la Segunda República española*, Madrid, Centro de Investigaciones Sociológicas, 1979.

France and the Croix de Feu

The Third French Republic was a far more solid democratic regime than the Second Spanish Republic or the German Weimar Republic. In the early 1930s, therefore, the Third French Republic was not threatened by any anti-republican military or paramilitary plots, as was the case in Spain. France did not witness the rise of any powerful fascist movement, as happened in Germany. Physical violence did not significantly characterize French politics, at least until 1934.[105] Nevertheless, fascism remained a latent force inside French politics at that time. Given the relevance of the veteran myth among the French fascist groups of the 1920s, it is interesting to observe the evolution of certain veteran discourses and organizations of the early 1930s, namely, the Croix de Feu and its veteran 'mystique', which were seen as fascist by many contemporaries and are considered as such by some historians today.

Historians have extensively debated whether or not the Croix de Feu was a fascist organization as part of wider scholarly discussions about the existence and importance of French fascism.[106] The patent lack of consensus is mainly due to the difficulty of employing the term 'fascism' as a label to statically categorize and classify political phenomena.[107] Furthermore, in the case of the Croix de Feu, the ambiguity about its fascist nature was characteristic of the movement from the outset, and it can be argued that this ambiguity was one of the keys to its success.[108] Here I will underline the role that the symbol of the veteran played in creating this ambiguity around the Croix de Feu as a fascist-inspired movement whilst also considering the group's radicalization.

The Croix de Feu was created as an association for French decorated veterans in 1927, but its origins cannot be understood without taking into account precedents such as the Faisceau. Indeed, the patron of the

---

[105] Cf. Serge Berstein, 'L'affrontement simulé des années 1930', *Vingtième Siècle. Revue d'histoire*, 5 (1985), pp. 39–54; Chris Millington, 'Street-Fighting Men: Political Violence in Inter-War France', *English Historical Review*, 129, 538 (2013), pp. 606–38.

[106] William D. Irvine, 'Fascism in France and the Strange Case of the Croix de Feu', *Journal of Modern History*, 63 (1991), pp. 271–95; Michel Dobry (dir.), *Le mythe de l'allergie française au fascisme*, Paris, Albin Michel, 2003; Sean Kennedy, *Reconciling France against Democracy: The Croix de Feu and the Parti Social Français 1927–1945*, Montreal, McGill-Queen's University Press, 2007, pp. 112–19; Samuel Kalman, *The Extreme Right in Interwar France: The Faisceau and the Croix de Feu*, Hampshire, Ashgate, 2008.

[107] Michel Dobry, 'Desperately Seeking "Generic Fascism"'; Passmore, 'L'historiographie du "fascisme" en France'.

[108] This argument was already suggested in the 1930s; see Comité de Vigilance des Intellectuels Antifascistes, *Qu'est-ce que le Fascisme? Le fascisme et la France*, Paris, 1935, pp. 5–9.

Figure 5.1 Croix de Feu emblem. '*Pourquoi nous sommes devenus Croix de Feu . . .*', Clermont, 1934.
(Bibliothèque nationale de France.)

original cell of the Croix de Feu, François Coty, a rich entrepreneur and director of the journal *Le Figaro*, had previously backed Valois' party. Marcel Bucard, a war veteran and organizer of the Faisceau's paramilitary branch, was also involved in the creation of the Croix de Feu. Another of its principal leaders, Maurice Genay, was a military officer who had been a member of the Jeunesses Patriotes. The first president of the Croix de Feu, Maurice d'Hartoy, a member of the Association des Écrivains Combattants, promoted a largely conservative agenda. But his group soon provoked accusations of 'fascism' from the left. This is scarcely surprising, given that even the emblem of the association was charged with ambiguity: a skull with flames – recalling the *arditi* symbology – on top of a cross with swords typical of French war medals (Figure 5.1). In the beginning, the organization grew very slowly, gathering support among the Parisian middle class, the military and aristocrats such as Joseph Pozzo di Borgo. Colonel François de La Rocque, an officer who had served for an extended period in Morocco, entered these circles in 1929. As the moderate d'Hartoy lost the support of François Coty, Maurice Genay and La Rocque gained control of the association.[109]

Can the Croix de Feu be considered a fascist organization? The answer largely depends on the conceptualization of fascism in use. If we consider

---

[109] Jacques Nobécourt, *Le colonel de La Rocque (1885–1946), ou, Les pièges du nationalisme chrétien*, Paris, Fayard, 1996, pp. 91–150.

that a certain style of self-representation that enhanced the identity of the veteran is characteristic of fascism, the Croix de Feu might be considered a fascist movement, though its discourse simultaneously maintained more conservative elements. In the first manifesto of the Croix de Feu, published in the opening issue of their journal *Le Flambeau*, the organization exalted the spirit of comradeship and discipline in the fight against the internal enemy; the organization aspired to be a 'great anti-revolutionary and anti-defeatist force'. Yet, there were no calls for the veterans to seize power, nor to impose a veterans' government. The organization's position regarding fascism was unclear. Members claimed to be 'fascists' if this epithet meant to 'defend the honour and prosperity of their beloved country', to be 'supporters of order and discipline' and enemies of 'vain agitations'. At the same time, members plainly denied being 'fascists' if that implied being 'supporters of brutal repression ... and of the perpetual militarisation of the nation'. Their declared readiness for 'civic' defensive action and their lack of incitation to violent aggression also hint at the intermediate position of the movement between fascism and traditional conservatism.[110]

If we assume a definition of fascism that stresses its transnational nature and foregrounds the transfers, entanglements and contacts, an ambiguous image of the Croix de Feu also emerges. It is important to note that as far as is known, the Croix de Feu did not establish direct contact with the Italian fascists. La Rocque publicly disavowed those in France who embraced Mussolini; he argued that French culture and thought were rich enough to render unnecessary the borrowing of 'expressions and ways of doing' from abroad.[111] The main ideological inspiration for La Rocque was French Army General Lyautey, who, in 1891, had written a renowned essay about the social role of the officer.[112] In 1930, Croix de Feu members travelled to Italy to participate in a ceremony for the Unknown Soldier, but this was an unexceptional activity done together with many other veteran associations, not to establish political relations.[113] However, it has been demonstrated that Croix de Feu members were interested in learning fascist practices.[114] Even though the Croix de Feu tried to accentuate its purely French character, Italian Fascism undoubtedly was a hidden source of inspiration.

---

[110] *Le Flambeau*, 1 (1 November 1929).
[111] 'Plan d'action pour l'exercise 1930', *Le Flambeau*, 9 (July 1930). See also 'Il faut serrer vos rangs!', *Le Flambeau*, 13 (November 1930).
[112] Kennedy, *Reconciling France*, p. 31.
[113] 'Notre participation au Pélerinage de "la flamme" en Italie en 1930', *Le Flambeau*, 3 (January 1930).
[114] See Passmore, 'L'historiographie du "fascisme" en France', p. 496.

Historical circumstances prevented collusion of the Croix de Feu with the international network of fascist veterans, but the league was not impermeable to the overall European context of fascist expansion. As we saw previously, the radicalization of the Croix de Feu was closely connected to the perception of the German menace embodied by the Stahlhelm. Subsequently, the rise of Hitler reinforced these fears. Yet, a growing anti-pacifism, anti-communism and xenophobia characterized the association from 1931, when La Rocque consolidated his leadership and took over the presidency. The organization grew substantially (28,903 members in January of 1933) and developed its own style of politics, the so-called Croix de Feu mystique, based on civic parades and patriotic celebrations. Much like the original Italian fascist movement or even the Stahlhelm, the Croix de Feu became open to non-combatants, such as sons of members. From the end of 1933, anti-parliamentarian unrest increased, so at the beginning of February 1934, the Croix de Feu was willing and ready to join the violent demonstrations that were going to jeopardize the stability of the Third Republic. Many Frenchmen justifiably regarded the league as a fascist threat within France. For if the Croix de Feu would not easily fit in any static, typological categorization of 'fascism', it did contain many elements (persons, entities, ideas, symbols, etc.) that either were entangled with French fascism or could easily integrate into it by means of a process of fascist permeation.

In general, the radicalization of the Croix de Feu was part of a broader process: the beginning of the 'second wave' of French fascism.[115] The scenario for such an evolution became possible after the return of the left to power as a new *cartel des gauches* following the elections of June 1932. The veterans' associations did not welcome this political change; they radicalized their stance against Herriot's government, as he attempted to reform the pension system.[116] This government fell within six months. Thus began a phase of instability and ineffectiveness in French politics. In 1933, new fascist organizations appeared: the Francistes created by Marcel Bucard, the Green Shirts of Henry Dorgères, and Solidarité Française founded by François Coty. Personal and ideological continuities existed between these groups and those which had gone before. The persistence of the veteran 'mystique' was not exclusive to the Croix de Feu; it was present in all these organizations. Fascist Italy was not just an ideological inspiration: Mussolini also provided Bucard' Francistes with funds. In short, it is not possible to understand the case of the Croix de

---

[115] Soucy, *French Fascism: The Second Wave 1933–1939*.
[116] Millington, *From Victory to Vichy*, pp. 42–3; Prost, *Les anciens combattants*, Vol. 1, pp. 148–53.

Feu without talking about fascism and the key role of the fascist-inspired veterans' mystique. Paramilitarism and French fascism, however, now had another source of inspiration outside Italy: Nazi Germany.

The Third Reich

The process by which the Nazis seized power and imposed a totalitarian dictatorship on Germany is one of the most investigated topics in modern European history. Accordingly, questions such as the role of the Stahlhelm in the last years of the Nazi struggle for power (*Kampfzeit*), the use of front soldiers as a symbol in Nazi propaganda before and after 1933 and the fate of the German veterans' organizations within the Third Reich have been widely studied.[117] For this reason, the process of nazification of the German veterans that took place between 1931 and 1934 will be succinctly described here. The main purpose of this section is to show the relevance of Italian Fascism in this process, as well as the high level of entanglement and the numerous cross-border contacts that marked consolidation of the Nazi dictatorship and its model of veteran politics.

The rise of the NSDAP in Germany implied the assimilation of other movements on the right into the Nazi movement, including war veterans' organizations. As we have seen, the Stahlhelm was one of the spearheads of the anti-republican reaction during the early 1930s; it was a competitor of the NSDAP. In October of 1931, the rally of Bad Harzburg, organized by the German nationalists together with the Nazis, presented a supposedly united national front against Weimar. The Stahlhelm, the DNVP, the NSDAP and other 'patriotic' organizations would participate. Yet, this attempt was a failure, as the uncooperative attitude of Hitler only deepened the existing divisions.[118] Hitler was not willing to establish an alliance. As a consequence of this division, the Stahlhelm nominated its leader, Theodor Duesterberg, as a candidate for the two-round presidential election of March–April 1932, in competition with Hitler and Hindenburg. While the conservative Hindenburg was re-elected president, and the second-ranked Hitler obtained more than 13 million votes; Duesterberg was defeated in the first round, with roughly 2.5 million votes – even less than the communist candidate,

---

[117] Among others, Berghahn, *Der Stahlhelm*; James M. Diehl, 'Victors or Victims? Disabled Veterans in the Third Reich', *Journal of Modern History*, 59, 4 (1987), pp. 705–36; Löffelbein, *Ehrenbürger der Nation*.
[118] Larry Eugene Jones, 'Nationalists, Nazis, and the Assault against Weimar: Revisiting the Harzburg Rally of October 1931', *German Studies Review*, 29, 3 (2006), pp. 483–94.

Ernst Thälmann. When it was revealed that Duesterberg had Jewish ancestors, this *völkisch* veteran leader was completely discredited. Rabidly attacked by the Nazis, the Stahlhelm reinforced its ties with the DNVP, but its political agency decreased.[119]

Furthermore, in the struggle to gain supporters, the NSDAP began to win at the expense of the Stahlhelm. Apart from the aggressive attitude of the SA towards the Stahlhelm, the main cause for this membership transfer was the Stahlhelm's doctrinal rigidity.[120] The Stahlhelm's restrictive concept of *Frontgemeinschaft* ('Front Community') had less political success than the Nazi ideal of *Volksgemeinschaft* ('National Community').[121] As the Stahlhelm was essentially an organization of men with war experience, the younger generation had much less prominence within the Stahlhelm than within the Nazi movement. As a result, many young men abandoned the veterans' organization to join the more attractive Nazi movement. During these years, the massive growth of the SA was paralleled by the sustained decline of the Jungstahlhelm organization.[122] Young people who had not directly experienced the war, inspired by the myth of the heroic front soldier, flocked to the SA, where more than 70 percent of the organizers were ex-soldiers, particularly ex-officers.

The SA was sociologically similar to the fascist *squadre*, but the input of veterans in the SA was much more reduced. As Sven Reichardt's comparative research on the fascist combat organizations has shown, the Italian squadrists of 1921–2 and the German SA men of 1930–2 were almost identical in their average age, despite a historical gap of a decade between both phenomena.[123] In the early 1930s, most German veterans were perhaps too old (between thirty and forty years of age) to be involved in political street fighting; their proclivity to join the NSDAP was not greater either, since the average age of NSDAP members was only a few years older than that of the SA. It is true that Nazism was a

---

[119] Berghahn, *Der Stahlhelm*, pp. 187–229.
[120] Anke Hoffstadt, 'Eine Frage der Ehre – Zur "Beziehungsgeschichte" von "Stahlhelm. Bund der Frontsoldaten" und SA', in Yves Müller and Reiner Zikenat (eds.), *Bürgerkriegsarmee: Forschungen zur nationalsozialistischen Sturmabteilung (SA)*, Frankfurt am Main, Peter Lang, 2013, pp. 267–96.
[121] Anke Hoffstadt, 'Frontgemeinschaft? Der "Stahlhelm. Bund der Frontsoldaten" und der Nationalsozialismus', in Krumeich (ed.), *Nationalsozialismus und Erster Weltkrieg*, pp. 191–206.
[122] Imtraud Götz von Olenhusen, 'Vom Jungstahlhelm zur SA: Die junge Nachkriegsgeneration in den paramilitärischen Verbänden der Weimarer Republik', in Wolfgang R. Krabbe (ed.), *Politische Jugend in der Weimarer Republik*, Cohum, Universitätsverlag Dr. N. Brockmezer, 1993, pp. 146–82.
[123] Reichardt, *Faschistische Kampfbünde*, pp. 346–89; Arndt Weinrich, *Der Weltkrieg als Erzieher*.

product of the Great War and that many of its main leaders had fought at the front. Even many Stahlhelm members and German veterans probably voted for Hitler and his party. But the majority of Nazis were younger people raised on the home front and therefore marked by the patriotic propaganda and often by the loss in combat of a father or brother, not by actual soldierly experience. By 1933, most probably, the mass basis of the Nazi movement was *not* predominantly composed of war veterans. Membership in these violent political groups therefore was not primarily determined by combat experience but by myths about such experiences, such as the myth of the fascist veteran.

Taking into account these facts, the self-representation of the NSDAP as a front soldiers' movement during the early 1930s should be understood above all as a propaganda strategy that responded to the need to widen the party's mass support during the numerous elections in this period. The sudden, not to say opportunistic, rise of the Nazis' veterans-related activities and policies during the early 1930s sharply contrasts with the limited importance that this question had within the NSDAP before 1929. Hitler's crafted image as a self-sacrificing *disabled* front soldier was systematically employed for the first time during the presidential elections of 1932, but it was swiftly abandoned after Hitler's seizure of power.[124] Certainly, the effects of the insistent appeals to front soldiers to vote for Hitler, through electoral posters, for example, should not be underestimated. Due to this campaign, not only an indeterminate number of ex-combatants and disabled veterans were converted to Nazism but also a characteristically Nazi political discourse about war veterans and an original Nazi policy for war victims slowly took shape. However, this was a protracted process that gained momentum only after 1933, and the antecedent of Italian Fascism was the original matrix of it, as I will demonstrate.

Before 1933, the Nazis were very cautious in their contacts and relationship with Italy, as being publicly identified with Fascism would have jeopardized the NSDAP's rise to power. French authorities feared an agreement between Italy and the Nazis, for such an understanding would be clearly detrimental for France.[125] In reality, the close affinity between Mussolini and Hitler was paralleled by the mutual sympathy that united many fascists and Nazis. They were prospective allies, but premature fraternization might prove problematic. Hence, the direct influence and contacts between the SA and the Italian fascists were sparse and not

---

[124] Cf. Löffelbein, *Ehrenbürger der Nation*, pp. 126–31.
[125] MAE-AD, Direction des Affaires Politiques et Commerciales, Politique, 329, Italie-Alemagne.

encouraged by the NSDAP leadership.[126] At the end of 1931, the head of the NSDAP Foreign Service (Auslandsabteilung), Hans Nieland, travelled to Italy.[127] The objective was to bring German Nazi sympathizers in Italy under the party's control. The subsequent establishment of a NSDAP organization in Italy, which was not devoid of internal controversies, was principally motivated by the desire to stop uncontrolled NSDAP members coming to Italy.[128] Hitler wished to meet Mussolini, but this visit was not possible yet. Although it was difficult to deny the lure of Italian Fascism among the Nazis, direct and overtly political contacts and transfers encountered important strategic obstacles.

In contrast, in the final crisis year of the Weimar Republic, an elite of nationalist war veterans furthered adoption of the fascist model of politics in Germany. The transfer of political ideology in this direction was constant. Stahlhelm members did not conceal their admiration for Mussolini. Franz Seldte and other Stahlhelm leaders maintained contacts with the Duce, who they visited in Rome; for example, on the occasion of the Reale Accademia d'Italia congress in April of 1932, they sent him an adulatory message when crossing the border back into Germany.[129] In April of 1932, Stahlhelm leader Heinrich Mahnken reported his research findings on the military education of Italian youths and on the methods of fascist politics. He affirmed that the Italian model had significance for the Stahlhelm in relation to not only 'fundamental concepts but also immediate practical measures'.[130] Specifically, on the basis of the Italian example, Mahnken suggested that the NSDAP should mobilize German students. As this case suggests, even if the Nazis were reluctant to appear as debtors of Italian Fascism, the permeability of the boundaries between the NSDAP and the fascist-inspired Stahlhelm contributed to the adoption of fascist political traits by the Nazis.

In close connection with nationalist veterans' groups, certain anti-republican personalities set up cultural institutions to systematize the study of Italian Fascism. These fascist-friendly circles included several notable or would-be Nazis. In December of 1931, the Society for the

---

[126] Reichardt, *Faschistische Kampfbünde*, p. 17.
[127] MAE-AD, Direction des Affaires Politiques et Commerciales, Politique, 330, Italie-Alemagne, pp. 144–6.
[128] Fleuris Groenendijk, 'The NSDAP's Local Organizations in Italy, 14 September 1930 to 30 January 1933', *Yearbook of European Studies*, 3 (1990), pp. 67–99.
[129] ACS, SPD, CO, 510.977, 'Germania. Associazione Combattentistica degli Elmi d'Acciaio (Stahlhelm)'.
[130] Letter from Landesverband Westmark (Mahnken) (6 April 1932), BArch (Berlin), R 72/28.

Study of Fascism (Gesellschaft zum Studium des Faschismus) was created. Its president was Charles Edward, Duke of Saxe-Coburg and Gotha, who had lost his nobility with the arrival of the Weimar Republic and had been involved in anti-republican paramilitary activity. The director of this cultural society was the Major Waldemar Pabst, one of the culprits of the Liebknecht and Luxemburg killings and later an organizer of the Austrian Heimwehr.[131] The Gesellschaft aimed to investigate the fascist model of state and economy with a view to offering this knowledge 'to the future leaders of the coming Germany'.[132] The membership, initially limited to 100 people, was composed of several Stahlhelm leaders, ex-officers and generals, including Theodor Duesterberg, the Nazi Hermann Göring, the erstwhile Freikorps leaders Wilhelm Faupel and Rüdiger von der Goltz and the militaristic writer Franz Schauwecker. The lectures that this group held were also attended and promoted by Renzetti, whose 'Italian Reports' publicized Fascism among the Germans at the time.[133] Through his constant contacts with the Nazis and the Stahlhelm, Renzetti worked to realize his project of 'transforming the Stahlhelm into Hitler's party militia'.[134] Renzetti's activity contributed to the union of German anti-republican forces, in support of the NSDAP, whilst laying the foundations for a future Italian-German alliance after the imminent arrival of the Third Reich.[135]

After Hitler was nominated as Chancellor on 30 January 1933, the transformation of Nazi veterans' policies, discourses and representations experienced a remarkable acceleration. In the first Nazi government, Franz Seldte was appointed Ministry of Labour. Stahlhelm members enthusiastically saluted Hitler's government and collaborated with the SA in political manoeuvres to entrench the Nazis in power.[136] The Third Reich was presented as the heir of the spirit of the front; it was declared that 'the right of the front soldiers' would be enforced, that the 'gratitude of the fatherland' owed to the former soldiers would finally reap its fruits. The Nazi project of transforming disabled veterans into the 'First Citizens of the State', reinforced by Strasser through the NSDAP sections, resulted in the creation of the National Socialist War Victims' Care Organization (Nationalsozialistische Kriegsopferversorgung (NSKOV)) in July of 1933. The NSKOV undertook the militarization of the disabled

---

[131] Klaus Gietinger, *Der Konterrevolutionär: Waldemar Pabst - eine deutsche Karriere*, Hamburg, Nautilus, 2009, pp. 266–74, 297–301.

[132] BArch (Berlin), R 72/260, pp. 118–19, 127–9, 130, 131, 139, and 163–170.

[133] Giuseppe Renzetti, *Italienische Berichte*, Berlin, 1932.

[134] Report of Magg. Renzetti (20 November 1931), quoted by De Felice, *Mussolini e Hitler*, p. 233.

[135] De Felice, *Mussolini e Hitler*, pp. 211–58.   [136] Berghahn, *Der Stahlhelm*, pp. 250–4.

Figure 5.2 Emblem of the NSKOV.

veterans' politics and strived to mobilize the veterans through propaganda rallies and meetings.[137]

Fascist Italy was an inspiration for the NSKOV project. It is no coincidence that the emblem of the NSKOV seems to have drawn on the *arditi* symbol of a sword surrounded by a laurel wreath (Figure 5.2). In February of 1933, the Nazi magazine for disabled veterans, *Deutsche Kriegsopferversorgung*, devoted a long article describing the Italian war pensions law. Apart from denigrating the socialist and pacifist approaches to the war victims' care, the Nazis argued that the legislation for disabled veterans reflected the national spirit of each country. In Italy, Mussolini had introduced legislative innovations that were praised by the Nazis, namely, preferential treatment for disabilities caused by service on the front.[138] The Italian disabled veterans of the ANMIG embraced these positive comments with enthusiasm. When Hermann Göring, Minister of Aviation of the Third Reich, made an official trip to Italy in April of 1933, he also visited the Casa Madre del Mutilato in Rome. Shortly after,

---

[137] *Völkischer Beobachter*, 21 February 1933; Löffelbein, *Ehrenbürger der Nation*, pp. 159–60, 173–253.

[138] Alfred Dick, 'Fascismus und Kriegsopfer', *Deutsche Kriegsopferversorgung. Monatschrift* (Munich), 5 (February 1933).

another article in the NSKOV magazine described these friendly contacts and exalted the 'spiritual bond' of Mussolini with disabled veterans.[139] This nascent alliance between Italian and German veterans was reinforced by both the private and public displays of friendship between Hitler and Mussolini and the numerous trips by Nazis to directly study Fascist Italy.[140]

Meanwhile, in Germany, the war veterans' organizations were going through a process of nazification, which recalls the *fascistizzazione* of the ANC a decade before. The Nazi celebration of the *Frontsoldaten* concealed the actual subjugation of German veterans: new medals and public homage went hand-in-hand with the destruction of liberties and diversity. These 'contradictory signs' led the Jewish veterans of the Reichsbund jüdischer Frontsoldaten to wrongly think that they could continue to live their lives without fear under Nazism.[141] The Stahlhelm was compelled to relinquish its influence to the benefit of the SA, and Seldte placed the organization under the control of Hitler. The accusation that the Stahlhelm was admitting 'enemies of the NSDAP, masons [and] half-Jews' as new members only helped nazification.[142] Röhm, leader of the SA, was expanding its paramilitary power,[143] whilst the Nazis gradually established a monopoly over the symbol of the front soldier. In December of 1933, during a talk to the diplomatic corps, Röhm declared that 'the roots of National Socialism lay in the trenches of the Great War'.[144] By 1934, this brutal way of understanding and representing the war experience was deeply ingrained in the minds of many Nazi veterans, as the collection of early Nazis' autobiographies assembled that year by Theodor Abel demonstrates.[145] Despite some resistance from Stahlhelm members to losing their particular identity, the nazification of discourses and organizations was unrelenting. In early 1934, the SA brown shirt replaced the green-grey Stahlhelm uniform. In April of

[139] Alfred Dick, 'Fascismus und Kriegsopfer', *Deutsche Kriegsopferversorgung. Monatschrift*, 9 (July 1933).
[140] Jens Petersen, *Hitler-Mussolini: Die Entstehung der Achse Berlin-Rom 1933–1936*, Tübingen, Max Niemeyer, 1973, pp. 112–20 and 183–5.
[141] Tim Grady, 'Fighting a Lost Battle: The Reichsbund jüdischer Frontsoldaten and the Rise of National Socialism', *German History*, 28, 1 (2010), pp. 1–20.
[142] Information from the Oberster SA Führung in Munich (15 December 1933), BArch (Berlin), NS 6/215, folios 69–71.
[143] Hancock, *Ernst Röhm*, pp. 132–140.
[144] Ernst Röhm, *Warum SA.? Rede vor dem Diplomatischen Korps am 7 Dezember 1933*, Berlin, 1933, p. 3.
[145] Patrick Krassnitzer, 'Die Geburt des nationalsozialismus im Schützengraben. Formen der Brutalisierung in den Autobiographien von nationalsozialistischen Frontsoldaten', in Jost Dülfer and Gerd Krumeich (eds.), *Der verlorene Frieden: Politik und Kriegskultur nach 1918*, Essen, Klartex-Verlag, 2002, pp. 119–48.

1934, the Stahlhelm was transformed into the National Socialist German Front Soldiers Association (Stahlhelm) (Der National-Sozialistische Deutsche Frontkämpferbund – NSDFB Stahlhelm).[146] In short, the German veterans' nazification process was swifter, deeper and farther reaching than the co-optation of the Italian veterans by the fascists.

Here what is most interesting to acknowledge is the role that the Nazis bestowed on the German veterans in the realm of international relations. In this question, the nazification of discourses and organizations had the same mid-term purpose as *fascistizzazione* in Italy: using the veterans as an instrument for the dictatorship's foreign policy. The Third Reich yearning for 'vital space' (*Lebensraum*), Nazi militarism and imperialism and Hitler's own ideology made the probabilities of war against France very high, even if the Third Reich first needed to consolidate within Germany and then rebuild a powerful army. The growing German menace, threatening to absorb Austria as one of the first steps towards hegemony in Europe, frightened Germany's Italian ideological ally. Hitler and Mussolini, in their first meeting in Venice in June of 1934, did not reach any agreement. Finding a balance of power in Europe would prove very difficult. So, in order to gain time for rearmament, Hitler's official attitude was that of striving for European peace. The discourse of peace helped the Nazis to succeed in the German elections of November 1933 and therefore allowed Hitler to obtain dictatorial powers. Talking about peace was useful against the French, when a plebiscite about the future of the Saar region as either a province of Germany or a part of France took place in January of 1935.[147]

Why did the veterans become the instrument of this peace strategy? This choice can be better understood by taking into account trans-national factors. These dynamics of veteran rapprochement could not have worked without the turning point of French politics on 6 February 1934. As is well known, a mass demonstration on that date held by the French conservative veterans – mainly UNC – and extreme right groups – including the Croix de Feu – on the Place de la Concorde in Paris ended in a violent attempt to invade the French Parliament. In the clashes that ensued, fourteen protesters died.[148] Through the German embassy in Paris, the Nazis were aware of this dramatic irruption of the French veterans onto the political scene. That month, Oberlindober

---

[146] Berghahn, *Der Stahlhelm*, p. 269.

[147] Christian Leitz, *Nazi Foreign Policy, 1933–1941: The Road to Global War*, London, Routledge, 2004, p. 38.

[148] Chris Millington, 'February 6, 1934: The Veterans' Riot', *French Historical Studies*, 33, 4 (2010), pp. 545–72.

highlighted for the first time the advantage to be gained from cultivating mutual understanding among veterans from different countries.[149] It was not coincidence that over the course of the following spring, the Nazis established their first contacts with representatives of the British Legion, although this connection remained undeveloped.[150]

To expand its foreign network among veterans, the NSDAP needed to complete the monopolization of German veteran politics, in which Röhm and the SA had attained too much independent leverage. Hitler's need to maintain internal order and to tighten ties with the German army led to the violent purge of the SA during the 'Night of the Long Knives' (30 June–2 July 1934), including the assassination of Röhm. Shortly after, Hitler's Deputy Führer Rudolf Hess, during a speech in Königsberg, invoked the allegedly proverbial discipline and loyalty of the veterans who, on that basis, had complied with Hitler's ruthless measures. Moreover, Hess also made an appeal for peace 'to the front soldiers of the whole world'. He argued that the 'front fighters' (*Frontkämpfern*) would be the only group able to establish peace, the 'peace of the front soldiers'.[151] From the summer of 1934 on, the Nazi Propaganda Ministry would implement this rapprochement. As we will see, all these events were key moments in an important developmental phase of transnational contacts, entanglement and transfers between fascist, national socialist and French veterans.

The Veterans' Connection in Italy, France and Germany

The series of cross-border contacts among veterans that began in 1933–4 were a result of the particular historical conjuncture after the establishment of Hitler's dictatorship. The new German regime complicated the state of affairs, for Italy was no longer the undisputed lodestar of the European extreme right. Fascist Italy saw that one of its pupils, Nazi Germany, was threatening to surpass it. During 1933, debates between those defending the essentially Italian, un-transferable nature of Fascism and those highlighting the necessity of exporting it came to the fore once more.[152] In July of 1933, after a long theoretical debate, the Action

---

[149] Holger Skor, '*Brücken über den Rhein': Frankreich in der Wahrnehmung und Propaganda des Dritten Reiches, 1933–1939*, Essen, Klartext, 2011, pp. 203–77; Löffelbein, *Ehrenbürger der Nation*, pp. 364–71.

[150] James J. Barnes and Patience P. Barnes, *Nazis in Pre-War London 1930–1939: The Fate and Role of German Party Members and British Sympathizers*, Brighton, Sussex Academic Press, 2005, pp. 147–50.

[151] *Der Stahlhelm*, 15 July 1934; *Völkischer Beobachter*, 10 July 1934.

[152] See, for example, several articles in *Critica fascista*, 1 and 15 February and 1 and 15 March 1933.

Committees for the Universality of Rome (Comitati d'Azione per l'Universalità di Roma (CAUR)), a kind of fascist international, were created.[153] Eugenio Coselschi, an ex-officer, erstwhile collaborator of D'Annunzio in Fiume and organizer since 1919 of the small pro-fascist War Volunteers Association (Associazione Volontari di Guerra), was entrusted with the direction of the CAUR. By February of 1934, the fascists were striving to enhance the originality of Italian Fascism, underlining the imitative nature of 'analogous foreign movements'.[154] Yet, the attractiveness of Fascist Italy had not decreased; indeed, the grandiose propaganda and architectural endeavours of Mussolini, particularly in Rome, combined with the touristic allure of the country to bring even more foreign visitors,[155] in a context of diplomatic rapprochement between Italy and France.[156]

If the idea of basing international collaboration in Europe on war veterans was not new, French veterans now turned to it with renewed interest. In June of 1932, UF leaders paid a visit to French veterans residing in Genoa, invited by the UF organizer in Italy, Henri Mirauchaux. This occasion allowed veteran leaders such as Paul Brousmiche to meet fascist veteran leaders in Rome.[157] André Gervais, a writer, veteran and UF member, was another initiator of these international contacts. In 1932 and 1933, he had travelled to Germany to research the German veterans' organizations, exploring the general mood for establishing peace-oriented contacts between German and French veterans.[158] His conversations with Seldte and other German leaders served only to uncover important obstacles to any agreement. Gervais discovered the troubling reality that German youths were being systematically told about the allegedly positive values of war. (Gervais also noticed the lack of originality in Hitler's programme for the veterans.[159]) However, Gervais' proposal of furthering contacts with German republican veterans' organizations would soon be rendered obsolete by Hitler's rise to power.

At that point, veterans of the UF focused on establishing friendly contacts with the Italian fascist veterans. In April of 1933, Henri Pichot

---

[153] Marco Cuzzi, *Antieuropa: Il fascismo universale di Mussolini*, Milan, M & B, 2006, pp. 161–70.
[154] Bruno Corra, 'L'originale e le copie', *Il Popolo d'Italia*, 10 February 1934.
[155] Cf. Guglielmo Tagliacarne, 'L'afflusso degli stranieri', *Il Popolo d'Italia*, 7 April 1934.
[156] Christophe Poupault, *À l'ombre des faisceaux: Les voyages français dans l'Italie des chemises noires (1922–1943)*, Rome, École française de Rome, 2014.
[157] *Cahiers de l'Union fédérale* (Paris), 1 August 1932.
[158] *Ibid.*, 15 June, 1 and 15 July, 1 August and 1 September 1932; André Gervais, *La tranchée d'en face: Enquête d'un combattant français chez les combattants allemands*, Paris, 1933.
[159] *Ibid.*, pp. 148–9.

and other French veteran leaders conducted a ten-day visit to Italy. They cordially met fascist veteran leaders, including Rossi and Delcroix. The delegation also paid homage to the *Milite Ignoto* and visited the Mostra della Rivoluzione Fascista. They celebrated the trip as an example of the 'Franco-Italian combatant fraternity'.[160] Later in 1933, UF President Paul Brousmiche went on holiday to Italy, where he cultivated his friendly contacts with fascist veterans. Thus, the French reinforced their belief in the old myth of the fascist veteran. For his part, André Gervais praised the Mostra della Rivoluzione Fascista and stated that Fascism had originally been a 'veterans movement': 'the blackshirts of the March on Rome', he wrote, 'were our comrades of the war.'[161] At the beginning of 1934, Gervais visited Fascist Italy. After meeting several fascist leaders, he was received by the Duce. The interview was published only two days before the events of 6 February. Mussolini told Gervais that education of the youth in pacifist values was useless. Asked whether he thought the veterans should contribute to create a kind of 'European spirit', Mussolini replied, '[T]hey should, unquestionably!'. When further questioned whether he was partisan of the international collaboration among veterans, Mussolini stated, 'Obviously!'.[162] Mussolini's support for this veteran connection was not self-motivated, but it encouraged the French veterans' impulses to engage with the Italian Fascists.

The constructed image of the fascist regime and the Duce embodied the long-standing political ideal of French conservatives and nationalists, to say nothing of the French fascist groupings. Politics in France was experiencing an ongoing process of radicalization towards authoritarianism, and the veterans' organizations were not an exception.[163] The events of 6 February were not only the product but also one of the catalysts of this process. In their immediate aftermath, Daladier's government resigned and was replaced by a conservative cabinet headed by Gaston Doumerge. While the riot of 6 February became a mobilizing myth for the right, the left considered it a kind of coup d'état attempted by French 'fascism'. In fact, after this political crisis, the veterans' associations' as well as the Croix de Feu clearly radicalized their programmes and discourses. UF leader Henri Pichot, who would retain the presidency of the association from May of 1934 onwards, noticeably set out on the path towards authoritarianism. In the case of the UNC, new leaders emerged who embodied this

---

[160] *Cahiers de l'Union Fédérale*, 34 (1 May 1933).   [161] *Ibid.*, 42 (1 October 1933).
[162] *L'Intransigeant* (Paris), 4 February 1934.
[163] Chris Millington, 'The French Veterans and the Republic: The Union nationale des combattants and the Union fédérale, 1934–1938', *European History Quarterly*, 42 (2012), pp. 50–70.

trend; Georges Lebecq and Jean Goy endorsed the formation of paramilitary sections – the Action Combattante. Furthermore, now there was another example of 'national restoration', that of Germany. The French veterans noted, with a certain envy, the new Nazi legislation for the German '*generation du feu*'.[164] Yet Italy was the principal referent.

The rapprochement between French and Italian fascist veterans was reflected in organizations, direct contacts, and publications. Towards mid-February 1934, the monthly magazine *Le Trait d'Union* appeared in Italy (Turin), as the organ of the Italian branch of the UF (Union Fédérale en Italie des Associations Françaises d'Anciens Combattants). Groups of French veterans who resided in Italy had fused in this single organization, with the aim of maintaining a relationship of 'comradeship and fraternity' with Italian veterans, and thus improving Italian-French relations. As the review's leading writer, the ex-captain Henri Mirauchaux, made clear from its first issue, this publication highlighted the examples of 'national renovation' from which those seeking to save France should draw inspiration.[165] The visit of a group of around 500 French veterans to Fascist Italy served to strengthen the connection between French and Italian fascist veterans. This visit, an example of political tourism, took place between the 30 March and the 7 April 1934, including visits to Turin, Rome, Naples, Venice and Milan. There was also a 'pilgrimage' to battlefields of the Carso. André Gervais led this mission, welcomed by fascist veteran leaders such as Carlo Delcroix and Amilcare Rossi. Mussolini received them warmly, testament to a spirit of comradeship.[166] In the following weeks, as noted in a confidential report sent by the French police in Nice, the 'manifestations of French-Italian friendship' in Italy proliferated.[167]

Correspondingly, the activities of fascist veterans in France stepped up. Around the symbolic date of 24 May 1934, fascist ceremonies took place, for example, in Lyon, Metz and Toulouse.[168] The celebration of the Italian intervention in the Great War recalled the friendship between France and Italy, with leaders of the PNF and ANC fraternizing with French UF and UNC representatives. The most important ceremonies took place in Paris. There an homage to the fallen Italian soldiers included igniting the flame dedicated to the French Unknown Soldier

---

[164] L. D., 'La génération du feu en Allemagne', *La Voix du Combattant*, 10 February 1934.
[165] *Le Trait d'Union. Revue mensuelle publiée par l'Union Fédérale en Italie des Associations Françaises d'Anciens Combattants* (Turin), February 1934.
[166] *Ibid.*, March–April 1934; *La Nuova Italia. L'Italie Nouvelle* (Paris), 12 April 1934; *L'Italia grigio-verde*, 10 April–5 May 1934.
[167] Report dated in Nice, 20 April 1934, AN, F/7, 13465, Italie.
[168] See several reports in AN, F/7, 13465, Italie.

at the Arc de Triomphe. Under the guise of a Garibaldian celebration, representatives of the Associazione Volontari di Guerra and fascists such as the president of the CAUR Eugenio Coselschi were able to express their 'Italian and fascist enthusiasm' in the French capital.[169] These public activities developed in a context marked by the rising anti-fascist mobilization of the French working class: leftist counter-demonstrations ended with anti-fascist slogans, stone throwing and, in the case of Paris, clashes between leftists and police.[170] Fears of fascism taking hold in France were not unfounded.

In June of 1934, the French members of the Italian-based Union Fédérale organized a congress in Milan. This meeting was intended to be another opportunity to reinforce the Italian-French friendship. Approximately 300 people participated, joined by prominent fascist veteran leaders such as Giovanni Baccarini. In his speech, the former French Ambassador Henry de Jouvenel, a pro-fascist journalist, stated that 'the time of the veterans, which already came in Italy and other countries, is going to come in France.' The fascist-friendly climate of the meeting meant that the planned projection of the 1932 film, *Les Croix de Bois* (based on the homonymous novel of Roland Dorgelès), was suspended because of the anti-German passages in the movie.[171]

Relations between French and Nazi veterans were not so easy. At the end of June 1934, the shocking news of the Nazi purge of the SA temporarily chilled the enthusiasm towards Hitler of some French groups.[172] For this reason, they received the above-mentioned Hess's suggestion for international veterans' meetings cautiously. Gustave Hervé was among the few enthusiasts.[173] Henri Pichot, whose previous relations with the German republican veterans had been frustrated, considered contacts with the Nazis as the only way to continue his campaign for peace.[174] Yet, Pichot still had faith in the League of Nations, and when his first meeting with Oberlindober took place in Baden-Baden in August of 1934, there was no agreement. For his part, UNC leader Jean Goy was more open; he declared that a direct contact between German and French veterans was 'infinitely desirable'; he said that Hitler's and Hess's offers should not be overlooked.[175] Finally,

---

[169] *La Nuova Italia. L'Italie Nouvelle*, 31 May 1934.   [170] *L'Humanité*, 21 May 1934.

[171] Report, 'Anciens combattants français en Italie' (12 June 1934), AN, F/7, 13465, Italie; *Le Trait d'Union*, 5 (June 1934); *Il Popolo d'Italia*, 16 June 1934.

[172] Dietrich Orlow, *The Lure of Fascism in Western Europe: German Nazis, Dutch and French Fascists, 1933–1939*, New York, Palgrave Macmillan, 2009, p. 56.

[173] *La Victoire*, 10 July 1934.   [174] Trichet, *Henri Pichot et l'Allemagne*, pp. 145–7.

[175] *Le Petit Journal* (Paris), 17 and 18 September 1934; *Völkischer Beobachter*, 19 September 1934.

during November and December 1934, conversations took place between, on the one hand, Hitler and Oberlindober, and, on the other hand, Goy and Pichot. While certain activists, such as Gustave Hervé, expressed satisfaction with the budding rapprochement,[176] French public opinion was divided on the topic. Many realized that Nazi propaganda was using French veterans, and they were not wrong.[177]

This Franco-German connection must be considered in tandem with the Franco-Italian link that veterans had established. French fascists observed this triangular entanglement as the key to European peace. Marcel Bucard, the leader of the Francistes, put it clearly in an interview published in *Völkischer Beobachter*. In his view, a Franco-German accord was a necessity, and for that, France needed an understanding ally; this was the reason why France strove for an alliance with Italy; on the basis of this alliance, a German-French accord would be agreed on and would subsequently flourish.[178] Were the veterans realizing the imagined fascist Europe that Mussolini had predicted in 1929?

Undoubtedly, the belief in the imminent consolidation of a kind of peaceful fascist-led international system, based on mutual understanding between veterans, proved misguided. In fact, rather than looking for a triple fascist connection between Italy, France and Germany, the leaders of the pro-fascist French veterans in Italy were trying to consolidate an alliance along traditional lines, namely, between the allies of the Great War, with Germany remaining isolated as a potential threat.[179] Furthermore, the Nazi coup in Austria and the murder of Chancellor Engelbert Dollfuss disturbed the relations between Germany and both Italy and France. In December of 1934, the CAUR organized an international fascist conference at Montreaux, drawing together the representatives of fascist movements from different nations, but the Nazis refused to attend. Although an international commission for international fascism was created, this project soon declined.[180] This would not be the mission of the fascist veterans abroad. The ultra-nationalist agendas of the main European fascist movements precluded an international understanding.

---

[176] *La Victoire*, 2 and 22 December 1934.
[177] Claire Moreau Trichet, 'La propagande nazie à l'égard des associations françaises d'anciens combattants de 1934 à 1939', *Guerres mondiales et conflits contemporains*, 205 (2002), pp. 55–70; Orlow, *The Lure of Fascism*, pp. 73–4; Prost, *Les anciens combattants*, Vol. 1, pp. 177–8.
[178] *Völkischer Beobachter*, 30–31 December 1934.
[179] *Le Trait d'Union*, 11 (December 1934), pp. 12–13.
[180] Ledeen, *Universal Fascism*, pp. 115–31.

Moreover, the duplicity of the discourse around peace promoted by Mussolini and Hitler became clear at the end of 1934 and during 1935. In September of 1934, the Italian government undertook important measures to reinforce citizens' military education: the avowed aim was to create 'a military and warlike nation'.[181] Mussolini's verbal threats to Abyssinia followed. The supposed veteran comradeship facilitated this escalation towards war. The fact that the Franco-Italian agreements of Rome, January 1935, between the French Foreign Minister Pierre Laval and Mussolini, were surrounded by fascist veteran rituals is telling.[182] This accord, praised by the veterans, was a French concession faced with Italian imperial aspirations. The French hoped to secure the friendship of Italy in the face of the German threat. For the French veterans, the conference of Stresa in April 1935 'reignited the old Latin friendship between France and Italy'. Immediately, around 1,700 French veterans – mainly UNC members – once more visited the fascists in Italy, celebrating their comradeship.[183] The UF also sent a delegation to Italy to reinforce their ties of 'fraternity' with the fascist veterans.[184]

In spite of the fascist military menace, over the course of 1935, and for the years to come, contacts between French veterans and Italian fascists continued. The increasingly friendly relations between the UF and the fascists drove a wedge between Henri Pichot and René Cassin, but it was the latter, not the former, who lost influence over the French veterans movement.[185] However, the 'Stresa front' to contain Germany while giving free rein to Italy would fail. If the goal of this relationship was the maintenance of peace, as many French veterans sincerely believed, their expectations would be completely frustrated within months. After the Italian invasion of Ethiopia in October 1935, the French veterans' Union fédérale en Italie supported this aggression and adopted a bitterly critical stance against the sanctions imposed on Italy by the League of Nations.[186] In France, while UNC generally supported the fascist aggression, the UF was more critical. For the UF was highly involved in the struggle for international peace. Not only was its president, Henri Pichot, committed to this ideal, but so too was René Cassin. Now, both leaders coincided in a critical position regarding the fascist aggression but they

---

[181] *Il Popolo d'Italia*, 20 September 1934.
[182] See, for example, *Le Trait d'Union*, 1 (January 1935).
[183] Charles Vilain, *Le voyage des combattants français en Italie (15–22 Avril 1935)*, Rouen, 1935.
[184] *Cahiers de l'Union Fédérale*, 15 May 1935.
[185] Winter and Prost, *René Cassin*, pp. 78–83.
[186] *Le Trait d'Union*, 11 (November 1935).

profoundly disagreed on the means to operate in favour of peace.[187] As we will see, French veterans' pacifism had entered a serious crisis.

In Germany, shortly after the incorporation of the Saar into the Third Reich in January of 1935, militarism came to the fore once more. While rumours of Italian preparation for a military attack on Abyssinia circulated, Hitler re-imposed military service in Germany. On this occasion once more, the ideal of international veteran comradeship was an argument for the Nazis to justify their rearmament. Asked during an interview what the reaction of foreign veterans would be, Oberlindober argued that they should accept that their German 'comrades' had the same right to security as they had.[188] During 1935, the Nazi strategy of talking of peace with foreign veterans continued, and thus the encounters persisted; even the British Legion visited Nazi Germany in July 1935.[189] However, the Nazis had plans for the forced unification of all veteran associations in Germany, and the utility of the NSDFB Stahlhelm was being questioned. Seldte objected the demise of his organization but he finally acquiesced to Hitler's demands.[190] In November 1935, the instrumental nature of the Nazi exaltation of the veterans became all too clear when, after Hitler had fully rebuilt a German army, he ordered the dissolution of the nazified Stahlhelm. Its 'mission' was considered 'fulfilled'.[191]

In the end, the hypocritical veteran diplomacy served only fascist and Nazi interests. It can be said that by the end of 1935, the myth of the fascist veteran, born in Fascist Italy and largely circulated throughout Europe, reworked and reinforced by Nazism, had fulfilled one of the missions it had in the wider international sphere: preparing the ground for the expansion of the fascist regimes. In 1929–30, Mussolini had decided to use the veterans abroad to make progress towards the ultimate goal of a fascist Europe. When a fascist-inspired regime was actually imposed in Germany, the panorama changed substantially. Veterans continued to be an instrument in foreign policy, but the Rome-centred project of a fascist Europe had vanished in the advent of the Third Reich. Subsequent veteran diplomacy served only the interest of the fascist powers and was, in the end, detrimental to the French.

---

[187] Winter and Prost, *René Cassin*, p. 89. Henri Pichot, 'A bas la guerre', *Cahiers de l'Union Fédérale*, 15 October 1935; cf. René Cassin, 'Pas de paix sans courage', *Cahiers de l'Union Fédérale*, 10 November 1935.

[188] *Völkischer Beobachter*, 19 March 1935.

[189] Löffelbein, *Ehrenbürger der Nation*, pp. 385–93; Barnes and Barnes, *Nazis in Pre-War London*, pp. 151–8.

[190] Volker R. Berghahn, 'Das Ende des "Stahlhelm"', *Vierteljahrshefte für Zeitgeschichte*, 13, 4 (1965), pp. 446–51.

[191] *Der Stahlhelm*, 10 November 1935.

However, the Italian-French veteran friendship was a major source of inspiration for the authoritarian political trends within France. The works of André Gervais, especially his book on Italian veterans under Mussolini's regime, conveyed an extremely positive impression of Fascism. Gervais portrayed the fascist ideology as reflecting the soul of the veterans and persuaded his readers that veterans – fascists – ruled the Italian state.[192] Consequently, Gervais developed his own theories about a kind of French veteran spirit. His ideas were clearly inspired by the Italian example, although he sharply differentiated the French 'veteran mystique' from the French 'fascist mystique'.[193] If French veterans had not yet adopted the cult of the leader, Marshal Pétain, appointed Minister of War after 6 February 1934, became an acclaimed political figure in the pro-Italian veterans' press.[194] Gustave Hervé praised Pétain as a potential president for an authoritarian republic, and conservative veterans' journals echoed Hervé's slogan, 'It's Pétain who we need!'.[195] Since 1934, the interaction between veterans' organizations, such as the UNC, and the French extreme-right leagues, including the Croix de Feu and its successor, the Parti Social Français, is well known.[196] As has been demonstrated here, this political evolution of French veterans was rendered possible by the powerful allure of the fascist veteran myth and by the symbolic appropriation of the veteran that Italian fascists had successfully implemented since 1921. A misleading belief in an inherent inclination of war veterans towards Fascism was nourished by multiple contacts with the Italians and served as the key cause of the increasing adoption by French veterans of fascist practices, symbols and discourses.

---

[192] André Gervais, *Les Combattants à l'ombre du faisceau*, Paris, 1935; see book review in *La Voix du Combattant*, 8 August 1934.
[193] André Gervais, *L'esprit combattant*, Paris, 1934, p. 66.
[194] See, for example, *Le Trait d'Union*, 11 (December 1934); see also *La Voix du Combattant*, 20 October 1934,
[195] Gustave Hervé, *C'est Pétain qu'il nous faut*, Paris, 1936; *La Voix du Combattant*, 23 February 1935; *Le Mutilé de l'Algérie* (Algiers), 22 and 29 November 1936.
[196] Millington, *From Victory to Vichy*, pp. 109–38.

6   Veterans between Fascism and Anti-Fascism, War and Peace, 1936–1940

From the fascist military invasion of Ethiopia in October of 1935 until the Nazi aggression against Poland in September of 1939, there was hardly a moment of total peace for Europe. It is not mistaken to state, as some historians have, that the outbreak of the Second World War took place with the beginning of the Ethiopian war.[1] Indeed, armed confrontation in former Abyssinia did not stop when the Italian troops entered Addis Ababa and Mussolini 'founded' the Italian Empire in May of 1936.[2] Only two months after this event, a group of Spanish officers executed a coup d'état in the Second Republic that sparked civil war in the Iberian Peninsula. This conflict was quickly internationalized. When the Spanish Civil War came to an end in April of 1939, Europe was already set on the path towards another great war, which would officially start within a few months. These three sequential wars were the product of different but highly interconnected dynamics driven by fascism. Therefore, the circle of violence that emerged from the end of the Great War and led to a new international armed conflict can be considered closed by 1935–6. In previous chapters I explained the role of the relationship between veterans and fascism in closing this circle.

There are two principal justifications for continuing our analysis beyond this period and into the early 1940s. First, the Ethiopian war allows us to see how the long relationship between Italian Fascism and the war veterans reached its peak in organizational and symbolic terms. I will assess whether Italian Fascism successfully perfected a totalitarian relationship with the veterans in the ideally fascist context of war. The 'fascist' wars of Ethiopia and Spain amplified the transnational confrontation between fascism and anti-fascism. For this reason, I will also

---

[1] Zaude Hailemariam, 'La vera data d'inizio della seconda guerra mondiale', in Angelo Del Boca (ed.), *Le guerre coloniali del fascismo*, Bari, Laterza, 2008, pp. 288–313.

[2] Angelo Del Boca, *La guerra d'Abissinia 1935–1941*, Milan, Feltrinelli, 1965; Matteo Dominioni, *Lo sfascio dell'impero. Gli italiani in Etiopia 1936–1941*, Rome-Bari, Laterza, 2008.

examine the anti-fascist attempts to break the supposed fascist monopoly of veteran politics in Europe in the second half of the 1930s. At that time, the fascist veterans continuously manipulated the transnational symbol of the ex-soldier whilst also trying to influence the political orientation of veterans living in non-fascist countries (i.e. France) through new international veterans' organizations and contacts.

The second justification for this chapter is that by 1939 and 1940, the fascist model of veteran politics had been effectively transferred, albeit with some adaptations, to two countries: Spain and France. This outcome was the culmination of the long history of the use of the myth of the fascist veteran in Italian foreign affairs and the result of the free circulation of this myth throughout Western Europe. The established relationship between veterans and fascism not only contributed to the provocation of wars, but it also therefore significantly contributed to the establishment of new fascist or authoritarian regimes in other European countries.

The Fascist Veterans and the Ethiopian War

The Ethiopian war was, first and foremost, a fascist war for empire.[3] It was fought by more than 200,000 Italian soldiers who arrived in the region and successfully waged their campaign there thanks to a huge logistical operation. The fascist regime attained its military objectives within seven months due to the Italian technical superiority and because of the use of modern war weapons – such as poison gas – with no regard for the enemy, who were considered to be inferior race. This war seemed like it would be an important victory for the fascist regime in terms of foreign policy.[4] In reality, it was a 'hollow success' that brought new problems and international tensions.[5] The League of Nations condemned the Italian aggression and imposed a set of economic sanctions. Yet, instead of impeding Italy's ability to wage war, the international sanctions contributed to a heightening of the emotional climate of nationalist, warlike exaltation and totalitarian mobilization that characterized the country at the time.

The role of the Italian fascist veterans in the origin, development and aftermath of the Ethiopian war is noteworthy. They not only helped to create a favourable foreign opinion about the war, particularly among French veterans – as we saw – but also contributed substantially to the

---

Nicola Labanca, *Una guerra per l'impero: Memorie della campagna d'Etiopia 1935–36*, Bologna, il Mulino, 2005.
De Felice, *Mussolini il duce, I.*, p. 642.   [5] Burgwyn, *Italian Foreign Policy*, pp. 125–44.

war propaganda and discretely to the military effort. New fascist and colonial functions were assigned to the fresh batch of veterans from the Ethiopian war. And the ritualized demobilization of the troops shows us how Fascism continued to use the image of the victorious soldier at that particular time of fascist evolution towards totalitarianism.

Participating in propaganda campaigns was the main activity of the fascist veterans during the war. Immediately after the campaign started, the ANC journal changed its title to *L'Italia combattente–L'Italia grigio-verde (The Fighting Italy)*, and more importantly, all the rest of the provincial ANC newspapers were suppressed.[6] The justification that was offered was the necessity to restrict consumption. This further limitation of the veterans' expression was another step towards totalitarianism. The ANC journal became basically one more mouthpiece for the regime's war propaganda. The ANC's main leader, Amilcare Rossi, was appointed director of the journal, and his numerous articles, written in an obscure, convoluted rhetoric, would echo the regime's propagandistic discourse. At that point, the veterans' association changed its activity and started collecting gold and medals from its members to be donated for the war effort. One of the first measures was asking the veterans to return their old inter-Allied medals, deemed to have lost their moral value after the League of Nations introduced the sanctions.[7] The ANC leaders also revoked war insurance policies for the veterans and used the funds to contribute to financing the war. Thus, in a few months, more than 7 million lira were transferred from the ANC to the Duce; and one year after the beginning of the war, the total amount collected by the ANC in the form of veterans' war insurance policies was 16 million lira.[8] If in the previous decade the ANC had basically assured medals and benefits to the Italian veterans, now they were forced to return this capital to the regime. Furthermore, the ANC provincial leaders made sure that veterans joined demonstrations in support of the combatant troops.[9] There were also veterans from the ANC among those who were fighting in the campaign.

Some Italian veterans of the Great War fought again in Ethiopia, embodying the Fascism-driven closed circle of war violence from 1919 to 1935. It is known that the soldiers that Mussolini sent to conquer the empire came from the oldest classes, since the regime did not want to debilitate the army in the Italian peninsula.[10] Only a portion of the military contingent was voluntary, and unemployment and poverty were

---

[6] *L'Italia combattente. L'Italia grigio-verde* (Rome), 20–1 (15–30 November 1935).
[7] *Ibid.*   [8] *Ibid.*, 1–2 (15–30 January 1936) and 18 (15 October 1936).
[9] *Ibid.*, 5 (15 March 1936).   [10] Labanca, *Una guerra per l'impero*, p. 59.

common reasons to volunteer. Yet, members of the fascist militia, the MVSN, also joined the campaign. One of the fascist military units, the 'Tevere' Division, was composed of four legions – one of veterans, another of disabled veterans, and two more with members of the Fasci all'Estero. The total number of veterans who enrolled for the fascist war is difficult to assess. It was claimed that one of the two battalions that formed the veterans' legion of the 'Tevere' Division included 524 ex-soldiers of the Great War.[11] Even if the total number of veterans serving in Oriental Africa numbered a few thousands (66,000 according to subsequent fascist propaganda),[12] it was a very small group with respect to the total military contingent during the campaign and in comparison to the number of ANC members, and indeed the number pales in comparison to the vast number of Italian Great War veterans.

Even though the participation of veterans in the Ethiopian war was reduced, a seven-month war was enough for Fascism to forge a new stock of experienced combatants. Mussolini wanted to create 'new men' out of the fascist war, though reality did not match this expectation. Only certain elite fascist soldiers understood and experienced the Ethiopian war in line with fascist ideology. Former squadrists and fascist cadres believed that they were continuing the fascist revolution in Africa.[13] Either way, both the men who remained in the conquered land and those who returned to Italy became instruments of the fascist regime.

After Mussolini's grandiose proclamation that the empire had been founded, the heroization of the victorious soldiers followed, through a set of discourses and rituals. The combatants of Ethiopia were represented as having renewed the spirit of the equally triumphant soldiers of the Great War.[14] In fascist rhetoric, 'the fallen soldiers, disabled veterans and ex-combatants of the African enterprise' had 'avenged the sacrifice and realized the hope of the 670,000 dead, 470,000 mutilated and 3 million fighters of the Great War.'[15] From the beginning of July 1936, the returning troops who arrived at the ports of Naples, Livorno or Genoa and the train stations of Rome and Florence were welcomed by cheerful, deferential crowds singing hymns and throwing flowers and by the authorities who depicted them as heroes.[16] In the climate of enthusiasm, the PNF decided to offer party membership to some returning volunteers.[17]

---

[11] *VI. Divisione Camicie Nere 'Tevere'. Il 219. battaglione cc. nn. in Africa Orientale*, Rome, 1937.
[12] *L'Italia combattente. L'Italia grigio-verde*, 23 (31 December 1940).
[13] Labanca, *Una guerra per l'impero*, pp. 73–225.   [14] *Il Popolo d'Italia*, 24 May 1936.
[15] *L'Italia combattente. L'Italia grigio-verde*, 9 (15 May 1936).
[16] For example, see *Il Popolo d'Italia*, 21 July and 18 August 1936.
[17] *La Nazione* (Florence), 9 July 1936.

Taking into account all this pride-inducing rhetoric and political measures, one might ask why the veterans from Ethiopia did not form any new particular veterans' organizations. Historian Nicola Labanca has advanced some arguments to explain this absence.[18] According to him, the few months of Ethiopian war experience were not comparable with the long-term suffering of Great War soldiers. Prior to the Ethiopian war, the Italian colonial campaigns in Africa had not produced any veterans' movements. Furthermore, Labanca points out that Mussolini would not have been interested in any renewed veterans' movements at that time because the regime hoped to reinforce the threatening image of fixed bayonets, not old ex-combatants. But the actual fate of the Ethiopian veterans under Fascism has remained rather unknown by historians until now.

The truth is that the veterans from Ethiopia were incorporated into the ANC and therefore were symbolically amalgamated with the Great War veterans. The regime took this decision in October of 1936 after a request from ANC leaders.[19] It was in consonance with the 'unitary and totalitarian function of the ANC' that the veterans from 'all victories' would be part of the same organization.[20] With this absorption, the fascists wanted to check the proliferation of uncontrolled veterans' groups. The insistence in the instructions of the ANC leaders in this respect shows that they pursued this goal very seriously. They made sure that the new veterans had devotedly served, even obtained some distinction in combat (medal, injury or mutilation), before being admitted to the association. The ANC also stipulated that combat volunteers were allowed to wear the emblem of the *arditi*.[21] In contrast, the ANC refused to affiliate labourers who had gone to the Horn of Africa and come back to Italy without combat experience.[22] Non-combatants might have envied the privileged position of the returning soldiers, even though there is evidence to believe that by July of 1937 the problem of unemployment still affected many of the veterans.[23] The combat veterans from Ethiopia gained access to benefits and privileges by joining the fascist ANC. But in the fascist plans, the war-experienced men were expected to continue serving Fascism, and the fascist leaders assigned them further functions.

In the fascist colonial dream, Ethiopia was a new and fertile land that would provide agricultural products for the autarchic empire; the

---

[18] Labanca, *Una guerra per l'impero*, pp. 217–18.   [19] *Il Popolo d'Italia*, 22 October 1936.
[20] *L'Italia combattente. L'Italia grigio-verde*, 18 (15 October 1936).
[21] *Ibid.*, 19 (31 October 1936).   [22] *Ibid.*, 6 (31 March 1937).
[23] Reports from the *prefettura* of Florence (1 June and 22 July 1937), ACS, MI, PS (G1), box 32, file 264, 'Volontari Guerra Associazione'.

veterans were seen as the archetype of the colonizer. The military conquerors of the region were viewed as settlers, and indeed, many of the soldiers were southern Italian peasants aspiring to own land. At the beginning of July 1936, the Army's High Command in Africa decreed that the soldiers – from the 1911 class and older – who found employment in Ethiopia would be immediately discharged.[24] They were also obliged to join the MVSN. Thus, the regime expected to give employment to 100,000 veterans whilst maintaining an armed force in the colony. After his return from Ethiopia in June of 1936, the fascist leader of the ANC, Amilcare Rossi, who had gone to war with the 'Tevere' Division,[25] elaborated a vague colonizing project. According to him, the veterans would assume a new mission: expansion of the Italian nation in Ethiopia and the agricultural exploitation of this land. In November of 1936, during the Tenth National Council of the ANC in Littoria, Rossi talked about the wealth and vastness of the new territory, predicting that Italian peasants would slowly colonize it. For this reason, he said, the next ANC National Council should be celebrated there. In reality, however, the colonization through peasant-soldiers was doomed to failure. According to fascist statements, of the 12,000 'volunteers' of the 'Tevere' Division, 5,000 requested to remain in Eastern Africa.[26] Yet, of the more than 200,000 veterans in Ethiopia, only 13,881 decided to stay. The result of the project was a failure, and Ethiopians resisted by constantly raiding settlements.[27]

Veterans and the Crisis of Anti-Fascism and Pacifism

One of the consequences of the Ethiopian war was a period of disorientation and demoralization for anti-fascists and pacifists in Italy and France. It is important to note that anti-fascism and pacifism were never interchangeable concepts, despite the numerous links between them. Pacifism should not be confused with non-violence nor with anti-militarism. In France, after the First World War, a traditional conception of pacifism understood as the international rule of law had been progressively eclipsed by a more radical, integral view of pacifism.[28] In this

---

[24] *Il Popolo d'Italia*, 9 July 1936.
[25] Amilcare Rossi, *Dalle Alpi alle Ambe*, Rome, 1937; id., *Figlio del mio tempo*, pp. 127–9.
[26] *La Nazione* (Florence), 30 May 1936.
[27] Alberto Sbacchi, *Il colonialismo italiano in Etiopia, 1936–1940*, Milan, Mursia, 1980, pp. 257–66. See also Fabienne Le Houreou, *L'Épopée des soldats de Mussolini en Abyssinie 1936–1938: Les 'Ensablés'*, Paris, L'Harmattan, 1994.
[28] Norman Ingram, *The Politics of Dissent: Pacifism in France 1919–1939*, Oxford, Clarendon Press, 1991.

country, during the second half of the 1930s, more than 200 pacifist organizations maintained diverse approaches to the question of peace.[29] Most veterans' associations claimed to be in favour of peace, but their concrete political positions varied widely. Conservative veterans scorned the left for having turned its 'pacifism' into 'bellicosity' after 6 February 1934.[30] At the end of August 1935, the sudden death of Henri Barbusse, the communist 'combatant of peace', was another blow to the leftist veterans' groups, just when war seemed to be 'at their doorstep'.[31] To complicate this panorama, when the fascists invaded Ethiopia, traditionally bellicose political sectors such as Action Française declared themselves to be pacifists, not because they opposed this war but rather because they very much supported it. The French extreme right accused the left and the supporters of the League of Nations of wanting to provoke a war against Italy.[32] Obviously, this right-wing attitude was opportunistic and hypocritical. But even genuinely anti-fascist and pacifist organizations differentiated between internal anti-fascism and external pacifism, thereby giving free rein to fascist and Nazi expansionism.[33]

This double crisis of anti-fascism and pacifism was the origin of renewed attempts to redefine the symbol of the war veteran in *both* pacifist and anti-fascist terms. The confusion that riddled the French pacifists and anti-fascists could be detected in Italy as well. The swift and dramatically successful campaign in Ethiopia and popular enthusiasm among Italians puzzled and temporally discouraged the clandestine opposition.[34] Nonetheless, the communists directly appealed to the Italian veterans to organize the resistance against the new war; they questioned the alleged fascist convictions of the volunteers and even called on them to fraternize with the Ethiopians.[35] Paradoxically, the new fascist aggression, with all its exaltation of the soldier and the veteran, seems to have led these anti-fascists to place their hopes in the Italian veterans' anti-war sentiments as the detonator for a popular reaction against Fascism.[36] As the available evidence suggests, however, these hopes were quixotic. Nevertheless, use of the veteran symbol with anti-fascist and pacifist objectives is worthy of analysis. During the second half of the

[29] *Ibid.*, p. 1.   [30] *La Voix du Combattant*, 24 August 1935.
[31] *L'Humanité*, 2 and 8 September 1935.
[32] Jacques Delarue, 'La guerra d'Abissinia vista dalla Francia: Le sue ripercussioni nella politica interna', in Del Boca (ed.), *Le guerre coloniali del fascismo*, pp. 317–39.
[33] Ingram, *The Politics of Dissent*, pp. 179–222; see also Pierre Laboire, *L'opinion française sous Vichy*, Paris, Seuil, 1990, pp. 88–109.
[34] De Felice, *Mussolini il Duce, I.*, pp. 768–73.
[35] *L'Unità. Organo del Partito Comunista d'Italia* (clandestine edition), 1, undated (1935?).
[36] *Ibid.*, 12, undated (1935?).

1930s, and especially after the Spanish Civil War broke out, the fascist symbolic appropriation of the war veteran came under attack from certain groups.

Different initiatives to challenge the fascist symbolic appropriation of the war veteran came from Italians abroad. In November of 1935, a group of Italians residing in New York launched a call for the formation of an Association of Anti-Fascist Italian Veterans of New York and Surroundings. They introduced themselves as men who had 'worn the green-grey' uniform and had made a promise to themselves never to let the sacrifices and horrors of war happen again. Now, a 'mad governor' in their country had 'dishonoured' the Italian 'race' by attacking the Ethiopian people. The veterans rebelled against this dishonour, aspiring fraternity among all men. They had fought and confronted dangers and horrors on the battlefield, and now they were 'the vanguard of an international army that demanded peace, justice and liberty'. Remembering 600,000 dead soldiers, they called for 'Peace, Peace, Peace!'.[37] This rhetoric reminds us of the fascist and Mussolinian discursive repertory ('race', invoking the fallen soldiers, 'the vanguard of ...', etc.), but they introduced key pacifist and democratic elements ('liberty', 'fraternity', etc.) to make an anti-fascist appeal. As we know, mythologizing narratives about veterans could be reworked to serve different aims, and this is exactly what some anti-fascist veterans were doing.

These kinds of small and splintered groupings of pacifist or anti-fascist veterans began to proliferate in France, joined by Italian exiles and migrants. The pacifist Silvio Schettini was the leader of an Italian association of veterans based in Paris. A similar cell appeared in Brussels in January of 1936 with a distinctive leftist orientation. This so-called Belgian-Italian Association of Veterans (Association Belgo-Italienne des Anciens Combattants) counted about thirty members and held weekly meetings. They were veterans who 'loved their country' and wanted to overthrow Fascism in order to establish 'a proletarian government'. Anarchist exiles rejected the invitation to join this organization, since they did not want to take part in a group that relived the war. The fascist authorities monitored this Belgian group and noticed that they had contacts with the anti-fascist veterans in France.[38] Confronting the wide European network of fascist veterans, a web of contacts among anti-fascist veterans was trying to emerge.

---

[37] ACS, MI, PS (G1), box 309, file 1081, 'Stati Uniti Associazione Sovversiva Ex combattenti'.
[38] ACS, MI, PS (G1), box 310, file 1106, 'Belgio Associazione ex combattenti antifascisti'.

The struggle over the symbol of the veteran, which was complexly linked to the idea of peace, was determined by the rapidly evolving European context. During the Ethiopian war, the climate of civil confrontation progressively worsened in France, whilst in Spain the political situation became extremely polarized and agitated.[39] In January of 1936, the French government decreed the dissolution of some paramilitary leagues, and shortly after, the pro-Italian Prime Minister Pierre Laval was obliged to resign. In February of 1936, the Spanish republican and leftist coalition known as the Popular Front (Frente Popular) won the national elections, and a period of social unrest followed. The Spanish fascist party Falange Española grew significantly, whilst the anti-republican military conspired to prepare a coup d'état. In May of 1936, it was the turn of the French Popular Front (Front Populaire) to win the elections. At virtually the same time, Italian troops entered Addis Ababa.

It is interesting to track the French veterans' political evolution during this period of change. One of the first measures of the Front Populaire was the dissolution of the Croix de Feu. At that time, the UNC, lured by the fascist-inspired mystique, had multiple friendly contacts and interactions with this extreme-right league.[40] The pages of the UNC journal exalted the fascist empire.[41] Hence, the UNC's aggressive attitude against the Front Populaire is not surprising. Many UNC veterans joined the Parti Social Français (PSF), the new party that Croix de Feu leader Colonel La Rocque, founded in reaction to the ban on the Croix de Feu. The PSF would rapidly become the largest party in France. Unsurprisingly defined as fascist by the left, the PSF was a significant threat to the main democracy of the Continent, though it was in fierce competition with other extreme-right parties.[42] However, in the case of the UF, there were no clear connections with the extreme right. Nevertheless, the 'patriotic pacifism' of UF veterans cannot be considered anti-fascist, even though they bitterly criticized the fascist breach of international law.[43]

The outbreak of the Spanish Civil War complicated the profound realignment of politics in France and Spain, two countries within Fascist Italy's sphere of geostrategic interest. At the end of July 1936, after the

---

[39] Rafael Cruz, *En el nombre del pueblo: República, rebelión y guerra en la España de 1936*, Madrid, Siglo XXI, 2006.
[40] Millington, *From Victory to Vichy*, pp. 123–9.
[41] *La Voix du Combattant*, 25 July and 1 August 1936.
[42] Kennedy, *Reconciling France*, pp. 120–56.
[43] See, for example, René Cassin, 'La France combattante et la paix', *Cahiers de l'Union Fédérale* (Paris), 20 April 1936.

swift request of Franco – one of the rebel leaders – both Hitler and Mussolini decided to send military help. German and Italian aircraft allowed the Spanish rebels to initiate a military offensive on Madrid. On both sides of the divided country there were hundreds of political assassinations. The rebels, assisted by Falangist volunteers, imposed a bloody regime of terror. In Catalonia and other parts of the country, revolutionaries held power, and the republican authorities lost control of the situation for several months. While nothing really impeded the Nazi and fascist support for the rebels, the initial intention of French Prime Minister Leon Blum to help the Spanish republicans was thwarted by the right's fierce opposition. The long Spanish Civil War constituted another source of division in French society.[44] In general, the French veteran movement advocated non-intervention and therefore narrowed the scope of its pacifism to the maintenance of peace within France. In contrast, French anti-fascists advocated for intervention in Spain in the name of international peace.

At this crucial international conjuncture, the fascists and Nazis turned once again to the veteran connection to exert influence abroad, employing pseudo-pacifist discourses. During the months prior to the Spanish Civil War, whilst the Italians conquered their empire, the Nazi veterans publicly declared their commitment to peace. Through this policy, the Nazis were taking advantage of the French veterans' priority of maintaining peaceful and friendly relations with Germany. Following this course of action, during the first half of 1936, Henri Pichot, leader of the UF, met and corresponded with Hans Oberlindober, leader of the NSKOV. The Germans also paid a visit to London, meeting the British Legion and thus enhancing the Germanophile stance of the British veterans. These kinds of contacts led to the international meeting on the former battlefield of Verdun in mid-July of 1936. There the Nazi veterans, together with French, British and comrades from other countries, 'swore to conserve and to desire peace'.[45] The Nazi commitment to this oath, taking into account the date of the partisan German intervention in the Spanish Civil War, lasted roughly ten days.

Just as Nazi Germany and Fascist Italy coincided in their masked, albeit indisputable intervention in Spain, they also harmoniously entangled their veteran foreign politics. The Nazi veterans maintained their hypocritical discourse of peace, and over the following months, they continued receiving friendly visits from French veteran leaders such as

---

[44] David Wingeate Pike, *France Divided: The French and the Civil War in Spain*, Portland, Sussex Academic Press, 2011.
[45] *Völkischer Beobachter*, 14 July 1936.

Pichot and Héraud.[46] The Italian fascist veterans dedicated themselves thoroughly to the same discursive strategy. Moreover, the fascists decided to create a new organization to control the veterans' international contacts. In this fashion, they tried to monopolize the proliferating discourses about peace. It is important to note that this manoeuvre took place shortly after creation of the Non-Intervention Committee. This committee was designed to isolate war within Spain but only served to suffocate the Spanish republicans whilst the fascist powers continued assisting the rebels.

The first fascist step in this direction was to regain influence over existing international veterans' organizations. As we know, since 1929, the FIDAC had ceased to represent the real fascist interests in foreign policy. During September of 1936, both FIDAC and CIAMAC congresses took place. First, the FIDAC Congress was held in Warsaw, in Pilsudski's Poland, with the participation of representatives from the ex-Allied nations. The French travelling to Poland used the occasion to pay another visit to NSKOV leader Hans Oberlindober. At the congress, an anti-leftist and conditional understanding of peace prevailed. The most important consequence of the congress was that the fascist Carlo Delcroix, leader of the ANMIG, was elected the new president of the FIDAC.[47] It was the second time during the inter-war period that the presidency of the FIDAC fell to a fascist member. Furthermore, the delegates agreed to continue their conversations *in Rome* during the following month, *outside* the framework of the FIDAC and CIAMAC, and *with participation of German representatives*.[48] All these unprecedented decisions were aimed at a rapprochement with the German former enemies, an outcome that fully corresponded with fascist interests. Thus, it is not surprising that the Italian disabled veterans openly ignored the CIAMAC conference in Copenhagen; so too did the Germans and Austrians. This international organization was deemed to be dominated by a 'prevalent socialist-mason tendency'.[49] Obtaining control of the FIDAC had been an important move.

At the same time, the Non-Intervention Committee held its inaugural meeting in London, although soon it became clear that it would not serve to stop the internationalization of the Spanish Civil War. The Soviet Union withdrew from the committee. Anti-fascist and communist

---

[46] Trichet, *Henri Pichot et l'Allemagne, passim*; id., 'La propagande nazie'; *Völkischer Beobachter*, 24 November 1936 and 23 September 1937.
[47] *Il Popolo d'Italia*, 5 September 1936.   [48] *La Voix du Combattant*, 19 September 1936.
[49] AMAE, Società delle Nazioni 1919–1932, box 66, file 'CIAMAC'.

volunteers from different parts of the world, but mainly from France, were arriving in Spain, where the carnage continued.

As proof of the widespread belief that the European expansion of fascism could only be stopped by armed force, the foreign anti-fascist volunteers in Spain joined the International Brigades, supported by the Komintern. The total number of volunteers has been estimated at 35,000.[50] According to George L. Mosse, a romantic myth of the war experience inspired these fighters.[51] This idealistic understanding of the Spanish Civil War represented a counter-model to the fascist glorification of war in and of itself. It demonstrates that by 1936 the heroic image of the combatant did not pertain exclusively to the fascists or to right-wing nationalists. The German anti-fascist volunteers formed the Thälmann Brigade, named after the communist and decorated war veteran who had been the leader of the RFB and who was at that time imprisoned by the Nazis. In this sense, it is interesting to note that, motivated by an anti-communist version of the idealization of war, only around 1,000 to 1,500 international volunteers came to Spain to fight for Franco.[52] However, if anti-fascists contested the symbol of the combatant, were the fascists able to keep their transnational symbolic hegemony over the veterans?

With the objective of dominating veteran politics, the fascists employed the same old tactic of discursive manipulation and organizational guile that they had always used. In the strained international conjuncture, the fascists reacted swiftly. The next key event was the veterans' meeting in Rome, on 7 November 1936.[53] By that date, in Spain, Franco's troops had arrived at the gates of Madrid. Nazi Germany and Fascist Italy had substantially increased their military aid to the rebels. A few days later, the International Brigades experienced combat for the first time, successfully defending the Republican capital. Meanwhile, at Palazzo Venezia, Mussolini received veterans' representatives from fourteen European nations, including Germany and the United States. The veterans' meeting was the occasion to launch a new Permanent International Committee of Veterans (Comitato Permanente Internazionale dei Combattenti (CIP)) presided over by Carlo Delcroix.

---

[50] Rémi Skoutelsky, *Novedad en el frente: Las brigadas internacionales en la guerra civil*, Madrid, Temas de Hoy, 2006.

[51] Mosse, *Fallen Soldiers*, pp. 185–95.

[52] Judith Keene, *Fighting for Franco: International Volunteers in Nationalist Spain during the Spanish Civil War, 1936–39*, London, Leicester University Press, 2001.

[53] *Il Popolo d'Italia*, 8 November 1936; *Deutsche Kriegsopferversorgung: Monatschrift der Frontsoldaten und Kriegsopfer der National-Sozialistischen Kriegsopferversorgung (NSKOV)* (Berlin), 4 (January 1937).

The representative from Nazi Germany to the CIP was the Duke of Saxe-Coburg, who had been appointed by Hitler as the head of the surviving German veterans' associations and was – according to Nazi sources – the author of the idea of creating the CIP.[54] For the first time, an international organization of First World War veterans was bringing together fascist and Nazi veterans under the hegemony of Fascism.

The fascists and the Nazis hastened to put the CIP to work for their interests. Rapidly, Carlo Delcroix prepared the statutes of the new institution secretly destined to supplant the old international veterans' platforms.[55] The declared aims of the CIP were, firstly, to strengthen the relations among veterans from all the nations; secondly, to ensure that the veterans' moral force would serve the rapprochement and collaboration of the different nations; and finally, to promote in all countries 'the spirit of understanding and solidarity which is the basis for the maintenance of peace'.[56] In record time, another congress was organized, which would take place in Berlin.[57] On 15 February 1937, Göring welcomed more than fifty international delegates. He reminded them, unoriginally, that having experienced the horrors of war, they were the guarantors of peace. The poet Carlo Delcroix was more imaginative; he argued that if war was necessary, it was sacred, but if it was avoidable, it was a crime.[58] Unsurprisingly, the delegates confirmed Delcroix as president. As Amilcare Rossi later reported, some opposition from certain delegates of democratic nations arose, but they were silenced, and thus, the institution consolidated on a 'totalitarian basis'.[59] Then the delegates went to visit Hitler in Berchtesgaden and publicly declared the necessity of defending peace.[60]

The CIP became the barefaced instrument of the Rome-Berlin Axis, whilst the war in Spain continued successfully in favour of the fascist powers. The next meeting of the CIP took place again in Rome in April of 1937. There Delcroix dared to say that until then, the institutions dedicated to the maintenance of peace had, in fact, exacerbated the misunderstanding between nations.[61] Some weeks later, in Spain, the German Condor Legion bombed Guernica.[62] By this time, the Italian

---

[54] *Völkischer Beobachter* (Munich), 9 November 1936.
[55] *L'Italia combattente. L'Italia grigio-verde*, 2 (31 January 1937).
[56] *Il Popolo d'Italia*, 3 January 1937.
[57] *Völkischer Beobachter* (Munich), 13, 15, 16 and 17 February 1937.
[58] *Il Popolo d'Italia*, 16 February 1937.
[59] *L'Italia combattente. L'Italia grigio-verde*, 4 (28 February 1937).
[60] *Il Popolo d'Italia*, 18 February 1937; *Völkischer Beobachter* (Berlin), 18 February 1937.
[61] *L'Italia combattente. L'Italia grigio-verde*, 7 (15 Abril 1937).
[62] On the Legion Condor, see Stephanie Schüler-Springorum, *Krieg und Fliegen: Die Legion Condor im Spanischen Bürgerkrieg*, Paderborn, Ferdinand Schöningh, 2010.

'voluntary' troops that Mussolini had been sending to Spain since January of 1937 numbered 50,000 men.[63] In Francoist Spain, there was a process of amalgamation of anti-republican sectors leading to the formation of the fascist unified party Falange Española Tradicionalista y de las JONS (FET-JONS). In contrast, within the Spanish republic, internal disputes provoked violent clashes between communists and anarchists in Barcelona. By now it was clear that the Non-Intervention Committee was a complete farce. Similarly, the CIP only benefitted the fascist powers, as it became clear on a number of occasions.

In October of 1937, the FIDAC Congress in Paris confirmed that the responsibility for advancing towards an international entente was now in the hands of the fascist-dominated Permanent Committee. At this point, the FIDAC's main concern was simply to maintain friendship among the former Allied countries. In his speech, outgoing FIDAC President Delcroix justified his efforts to make a rapprochement with the former enemies. He also described the kind of peace that the veterans should construct – neither a peace that repudiated sacrifice nor one of oppression that ignored the necessities of other nations. Instead, Delcroix praised a 'militant' peace 'of dignity and justice' after 'having set the conditions for its existence'.[64] Implicitly, Delcroix was talking of a peace conditioned by the priority of the imperial and territorial expansion of the fascist powers. The idea of peace that the fascists were defending at the international veterans' meetings was one subservient to the idea of international justice,[65] though this conception of justice was concealing their intention of redesigning the map of Europe and the world in accordance with the fascist and Nazi wishes. Some weeks later, the fascists would have yet another opportunity to defend their position at an international veterans' meeting.

Held in Paris between November and December of 1937, the first official CIP Congress marked an important victory for the fascist veterans.[66] Among the French delegates were Henri Pichot and Jean Goy, whilst Oberlindober was part of the German delegation.[67] The

[53] John F. Coverdale, *Italian Intervention in the Spanish Civil War*, Princeton, NJ, Princeton University Press, 1975.
[54] *L'Italia combattente. L'Italia grigio-verde*, 18 (15 October 1937). Due to a gap in the sources, I have examined the activities of the congress through *Le Combattant des Deux-Sèvres. Organe des combattants ... Organe de l'Union nationale des combattants* (Niort), 210 (November 1937); see also *Cahiers de l'Union Fédérale* (Paris), 20 October 1937.
[55] See the replies of Delcroix and Rossi to Henri Pichot's survey about the peace in *Cahiers de l'Union Fédérale*, 20 November 1937.
[56] The minutes of the congress in National Archives (Kew), FO370/529, L 164.
[57] *La Voix du Combattant*, 4 December 1937; *Cahiers de l'Union Fédérale*, 10 December 1937.

representatives from the United States were the only ones to decline participation, correctly understanding that the meeting corresponded with the interests of the dictatorships. Carlo Delcroix, in his confidential report written for the Italian Ministry of Foreign Affairs, considered that the withdrawal of the American Legion was a consequence of Jewish pressure. In general, though, Delcroix was delighted with the good result of the congress. The unenthusiastic French government had been unable to oppose it, and 'for the first time the German flag had appeared in a parade through the streets of Paris.' Delcroix considered 'useful that in the capital of masonry, Judaism and Socialism, the spirit and style of fascism were affirmed, in a meeting of veterans from across Europe, to whom we have taught to what extent and in which tone the soldiers may talk about peace'.[68] Since the messages sent to the French authorities at the end of the meeting captured the fascist views on peace, Delcroix celebrated that in only one year they had succeeded in affirming the principles, methods and style of fascism in veteran diplomacy. At the congress, there had even been cordial conversations about the need to 'suppress every other organization, starting with the [FIDAC]'.[69] And the fascists also prepared the terrain to make sure that the next president of the Permanent Committee would be the Duke of Saxe-Coburg – the Nazi representative. Delcroix insisted that the organization should not 'escape from the hands of its founders, in order to prevent the moral force of the veterans from becoming subjugated to the socialist politics of the so-called democracies'.[70] The fascists not only continued to try to monopolize the symbol of the veteran in the international sphere and to control the organizations, but they also misappropriated the discourse about peace.

A few days after this meeting in Paris, Mussolini announced to the world that Italy was withdrawing from the League of Nations. The Duce had recently visited Germany, and now the foreign policies of both countries started to clearly and publicly converge. As we have seen, the veteran connections played a role in the evolution towards the formation of the Rome-Berlin Axis. The developing anti-French military threat coming from Germany and Italy was fairly clear for the French left, and the terrible events taking place in Spain corroborated this threat. During this time, for most French leftists, war and fascism fused into one menace, and fighting against fascism in Spain meant fighting for peace and democracy.

---

[68] AMAE, Società delle Nazioni 1919–1932, box 66, file 'Comitato internazionale permanente dei combattenti'.
[69] Ibid.   [70] Ibid.

Despite these disheartening events, sectors of anti-fascism did not renounce the symbol of the veteran. However, anti-fascist and pacifist veterans in France were not united. In November of 1937, the French League of Pacifist Veterans, headed by socialist MP and veteran Camille Planche, launched an appeal to Italian veterans to create a unique anti-war and anti-fascist veterans' front. Actually, this new initiative competed against the communist-inspired veterans' associations. In any case, the chief concern was to divest the Italian veterans of their fascist stigma. One of the final lines of the call stated, 'It is false to say that all Italian veterans want to support the fascist regime!'.[71] Similarly, during 1938, the anti-fascist Association Franco-italienne des Anciens Combattants issued important propaganda to attract Italian veterans to their ranks, questioning the fascist promises to the veterans.[72] However, all these anti-fascist efforts show precisely the extent to which Fascism had monopolized the symbol of the veteran by 1938.

Fascist Italy, Francoist Spain and the Culmination of the Model

The case of Spain was the first in which the fascist model of veterans' politics was transferred into another country, contributing to the establishment of a dictatorship. The Spanish Civil War experience involved the arrival of fascist politics on the Francoist side, and the discourses and organizations for war veterans were no exception. Now, as a 'total' war experience was ending, Spanish fascism could construct a mass base of support composed of many men with combat records. In this section I will show that fascist veteran politics was a fundamental element in the incorporation of Francoist Spain into the wider phenomenon of transnational fascism. The state of war and the formation of the Axis were the key historical events in the process that enabled Fascist Italy's model of veteran politics reach its peak.

During the war, the fascist influence in Spain was not only military but also political. At the end of 1937, it became evident that Soviet help was not enough to sustain the republican counterattacks and that German and Italian military aid to Franco was enabling him to slowly win the war. This reality ensured that the fascist powers had a great reputation among the combatants on the rebel side. In March of 1938, the Francoists published a fundamental programmatic text, the *Fuero del Trabajo*,

---

[71] ACS, MI, PS (G1), box 320, file 1225, 'Associazione franco-italiana ex combattenti'.
[72] ACS, MI, PS (G1), box 315, file 1169, 'Ass. Franco-italiana excombattenti antifascisti'.

clearly inspired by the Italian regime.[73] In this text it was stated that after the war, the new Spain would give 'positions of work, honour and command' to the heroic young combatants. Notwithstanding the persistence of conservative military men in the power structures, the renewed fascist party, the FET-JONS, was attaining an important position of power. The ideological evolution of the anti-republican coalition during the war can be perfectly understood as a process of 'fascistization' (*fascistización*).[74] And the Falangists showed great interest in instilling their ideology into the combatants, something that was particularly evident in their own militia units. These combating soldiers were told about the 'National Syndicalist Revolution' (*Revolución Nacionalsindicalista*), yet loyalty to Franco – the Caudillo – was the key point.[75] Franco had nominated himself as head of the FET-JONS, while the founder of Falange, José Antonio Primo de Rivera, had been executed in a republican prison. Around 1.2 million men fought in the Francoist army. While the military preferred to protect its soldiers from excessive politicization, the FET-JONS saw the veterans as a potential group of trustworthy supporters.[76] They would be agents of the construction of the Spanish fascist regime.

Meanwhile, the war evolved towards a Francoist victory. The fate of the Spanish Second Republic was not so much decided on the battlefields as it was in the international conference of Munich in September of 1938. Earlier, in March of 1938, the Nazis had annexed Austria to the Third Reich, whilst German air support facilitated the sweeping Francoist offensive on the front at Aragon. Now faced with the Nazi intention to absorb the German-speaking portions of Czechoslovakia, France and Britain decided to maintain their policy of appeasement. Together with Mussolini, they signed the Munich Pact on 30 September, thus allowing the Germans to proceed with the occupation. British Legion veterans, indeed, had contributed substantially to reaching an agreement with the Nazis.[77] Opposition from the democratic countries would have probably meant war, and it was said that the agreement ensured peace. However, for the Spanish Second Republic, it was a death sentence, since it could

---

[73] See Javier Tusell, *Franco en la guerra civil: Una biografía política*, Barcelona, Tusquets, 1992, pp. 256–64.

[74] Ferran Gallego, *El Evangelio fascista: La formación de la cultura política del franquismo (1930–1950)*, Barcelona, Crítica, 2014.

[75] See the brochure edited by the propaganda office of FET-JONS, 'Los combatientes y el Caudillo', Bilbao, 1938.

[76] Alcalde, *Los excombatientes franquistas*.

[77] Niall Barr, '"The Legion that Sailed but Never Went": The British Legion and the Munich Crisis of 1938', in Eichenberg and Newman (eds.), *The Great War and Veterans' Internationalism*, pp. 32–52.

no longer expect a general European conflict between democracies and fascist powers. This scenario would have allowed Spanish republicans to receive military help against Franco. Nothing hampered the constant inflow of support from the fascist powers to Franco, whilst the International Brigades had been withdrawn from Spain on the poor advice of the farcical Non-Intervention Committee.

In early 1939, contact between the Falangists and the fascists increased, whilst the Spanish Second Republic lay on its deathbed. These connections transcended the meetings between just a few important personalities and largely helped shape Francoist veteran politics. The FET-JONS created a network of headquarters abroad to maintain relations with the Nazis in Germany and the fascists in Italy.[78] Collaboration was closer with the latter country. In a climate of fascist friendship, some of the Italian soldiers of the Corpo di Truppe Volontarie became members of the FET-JONS during their stay in Spain.[79] Among them, there were a few old veterans of the Great War, who thus embodied the fascist ideal of eternal combatant.[80] Furthermore, relevant political representatives of the Francoist coalition visited Fascist Italy during the war. For example, during 1938, Millán Astray, co-founder – along with Franco – of the Spanish Legión and then leader of the Francoist organization of disabled veterans (the Benemérito Cuerpo de Mutilados de Guerra por la Patria), travelled to Italy along with José María Pemán, a conservative writer who developed the exalting mystique about the 'provisional junior officers' (alféreces provisionales) of the Francoist army.[81] Likewise, an important number of FET-JONS leaders visited Italy, learning first-hand about the functioning of a fascist regime. For example, José Antonio Girón, a young Falangist from Valladolid, who was a commander of fighting militia units, spent the last months of the Spanish Civil War in Italy as part of a political mission.[82] After the war, he would become the main leader of the Falangist organization for war veterans. Evidently, all these contacts contributed much to the institutional and political construction of Franco's regime, including the organizational structure for Spanish Civil War veterans.

[78] Eduardo González Calleja, 'El Servicio Exterior de Falange y la política exterior del primer franquismo: consideraciones previas para su investigación', Hispania. Revista española de historia, LIV/1, 186 (1994), pp. 279–307; Wayne H. Bowen, Spaniards and Nazi Germany: Collaboration in the New Order, Columbia, University of Missouri Press, 2000, pp. 22–55.

[79] AGA, DNSE, caja 51/20911, carpeta 'Excombatientes italianos'.

[80] AGA, DNSE, caja 51/20912, carpeta 'Afiliados extranjeros'.

[81] AMAE, Gabinetto del Ministro e del Segretario Generale 1923–1943, box 1217, file Us 6.

[82] José Antonio Girón, Si la memoria no me falla, Barcelona, 1994, pp. 44–7 and 56–8.

In ideological terms, the closeness to Fascist Italy resulted in a clear incorporation of fascist discourses into the Franco regime. As we know, since the early 1920s, some promoters of Falange, such as Rafael Sánchez Mazas and Ernesto Giménez Caballero, had admired Mussolini and the Italian fascists and emulated fascist culture. Both intellectuals would be figures of reference for the regime during the early 1940s. Falangist rituals and discourses of war were of fascist heritage; therefore, during the war, the exaltation of youth, the sacralization of violence and the cult of sacrifice and death became important elements of the Falangist ideology. Consequently, the Francoists also turned to the fascist model of discourse to approach the war veterans. Since 1938, the Francoist trench newspapers published articles insisting that after the war the soldiers were obliged to maintain their loyalty to the Caudillo and to transform themselves into obedient and selfless workers.[83] Not only the organizational structure, therefore, but also the discourses employed to address the war veterans in Francoist Spain had their origins in Fascist Italy.

The European context marked this long process of transfer, ending with the consolidation of the National Delegation of Veterans of the FET-JONS (Delegación Nacional de Excombatientes (DNE)), the key Francoist veterans' organization (Figure 6.1).[84] On 1 April 1939, with the republic defeated, Franco announced the end of the war, and a period of military and fascist celebrations followed. The Francoist authorities paid friendly homage to the German and Italian troops, and Spanish emissaries accompanied them on their return home. They were welcomed with great pomp and ceremony in Germany and Italy in a climate of soldierly brotherhood between the three countries. It was at this time that the Nazis and the fascists signed the Pact of Steel. The display of victorious combatants parading through Spanish, German and Italian cities was a warning to the rest of Europe. When Franco formed a new government in August of 1939, the fascists of the FET-JONS obtained important positions of power, and some sectors of the army fused with them. Falangist military officer Agustín Muñoz Grandes was appointed secretary general of the party. It was at this time that José Antonio Girón became the leader (*Delegado Nacional*) of the new

---

[83] Alcalde, *Los excombatientes franquistas*, pp. 84–9; see also Ángel Alcalde, 'Los excombatientes en el mundo rural de la posguerra: del mito del campesino soldado a la realidad social de la España franquista', in Óscar Rodríguez Barreira (ed.), *El franquismo desde los márgenes: Campesinos, mujeres, delatores, menores . . .*, Lleida-Almería, UdLl & UAL, 2013, pp. 113–29.

[84] Ángel Alcalde, 'Los orígenes de la Delegación Nacional de Excombatientes de FET-JONS: la desmovilización del ejército franquista y la Europa de 1939', *Ayer*, 97 (2015), pp. 169–94.

Figure 6.1 'At war, your blood. At peace, your work' – emblem and motto of the Delegación Nacional de Excombatientes.

Falangist organization for war veterans.[85] Francoist veteran policy was designed in a context of intense entanglement between the European fascist powers.

The setting up of the DNE was slow, but it was fully in line with the Italian example. If in Italy in November 1938 both the ANC and the ANMIG had officially become subordinate to the PNF,[86] in Spain, the DNE was directly created as a dependent organization of the FET-JONS. The Spanish army kept the disabled veterans' organization under control, but the organizational duality between disabled and non-disabled veterans was similar in Spain and Italy. The Nazis followed the same principle in Germany after Hitler decided, in March of 1938, that all veterans' organizations apart from the NSKOV would be fused into a National Socialist 'Kyffhäuser'.[87] The Spanish DNE was a totalitarian structure based on local and provincial cells subordinate to the national leadership, the same as the Italian ANC. As for the leaders, ex-officers coming from bourgeois backgrounds predominated in both the Spanish and Italian organizations. Moreover, the Spanish regime developed a system of material privileges for the veterans, reserving for them a significant quota of job vacancies, as had been the norm in Fascist Italy. In conclusion, the Francoist system

[5] Alcalde, *Los excombatientes franquistas*, pp. 139–55.
[6] *Il Popolo d'Italia*, 6 November 1938.   [87] Diehl, *The Thanks of the Fatherland*, p. 42.

of management of veterans' benefits with political objectives had a precedent in Fascist Italy.

The most striking similarities between the DNE and the ANC relate to the political discourse employed at that time. Both organizations insisted on the blind loyalty of the veterans to the Caudillo and the Duce. Both organizations exalted the alleged military virtues of the veterans: obedience and the will to sacrifice. The Italian fascists had employed this kind of discourse before, for example, during the worst years of the economic depression. In Spain, the economic conditions in the aftermath of war were no better. The situation of the defeated was appalling, suffering both hunger and political persecution. Apart from certain political elites who occupied positions of power at the local and provincial levels, the great majority of Francoist veterans were told to return silently to work. As was written in the main Falangist journal *Arriba*, the veterans should 'return to work wherever they were ordered, without any other demand than being the vanguard of this distressing moment'.[88] In Italy, Amilcare Rossi had employed exactly the same kind of discourse to explain what the duty of the veterans was – 'to work and to shut up', in line with the fascist consign 'believe, obey, fight'.[89] These discourses acquired prominence with the outbreak of the Second World War.

The Italian fascist model of veteran politics culminated during the period between the beginning of the Second World War and the Italian intervention in June of 1940. At this point, the fascist model became totalitarian in nature. What marked the context of this final development was the entanglement with Nazi Germany, including the fascist veterans' week-long visit to the Third Reich in June of 1939[90] and the friendship with the Spanish Falangists, exemplified by the huge metal wreath that Mussolini sent to Spain for the funeral of José Antonio Primo de Rivera in November of 1939.[91]

The fascist model of political organization of war veterans can be described as totalitarian because it implied elimination of the boundaries between the category of veteran and that of member of the fascist party. This fusion happened almost simultaneously in both Spain and Italy. The Spanish FET-JONS party was first to take the significant decision of opening party membership to all ex-combatants who had fought in

---

[88] *Arriba* (Madrid), 31 January 1940.
[89] *L'Italia Combattente. L'Italia Grigio-Verde*, 15 September 1939.
[90] Luigi E. Gianturco, *Sette giorni in Germania: Impressioni sul viaggio dei combattenti in Germania*, Milan, 1939.
[91] AMAE, Gabinetto del Ministro e del Segretario Generale 1923–1943, box 1217, file 'Sepoltura e onoranze spoglia JA Primo de Rivera all'Escuriale a Madrid - Novembre 1939'; *Arriba*, 2 December 1939.

the war. On 4 December 1939, FET-JONS Secretary General Agustín Muñoz Grandes signed a memorandum that awarded this right to veterans who applied for it.[92] Soon afterwards, in Italy, Mussolini took an equivalent decision, awarding all Italian veterans the right to become members of the PNF if they applied for it. On 7 December 1939, the ANC leaders visited the Duce to declare the immutable loyalty of the Italian veterans and to request that they be admitted to the PNF.[93] Mussolini immediately accepted. Significantly, the veterans would obtain membership in the PNF with seniority dating back to 3 March 1925, the date of the ANC *fascistizzazione*. Thus, Fascism was reaching the long-awaited symbolic and real fusion between the fascist and the veteran. According to the fascists, this amalgamation demonstrated that 'war and Fascism [were] two inseparable terms and factors'.[94]

What was the meaning of the direct integration of the veterans into the fascist parties? Firstly, it was a measure coherent with the radicalization of politics within the fascist regime and the Spanish dictatorship, as well as a reflection of the fascist ideological worldview. The fascists explained the adhesion of the war veterans from all the Italian 'victories' to the PNF as a 'truly totalitarian' measure.[95] In a pamphlet probably written by Amilcare Rossi, it was said that there could not be *combattentismo* outside Fascism and that the true combatant was necessarily fascist. Fascism was, in fact, 'a real army', the expression of the best of the nation; for this reason, Fascism must embrace the veterans. The signing up of veterans into the PNF matched all the requirements of morality and security because the fascists considered the veterans not only 'excellent citizens' but also 'faithful fascists'.[96] In their explanation of the measure, the fascists recalled the veterans' role in the origin of Fascism. Yet, the fascists had not undertaken the direct integration of veterans into the PNF until that point. It was only after nearly twenty years of propaganda and political violence that the fascists felt safe enough to consider any war veteran as a potential fascist militant without further scrutiny. By 1940, the fascists were fully convinced of the veterans' trustworthiness.

The fascists had other reasons to take the decision of considering all veterans as potential fascist militants. This measure not only served to recognize the veterans' fascist credentials but also served as a mechanism to attract more veterans to the fascist creed. Of course, being a member

[92] *Arriba*, 7 December 1939.   [93] *La Stampa*, 7 December 1939.
[94] *Il Popolo d'Italia*, 9 December 1939.
[95] Angelo Amico [Amilcare Rossi], *Il significato dell'ammissione dei combattenti nel Partito*, Caltanisetta, 1940.
[96] *Ibid.*

of the party implied benefits and privileges, and therefore, material interests probably motivated thousands of Italian veterans who joined the PNF at that time. In Italy, by 24 May 1940, the fascists claimed that more than 1 million veterans had asked to join the PNF.[97] At a moment when the state imposed the rationing of food,[98] being a member of the fascist party could be useful for survival. This situation was particularly decisive in Francoist Spain.[99] There starving veterans often begged the Falangist leaders for help.[100] The virtually totalitarian control of the media that characterized these fascist dictatorships makes it extremely difficult to examine the real opinions of the veterans, but the fascist organizational structures were able to perform their duties no matter what the intimate feelings of their members were. The fascist veteran discourse, both in Italy and in Spain, was created and delivered by a very restricted elite group of fascist leaders who were, in the end, mere megaphones for the regime's official discourse. Even in Nazi Germany, the veterans would be used for propaganda purposes during the war.[101] War veterans' organizations and discourses were perhaps put under total fascist control in Italy, Spain and Germany, but this process only converted veterans, by and large, into a purely symbolic reference, ready for the war propaganda, a mute pawn in the hands of fascist regimes.

Finally, merging fascists and veterans helped to bridge the gap between one war and another, creating a society constantly ready for war, which was what the fascists had wanted. Fascism was creating a system in which war service was rewarded in such a way that new sectors of the population would be prepared and willing to become combatants in subsequent wars, even if not necessarily sharing the fascist ideology. The whole fascist regime, with its multiple organizations and efforts at military education of the new generations, served this purpose, and the role of the fascist discourses and organizations for war veterans can be considered a crucial instrument to reach these goals. The actual extent to which the various regimes succeeded in this objective was neither total nor insignificant but rather somewhere in between.

Probably the level of fascist political commitment and ideological conviction among war veterans simply reflected that of society as a whole. 'Consent' to fascism cannot be separated from notions such as

---

[97] *L'Italia combattente. L'Italia grigio-verde*, 10 (31 May 1940).
[98] *Ibid.*, 2 (31 January 1940).
[99] Miguel Ángel del Arco, 'Hunger and the Consolidation of the Francoist Regime (1939–1951)', *European History Quarterly*, 40, 3 (2010), pp. 458–83.
[100] Alcalde, *Los excombatientes franquistas*, p. 169.
[101] Löffelbein, *Ehrenbürger der Nation*, pp. 414–37.

'coercion', 'collusion' and 'evasion'.[102] In June of 1940, Italians went to war again, and according to the fascists, more than 140,000 former veterans of the Great War served once more.[103] However, most of them were obliged to do so. In June of 1941, when the Germans attacked the Soviet Union, the FET-JONS organized a Spanish military unit to join the Russian campaign: the Blue Division. Thousands of Falangist young men joined it, thus obtaining the coveted condition of *excombatiente* following their eventual return.[104] Still, many Spanish soldiers were forced to fight in Russia, and hundreds of former leftists joined the endeavour in order to expiate an inconvenient political past.[105] All these nuances notwithstanding, the veterans had become a necessary symbolic link for the reproduction and military expansion of fascism.

Fascist and French Veterans and the Path towards Vichy France

France was the second case in which fascist veteran politics substantially contributed to the establishment of a dictatorship. On 17 June 1940, after the French Third Republic had collapsed in the face of the overwhelming German invasion and the opportunistic Italian attack, Marshall Pétain offered himself as the new governor of the country in his message to French citizens. Pétain invited the French to cease resistance against the invaders whilst stating that he was 'sure of the support of the war veterans whom he had the honour of commanding'. The French veterans, organized in the Légion Française des Combattants, would become one of the pillars of the new collaborationist Vichy regime. Even if both the Spanish and French republics were destroyed by war, the historical process by which a dictatorship was established in France was very different from the Spanish path towards a fascist-inspired regime. Correspondingly, the role of the veterans in this French evolution, though fundamental as in Spain, was also quite distinct. In the case of France, the fascist veterans had a very prominent role. Yet, one key factor operated in both cases: the influence of Fascist Italy.

My main argument here is that without the precedent of Fascist Italy and without the previous numerous contacts and exchanges established

---

[102] Alf Lüdtke (ed.), *Everyday Life in Mass Dictatorship: Collusion and Evasion*, New York, Palgrave Macmillan, 2016; Paul Corner (ed.), *Popular Opinion in Totalitarian Regimes: Fascism, Nazism, Communism*, Oxford University Press, 2009, pp. 8–9.

[103] *L'Italia combattente. L'Italia grigio-verde*, 23 (31 December 1940).

[104] Alcalde, *Los excombatientes franquistas*, pp. 171–8.

[105] José Luis Rodríguez Jiménez, *De héroes e indeseables: La División Azul*, Madrid, Espasa, 2007.

between relevant veteran elites from France and Italy, it would not have been possible to establish an authoritarian collaborationist regime in France with the participation of war veterans in 1940. The introduction of fascist-inspired veteran politics into France presents many particularities, for it was not only an adaptation but also the end of an endogenous French evolution.[106] Therefore, the transfer did not imply the creation of veterans' structures that would be directly equivalent to the Italian system, as had been the case in Spain. Previous unsuccessful attempts to unify veterans' organizations, comparable to the unification processes of British and American veterans' groups, must be taken into account. Yet, saying that the LFC was the natural and long-awaited culmination of the French veterans' desires for unification would be a fully teleological explanation not sustained by comparative or transnational analysis. The origin of the Légion Française des Combattants cannot be understood without the Italian fascist factor, and as an organization and political entity, it had much more to do with the fascist veterans' associations than with the British or American Legions. However, the transfer that we are uncovering also took place in the realm of discourses, practices and representations.

It may be surprising that adaptation of the fascist model of veteran politics to France culminated amidst a full rupture between French and Italian fascist veterans. The status of the bilateral relations between France and Italy provoked this break. In the advent of the Front Populaire, Italian-French relations had clearly cooled. With the intervention in Spain, the Italian-German alliance took shape, whilst Italy's ties with its 'Latin sister' France loosened. During 1937, the meetings between French and fascist veterans on French soil became occasions to reveal profound divergences, particularly with the UF. Even though UF leader Henri Pichot maintained cordial relations with the Nazi Oberlindober, the French veteran was critical of the totalitarian style of politics.[107] In contrast, the UNC still tried to maintain friendly relations with the fascist veterans.[108]

Then other international events worsened the situation. The German *Anschluss* pushed the Italians to focus on the Mediterranean as their main, if not only, sphere of influence and expansion. And in this region,

---

[106] Cf. Millington, *From Victory to Vichy*.
[107] AMAE, Società delle Nazioni 1919–1932, box 66, file 'Combattenti – Mutilati e Reduci di guerra', folder 'Riunione degli ex-combattenti francesi a Aix-les Bains (Maggio 1937)'.
[108] Report from the Central Committee of the ANMIG to the Ministry of Foreign Affairs (31 May 1937), AMAE, Società delle Nazioni 1919–1932, box 66, file 'Combattenti – Mutilati e Reduci di guerra', folder 'Parte generale'.

he fascists clashed with French and British interests. The German annexation of Austria had been a clear defeat for Italy's traditional interests on its northern border, but the Italian alliance with Germany was unquestionable. A friendly visit of 500 Nazi veterans to Rome shortly after the *Anschluss* served to confirm the alliance.[109] And while Mussolini reached a favourable agreement with the British regarding the Mediterranean, relations with France deteriorated further. In May of 1938, the London meeting of the CIP, where the fascists and the Nazis consolidated their power in international veteran politics,[110] ended with the withdrawal of the French representatives, Pichot, Goy and Desbons, who understood that the Nazi representative – the Duke of Saxe-Coburg – had been appointed as the new president as a result of the fascist plan despite open French opposition.[111] This was a serious obstacle for the French-Italian friendship. Even the Italy-based Union d'Anciens Combattants France-Italie, led by Henri Mirauchaux, was unable to maintain the unity of French and fascist veterans. Yet, the admiration of French veterans for Fascist Italy did not really fade. In February of 1938, the last amicable meeting of the Union d'Anciens Combattants France-Italie took place, with a banquet, a speech given by Delcroix and André Gervais' praise of the fascist motto 'believe, obey, fight' in the name of French veterans.[112] As we will see, the end of the fraternal relationship did not mean the abandonment of fascist discourses among certain groups of French veterans.

The Munich Pact momentarily satisfied the pro-Italian groups of French veterans who still believed in friendship with the fascists,[113] but the final rupture came just a few weeks later. Until then, fascist-friendly French veterans had observed the increasing Italian verbal attacks on France with a certain amount of incredulity.[114] Still it could not have come as a total surprise that, at the end of December 1938, following orders from the PNF, the fascist veterans abandoned the Union d'Anciens Combattants France-Italie.[115] (As we know, the Italian veterans' organizations had been submitted to the authority of the PNF in November of 1938.) By then, as Henri Mirauchaux regretfully wrote, the international

---

[109] *L'Italia combattente. L'Italia grigio-verde*, 4 (28 February 1938); *Il Popolo d'Italia*, 19 March 1938; *Deutsche Kriegsopferversorgung*, 8 (May 1938).
[110] National Archives (Kew), FO370/529, L 169ff., and FO370/530, L 203ff.
[111] *Cahiers de l'Union Fédérale*, 10–20 June 1938.
[112] *Le Trait d'Union*, 2 (February 1938).   [113] *Ibid.*, 9–10 (September–October 1938).
[114] *Ibid.*, 8 (August 1938).
[115] *L'Italia combattente. L'Italia grigio-verde*, 23 (suppl. 11) (31 December 1938); *La Voix du Combattant*, 21 January 1939.

action of the war veterans was 'dead'.[116] Within a few months, Mirauchaux saw his own organization disappear. During 1939, the official position of the fascist veterans became obviously hostile to the French, and this reality shows the extent to which the ANC and its newspaper had become mere tools of the regime's propaganda.[117] Veterans such as Mirauchaux, and probably also Delcroix, regretted the end of their long-lasting friendly relationship, but the decision of the fascist regime prevailed, and not even a last farewell encounter between French and Italian veterans – planned for in Sardinia in January of 1939 – was allowed to take place.[118] An exchange of reproachful letters between, on the one hand, Delcroix and Rossi and, on the other hand, Gervais, Mirauchaux and the French representatives of the FIDAC did nothing but confirm the official bitter rupture between the fascists and the French veterans.[119]

Despite the severed ties with Italy, the French veterans' organizations were set on adopting authoritarian traits. The French UF had started to transform its organizational structure in a way that brought it ideologically closer to the UNC.[120] In other words, the largest French centre-left veterans' organization acquired right-wing qualities. The leader, Henri Pichot, despite his republican and democratic convictions, began to strive for the formation of a new national government to concentrate all the forces of French society. Hence, on 20 April 1938, Pichot made a call for the formation of a government of 'public safety' formed by the veterans.[121] Recognizing that parliamentary democracy was exhausted, he proposed that the veterans help to form a capable government. On this basis, the rapprochement between the UF and the UNC was easier, and after the Munich Pact, both associations converged in a common campaign of 'civic action'.[122] In an international context where the security of France was in danger, both associations began to collaborate. After the proposal of Henri Pichot, Jean Goy and the UNC joined this project of 'national reconciliation'.[123] Both veteran leaders, supported by other minor associations, launched a joint programme of 'national concentration' (*rassemblement national*), which implied working for the rearmament of France and the preparation for its defence.[124] Finally, as a

---

[116] *Le Trait d'Union*, 12 (December 1938).
[117] See, for example, *L'Italia combattente. L'Italia grigio-verde*, 1 (15 January 1939), 4 (28 February 1939), and 5 (15 March 1939); cf. *La Voix du Combattant*, 28 January 1939.
[118] ACS, MI, PS, G1, box 30, file 330, 'Unione Combattenti Francia-Italia'.
[119] *La Voix du Combattant*, 11 February and 25 March 1939.
[120] Prost, *Les anciens combattants*, Vol. 1, pp. 195–6.
[121] *Cahiers de l'Union Fédérale*, 20 April 1938.
[122] Prost, *Les anciens combattants*, Vol. 1, pp. 197–8.
[123] *La Voix du Combattant*, 7 January 1939.   [124] *Ibid.*, 4 February 1939.

consequence of this convergence, on 12 November 1939, both the UF and the UNC founded the Légion des Combattants Français. This was a reflection of their shared desire for a 'moral revival' and 'economic resurrection'.[125] Meanwhile, the French Confederation of Veterans' Associations gathered the remaining organizations in a similarly named platform, the Légion Française des Combattants (not to be confused with Vichy's posterior organization with the same name). Yet, the most important historical development was, in short, the fact that the two main French veterans' associations had moved together towards authoritarianism.[126]

Although the political orientation of the main French veterans' associations during this period cannot be defined as fascist, it seems clear that the calls for participation of the veterans in the government of France cannot be understood without the precedent of Fascism. Deeply ingrained beliefs about the leading role that war veterans had allegedly attained in Fascist Italy and even Nazi Germany – the old myth of the fascist veteran – had long since become part of the French veteran worldview. This preconception operated in the minds of French veteran leaders, who, furthermore, had direct and frequent contact with both fascists and Nazis. It was largely thanks to the fascist example that the possibility of practicing authoritarian politics was part of the veterans' horizon of expectations. However, despite the French veterans' drift towards authoritarianism, these political projects still lacked clear fascist-inspired traits. It would only be after June of 1940 that French veteran politics would be reshaped in a manner that incorporated fascist characteristics more clearly, both in organizational and in discursive aspects.

Does the prominence of veteran politics in Vichy allow us to speak about fascism? The answer is not straightforward. The Vichy regime was an opportunity to put into practice a 'National Revolution' in which war veterans would play a key role. In theory, this project matched the fascist experience. Nevertheless, while authoritarian tendencies had undoubtedly motivated Pétain's call for support from veterans, it is also true that, by June of 1940, the real influence of the veterans' movement over the country had substantially diminished.[127] Demanding that war veterans be the basis of a new France did not have the same connotations that such an appeal would have had in the aftermath of the Great War. Veterans were far from being the only group rallied by Pétain; many other sectors of society backed the new collaborationist regime, built on

---

[125] *Ibid.*, 18 November 1939.   [126] Millington, *From Victory to Vichy*, pp. 194–217.
[127] Prost, *Les anciens combattants*, Vol. 1, pp. 190 and 201–2.

the ruins of a discredited republic.[128] The new Légion Française des Combattants (LFC), created by the law of 29 August 1940, signed by Pétain, would channel this popular support into a structure under the control of the regime, yet this organization implied leaving aside the option of a single party.[129] Xavier Vallat, a one-eyed veteran and former member of the Faisceau and the Croix de Feu, was appointed head of Vichy's general secretariat for war veterans and was the principal mind behind the organization of the LFC. Later, he would become the general commissary for the Jewish question, being responsible for the persecution of Jews under the regime.[130] Yet, if important personalities of the veterans' movement made up the leading cadres of Vichy, the main leaders of the French fascist leagues remained in German-occupied Paris during the war. When compared with the fascist powers, the public role of the French veterans in Vichy seems to simultaneously represent a commonality and a distinguishing feature.

However, Vichy endowed the LFC with duties and functions that in some aspects matched those of the fascist veterans in Italy. The fundamental common point was the declared obedience and loyalty to the leader of the nation. In the French case, this charismatic figure was Marshall Pétain, who also became the honorific head of the veterans' organization. If not a single party, the LFC assumed the functions of a single political organization, where the position of Pétain was homologous to that of Franco and Mussolini. Meanwhile, in France, Xavier Vallat, as secretary general for war veterans, played the role that the secretary general of the FET-JONS and the PNF played in Spain and Italy, respectively. (Later, Vallat appointed the anti-communist officer Georges Loustaunau-Lacau as head of the LFC. He would soon be replaced by Émile Meaux.) The legionnaires had to be the 'partisans of the National Revolution'.[131] A rhetoric insisting on the sacrifice and selfless work of the legionnaires was the most common expression of this allegedly revolutionary task, thus paralleling the Spanish and Italian cases. Apart from these aspects, the members of the LFC, with their uniforms and martial symbolism, were omnipresent in the militaristic

---

[128] Robert O. Paxton, *Vichy France: Old Guard and New Order, 1940–1944*, New York, Alfred A. Knopf, 1972.

[129] Jean-Paul Cointet, *La Légion Française des Combattants, 1940–1944: La tentation du fascisme*, Paris, Albin-Michel, 1995; Jean-Marie Guillon, 'La Légion française des combattants, ou comment comprendre la France de Vichy', *Annales du Midi: revue archéologique, historique et philologique de la France méridionale*, 116, 245 (2004), pp. 5–24

[130] Paxton, *Vichy France*, pp. 250–7; Cointet, *La Légion Française des Combattants*, pp. 27–40.

[131] *La Légion. Organe officiel de la Légion Française des Combattants* (Vichy), 20 November 1940.

Figure 6.2 Emblem of the Légion Française des Combattants.

and fascist-inspired rituals of the regime. From November of 1941, in a typically fascist organizational development, the LFC accepted members without war experience and organized them in the Volunteers of the National Revolution. Furthermore, an armed militia was created out of the LFC. Despite a yawning gap between a committed leadership and a reluctant sector of the rank and file, at its peak, the LFC would reach 1.4 million members in Vichy France, including the colonies.[132]

The construction of the LFC cannot be fully understood without the precedent of the fascist veterans' organizations and discourses. Although French veteran leaders did not want to 'copy' anything from the Nazis and the fascists, it is clear that they understood the LFC as a 'partisan organization' to sustain a 'national order' similar to those of Germany and Italy.[133] The emblem of the organization had a clearly fascist aesthetic, particularly as it introduced the sword into the traditional symbolic system of the French veterans (Figure 6.2). The LFC, a highly

---

[132] Cointet, *La Légion Française des Combattants*.
[133] Letter of F. Boissin to Henri Pichot (26 August 1940), AN, Fonds Pichot (43AS), box 3, 'Affaire UF'.

centralized and hierarchical structure, was set up, turning on many occasions to the same former leaders of the veterans' movement, particularly the UNC, or former leagues such as the Croix de Feu and the Jeunesses Patriotes.[134] In fact, most of the political discourse and doctrine of Vichy came from the PSF, heir of the Croix de Feu.[135] Moreover, other characteristics of Vichy's political organization for the *anciens combattants* had their origins in the long friendship between conservative French veterans and the fascists.

The case of André Gervais is perhaps the most significant. As we know, he had been one of the leading figures of the friendship between French and fascist veterans. Particularly during 1934–5, several of his publications in French and Italian had praised the Italian model of veterans' organization. In 1936, Gervais, a member of the UF, had written a programmatic text for the new youth section of this association. This organizational development recalls, for example, the youth section that the Stahlhelm had created during its fascist-inspired evolution. In fact, André Gervais had underlined the need for a national 'mystique' for French youth, similar to the spirit of the Italian fascists and the German National Socialists.[136] When the LFC was created, Gervais became a departmental leader and continued publishing his writings in LFC publications.[137] For him, the LFC was the hope of France.[138] In 1942, Gervais' book, *L'esprit légionnaire*, synthesized his thoughts about renewing the spirit of the Great War combatants in order to reconstruct France on Pétain's orders.[139] For his part, Henri Pichot, after a period of withdrawal from veteran politics following his resignation as president of the UF in July of 1940, joined the endeavour of providing the LFC with an a ideology and political programme. According to him, this was a matter of placing 'the veterans' spirit at the service of the National Revolution'.[140] These were attempts to create an original doctrine for the LFC, yet Fascist Italy was an influential precedent that is impossible to ignore.

---

[134] Jean-Paul Cointet and Michèle Cointet, 'Contribution a une socio-politique de l'État français: La Légion française des combattants dans la Vienne (1940–1943)', *Revue d'histoire moderne et contemporaine*, 20, 4 (1973), pp. 595–618; see also the contributions to the special issue *Voyage dans la France de Vichy: La Légion française des combattants* in *Annales du Midi*, 116, 245 (2004).

[135] Kennedy, *Reconciling France*, pp. 225ff.

[136] André Gervais, *Jeunesses*, Paris, 1936, p. 19.

[137] See, for example, *La Légion. Revue Mensuelle Illustrée publiée par la Légion Française des Combattants* (Vichy), 3 (August 1941).

[138] André Gervais, *Légion, espoir de la France*, Paris, 1941.

[139] André Gervais, *L'esprit légionnaire*, Paris, 1942.

[140] AN, Fonds Henri Pichot (43AS), box 3, file 4, 'La Légion des Combattants'.

For all these reasons, it is not surprising that historians have described
he LFC as part of the fascist 'temptation' in France.[141] Whether the
_FC represented only a 'temptation' or a fully fledged French fascist
phenomenon is a matter of discussion as part of the wide scholarly debate
about the existence and relevance of fascism in France. Here I have
underlined the fact that such a political evolution of the French veterans'
movement would have been impossible without the imposing precedent
of Fascist Italy. France was not 'allergic' to fascism but rather was a
country in which ample social and political sectors had assumed the
fascist style of politics and fascist political postulates such as the
National Revolution' by direct contagion from the original source: Italy.
And this contagion, as I have demonstrated here, was partially caused by
he long history of friendly relationships between French and Italian
fascist veterans, which introduced fascist discourses and organizational
principles into France.

[41] Cointet, *La Légion Française des Combattants.*

Conclusion

Historians have discussed on many occasions the link that seemingly existed between individual former combatants, veterans' groups and organizations and the origin of the fascist movements in Italy, Germany and even France. Scholars assumed that as the conspicuous cases of Hitler, Mussolini, Röhm, Balbo, Hess, Bottai and many others suggest, the fascists and the Nazis had very often been former soldiers, having served in the trenches of the Great War or joined paramilitary formations after November of 1918. Such realities would reveal the 'brutalizing' effect that, according to George L. Mosse, the Great War had on an entire generation. However, specialists of the history of the veterans' movements recalled that as the examples of Henri Pichot, René Cassin, Erich Maria Remarque, Emilio Lussu, Erich Kuttner, Ferruccio Parri and many others demonstrate, former combatants of the First World War predominantly became committed pacifists and democrats. If we concede the utility of Mosse's notion, we can say that one side of the coin included the fascists and National Socialists, and the other those internationalists and pacifists who escaped or were not responsive to 'brutalization'. Yet, in reality, the number of people who served as soldiers during the First World War was so high that, by the same token, we might find examples of war veterans involved in any facet human activity, whether political or not, during the interwar period. And furthermore, thousands of people *without* combat experience became fascists and National Socialists. It is true that the veterans' know-how was a coveted asset for the fascists in their violent quest for political power, but veterans could also employ their combat skills against the fascists, as they did in Italy and Germany. Put simply, it is misleading to categorize war veterans into defined ideologies or political sectors, to affirm that veterans were more inclined to certain behaviours or mind-sets.

Whereas it is true that many war veterans shared a set of common experiences related to mass warfare and that they showed in different societies a rather similar tendency to spontaneously create associations and defend their material interests, there was no universality of feelings and ideals that united them. Even in countries where veterans' associations mobilized hundreds of thousands of men, the majority of people who actually had been soldiers during the First World War never joined these groups or did so without a real commitment. It was not only the typical young, bourgeois, nationalist war volunteer – a figure common to France, Britain, Germany and Italy – who had the right to be labelled a 'veteran'. Illiterate peasant servicemen also were veterans, and their opinions and emotions often differed much from those of their officers. Moreover, the political diversity of the veterans' associations in the aftermath of war is impressive. Only as time passed, when the transnational symbol of the veteran acquired certain meanings, did the veterans' organizations in Europe become more homogeneously patriotic, nationalistic and right wing and less democratic, pacifist and orientated to the left. Pacifist and republican combatant writer Henri Barbusse, a famous figure in early 1919 among European veterans, was gradually eclipsed by fascist veteran 'stars' over the course of the interwar period. During the 1930s, while anti-fascism also embraced paramilitarism and the myth of the combatant, it was the stereotypical image of the fascist veteran that dominated international veteran politics. This evolution was, however, by no means pre-ordained.

Having recognized the constructed nature of the category of veteran, a substantial part of this book has explained the transnational process of symbolic appropriation of the idea of the war veteran by nationalist, counter-revolutionary and fascist forces. Symbolic appropriation was the core reason why, despite the fact that millions of European ex-soldiers did not become ardent warmongers but rather instinctive pacifists during the interwar period, people easily associated the image of the fascist with the symbol of the veteran.

I have argued that it was in Italy during the early post-war period that the process of symbolic appropriation was most consequential. In Italy, the controversy about the meaning of the war was particularly significant, given the bitter confrontation between interventionists and neutralists. The inception of Fascism, therefore, must be understood in its context. Only by simultaneously taking into account Mussolini's particular ideological position during the war, the precedent of the Russian Revolution and the anxieties after Caporetto can the connection between the symbol of the veteran and the nascent ideology of Italian Fascism be fully understood. After 1917, preventing the transformation of soldiers into socialist revolutionaries became an urgent task in the main belligerent countries and even more so in Italy. Yet, whereas in a France spurred on by victory, the conservative, patriotic and nationalist forces embodied by Clemenceau partially succeeded in maintaining, both practically and symbolically, the republican allegiance of the masses of soldiers,[1] in a crisis-ridden Italy, former combatants' opinions were much more fragmented and inclined towards extremes. By the end of 1919 in Italy, after violent physical and discursive confrontations, it was not only the symbol of the *arditi* but also the symbol of the veteran that had acquired a strong anti-Bolshevik bias. Paradoxically, the as yet unsuccessful fascist movement would go on to be the main beneficiary of this process. Significantly, Italo Balbo wrote in his 1922 diary that 'without Mussolini, three-quarters of the Italian youth returning from the trenches would have become Bolsheviks.'[2]

The precedent of paramilitary formations crushing revolutions in Central Europe became an important element of the transnational process of symbolic appropriation of the veteran as an anti-Bolshevik. Yet, in Germany, the connection between veterans and proto-fascist movements and ideologies is not as clear as is often supposed. The conservative Stahlhelm slowly defined its political stance regarding Weimar. By the time Hitler started his political career in the DAP (later NSDAP), the symbolic appropriation of the veteran by the Italian fascist movement was already crystallizing. In early and mid-1921, the stereotype of the 'fascist veteran' – commonly a patriotic, young, decorated ex-officer with front experience willing to restore 'victory' and exterminate socialism – was already circulating from Italy to Switzerland, Austria, France, Spain and Germany, particularly Bavaria. I have argued that this communicative process illuminates the transnational formation of non-Italian fascisms, including the case of Germany. Even in Italy, real ex-soldiers began to positively believe that Fascism was the archetypical expression of the veteran spirit, thus reinforcing the nascent stereotype. The self-fulfilling prophecy of Mussolini's *trincerocrazia* was becoming true not only in Italy but also in countries where the Italian example gained currency.

After the March on Rome, what had once been a stereotype became an outright political myth, reinforcing the transformation of fascism into a transnational phenomenon. The myth of the fascist veteran, drawn from the self-representation and self-stylization of the fascists as veterans and heirs to the fallen soldiers, stimulated the proliferation of fascist-inspired political groups in some of the European regions closest to Italy. Whereas under Mussolini's government the veterans' organizations were ruthlessly forced to accept PNF control and the preponderance of the fascist discourse, symbols and commemorative framework, in France and Germany, fascism was not initially imposed from above. Legends about

---

[1] See Pierre Vilar, 'Reflexions sur les années 20', in VV.AA., *Piero Gobetti e la Francia: Atti del colloquio italo francese*, Milan, Franco Angeli, 1985, pp. 15–25.
[2] Italo Balbo, *Diario 1922*, Milan, 1932, p. 6.

the Italian regime and the supposed good life veterans enjoyed under Mussolini's leadership led to the progressive fascist permeation of veterans' organizations such as the Stahlhelm or to the foundation of fascist parties of self-described former combatants such as the French Faisceau. Not even the main international organization of veterans – the FIDAC – was immune to fascist myths. In this context, the fascist regime could even further reinforce its monopoly over the symbol of the war veteran, advancing towards new totalitarian goals.

The turn of the decade witnessed the transformation of the fascist symbol of the war veteran that had hitherto been prevalent in Europe. The early fascist notion of a national revolutionary ex-combatant returned from the front, willing to crush the Bolshevik menace, to impose the politics of victory and to compose the leading aristocracy of a new state had always coexisted with a more conservative vision of the obedient and self-sacrificed soldier who should be rewarded for his service by society but who should maintain his loyalty to the state upon his return to civil life. In purely iconographic terms, the sword – or other icons such as the laurel wreath and the skull – was representative of the former model and the helmet of the latter. During the 1930s, these two models – the national revolutionary and the conservative – became fused into the totalitarian symbol of the fascist veteran: a fanatic servant of the state and the 'national revolution' who not only silently returns to his former occupation after fiercely fighting in war but also is ready to blindly obey, whatever the ultimate consequences, the eventual orders of a national leader to construct a greater nation or to save it from its enemies once again. Correspondingly, the emblems of totalitarian organizations for veterans mostly fused the national revolutionary and conservative veteran icons into a single iconographic symbol for the fascist veterans.

These new symbolic elements and practical roles of fascist veterans emerged in the 1930s as the European context changed fundamentally. The Nazi movement irrupted onto the scene, whilst the Stahlhelm became the main German interlocutor of Italian Fascism. New actors also played a role in this international scenario; in particular, French and Spanish fascist movements that had to define their position regarding the transnational symbol of the fascist veteran. This symbolic reference was, in practice, personified by active fascist politicians such as Carlo Delcroix and Amilcare Rossi, around whom a network of contacts between European fascist-friendly veterans and would-be fascists was built. It was a period of wide intellectual struggles around the meaning of the war experience. An important backlash rejected the great success of Remarque, and fascism continued to be the most influential political option in veteran politics. With the coming of the Third Reich, Germany experienced an upsurge in the special treatment doled out to honour war veterans. Veteran organizations were nazified. Nazi Germany defined its veteran politics following the model of Fascist Italy. Even in France, around 1934, the essentially republican veteran associations moved towards authoritarianism and paramilitarism. The events in Paris on 6 February 1934 must be understood in relation not only to these processes but also to the subsequent fascist and National Socialist attempts to construct a fascist European entente in which veterans had a prominent position. However, geostrategic issues left this dream unfulfilled.

In the end, the persisting transnational identification between war veterans and fascism in the symbolic realm contributed to bringing war to Europe once more. If the Italian attack on Ethiopia shocked many citizens across the world into realizing the fascist threat to peace, veteran politics remained an instrument through which Italian Fascism could reinforce its power and influence both within Italy and in the international sphere. Pacifism and anti-fascism suffered a long crisis throughout the Ethiopian conflict and the Spanish Civil War. The anti-fascists' attempts to divest the transnational symbol of the veteran of its ultra-nationalist, aggressive and anti-democratic connotations were not successful. People across the world denounced the clear relation between fascism and war, but the struggle of international groups of pacifist veterans ultimately failed. The fascists' and the Nazis' cunning political manoeuvres fundamentally undermined the functioning of the transnational networks of veterans, whose supposed objective was the preservation of peace.

Finally, in 1939–40, when war waged against democratic states resulted in the imposition of fascist and authoritarian dictatorships in Spain and France, the long-developed fascist model of veteran politics was transferred to these countries. This process, however, was not without selection, adaptation and transformation. It is reasonable to state that the Spanish and Italian fascist models of veterans' organization evolved in parallel over the course of some months. Both the FET-JONS and the PNF decided, at the same time – December 1939 – to promote the transformation of all veterans into members of the party. Veterans had almost identical symbolic roles in Fascist Italy, Nazi Germany and Francoist Spain. After June 1940, it is not surprising, therefore, that Pétain summoned the French veterans to endorse the regime of Vichy: the French dictatorship was attempting to enforce a 'National Revolution'. By that time, even if most individuals who had fought in the First World War had never been the violent anti-democrats, ultra-nationalists and anti-Bolsheviks that fascism claimed, the symbol of the fascist and the symbol of the veteran had coalesced in the minds of many Europeans.

Sources

La Vanguardia, www.lavanguardia.com/hemeroteca/index.html
La Stampa archivio, www.lastampa.it/archivio-storico/
Archivio Luce, www.archivioluce.com/

PERIODICALS

DAILY NEWSPAPERS

Published in Italy

Avanti! (Milan and Turin)
Corriere della Sera (Milan)
Cremona Nuova (Cremona)
Giornale del Mattino (Bologna)
Il Popolo d'Italia (Milan)
Il Popolo di Trieste (Trieste)
Il Popolo di Roma (Rome)
Il Paese (Rome)
L'Idea Nazionale (Rome)
L'Impero (Rome)
La Nazione (Florence)
La Stampa (Turin)

Published in France

La Presse de Paris. Édition du soir (Paris)
L'Action française (Paris)
La Victoire (Paris)
Le Figaro (Paris)
Le Matin (Paris)
Le Petit Journal (Paris)
Le Populaire (Paris)
L'Humanité (Paris)
L'Intransigeant (Paris)

Published in Germany

Berliner Tageblatt (Berlin)
Münchner Neueste Nachrichten (Munich)
Münchener Post (Munich)
Neue Zeitung. Organ für das arbeitende Volk (Munich)
Rote Fahne (Berlin)
Vorwärts (Berlin)
Vossische Zeitung (Berlin)
Völkischer Beobachter (Munich and Berlin)

Published in Spain

Arriba (Madrid)
La Voz (Madrid)

La Vanguardia (Barcelona)
ABC (Madrid)
El Socialista (Madrid)
El Debate (Madrid)

Published Elsewhere

The Times (London)
New York Times (New York)
Arbeiterville (Graz)
Arbeiter-Zeitung (Vienna)
Gazette de Lausanne (Lausanne)
Neues Montagblatt (Vienna)
Rote Fahne (Vienna)
Wiener Bilder (Vienna)

MAGAZINES, BULLETINS AND OTHER PERIODICALS

Published in Italy

A Noi! Organo dell'Associazione Nazionale Reduci Zona Operante (Turin)
Antieuropa. Rassegna mensile (Rome)
Battaglie. Libera voce dei combattenti della provincia di Alessandria (Alessandria)
Bollettino Associazione Nazionale Combattenti (Pavia)
Bollettino della Federazione Provinciale di Terni dell'Associazione Nazionale Combattenti (Terni)
Bollettino della Federazione Provinciale Mantovana dell'Associazione Nazionale Combattenti (Mantova)
Bollettino della Federazione Provinciale Valtellinese dell'Associazione Nazionale Combattenti (Sondrio)
Bollettino della Sezione Provinciale fra Mutilati ed Invalidi di Guerra (Rovigo)
Bollettino della sezione provinciale di Ferrara fra mutilati e invalidi di guerra (Ferrara)
Bollettino dell'Associazione Nazionale Combattenti. Federazione della Tripolitania (Tripoli)
Bollettino mensile. Associazione Nazionale fra Mutilati e Invalidi di Guerra. Sezione di Modena (Modena)
Critica fascista (Rome)
Critica Sociale. Rivista quindicinale del socialismo (Milan)
Esercito e Nazione. Rivista per l'ufficiale italiano (Rome)
Fanteria (Florence)
I Combattenti (Genoa)
I Combattenti. La Nuova Giornata (Genoa)
Il Bollettino. Organo Mensile dell'Associazione Nazionale Mutilati e Invalidi di Guerra (Rome)
Il Bollettino dell'Associazione Nazionale Combattenti (Rome)
Il Bolscevico. Organo settimanale del Partito Comunista d'Italia (Novara)

Il Combattente (Bologna)

Il Combattente d'Italia. Periodico mensile dei combattenti di Terni (Terni)

Il Combattente. Giornale letterario assistenziale apolitico organo uffciale della federazione provinciale combattenti (Naples)

Il Combattente Maremmano (Grosseto)

Il Combattente. Organo dell'Associazione Nazionale dei Combattenti - Federazione regionale Siciliana (Messina)

Il Combattente. Organo Provinciale dell'Associazione Nazionale Combattenti (Cremona)

Il Combattente. Organo letterario assistenziale apolitico (Naples)

Il Combattente. Politico indipendente dell'Italia Meridionale (Naples)

Il Combattente Romagnolo (Ravenna)

Il Combattente. Settimanale delle Sezioni Mutilati, Invalidi e Combattenti di Capitanata (Capitanata)

Il Combattente. Settimanale. Organo dei Combattenti Mantovani (Mantova)

Il Fascio. Organo dei Fasci italiani di combattimento (Milan)

Il Giornale dei Combattenti. Organo Ufficiale dell'Unione Nazionale Combattenti (Turin)

Il Giornale dei Combattenti. Organo dei Combattenti Nazionali del Piemonte (Turin)

Il giornale del soldato (Milan)

Il Maglio. Giornale Settimanale degli ex Combattenti e Smobilitati (Varese)

Il Mutilato (Cremona)

Il Primato. Settimanale dei Combattenti (Turin)

Il Soviet. Organo delle Sezioni del Partito Socialista Italiano nella Provincia di Napoli (Naples)

Italia Augusta. Problemi d'Italia. Rassegna dei combattenti (Rome)

'Italia Augusta'. Rassegna dell'Opera Nazionale per i Combattenti (Rome)

La Conquista dello Stato (Rome)

La Critica Politica (Rome)

La Libera Parola. Giornale settimanale dei Mutilati, dei Combattenti e delle nuove coscienze (Parma)

La Nuova Giornata (Milan)

L'Ardito (Milan)

La Vittoria. Organo dell'Associazione Nazionale Combattenti di Palermo (Palermo)

La Voce dei Reduci. Giornale dei mutilati e invalidi di guerra (Bologna)

Le Fiamme. Organo dell'arditismo (Rome)

L'elmetto. Trimensile dei combattenti di Terra di Lavoro (Caserta)

Le Trait d'Union. Revue mensuelle publiée par l'Union Fédérale en Italie des Associations Françaises d'Anciens Combattants (Turin)

L'Intrepido (Lucca)

L'Italia combattente. L'Italia grigio-verde (Rome)

L'Italia grigio-verde. Periodico di disciplina nazionale (Rome)

L'Italia Libera. Organo dei gruppi combattenti 'Italia Libera' (Rome)

L'Unità (Florence)

L'Unità. Organo del Partito Comunista d'Italia (clandestine edition)

Problemi d'Italia. Rassegna mensile dei combattenti (Rome)
Roma fascista. Settimanale politico (Rome)
Roma Futurista. Giornale del Partito Politico Futurista (Rome)
Settimanale dei Fasci di Combattimento della Lombardia (Varese)
Spartacus. Organo della Lega Proletaria (Milan)
Volontà (Rome)

Published in France

Bollettino dell'Associazione Nazionale Combattenti per la zona del nord (Nord, Pas-de-Calais e Somme) (Lille)
Cahiers de l'Union Fédérale (Paris)
FIDAC. Bulletin mensuel de la Fédération Interalliée des Anciens Combattants (Paris)
FIDAC. Bulletin of the Allied Legions (Paris)
Journal des Mutilés et Combattants (Paris)
Journal des mutilés et reformés des anciens combattants et des victimes de la guerre (Paris)
La France Mutilée. Bulletin de l'Union Fédérale (Paris)
La Légion. Organe officiel de la Légion Française des Combattants (Vichy)
La Légion. Revue Mensuelle Illustrée publiée par la Légion Française des Combattants (Vichy)
La Nuova Italia. L'Italie Nouvelle (Paris)
La Revue des vivants. Organe des générations de la guerre (Paris)
La Voix du Combattant (Paris)
Le Combattant des Deux-Sèvres. Organe des combatants ... Organe de l'Union nationale des combattants (Niort)
L'étudiant français. Organe mensuel de la Féderation Nationale des Étudiants d'Action Française (Paris)
Le Flambeau. Organe des 'Croix de Feu' (Paris)
Le Nouveau Siècle. Journal de la Fraternité Nationale, veut la politique de la Victoire (Paris)
Le Mutilé de l'Algérie (Algiers)
L'Illustration (Paris)

Published in Germany

Arminius. Kampfschrift für deutsche Nationalisten (Berlin)
Der Angriff. Das deutsche Abendblatt in Berlin (Berlin)
Der Stahlhelm. Organ des 'Stahlhelm', Bund der Frontsoldaten (Berlin)
Deutsche Kriegsopferversorgung.Monatschrift der Frontsoldaten und Kriegsopfer der Deutsche Kriegsopferversorgung. Monatschrift (Munich and Berlin)
Die Grenzboten. Zeitschfit für Kunst, Politik, Literatur (Berlin)
Gewissen (Berlin)
Nachrichtenblatt des Gaues Postdam des 'Stahlhelm' Bund der Frontsoldaten (Postdam)
National-Sozialistischen Kriegsopferversorgung (NSKOV) (Berlin)

*Reichsbund. Organ des Reichsbundes der Kriegsbeschädigten, Kriegsteilneh-
mer und Kriegshinterbliebenen* (Berlin)
Simplicissimus (Stuttgart)
Sozialistische Monatshefte (Berlin)
Standarte. Wochenschrift des neuen Nationalismus (Berlin)
Zeitbilder. Beilage zur Vossischen Zeitung (Berlin)

Published in Spain

Acción Española (Madrid)
*La Acción. Periódico republicano. Órgano de las izquierdas de Tarrasa y su
distrito* (Tarrasa)
La Gaceta Literaria (Madrid)

Published Elsewhere

Wiener Bilder. Illustriertes Familienblatt (Vienna)

BOOKS AND PAMPHLETS

L'Opera Nazionale Combattenti, Rome, 1926
'Codice della terra'. Biblioteca agraria dell'Opera Nazionale Combattenti, Rome,
1928
Chi è? Dizionario degli italiani d'oggi, Rome, 1936 and 1940
Numero unico per l'inaugurazione. Monumento della Vittoria, Bolzano, 1928
Der Stahlhelm am Rhein. 11. Reichsfrontsoldatentag am 4–5. Oktober in Koblenz,
Berlin, 1930
*Cahiers des États Generaux. Première Assemblée Nationale des Combattants, des
Producteurs et des Chefs de Famille tenue à Reims le 27 juin 1926 sur l'initiative du
Faisceau des Combattants et des Producteurs. Compte rendu des travaux de
l'assemblée*, Paris, Nouvelle Librairie Nationale, 1926
*Le Celebrazioni della Patria. Orazioni dell'On. Nicola Sansanelli pronunziate in
presenza di S. M. il Re*, Naples [1930]
Pourquoi nous sommes devenus Croix de Feu . . ., Clermont [1934]
VI. Divisione Camicie Nere 'Tevere'. Il 219. battaglione cc. nn. in Africa Orientale,
Rome, 1937
Acerbo, Giacomo, *Fra due plotoni di esecuzione. Avvenimenti e problemi dell'epoca
fascista*, Bologna, Cappelli, 1969
  Tre discorsi politici. Chieti (1920) – Teramo, Aquila (1923), Florence, 1923
Amendola, Giovanni, *L'Aventino contro il fascism: Scritti politici (1924–1926)*,
Milan, 1976
Amico, Angelo, *Combattentismo e Fascismo*, Milan, 1932
  Il significato dell'ammissione dei combattenti nel Partito, Caltanisetta, 1940
Arthuys, Jacques, *Les Combattants*, Paris, Nouvelle Librairie Nationale, 1925
  Les combattants, Paris, Nouvelle Librairie Nationale, 1925
Ass. Naz. Combattenti Federazione Provinciale di Torino, *Canti di guerra. diretti
dal Maestro Gaetano Salvadego ed eseguiti da ex Combattenti*, Turin, 1929

Associazione Nazionale Combattenti. Direttorio Nazionale, *VIII Consiglio Nazionale. Trieste 15–21 Giugno 1932-X. Atti Ufficiali*, Rome, 1932.
Associazione Nazionale Combattenti. Federazione Provinciale di Firenze, *Relazione Morale e Finanziaria. Ottobre XIV*, Florence [1935]
Aymar, Camille, *Bolchevisme ou Fascisme? ... Français, il faut choisir!*, Paris, Flammarion, 1925
Baiocchi, Adolfo, *Generazioni. Romanzo della guerra*, Milan, 1930
    Uno dei tanti, Rome, 1931
Balassa, Imre, *Fronte: Romanzo di guerra*, Milan, 1931
Balbo, Italo, *Diario 1922*, Milan, 1932
Barbusse, Henri, *Paroles d'un combattant: Articles et Discours (1917–1920)*, Paris, 1920
Bartolini, Luigi, *Il Ritorno sul Carso*, Verona, 1930
Berry, François, *Le fascisme en France*, Paris, 1926
Bolzon, Piero, *Fiamma nera*, Milan, 1921
Brancaccio, Nicola, *et al.*, *Le Medaglie d'Oro (1833–1925)* [1925]
Campese, Ernesto, *Il Fascismo contro la disoccupazione*, Rome, 1929
Calamandrei, Piero, Calamandrei, Silvia and Casellato, Alessandro (eds.), *Zona di Guerra: Lettere, scritti e discorsi (1915–1924)*, Rome-Bari, Laterza, 2006
Carli, Mario, *Noi arditi*, Milan, 1919
    Codice della vita fascista, Rome, 1928
C. C. dei Fasci Italiani di Combattimento, *Barbarie rossa: Riassunto cronologico delle principali gesta commesse dai socialisti italiani dal 1919 in poi ...*, Rome, 1921
Cebreiros, Nazario, *El Fascismo: Su origen, organización, doctrina, lucha y triunfo de Mussolini en Italia (1919–1922)*, Madrid, 1933
Ceci, Paolo, *I Gerarchi dell'Associazione Nazionale Combattenti*, Rome, 1928
Charles-Roux, François, *Souvenirs diplomatiques: Une Grande Ambassade à Rome, 1919–1925*, Paris, 1961
Codignola, Arturo, *La resistenza de 'I combattenti di Assisi'*, Modena, 1965
Colonna, Giuseppe (ed.), *Raccolta delle disposizioni di legge a favore degli ex combattenti*, Siena, 1954
Comité de Vigilance des Intellectuels Antifascistes, *Qu'est-ce que le Fascisme? Le fascisme et la France*, Paris, 1935
De Vecchi di Val Cismon, Cesare Maria and Romersa, Luigi (ed.), *Il Quadrumviro scomodo: Il vero Mussolini nelle memorie del più monarchico dei fascisti*, Milan, Mursia, 1983
Dini, Vicenzo, *Dalla scuola alla trincea: Commedia in quattro atti*, Florence, 1930
Dresler, Adolf, *Mussolini*, Leipzig, 1924
Duesterberg, Theodor, *Der Stahlhelm und Hitler*, Wolfenbüttel & Hannover, 1949
Farinacci, Roberto, *Andante mosso, 1924–25*, Milan, 1929
Fasci italiani all'estero, *Trentacinque morti: Duecentododici feriti*, [Rome] 1930
FET-JONS, *Los combatientes y el Caudillo*, Bilbao, 1938
Franke, Helmut, *Staat im Staate: Aufzeichnungen eines Militaristen*, Magdeburg, 1924
Gabelli, Federico, *Adolfo Schiavo e la 'Romana combattenti' dall'apoliticità al fascismo*, Rome, 1930
Gallo, Arturo, *Stirpe eroica*, Naples, 1929

Gay, Vicente, *La revolución nacional-socialista: Ambiente, Leyes, Ideología,* Barcelona, 1934

Giménez Caballero, Ernesto, *Notas marruecas de un soldado,* Madrid, 1923

Circuito Imperial, Madrid, 1929

La nueva catolicidad: Teoría general sobre el Fascismo en Europa: en España, Madrid, 1933

Gervais, André, *La tranchée d'en face: Enquête d'un combattant français chez les combattants allemands,* Paris, 1933

L'esprit combattant, Paris, 1934

Les Combattants à l'ombre du faisceau, Paris, 1935

Jeunesses, Paris, 1936

Légion, espoir de la France, Paris, 1941

L'esprit légionnaire, Paris, 1942

Gianturco, Luigi E., *Sette giorni in Germania: Impressioni sul viaggio dei combattenti in Germania,* Milan, 1939

Girón, José Antonio, *Si la memoria no me falla,* Barcelona, 1994

Giunta, Francesco, *Un po' di fascismo,* Milan, 1935

Goebbels, Joseph and Fröhlic, Elke (eds.), *Die Tagebücher von Joseph Goebbels: Sämtliche Fragmente,* Munich, K.G. Saur, 1987

Gorgolini, Pietro, *La Révolution fasciste: Avec le texte intégral des principaux discours de Benito Mussolini,* Paris, Nouvelle Librairie Nationale, 1924

Hazard, Paul, *L'Italie vivante,* Paris, 1923

Hervé, Gustave, *C'est Pétain qu'il nous faut,* Paris, 1936

Hitler, Adolf, *Mein Kampf,* Munich, 1936 (1st edn. 1925)

Sämtliche Aufzeichnungen 1905–1924, Stuttgart, Deutsche Verlag-Anstalt, 1980

Reden, Schriften, Anordnungen, Februar 1925 bis Januar 1933, Munich, K.G. Saur, 1992–2006

Istituto Centrale di Statistica del Regno d'Italia, *VII censimento generale della popolazione, 21 Aprile 1931,* Rom3, 1933–4.

Jünger, Ernest [*sic*], *Tempestades de Acero,* Barcelona, 1930

Jünger, Ernst, *Politische Publizistik, 1919 bis 1933,* Stuttgart, Klett, 2001

Kaminski, Hanns-Erich, *Fascismus in Italien,* Berlin, 1925

Kampffmeyer, Paul. *Der Fascismus in Deutschland,* Berlin, 1923

Kleinau, Wilhelm(ed.), *Echo aus dem Westen: Berichte der französischen Presse über den XI. Reichsfrontsoldatentag am Rhein (Koblenz, 4–5 Oktober 1930),* Berlin, 1930

Lanzillo, Agostino, *La disfatta del Socialismo: Critica della guerra e del socialismo,* Florence, 1918

Ledesma Ramos, Ramiro, *¡Hay que hacer la revolución hispánica!,* Madrid, 1931

Lussu, Emilio, *Marcia su Roma e dintorni,* Turin, Einaudi, 2002 (1st edn. 1945)

Lüdecke, Kurt, *I Knew Hitler,* London, 1938

Mannhardt, J. W., *Der Faschismus,* Munich, 1925

Marchese, Alberto, *Vademecum per l'Avanguardista d'Italia,* Naples, 1928

Marpicati, Arturo, *La coda di Minosse: Romanzo di guerra,* Bologna, 1931 (1st edn. 1925)

Matteotti, Giacomo, *Un anno di dominazione fascista,* Sala Bolognese, Arnaldo Forni, 1980 (1st edn. 1923)

Sources 287

Maurras, Charles, *La part du combattant*, Paris, 1917
Migliore, Benedetto, *Le convulsioni dell'arditismo*, Milan, 1921
Ministero della Guerra. Ufficio stadistico, *La forza dell'esercito: Statistica dello sforzo militare italiano nella guerra mondiale*, Rome, 1927
Mosley, Oswald, *The Greater Britain*, London, 1931
Mussolini, Benito, *Mussolini ai combattenti d'Italia*, Rome, 1923
Mussolini, Benito, Susmel, Edouardo and Susmel, Duilio (eds.), *Opera Omnia di Benito Mussolini*, Florence, La Fenice, 1961
Norton-Cru, Jean, *Témoins*, Nancy, Presses Universitaires de Nancy, 2006 (1st edn. 1929)
Olberg, Oda, *Der Fascismus in Italien*, Jena, 1923
Omodeo, Adolfo, *Momenti della vita di guerra (dai Diari e dalle Lettere dei Caduti)*, Bari, Laterza, 1934
Pezet, Ernest, *Combattants et Citoyens: Les Combattants dans la Cité branlante devant la Victoire mutilée*, Paris [1925]
Piazzesi, Mario, *Diario di uno squadrista toscano 1919–1922*, Rome, Bonacci, 1980
Pironti, Francesco, *Manuale di cultura fascista: Ad uso delle scuole medie*, Rome, 1929
Pocaterra, Giuglielmo, *La pensione di guerra nella sua legge base (R. Decreto 12 luglio 1923 n. 1491) e successive integrazioni, modifiche e aggiunte (preparazione a un testo unico)*, Rome, 1936
Redondo, Onésimo, *Obras completas: Edición cronológica*, 2 vols., Madrid, 1954–5
Remarque, Erich Maria, *Der Weg zurück*, Köln, Kiepenheuer & Witsch, 2012 (1st edn. 1931)
  La via del ritorno, Milan, Mondadori, 1932
Renzetti, Giuseppe, *Italienische Berichte*, Berlin, 1932
Río Cisneros, Agustín del (ed.), *Obras completas de José Antonio Primo de Rivera: Edición Cronológica*, Madrid, 1959
Rossi, Amilcare, *Le tappe gloriose*, Rome, 1933
  Dalle Alpi alle Ambe, Rome, 1937
  Figlio del mio tempo: Prefascismo-Fascismo-Postfascismo, Rome, 1969
Röhm, Ernst, *Die Geschichte eines Hochverräters*, Munich, 1934 (1st edn. 1928)
  Warum SA? Rede vor dem Diplomatischen Korps am 7 Dezember 1933, Berlin, 1933
Salvatorelli, Luigi, *Nazionalfascismo*, Turin, 1923
Santa Marina, Luys, *Tras el águila del César: elegía del tercio*, Duero, 1924
Sapori, Francesco, *La Trincea. Romanzo*, Milan, 1931 (1st edn. 1917)
Schotthöfer, Fritz, *Il Fascio: Sinn und Wirklichkeit des italienischen Fascismus*, Frankfurt am Main, 1924
Sezione 'P' del Governo della Dalmazia, *Battute di propaganda: Per i giovani Ufficiali nelle conversazioni coi soldati*, Ancona, 1919
Strasser, Georg, *Freiheit und Brot*, Berlin, 1928
  Hammer und Schwert, Berlin, 1928
Taittinger, Pierre, *Les Cahiers de la Jeune France*, Paris, 1926
Van den Bruck, Moeller, *Das Recht der Jüngen Volker: Sammlung politische Aufsätze*, Berlin, 1932.
Valois, Georges, *La réforme économique & sociale*, Paris, 1918

D'un siècle a l'autre: Chronique d'une génération 1885–1920, Paris, Nouvelle Librairie Nationale, 1921
La Révolution Nationale, Paris, Nouvelle Librairie Nationale, 1924
La politique de la victoire, Paris, Nouvelle Librairie Nationale, 1926
Il fascismo francese, Rome, 1926
Le fascisme, Paris, Nouvelle Librairie Nationale, 1927
Vecchi, Ferruccio, *Arditismo civile*, Milan, 1920
Viola, Ettore, *Combattenti e Mussolini dopo il congresso di Assisi*, Florence, 1975
Vilain, Charles, *Le voyage des combattants français en Italie (15–22 Avril 1935)*, Rouen, 1935
Von Salomon, Ernst, *Die Geächteten*, Berlin, 1935 (1st edn. 1930)
Zibordi, Giovanni, *Critica socialista del fascismo*, Bologna, Cappelli, 1922

PUBLISHED DOCUMENT COLLECTIONS

Akten zur Deutschen Auswärtigen Politik 1918–1945. Serie A: 1918–1925. 1. März bis 31. Dezember 1922, Göttingen, Vandenhoeck & Ruprecht, 1988
Commission Nationale pour la Publication de Documents Diplomatiques Suisses, *Documents diplomatiques suisses/Diplomatische Dokumente der Schweiz/Documenti diplomatici Svizzeri 1848–1945*, Bern, Benteli Verlag, 1988
Documents on British Foreign Policy, 1919–1939. First Series, Vol. IV, 1919, London, Her Majesty's Stationery Office, 1952.
Könnemann, Erwin and Schulze, Gerhard (eds.), *Der Kapp-Lüttwitz-Ludendorff-Putsch: Dokumente*, Munich, Olzog Verlag, 2002
Ministero degli Affari Esteri, *I documenti diplomatici italiani: Settima serie, 1922–1935. Vol. I (31 ottobre 1922–26 aprile 1923)*, Rome, 1953
Riddel, John (ed.), *Toward the United Front: Proceedings of the Fourth Congress of the Communist International, 1922*, London, Leiden, 2012

Bibliography

Adamson, Walter L., *Avant-Garde Florence: From Modernism to Fascism* (Cambridge, MA, Harvard University Press, 1993)

Alares, Gustavo, 'Ruralismo, fascismo y regeneración: Italia y España en perspectiva comparada', *Ayer*, 83 (2011), pp. 127–47

Albanese, Giulia, 'Brutalizzazione e violenza alle origini del fascismo', *Studi Storici*, 55, 1 (2014), pp. 3–14

Alle origini del fascismo: La violenza politica a Venezia 1919–1922 (Padua, Il Poligrafo, 2001)

La marcia su Roma (Rome-Bari, Laterza, 2006)

'Alla scuola del fascismo: la Spagna dei primi anni venti e la marcia su Roma', in Mario Isnenghi (ed.), *Pensare la nazione. Silvio Lanaro e l'Italia contemporanea* (Roma, Donzelli, 2012), pp. 111–122

Albert, Mathias, et al., *Transnational Political Spaces: Agents, Structures, Encounters* (Frankfurt, Campus Verlag, 2009)

Alcalde, Ángel, *Los excombatientes franquistas: La cultura de guerra del fascismo español y la Delegación Nacional de Excombatientes (1936–1965)* (Zaragoza, Prensas de la Universidad de Zaragoza, 2014)

'Los excombatientes en el mundo rural de la posguerra: del mito del campesino soldado a la realidad social de la España franquista', in Óscar Rodríguez Barreira (ed.), *El franquismo desde los márgenes: Campesinos, mujeres, delatores, menores . . .*, Lleida-Almería, UdLl & UAL, 2013, pp. 113–29

'Los orígenes de la Delegación Nacional de Excombatientes de FET-JONS: la desmovilización del ejército franquista y la Europa de 1939', *Ayer*, 97 (2015), pp. 169–94

'War veterans and the transnational origins of Italian Fascism (1917–1919)', *Journal of Modern Italian Studies*, 21, 4 (2016), pp. 565–83.

Arco, Miguel Ángel del, 'Hunger and the Consolidation of the Francoist Regime (1939–1951)', *European History Quarterly*, 40, 3 (2010), pp. 458–83

Audoin-Rouzeau, Stéphane, *Combattre: Une anthropologie historique de la guerre moderne, XIXe–XXIe siècle* (Paris, Seuil, 2008)

Audoin-Rouzeau, Stéphane and Becker, Annette, *14–18, retrouver la Guerre* (Paris, Gallimard, 2000)

Baird, Jay W., *Hitler's War Poets: Literature and Politics in the Third Reich* (New York, Cambridge University Press, 2008)

Baldassari, Marco, 'La memoria celebrata: La festa del 4 novembre a Lucca tra dopoguerra e fascismo', *Italia contemporanea*, 242 (2006), pp. 23–43

Ballini, Pier Luigi, *Le elezioni nella storia d'Italia dall'Unità al fascismo: Profilo storico-statistico* (Bologna, Il Mulino, 1988)

Baravelli, Andrea, *La vittoria smarrita: Legittimità e rappresentazioni della Grande Guerra nella crisi del sistema liberale (1919–1924)* (Rome, Carocci, 2006)

Barnes, James J. and Patience P. Barnes, *Nazis in Pre-War London 1930–1939: The Fate and Role of German Party Members and British Sympathizers* (Brighton, Sussex Academic Press, 2005)

Barone, Giuseppe, 'Statalismo e riformismo: l'Opera Nazionale Combattenti (1917–1923)', *Studi Storici*, 25 (1984), pp. 203–44

Barr, Niall, *The Lion and the Poppy: British Veterans, Politics, and Society, 1921–1939* (London, Praeger, 2005)

'"The Legion that Sailed but Never Went": The British Legion and the Munich Crisis of 1938', in Julia Eichenberg and John Paul Newman (eds.), *The Great War and Veterans' Internationalism* (New York, Palgrave, 2013), pp. 32–52

Barth, Boris, *Dolchstoßlegenden und politische Desintegration: Das Trauma der deutschen Niederlage im Ersten Weltkrieg 1914–1933* (Düsseldorf, Droste, 2003)

Bartov, Omer, *Mirrors of Destruction: War, Genocide, and Modern Identity* (Oxford University Press, 2000)

Bauerkämper, Arnd, 'Transnational Fascism: Cross-Border Relations between Regimes and Movements in Europe, 1922–1939', *East Central Europe*, 37 (2010), pp. 214–46

Beaupré, Nicolas, *Écrire en guerre, écrire la guerre, France, Allemagne 1914–1920* (Paris, CNRS, 2006)

Becker, Annette, 'Du 14 Julliet 1919 au 11 novembre 1920: Mort, où est la victoire?', *Vingtième siècle, Revue d'histoire*, 49 (1996), pp. 31–44

Ben-Ghiat, Ruth, *Fascist modernities: Italy, 1922–1945* (Berkeley, University of California Press, 2001)

Berardi, Roberto, *Dizionario di termini storici politici ed economici moderni* (Florence, Felice Le Monier, 1976)

Berghahn, Volker R., *Der Stahlhelm: Bund der Frontsoldaten* (Düsseldorf, Droste, 1966)

'Das Ende des "Stahlhelm"', *Vierteljahrshefte für Zeitgeschichte*, 13, 4 (1965), pp. 446–51

Berghaus, Günter, *Futurism and Politics: Between Anarchist Rebellion and Fascist Reaction, 1909–1944* (Oxford, Berghahn Books, 1996)

Bers, Günter (ed.), *'Rote Tage' im Rheinland: Demonstrationen des Roten Frontkämpfer-Bundes (RFB) im Gau Mittelrhein 1925–1928* (Hamburg, Einhorn Presse Verlag, 1980)

Berstein, Serge, 'L'affrontement simulé des années 1930', *Vingtième Siècle. Revue d'histoire*, 5 (1985), pp. 39–54

Bessel, Richard, *Germany after the First World War* (Oxford, Clarendon Press, 1993)

'Die Heimkehr der Soldaten: Das Bild der Frontsoldaten in der Öffentlichkeit der Weimarer Republik', in Gerhard Hirschfeld, Gerd Krumeich and Irina Renz (eds.), *'Keiner fühlt sich hier mehr als Mensch . . .' Erlebnis und Wirkung des Ersten Weltkriegs* (Frankfurt am Main, Fischer Taschenbuch, 1996), pp. 260–82

'The Front Generation and the Politics of Weimar Germany', in Mark Roseman (ed.), *Generations in Conflict: Youth Revolt and Generation Formation in Germany, 1770–1968* (Cambridge University Press, 2005), pp. 121–36

Bianchi, Roberto, *Pace, pane, terra: Il 1919 in Italia* (Rome, Odradek, 2006)

Boca, Angelo Del, *La guerra d'Abissinia 1935–1941* (Milan, Feltrinelli, 1965)

Bottici, Chiara, *A Philosophy of Political Myth* (New York, Cambridge University Press, 2007)

Bowen, Wayne H., *Spaniards and Nazi Germany: Collaboration in the New Order* (Columbia, University of Missouri Press, 2000)

Bullón de Mendoza, Alfonso, *José Calvo Sotelo* (Barcelona, Ariel, 2004)

Bracco, Barbara, *La patria ferita: I corpi dei soldati italiani e la Grande guerra* (Florence, Giunti, 2011)

Burgwyn, H. James, *The Legend of the Mutilated Victory: Italy, the Great War, and the Paris Peace Conference, 1915–1919* (Westport, CT, Greenburg Press, 1993)

Italian Foreign Policy in the Interwar Period 1918–1940 (Westport, CT, Praeger, 1997)

Cabanes, Bruno, *La Victoire endeuillée: La sortie de guerre des soldats français (1918–1920)* (Seuil, Paris, 2004)

'"Génération du feu": aux origines d'une notion', *Revue historique*, CCCIX, 1 (2007), pp. 139–50

Cadorza, Anthony L., *Agrarian Elites and Italian Fascism: The Province of Bologna 1901–1926* (Princeton, NJ, Princeton University Press, 1982)

Calí, Vincenzo, 'Il monumento alla Vittoria di Bolzano: Un caso di continuità fra fascismo e post-fascismo', in Diego Leoni and Camillo Zadra (eds.), *La Grande Guerra: Esperienza, memoria, immagini* (Bologna, Il Mulino, 1986), pp. 663–70

Canali, Mauro, *Il delitto Matteotti: Affarismo e politica nel primo governo Mussolini* (Bologna, Il Mulino, 1997)

Caprariis, Luca De, '"Fascism for Export"? The Rise and Eclipse of the Fasci Italiani all'Estero', *Journal of Contemporary History*, 35, 2 (2000), pp. 151–83

Carbajosa, Mónica and Carbajosa, Pablo, *La corte literaria de José Antonio: la primera generación cultural de la Falange* (Barcelona, Crítica, 2003)

Casanova, Julián, *Europa contra Europa 1914–1945* (Barcelona, Crítica, 2011)

Chini, Chiara, 'Fascismo britannico e fascismo italiano: La British union of fascists, Oswald Mosley e i finanziamenti stranieri', *Contemporanea*, XI, 3, (2008), pp. 433–57.

Clausewitz, Carl von, *On War* (ed. and trans. Michael Howard and Peter Paret) (Princeton, NJ, Princeton University Press, 1984)

Cohen, Deborah, *The War Come Home: Disabled Veterans in Britain and Germany, 1914–1939* (Berkeley, University of California Press, 2001)

Cohrs, Patrick O., 'The First "Real" Peace Settlements after the First World War: Britain, the United States and the Accords of London and Locarno, 1923–1925', *Contemporary European History*, 12, 1 (2003), pp. 1–31

Cointet, Jean-Paul, *La Légion Française des Combattants, 1940–1944: La tentation du fascisme* (Paris, Albin-Michel, 1995)

Cointet, Jean-Paul and Cointet, Michèle, 'Contribution a une socio-politique de l'État français: La Légion française des combattants dans la Vienne (1940–1943)', *Revue d'histoire moderne et contemporaine*, 20, 4 (1973), pp. 595–618

Colarizi, Simona, *Dopoguerra e fascismo in Puglia (1919–1926)* (Bari, Laterza, 1971)

L'opinione degli italiani sotto il regime 1929–1943 (Rome, Laterza, 1991)

Coppola, Salvatore, *Conflitti di lavoro e lotta politica nel Salento nel primo dopoguerra (1919–1925)* (Lecce, Salento Domani, 1984)

Cordova, Ferdinando, *Arditi e legionari Dannunziani* (Padua, Marsilio, 1969)

Corner, Paul, *Fascism in Ferrara, 1915–1925* (London, Oxford University Press, 1975)

Correia, Silvia, 'The Veterans' Movement and First World War Memory in Portugal (1918–33): Between the Republic and Dictatorship', *European Review of History*, 19 (2012), pp. 531–51

Corsini, Paolo, *Il feudo di Augusto Turati: Fascismo e lotta politica a Brescia (1922–1926)* (Milan, Franco Angeli, 1988)

Crotty, Martin and Edele, Mark, 'Total War and Entitlement: Towards a Global History of Veteran Privilege', *Australian Journal of Politics and History*, 59, 1 (2013), pp. 15–32

Cruz, Rafael, *En el nombre del pueblo: República, rebelión y guerra en la España de 1936* (Madrid, Siglo XXI, 2006)

Coverdale, John F., *Italian Intervention in the Spanish Civil War* (Princeton, NJ, Princeton University Press, 1975)

Cuzzi, Marco, *Antieuropa: Il fascismo universale di Mussolini*(Milan, M&B, 2006)

Delarue, Jacques, 'La guerra d'Abissinia vista dalla Francia: Le sue ripercussioni nella politica interna', in Angelo Del Boca (ed.), *Le guerre coloniali del fascismo* (Rome, Laterza, 2008), pp. 317–39

Demiaux, Victor, 'Dov'è la vittoria? Le rôle de la référence interalliée dans la construction rituelle de la sortie de guerre italienne (1918–1921)', *Mélanges de l'École française de Rome, Mélanges de l'École française de Rome–Italie et Méditerranée modernes et contemporaines* [on-line], 125, 2 (2013), available at http://mefrim.revues.org/1426 (accessed 22 February 2014)

Diehl, James M., 'Germany: Veterans' Politics under Three Flags', in Stephen R. Ward (ed.), *The War Generation: Veterans of the First World War* (Port Washington, NY, Kennikat Press, 1975), pp. 135–86

Paramilitary Politics in Weimar Germany (Bloomington, Indiana University Press, 1977)

The Thanks of the Fatherland: German Veterans after the Second World War (Chapel Hill, University of North Carloina Press, 1993)

'Von der "Vaterlandspartei" zur "Nationalen Revolution": Die "Vereinigten Vaterländischen Verbände Deutschlands (VVVD)" 1922–1932', *Vierteljahrshefte für Zeitgeschichte*, 33, 4 (1985), pp. 617–39

'Victors or Victims? Disabled Veterans in the Third Reich', *Journal of Modern History*, 59, 4 (1987), pp. 705–36

Dobry, Michel, 'Desperately Seeking "Generic Fascism": Some Discordant Thoughts on the Academic Recycling of Indigenous Categories', in António Costa Pinto (ed.), *Rethinking the Nature of Fascism: Comparative Perspectives* (Basingstoke, Palgrave Macmillan, 2011), pp. 53–84

(dir.), *Le mythe de l'allergie française au fascisme* (Paris, Albin Michel, 2003)

Dominioni, Matteo, *Lo sfascio dell'impero: Gli italiani in Etiopia 1936–1941* (Rome-Bari, Laterza, 2008)

Douglas, Allen, *From Fascism to Libertarian Communism: Georges Valois against the Third Republic* (Berkeley, University of California Press, 1992)

'Violence and Fascism: The Case of the Faisceau', *Journal of Contemporary History*, 19, 4 (1984), pp. 689–712

Drábik, Jakub, '"We're of Their Blood and Spirit of Their Spirit": Ex-Servicemen and the British Union of Fascists', in Salvador Alessandro and Anders G. Kjøstvedt (eds.), *New Political Ideas in the Aftermath of the Great War* (Cham, Palgrave Macmillan, 2017), pp. 151–74.

Dunker, Ulrich, *Der Reichsbund jüdischer Frontsoldaten 1919–1938: Geschichte eines jüdischen Abwehrvereins* (Düsseldorf, Droste, 1977)

Durham, Martin and Power, Margaret (eds.), *New Perspectives on the Transnational Right* (New York, Palgrave Macmillan, 2010)

Edele, Mark and Robert Gerwarth (eds.), Special Issue: 'The Limits of Demobilization', *Journal of Contemporary History*, 50, 1 (2015)

Eichenberg, Julia, *Kämpfen für Frieden und Fürsorge: Polnische Veteranen des Ersten Weltkriegs und ihre internationalen Kontakte, 1918–1939* (Munich, Oldenbourg, 2011)

Eichenberg, Julia and Newman, John Paul (eds.), *The Great War and Veterans' Internationalism* (New York, Palgrave, 2013)

Eksteins, Modris, 'War, Memory, and Politics: The Fate of the Film *All Quiet on the Western Front*', *Central European History*, 13 (1980), pp. 60–82

Elliot, C. J., 'The Kriegervereine and the Weimar Republic', *Journal of Contemporary History*, 10, 1 (1975), pp. 109–29

Erger, Johannes, *Der Kapp-Lüttwitz-Putsch: Ein Beitrag zur deutschen Innenpolitik 1919/20* (Düsseldorf, Droste Verlag, 1967)

'War, Memory, and Politics: The Fate of the Film *All Quiet on the Western Front*', *Central European History*, 13 (1980), pp. 60–82

Fabbri, Fabio, *Le origini della guerra civile: L'Italia dalla Grande Guerra al fascismo, 1918–1921* (Milan, Utet, 2009)

Fagerberg, Elliott Pennell, 'The "Anciens Combattants" and French Foreign Policy', unpublished PhD thesis, Université de Genève, 1966

Falasca-Zamponi, Simonetta, *Fascist Spectacle: The Aesthetics of Power in Mussolini's Italy* (Berkeley, University of California Press, 1997)

Fava, Andrea, 'Assistenza e propaganda nel regime di guerra (1915–1918)', in Mario Isnenghi (ed.): *Operai e contadini nella Grande Guerra* (Bologna, Cappelli, 1982), pp. 174–212

Felice, Renzo de, *Mussolini il rivoluzionario, 1883–1920* (Turin, Einaudi, 1965)
Il Fascismo: Le interpretazioni dei contemporanei e degli storici, (Rome-Bari, 1998)
Mussolini e Hitler: I rapporti segreti (1922–1933) (2nd edn.) (Florence, Felice Le Monnier, 1983)
Mussolini il fascista. I. La conquista del potere 1921–1925 (Turin, Einaudi, 1966)
Mussolini il fascista. II. L'organizzazione dello Stato fascista 1925–1929 (Turin, Einaudi, 1968)
Mussolini il duce. I. Gli anni del consenso 1929–1936 (Turin, Einaudi, 1974)

Figlia, Matteo di, *Farinacci: Il radicalismo fascista al potere* (Rome, Donzelli, 2007)

Fincardi, Marco, 'I reduci risorgimentali veneti e friulani', *Italia contemporanea*, 222 (2001), pp. 79–83

Kurt Finker, *Geschichte des Roten Frontkämpferbundes* (Berlin, Dietz Verlag, 1982)

Francescangeli, Eros, *Arditi del Popolo: Argo Secondari e la prima organizzazione antifascista (1917–1922)* (Rome, Odradek, 2000)

Finchelstein, Federico, *Transatlantic Fascism: Ideology, Violence, and the Sacred in Argentina and Italy, 1919–1945* (Durham, NC, Duke University Press, 2010)

Franz-Willing, Georg, *Die Hitlerbewegung: Der Ursprung 1919–1922* (Berlin, Deckers Verlag G. Schenk, 1962)

Franzina, Emilio and Sanfilippo, Matteo (eds.), *Il fascismo e gli emigrati: La parabola dei Fasci italiani all'estero (1920–1943)* (Rome, Laterza, 2003)

Franzinelli, Mimmo, *Squadristi: Protagonisti e tecniche della violenza fascista, 1919–1922* (Milan, Mondadori, 2003)

Fussell, Paul, *The Great War and Modern Memory* (Oxford University Press, 1975)

Galey, John H., 'Bridegrooms of Death: A Profile Study of the Spanish Foreign Legion', *Journal of Contemporary History*, 4, 2 (1969), pp. 47–64

Gallego, Ferran, *El Evangelio fascista: La formación de la cultura política del franquismo (1930–1950)* (Barcelona, Crítica, 2014)
Ramiro Ledesma Ramos y el fascismo español (Madrid, Síntesis, 2005)

Salvatore Garau, 'The Internationalisation of Italian Fascism in the Face of German National Socialism, and Its Impact on the British Union of Fascists', *Politics, Religion & Ideology*, 15, 1 (2014), pp. 45–63

Gentile, Emilio, *Le origini dell'ideologia fascista (1918–1925)* (Bari, Laterza, 1975).
Storia del partito fascista, 1919–1922: Movimento e milizia (Rome-Bari, Laterza, 1989)
Il culto del Littorio: La sacralizzazione della politica nell'Italia fascista (Rome, Laterza, 1993)
La via italiana al totalitarismo: Il partito e lo Stato nel regime fascista (Rome, Carocci, 2008)

Gerber, David A. (ed.), *Disabled Veterans in History* (Ann Arbor, University of Michigan Press, 2000)

Gerwarth, Robert, 'The Central European Counter-Revolution: Paramilitary Violence in Germany, Austria and Hungary after the Great War', *Past and Present*, 200 (2008), pp. 175–209

Gerwarth, Robert and John Horne (eds.), *War in Peace: Paramilitary Violence in Europe after the Great War* (Oxford University Press, 2012)

Gietinger, Klaus, *Der Konterrevolutionär: Waldemar Pabst – eine deutsche Karriere* (Hamburg, Nautilus, 2009)

Goeschel, Christian, 'Italia Docet? The Relationship between Italian Fascism and Nazism Revisited', *European History Quarterly*, 42 (2012), pp. 480–92

González Calleja, Eduardo, *El máuser y el sufragio: Orden público, subversión y violencia política en la crisis de la Restauración (1917–1931)*, (Madrid, CSIC, 1999)

'El Servicio Exterior de Falange y la política exterior del primer franquismo: Consideraciones previas para su investigación', *Hispania. Revista española de historia*, LIV, 1 (1994), pp. 279–307

Contrarrevolucionarios: Radicalización violenta de las derechas durante la Segunda República, 1931–1936 (Madrid, Alianza, 2011)

González Calleja, Eduardo and Fernando del Rey, *La defensa armada contra la revolución: Una historia de las guardias cívicas en la España del siglo XX* (Madrid, CSIC, 1995)

Gooch, John, *Army, State and Society in Italy, 1870–1915* (Houndmills, Macmillan, 1989)

Goodfellow, Samuel Huston, 'Fascism as a Transnational Movement: The Case of Inter-War Alsace', *Contemporary European History*, 22, 1 (2013), pp. 87–106

Gordon, Harold J., Jr., *Hitlerputsch 1923: Machtkampf in Bayern 1923–1924* (Munich, Bernard & Graefe Verlag, 1978)

Götz von Olenhusen, Imtraud, 'Vom Jungstahlhelm zur SA: Die junge Nachkriegsgeneration in den paramilitärischen Verbänden der Weimarer Republik', in Wolfgang R. Krabbe (ed.), *Politische Jugend in der Weimarer Republik* (Cohum, Universitätsverlag Dr. N. Brockmezer, 1993), pp. 146–82

Grady, Tim, 'Fighting a Lost Battle: The Reichsbund jüdischer Frontsoldaten and the Rise of National Socialism', *German History*, 28, 1 (2010), pp. 1–20

Griffin, Roger, *The Nature of Fascism* (London, Printer Publishers, 1991)

Groenendijk, Fleuris, 'The NSDAP's Local Organizations in Italy, 14 September 1930 to 30 January 1933', *Yearbook of European Studies*, 3 (1990), pp. 67–99

Gruber, Alfons, *Südtirol unter dem Faschismus* (Bozen, Verlagsanstalt Athesia, 1974)

Guillon, Jean-Marie, 'La Légion française des combattants, ou comment comprendre la France de Vichy', *Annales du Midi: revue archéologique, historique et philologique de la France méridionale*, 116, 245 (2004), pp. 5–24

Hailemariam, Zaude, 'La vera data d'inizio della seconda guerra mondiale', in Angelo Del Boca (ed.), *Le guerre coloniali del fascismo* (Bari, Laterza, 2008), pp. 288–313

Hall, Alex, 'The War of Words: Anti-Socialist Offensives and Counter-Propaganda in Wilhelmine Germany 1890–1914', *Journal of Contemporary History*, 11, 2–3 (1976), pp. 11–42

Hancock, Eleanor, *Ernst Röhm: Hitler's SA Chief of Staff* (New York, Palgrave Macmillan, 2008)

Hannover, Heinrich and Elisabeth Hannover-Drück (eds.): *Der Mord an Rosa Luxemburg und Karl Liebknecht. Dokumentation eines politischen Verbrechens* (Göttingen, Lamuv, 1989)

Hinton, Perry R., *Stereotypes, Cognition and Culture* (East Sussex, Psychology Press, 2000)

Hippler, Thomas, *Citizens, Soldiers and National Armies: Military Service in France and Germany, 1789–1830* (London, Routledge, 2008)

Hoepke, Klaus-Peter, *Die deutsche Rechte und der italiensiche Faschismus* (Düsseldorf, Droste Verlag, 1968)

Hoffstadt, Anke, 'Eine Frage der Ehre – Zur "Beziehungsgeschichte" von "Stahlhelm. Bund der Frontsoldaten" und SA', in Yves Müller and Reiner Zikenat (eds.), *Bürgerkriegsarmee: Forschungen zur nationalsozialistischen Sturmabteilung (SA)* (Frankfurt am Main, Peter Lang, 2013), pp. 267–96

'Frontgemeinschaft? Der "Stahlhelm. Bund der Frontsoldaten" und der Nationalsozialismus', in Gerd Krumeich (ed.), *Nationalsozialismus und Erster Weltkrieg*, (Broschiert, 2010), pp. 191–206

Hömig, Herbert, *Brüning. Kanzler in der Krise der Republik: Eine Wiemarer Biographie* (Paderborn, Ferdinand Schöningh, 2000)

Horne, John, 'Remobilising for "total war": France and Britain, 1917–1918', in John Horne (ed.), *State, Society and Mobilization in Europe during the First World War* (Cambridge University Press, 2002), pp. 195–211

(dir.), 'Démobilisations culturelles après la Grande Guerre', *14–18 Aujourd'hui, Today, Heute*, 5 (2002)

Houreou, Fabienne Le, *L'Épopée des soldats de Mussolini en Abyssinie 1936–1938: Les 'Ensablés'* (Paris, L'Harmattan, 1994)

Ingram, Norman, *The Politics of Dissent: Pacifism in France 1919–1939* (Oxford, Clarendon Press, 1991)

Iriye, Akira, *Global and Transnational History: The Past, Present and Future* (Basingstoke, Palgrave Macmillan, 2012)

Irvine, William D., 'Fascism in France and the Strange Case of the Croix de Feu', *Journal of Modern History*, 63 (1991), pp. 271–95

Isola, Gianni, *Guerra al regno della Guerra: Storia della Lega proletaria mutilati invalidi reduci orfani e vedove di guerra (1918–1924)* (Florence, Le Lettere, 1990)

'Socialismo e combattentismo: La Lega proletaria. 1918–1922', *Italia contemporanea*, 141 (1980), pp. 5–29

'Immagini di guerra del combattentismo socialista', in Diego Leoni and Camillo Zadra (eds.), *La Grande Guerra: Esperienza, memoria, immagini* (Bologna, Il Mulino, 1986), pp. 519–43

Isnenghi, Mario, *Il mito della Grande Guerra* (Bari, Laterza, 1970)

Jiménez Campo, Javier, *El fascismo en la crisis de la Segunda República española* (Madrid, Centro de Investigaciones Sociológicas, 1979)

Johansen, Anja, 'Violent Repression or Modern Strategies of Crowd Management? Soldiers as Riot Police in France and Germany, 1890–1914', *French History*, 15 (2001), pp. 400–20

ones, Larry Eugene, 'Nationalists, Nazis, and the Assault against Weimar: Revisiting the Harzburg Rally of October 1931', *German Studies Review*, 29, 3 (2006), pp. 483–94

ones, Mark, *Founding Weimar: Violence and the German Revolution of 1918-1919* (Cambridge University Press, 2016).

'From "Skagerrak" to the "Organisation Consul": War Culture and the Imperial German Navy, 1914–1922', in James E. Kitchen, Alisa Miller and Laura Rowe (eds.), *Other Combatants, Other Fronts: Competing Histories of the First World War* (Newcastle, Cambridge Scholars Publishing, 2011), pp. 249–74

Kallis, Aristotle A, '"Fascism", "Para-fascism" and "Fascistization": On the Similarities of Three Conceptual Categories', *European History Quarterly*, 33, 2 (2003), pp. 219–49

Fascist Ideology: Territory and Expansionism in Italy and Germany, 1922-1945 (London, Routledge, 2000)

Kalman, Samuel, 'Georges Valois et le Faisceau: Un mariage de convenance', in Olivier Dard (ed.), *Georges Valois, itinéraire et réceptions* (Internationaler Verlag der Wissenschaften, 2011), pp. 37–53

The Extreme Right in Interwar France: The Faisceau and the Croix de Feu (Hampshire, Ashgate, 2008)

Keene, Judith, *Fighting for Franco: International Volunteers in Nationalist Spain during the Spanish Civil War, 1936–39* (London, Leicester University Press, 2001)

Kemper, Claudia, *Das 'Gewissen' 1919–1925: Kommunikation und Vernetzung der Jungkonservativen* (Munich, Oldenbourg Verlag, 2011)

Kennedy, Sean, *Reconciling France against Democracy: The Croix de Feu and the Parti Social Français 1927–1945* (Montreal, McGill-Queen's University Press, 2007)

Kiesel, Helmut, *Ernst Jünger: Die Biographie* (Munich, Siedler, 2007)

Klotzbücher, Alois, 'Der politische Weg des Stahlhelm, Bund der Frontsoldaten in der Weimarer Republik: Ein Beitrag zur Geschichte der "Nationalen Opposition" 1918–1933', PhD dissertation, Friedrich Alexander-Universität zur Erlangen-Nürnberg, 1964

Kluge, Ulrich, *Soldatenräte und revolution: Studien zur Militärpolitik in Deutschland 1918/19* (Göttingen, Vandenhoeck & Ruprecht, 1975)

Koon, Tracy H., *Believe, Obey, Fight: Political Socialization of Youth in Fascist Italy, 1922–1943* (Chapel Hill, University of North Carolina Press, 1985)

Krassnitzer, Patrick, 'Die Geburt des nationalsozialismus im Schützengraben: Formen der Brutalisierung in den Autobiographien von nationalsozialistischen Frontsoldaten', in Jost Dülfer and Gerd Krumeich (eds.), *Der verlorene Frieden: Politik und Kriegskultur nach 1918* (Essen, Klartex, 2002), pp. 119–48

Krimmer, Elisabeth, *The Representation of War in German Literature* (Cambridge University Press, 2010)

Krüger, Gabriele, *Die Brigade Ehrhardt* (Hamburg, Leibniz-Verlag, 1971)

Krumeich, Gerd (ed.), *Nationalsozialismus und Erster Weltkrieg* (Essen, Klartext, 2010)

Kühne, Thomas, *Kameradschaft: Die Soldaten des nationalsozialistischen Krieges und das 20 Jahrhundert* (Göttingen, Vandenhoeck & Ruprecht, 2006)

Labanca, Nicola, *Una guerra per l'impero: Memorie della campagna d'Etiopia 1935–1936* (Bologna, Il Mulino, 2005)

Laboire, Pierre, *L'opinion française sous Vichy* (Paris, Seuil, 1990)

Lawrence, Jon, 'Forging a Peaceable Kingdom: War, Violence, and Fear of Brutalization in Post–First World War Britain', *Journal of Modern History*, 75, 3 (2003), pp. 557–89

Layton, Roland V., Jr., 'Kurt Ludecke and 'I Knew Hitler': An Evaluation', *Central European History*, 12, 4 (1979), pp. 372–86

Ledeen, Michael, *The First Duce: D'Annunzio at Fiume* (Baltimore, Johns Hopkins University Press, 1977)

Universal Fascism: The Theory and Practice of the Fascist International, 1928–1936 (New York, Howard Fertig, 1972)

Leed, Eric J., *No Man's Land: Combat and Identity in World War I* (Cambridge University Press, 1979)

Leitz, Christian, *Nazi Foreign Policy, 1933–1941: The Road to Global War* (London, Routledge, 2004)

Leoni, Diego and Zadra, Camillo (eds.), *La Grande Guerra: Esperienza, memoria, immagini* (Bologna, Il Mulino, 1986)

Linder, Ann P., *Princes of the Trenches: Narrating the German Experience of the First World War* (Columbia, Camden House, 1996)

Linehan, Thomas, *British Fascism 1918–39: Parties, Ideology and Culture* (Manchester University Press, 2000)

Loez, André and Mariot, Nicolas, *Obéir/desobéir: Les mutineries de 1917 en perspective* (Paris, Éditions La Découverte, 2008)

Löffelbein, Niels, *Ehrenbürger der Nation: Die Kriegsbeschädigten des Ersten Weltkriegs in Politik und Propaganda des Nationalsozialismus* (Essen, Klartext, 2013)

Longerich, Peter, *Die braunen Bataillone: Geschichte der SA* (Munich, C.H. Beck, 1989)

Lönne, Karl-Egon, *Faschismus als Herausforderung: Die Auseinandersetzung der 'Roten Fahne' und des 'Vorwärts' mit dem italienischen Faschismus 1920–1933* (Cologne, Böhlau-Verlag, 1981)

Loughlin, Michael B., 'Gustave Herve's Transition from Socialism to National Socialism: Another Example of French Fascism?', *Journal of Contemporary History*, 36, 1 (2001), pp. 5–39

Alf Lüdtke (ed.), *Everyday Life in Mass Dictatorship: Collusion and Evasion* (New York, Palgrave Macmillan, 2016)

Lupo, Salvatore, *Il Fascismo: La politica in un regime totalitario* (Rome, Donzelli, 2000)

Lyons, Anthony, Clark, Anna, Kashima, Yoshihisa and Kurz, Tim, 'Cultural Dynamics of Stereotypes: Social Network Processes and the Perpetuation of Stereotypes', in Yoshihisa Kashima, Klaus Fiedler and Peter Freytag (eds.), *Stereotype Dynamics: Language-Based Approaches to the Formation, Maintenance, and Transformation of Stereotypes* (New York, Erlbaum Associates, 2008), pp. 59–92

Lyttelton, Adrian, *The Seizure of Power: Fascism in Italy 1919–1929* (Princeton, NJ, Princeton University Press, 1987) (1st edn. 1973)
'Fascism in Italy: The Second Wave', *Journal of Contemporary History*, 1, 1 (1966), pp. 75–100
Maier, Charles S., *Recasting Bourgeois Europe: Stabilization in France, Germany, and Italy in the Decade after World War I* (Princeton, NJ, Princeton University Press, 1975)
März, Markus, *Nationale Sozialisten in der NSDAP* (Graz, Ares Verlag, 2010)
Mann, Michael, *Fascists* (Cambridge University Press, 2004)
Maser, Werner, *Frühgeschichte der NSDAP: Hitler's Weg bis 1924* (Frankfurt am Main, Athenäum Verlag, 1965)
McGarty, Craig, Yzerbyt, Vincent Y. and Spears, Russell, *Stereotypes as Explanations: The Formation of Meaningful Beliefs about Social Groups* (Cambridge University Press, 2002)
Mesching, Alexander, *Der Wille zur Bewegung: Militärischer Traum und totalitäres Programm. Eine Mentalitätsgeschichte vom Ersten Weltkrieg zum Nationalsozialismus* (Bielefeld, Transcript, 2008)
Millan, Matteo, *Squadrismo e squadristi nella dittatura fascista* (Rome, Viella, 2014)
Millington, Chris, *From Victory to Vichy: Veterans in Inter-War France* (Manchester University Press, 2012a)
'The French Veterans and the Republic: The Union nationale des combattants and the Union fédérale, 1934–1938', *European History Quarterly*, 42 (2012b), pp. 50–70
'February 6, 1934: The Veterans' Riot', *French Historical Studies*, 33, 4 (2010), pp. 545–72
'Street-Fighting Men: Political Violence in Inter-War France', *English Historical Review*, 129, 538 (2013), pp. 606–38
'Communist Veterans and Paramilitarism in 1920s France: The Association républicaine des anciens combattants', *Journal of War & Culture Studies*, 8, 4 (2015), pp. 300–14.
Milza, Pierre, *L'Italie fasciste devant l'opinion française 1920–1940* (Paris, Armand Colin, 1967)
(ed.), *Les italiens en France de 1914 à 1940* (Rome, École française de Rome, 1986)
Mohler, Armin, *Die Konservative Revolution in Deutschland 1918–1932* (Darmstadt, Wissenschaftliche Buchgesellschaft, 1994) (1st edn. 1949)
Mondini, Marco, *La politica delle armi: Il ruolo dell'esercito nell'avvento del fascismo*, (Rome-Bari, Laterza, 2006)
'La festa mancata: I militari e la memoria della Grande Guerra, 1918–1923', *Contemporanea*, 4 (2004), pp. 555–78
Mondini, Marco and Schwarz, Guri, *Dalla guerra alla pace: Retoriche e pratiche della smobilitazione nell'Italia del Novecento* (Verona, Cierre Edizioni/Istrevi, 2007)
Monteleone, Renato and Sarasini, Pino, 'I monumenti italiani ai caduti della Grande Guerra', in Diego Leoni and Camillo Zadra (eds.), *La Grande Guerra: Esperienza, memoria, immagini* (Bologna, Il Mulino, 1986), pp. 631–62

Moreau-Trichet, Claire, *Henri Pichot et l'Allemagne de 1930 à 1945* (Bern, Peter Lang, 2004)

'La propagande nazie à l'égard des associations françaises d'anciens combattants de 1934 à 1939', *Guerres mondiales et conflits contemporains*, 205 (2002), pp. 55–70

Morgan, Philip, *Italian Fascism, 1915–1945* (New York, Palgrave Macmillan, 2004)

Fascism in Europe, 1919–1945 (London, Routledge, 2003)

Morton, Desmond, and Wright, Glenn, *Winning the Second Battle: Canadian Veterans and the Return to Civilian Life 1915–1930* (University of Toronto Press, 1987)

Mosse, George L., *The Crisis of German Ideology: Intellectual Origins of the Third Reich* (New York, Universal Library, 1964)

'Two World Wars and the Myth of the War Experience', *Journal of Contemporary History*, 21, 4 (1986), pp. 491–513

Fallen Soldiers. Reshaping the Memory of the World Wars (New York, Oxford University Press, 1990)

Murdoch, Brian, 'Innocent Killing: Erich Maria Remarque and the Weimar Anti-War Novels', in Karl Leydecker (ed.), *German Novelists of the Weimar Republic. Intersections of Literature and Politics* (New York, Candem House, 2006), pp. 141–168

Musiedlak, Didier, 'L'Italie fasciste et Georges Valois' in Olivier Dard (ed.), *Georges Valois, itinéraire et réceptions* (Berne, Peter Lang, 2011), pp. 205–214

Nello, Paolo *L'avanguardismo giovanile alle origini del fascismo* (Bari, Laterza, 1978)

Nelson, Tood D., *Handbook of Prejudice, Stereotyping, and Discrimination* (New York, Psychology Press, 2009)

Newman, John Paul, *Yugoslavia in the Shadow of War: Veterans and the Limits of State Building, 1903–1945* (Cambridge University Press, 2015)

Nicolò, Mario De (a cura di): *Dalla trincea alla piazza: L'irruzione dei giovani nel Novecento* (Rome, Viella, 2011)

Nieddu, Luigi, *Dal combattentismo al fascismo in Sardegna* (Milan, Vangelista, 1979)

Nobécourt, Jacques, *Le colonel de La Rocque (1885–1946), ou, Les pièges du nationalisme chrétien* (Paris, Fayard, 1996)

Núñez Florencio, Rafael, *Militarismo y antimilitarismo en España* (Madrid, CSIC, 1990)

O'Brien, Paul, *Mussolini in the First World War: The Journalist, the Soldier, the Fascist* (Oxford, Berg, 2005)

Orlow, Dietrich, The History of the Nazi Party, *Vol. I:* 1919–1933 (Newton Abbot, David & Charles, 1971) (1st edn. 1969)

The Lure of Fascism in Western Europe: German Nazis, Dutch and French Fascists, 1933–1939 (New York, Palgrave Macmillan, 2009)

Parejo, Fernández and Antonio, José, *Señoritos, jornaleros y falangistas* (Seville, Bosque de Palabras, 2008)

Passerini, Luisa, *Mussolini immaginario: Storia di una biografia 1915–1939* (Bari, Laterza, 1991)

Passmore, Kevin, 'L'historiographie du "fascisme" en France', *French Historical Studies*, 37, 3 (2014), pp. 466–99

Pavan Dalla Torre, Ugo, 'L'Anmig fra D'Annunzio e Mussolini (ottobre 1922): Note e prospettive di ricerca', *Italia Contemporanea*, 278 (2015), pp. 325–52

Paxton, Robert O., *Vichy France: Old Guard and New Order, 1940–1944* (New York, Knopf, 1972)

The Anatomy of Fascism (New York, Knopf, 2004)

'The Five Stages of Fascism', *Journal of Modern History*, 70, 1 (1998), pp. 1–23.

Peloille, Manuelle, *Fascismo en ciernes: España 1922–1930, textos recuperados* (Tolouse, Presses Universitaires du Mirail, 2005)

Pencak, William, *For God and Country: The American Legion, 1919–1941* (Boston, Northeastern University Press, 1989)

Perfetti, Francesco, *Fiumanesimo, sindacalismo e fascismo* (Rome, Bonacci, 1988)

Pese, Walter Werner, 'Hitler und Italien 1920–1926', *Vierteljahrshefte für Zeitgeschichte*, 2 (1955), pp. 113–26

Petersen, Jens, *Hitler-Mussolini: Die Entstehung der Achse Berlin-Rom 1933–1936* (Tübingen, Max Niemeyer, 1973)

Piano, Lorenzo Del and Atzeni, Francesco, *Combattentismo, fascismo e autonomismo nel pensiero di Camillo Bellieni* (Rome, Edizioni dell'Ateneo, 1986)

Plöckinger, Othmar, *Unter Soldaten und Agitatoren: Hitler's prägende Jahre im deutschen Militär 1918–1920* (Paderborn, Ferdinand Schöningh, 2013)

Poesio, Camilla, *Reprimere le idee: Abusare del potere. La Milizia e l'instaurazione del regime fascista* (Rome, Quaderni della Fondazione Luigi Salvatorelli, 2010)

Porte, Pablo La, 'The Moroccan Quagmire and the Crisis of Spain's Liberal System, 1917–23', in Francisco J. Romero Salvadó and Angel Smith (eds.), *The Agony of Spanish Liberalism*, pp. 230–54

Christophe Poupault, *À l'ombre des faisceaux: Les voyages français dans l'Italie des chemises noires (1922–1943)* (Rome, École française de Rome, 2014)

Procacci, Giovanna, *Soldati e prigionieri italiani nella Grande Guerra: Con una raccolta di lettere inedite* (Rome, Editori Riuniti, 1993)

Prost, Antoine, *Les Anciens Combattants et la Societé Française 1914–1939*, 3 vols. (Paris, Presses de la Fondation Nationale des Sciences Politiques, 1977)

In the Wake of War: The 'Anciens Combattants' and French Society (Oxford, Berg, 1992)

'Les limites de la brutalisation: Tuer sur le front occidental, 1914–1918', *Vingtième Siècle. Revue d'histoire*, 81 (2004), pp. 5–20

Puymége, Gérard de, *Chauvin, le soldat-laboureur: Contribution à l'étude des nationalismes*, (Paris, Gallimard, 1993)

Quiroga, Alejandro, *Making Spaniards: Primo de Rivera and the Nationalization of the Masses, 1923–30* (New York, Palgrave, 2007)

Reichardt, Sven, *Faschistische Kampfbünde: Gewalt und Gemeinschaft im italienischen Squadrismus und in der deutschen SA* (Cologne, Böhlau, 2002)

Reichardt, Sven and Nolzen, Armin (eds.), *Faschismus in Italien und Deutschland: Studien zu Transfer und Vergleich* (Göttingen, Wallstein, 2005)

Relinger, Jean, *Henri Barbusse: Écrivain combattant* (Paris, PUF, 1994)

Remond, René, 'Les anciens combattants et la politique', *Revue française de science politique*, 5, 2 (1955), pp. 267–90

Répaci, Antonino, *La Marcia su Roma* (Milan, Rizzoli, 1972)

Ridolfi, Maurizio, *Le feste nazionali* (Bologna, Il Mulino, 2003)

Rochat, Giorgio, *L'esercito italiano da Vittorio Veneto a Mussolini (1919–1925)* (Bari, Laterza, 1967)

Gli arditi della Grande Guerra: Origini, battaglie e miti, Milan, Feltrinelli, 1981

'Antimilitarismo ed esercito rosso nella stampa socialsita e comunista del primo dopoguerra (1919–1925)', *Il movimento di liberazione in Italia*, 76 (1964), pp. 3–42

Rodríguez Jiménez, José Luis, *Historia de Falange Española de las JONS* (Madrid, Alianza, 2000)

Rodríguez Jiménez, *¡A mi la Legión! De Millán Astray a las misiones de paz* (Barcelona, Planeta, 2005)

'Una unidad militar en los orígenes del fascismo en España: la Legión', *Pasado y Memoria. Revista de Historia Contemporánea*, 5 (2006), pp. 219–40

De héroes e indeseables: La División Azul (Madrid, Espasa, 2007)

Rohe, Karl, *Das Reichsbanner Schwarz Rot Gold: Ein Beitrag zur Geschichte und Struktur der politischen Kampfverbaende zur Zeit der Weimarer Republik* (Düsseldorf, Droste, 1966)

Romero Salvadó, Francisco J., *Spain 1914–1918: Between War and Revolution* (London, Routledge, 1999)

The Foundations of Civil War: Revolution, Social Conflict and Reaction in Liberal Spain, 1916–1923 (London, Routledge, 2008)

Romero Salvadó, Francisco J. and Smith, Angel (eds.), *The Agony of Spanish Liberalism: From Revolution to Dictatorship, 1913–23* (New York, Palgrave, 2010)

Rossi, Marco, *Arditi, non gendarmi! Dalle trincee alle barricade: Arditismo di guerra e arditi del popolo (1917–1922)* (Pisa, BFS, 2011)

Roux, Christophe, 'De la Grande Guerre à la démocratie: Les anciens combattants et le mouvement autonomiste sarde', in Natale Duclos (dir.), *L'adieu aux armes: Parcours d'anciens combattants* (Paris, Karthala, 2010), pp. 299–323

Sabbatucci, Giovanni, *I combattenti nel primo dopoguerra*, Rome-Bari, Laterza, 1974.

La stampa del combattentismo (1918–1925) (Bologna, Cappelli, 1980)

'Il "suicidio" della classe dirigente liberale: La legge Acerbo 1923–1924', *Italia contemporanea*, 174 (1989), pp. 57–80

Salvador, Alessandro, *La guerra in tempo di pace: Gli ex combattenti e la politica nella Repubblica di Weimar* (Trento, Università degli Studi di Trento, 2013)

'Il nazionalsocialismo e la destra nazionalista tedesca: 1925–1933', PhD dissertation, Università degli Studi di Trento, 2009

Salvador, Alessandro, and Anders G. Kjøstvedt (eds.), *New Political Ideas in the Aftermath of the Great War* (Cham, Palgrave Macmillan, 2017).

alvante, Martina, 'The Italian Associazione Nazionale Mutilati e Invalidi di Guerra and Its International Liaisons in the Post Great War Era', in Julia Eichenberg and John Paul Newman (eds.), *The Great War and Veterans' Internationalism* (New York, Palgrave, 2013), pp. 162–83

andu, Traian, *Un fascisme roumain: Histoire de la Garde de fer* (Paris, Perrin, 2014)

aunier, Pierre-Yves, *Transnational History* (New York, Palgrave Macmillan, 2013)

az, Ismael, *Mussolini contra la II República: Hostilidad, conspiraciones, intervención (1931–1936)* (Valencia, Edicions Alfons el Magnànim, 1986)

bacchi, Alberto, *Il colonialismo italiano in Etiopia, 1936–1940* (Milan, Mursia, 1980)

chieder, Wolfgang, 'Fatal Attraction: The German Right and Italian Fascism', in Hans Mommsen (ed.), *The Third Reich between Vision and Reality: New Perspectives on German History 1918–1945* (Oxford, Berg, 2002), pp. 39–57

'Faschismus im politischen Transfer: Giuseppe Renzetti als faschistischer Propagandist und Geheimagent in Berlin 1922–1941', in *Faschistische Diktaturen: Studien zu Italien und Deutschland* (Göttingen, Wallstein Verlag, 2008), pp. 223–49

chüler-Springorum, Stephanie, *Krieg und Fliegen: Die Legion Condor im Spanischen Bürgerkrieg* (Paderborn, Ferdinand Schöningh, 2010)

chumann, Dirk, 'Europa, der Erste Weltkrieg und die Nachkriegszeit: Eine Kontinuität der Gewalt?', *Journal of Modern European History*, 1, 1 (2003), pp. 24–43

chuster, Kurt G. P., *Der Rote Frontkämpferbund 1924–1929* (Düsseldorf, Droste Verlag, 1975)

elva, Enrique, *Ernesto Giménez Caballero: Entre la vanguardia y el fascismo* (Valencia, Pre-textos/Instituciò Alfons el Magnànim, 2000)

egré, Claudio G., *Italo Balbo: Una vita fascista* (Bologna, Il Mulino, 1988)

eipp, Adam R., *The Ordeal of Peace: Demobilization and the Urban Experience in Britain and Germany, 1917–1921* (Farnham, Ashgate, 2009)

'"Scapegoats for a Lost War": Demobilisation, the Kapp Putsch, and the Politics of the Streets in Munich, 1919–1920', *War & Society*, 25, 1 (May 2006), pp. 35–54

errano, Carlos and Salaün, Serge (eds.), *Los felices años veinte: España, crisis y modernidad* (Madrid, Marcial Pons, 2006)

gueglia della Marra, Sabrina, 'Le aggressioni agli ufficiali nel primo dopoguerra', *Nuova Storia Contemporanea*, 3 (2012), pp. 117–34

herman, Daniel J., *The Construction of Memory in Interwar France* (University of Chicago Press, 1999)

horrock, William I., 'France and the Rise of Fascism in Italy', *Journal of Contemporary History*, 10, 4 (1975), pp. 591–610

imms, Brendan, 'Against a "World of Enemies": The Impact of the First World War on the Development of Hitler's Ideology', *International Affairs*, 90, 2 (2014), pp. 317–36

kor, Holger, *Brücken über den Rhein': Frankreich in der Wahrnehmung und Propaganda des Dritten Reiches, 1933–1939* (Essen, Klartext, 2011)

Skoutelsky, Rémi, *Novedad en el frente: Las brigadas internacionales en la guerra civil* (Madrid, Temas de Hoy, 2006)

Sluga, Glenda, 'Fascism and Anti-Fascism', in Akira Iriye and Pierre-Yves Saunier (eds.), *The Palgrave Dictionary of Transnational History* (Basingstoke, Palgrave Macmillan, 2009)

Smith, Leonard V., 'Jean Norton Cru et la subjectivité de l'objectivité', in Jean-Jacques Becker (dir.), *Histoire culturelle de la Grande Guerre* (Paris, Armand Colin, 2005), pp. 89–100

Snowden, Frank M., *The Fascist Revolution in Tuscany 1919–1922* (Cambridge University Press, 1989)

Soucy, Robert, *French Fascism: The First Wave, 1924–1933* (New Haven, CT, Yale University Press, 1986)

French Fascism: The Second Wave 1933–1939 (New Haven, CT, Yale University Press, 1995)

'France: Veterans' Politics between the Wars', in Stephen R. Ward (ed.), *The War Generation: Veterans of the First World War* (Port Washington, NY, Kennikat Press, 1975), pp. 59–103

Sprenger, Matthias, *Landsknechte auf dem Weg ins Dritte Reich? Zu Genese und Wandel des Freikorpsmythos* (Paderborn, Ferdinand Schöning, 2008)

Stachura, Peter D. *Gregor Strasser and the Rise of Nazism* (London, Allen & Unwin, 1983)

Stephenson, Scott, *The Final Battle: Soldiers of the Western Front and the German Revolution of 1918* (Cambridge University Press, 2009)

Sternhell, Zeev, 'Anatomie d'un mouvement fasciste en France: Le faisceau de Georges Valois', *Revue française de science politique*, 1 (1976). pp. 5–40

La droite révolutionnaire 1885–1914: Les origines françaises du fascisme (Paris, Fayard, 1997)

Tasca, Angelo *Nascita e avvento del fascismo* (Milan, La Nuova Italia, 2002) (1st edn. 1950)

Theweleit, Klaus, *Männerphantasien* (Frankfurt am Main, Verlag Roter Stern, 1977–8)

Thompson, Mark, *The White War: Life and Death on the Italian Front, 1915–1919* (New York, Basic Books, 2009)

Thöndl, Michael, *Oswald Spengler in Italien: Kulturexport politischer Ideen der 'Konservativen Revolution'* (Leipziger Universitätsverlag, 2010)

Tobia, Bruno, *L'Altare della Patria* (Bologna, Il Mulino, 1998)

Tognotti, Eugenia, *L'esperienza democratica del combattentismo nel Mezzogiorno: Il movimento degli ex-combattenti e il Partito Sardo d'Azione a Sassari (1918–1924)* (Cagliari, Edizioni Della Torre, 1983)

Traverso, Enzo, *A ferro e fuoco: La guerra civile europea, 1914–1945* (Bologna, Il Mulino, 2007)

Tusell, Javier, *Franco en la guerra civil: Una biografía política* (Barcelona, Tusquets, 1992)

Ungari, Andrea, 'Tra mobilitazione patriottica e suggestioni eversive: La vicenda dell'Unione Nazionale Ufficiali e Soldati nel primo dopoguerra', *Nuova Storia Contemporanea*, 5 (2001), pp. 41–76

Valli, Roberta Suzzi, 'The Myth of *Squadrismo* in the Fascist Regime', *Journal of Contemporary History*, 35 (2000), pp. 131–50

Vanzetto, Livio, 'Contadini e grande guerra in aree campione del Veneto (1910–1922)', in Mario Isnenghi (a cura di), *Operai e contadini nella Grande guerra* (Bologna, Cappelli, 1982), pp. 72–103

Ventrone, Angelo, *La seduzione totalitaria: Guerra, modernità, violenza politica (1914–1918)* (Rome, Donzelli, 2003)

Venza, Claudio, 'El consulado italiano de Barcelona y la comunidad italiana en los inicios del fascismo (1923–1925)', *Investigaciones Históricas*, 17 (1997), pp. 265–83

Verhey, Jeffrey, *The Spirit of 1914: Militarism, Myth and Mobilization in Germany* (Cambridge University Press, 2000)

Vilar, Pierre, 'Reflexions sur les années 20', in VV.AA., *Piero Gobetti e la Francia: Atti del colloquio italo francese* (Milan, Franco Angeli, 1985), pp. 15–25

Viscarri, Dionisio, *Nacionalismo autoritario y orientalismo: La narrativa prefascista de la guerra de Marruecos (1921–1927)* (Bolonia, Il Capitello del Sole, 2004)

Vivarelli, Roberto, *Storia delle origini del fascismo: L'Italia dalla grande guerra alla marcia su Roma* (Bologna, Il Mulino, 2012), Vol. 1, pp. 436–60

Wachsam, Nikolaus, 'Marching under the Swastika? Ernst Junger and National Socialism', in *Journal of Contemporary History*, 33, 4 (1998), pp. 573–89

Whalen, Robert Weldon, *Bitter Wounds: German Victims of the Great War, 1914–1939* (Ithaca, NY, Cornell University Press, 1984)

Waite, Robert G. L., *Vanguard of Nazism: The Free Corps Movement in Postwar Germany 1918–1923* (Cambridge, MA, Harvard University Press, 1952)

Wanrooij, Bruno, 'The Rise and Fall of Italian Fascism as a Generational Revolt', *Journal of Contemporary History*, 22, 3 (1987), pp. 401–18

Ward, Stephen R., 'The British Veterans' Ticket of 1918', *Journal of British Studies*, 8, 1(1968), pp. 155–69

    (ed.), *The War Generation: Veterans of the First World War* (Port Washington, NY, Kennikat Press, 1975)

Weber, Thomas, *Hitler's First War. Adolf Hitler, the Men of the List Regiment, and the First World War* (Oxford University Press, 2010)

Weiß, Christian, '"Soldaten des Friedens": Die pazifistischen Veteranen und Kriegsopfer des "Reichsbundes" und ihre Kontakte zu den französischen anciens combattatns 1919–1933', in Wolfgang Hardtwig (ed.), *Politische Kulturgeschichte der Zwischenkriegszeit 1918–1939* (Göttingen, Vandenhoeck & Ruprecht, 2005), pp. 183–204

Wingeate Pike, David, *France Divided: The French and the Civil War in Spain* (Portland, Sussex Academic Press, 2011)

Winter, Jay and Prost, Antoine, *René Cassin and Human Rights: From the Great War to the Universal Declaration* (Cambridge University Press, 2013)

Wohl, Robert, *The Generation of 1914* (Cambridge, MA, Harvard University Press, 1979)

Woller, Hans, Rom. 28–Oktober 1922: Die faschistische Herausforderung (München, DTV, 1999)

Wootton, Graham, *The Politics of Influence: British Ex-Servicemen, Cabinet Decisions and Cultural Change (1917–57)* (London, Routledge & Kegan Paul, 1963)

Zani, Luciano, *Italia Libera: Il primo movimento antifascista clandestino 1923–1925* (Bari, Laterza, 1975)

Zavatti, Francesco, *Mutilati ed invalidi di guerra: una storia politica. Il caso modenese* (Milan, Unicopli, 2011)

Zenobi, Laura, *La construcción del mito de Franco: De jefe de la Legión a Caudillo de España* (Madrid, Cátedra, 2011)

Ziemann, Benjamin, *War Experiences in Rural Germany 1914–1923* (Oxford, Berg, 2007)

Contested Commemorations, Republican War Veterans and Weimar Political Culture (Cambridge University Press, 2013)

'Die Konstruktion des Kriegsveteranen und die Symbolik seiner Erinnerung 1918–1933', in Jost Dülffer and Gerd Krumeich (eds.), *Der verlorene Frieden. Politik und Kriegskultur nach 1918* (Essen, Klartex-Verlag, 2002), pp. 101–18

Index